ORDEAL BY FIRE
Canada, 1910–1945

THE CANADIAN HISTORY SERIES

Edited by Thomas B. Costain

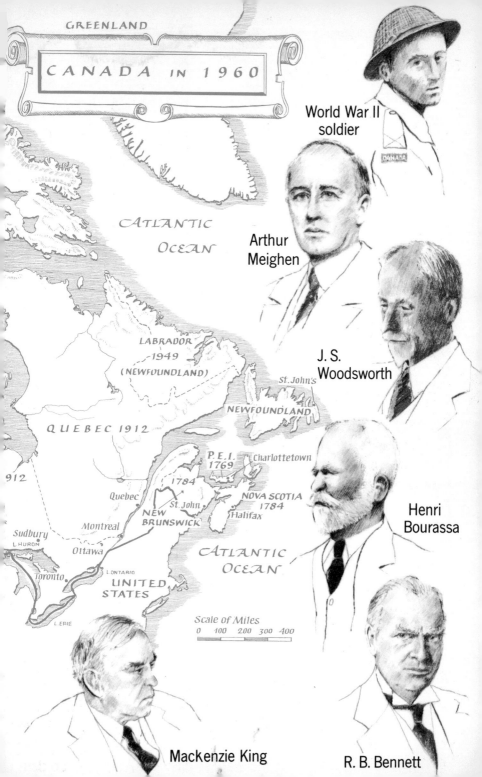

GREENLAND

CANADA IN 1960

ATLANTIC OCEAN

World War II soldier

Arthur Meighen

J. S. Woodsworth

LABRADOR 1949 (NEWFOUNDLAND)

St. John's

NEWFOUNDLAND

QUEBEC 1912

912

P.E.I. 1769   Charlottetown

1784

Quebec   St. John

NEW BRUNSWICK   NOVA SCOTIA 1784   Halifax

Montreal

Sudbury   Ottawa

L. HURON

L. ONTARIO

Toronto   UNITED STATES

Henri Bourassa

ATLANTIC OCEAN

L. ERIE

Scale of Miles
0   100   200   300   400

Mackenzie King

R. B. Bennett

ORDEAL BY FIRE

Canada, *1910-1945*

BY RALPH ALLEN

Garden City, New York
DOUBLEDAY & COMPANY, INC.

F
1034
A6
Copy 2

74812

CONTENTS

ORDEAL BY FIRE
Canada, 1910–1945

I

A sunny people, and a sunny year—
"One Flag, One Fleet, One Throne"

IN the sunlit year of 1910 an unsuspecting Canada began the most painful and momentous years of its education for nationhood. For all it knew of what lay ahead, it might have been a happy child swinging a five-cent scribbler in one hand and a shiny new pencil box in the other on the way to the first day of school.

Canada's nationhood was already more than half won and the rest was within certain grasp. But the education needed to make it fruitful had a long way yet to go. The phase now beginning on the threshold of a new general election was to see bitter conflicts within the country's borders and draw it deeply into two wars beyond them. It was to revolutionize Canada's economy, its individual ways of living, its philosophy of government, and its whole attitude and relation to the world.

But in 1910 the impending deluge of events was not discernible even at its sources, much less on the far-off tidal flats of North America. For most Canadians their country's greatest hazards were securely lost in the past, among the shadows of the Hurons and Iroquois, the Plains of Abraham, the Family Compact, and the War of 1812. The most serious of them all, the affair between Wolfe and Montcalm, was not quite forgotten, but its scars had nearly ceased to throb and what new grains of salt fell on them were apt to be directed more by carelessness than by malice.

For almost a decade and a half the Protestant English "conquerors" had loyally accepted and indeed helped to elect as their Prime Minister one of the Catholic French "conquered."

It was true that there recently had been a not well resolved altercation between the two main branches of the Canadian family concerning the country's involvement in the South African War of 1899–1902; English Canada had wanted more involvement, French Canada had wanted none. Too, there were fresh quarrels about separate Catholic schools in the fast-growing West. By and large, nevertheless, Canada was living comfortably in its two solitudes in the golden, unauspicious year of 1910.

The wondrous new age of gadgetry and gingerbread was well under way, and new shrines and talismans, and slightly old ones grown in splendor, gleamed and beckoned from every quarter of the compass: the Model T and the gasoline tractor, the Comptometer, the time clock, the alarm clock; Palmolive soap and Blue Jay corn plasters; Puffed Wheat, Shredded Wheat, and ketchup; the electric iron, the electric toaster, the soda fountain, the fountain pen, the flashlight; the portable outboard motor and the waterproof, gentleman's washable collar, the Dictaphone and the Gramophone. Not all these benefices, to be sure, were within the reach of everyone—not with farm labor running around twenty-five dollars a month, a good hired girl half that much, and six-room houses renting at twenty dollars and more. It was also true that behind the glittering façade a person with a sharp eye could detect intimations of decay. The turkey trot, the bunny hug, and the puppy snuggle were imminent and implicit in the nature of the times, and the Woman's Christian Temperance Union was able to report with even more assurance than usual that in the past twelve months another fifteen hundred once wholesome Canadian girls had been spirited away to white slavery, mostly in Chicago, and mostly because of drink or drugs. As against this testimony to social malaise it could be proved by government statistics that in the entire forty-three years since Confederation only 305 divorces had been granted in the whole Dominion and that the average adult was drinking no more than a gallon and a half of whisky a year and smoking only four cigarettes a week.

The year before had not been a prosperous one, but the coal strikes had ended in Nova Scotia and new railway lines were stretching farther into the growing West. The railways were still a—perhaps still *the*—prime source of public satisfaction. Even poets stood before their builders in self-abnegating reverence; the well-known literary man Arthur Stringer wrote in the Toronto *Globe*'s New Year's Day edition: "The sad truth is our whole busy bunch of novelists and storytellers and verse-writers today constitute nothing more than an attenuated choir of street sparrows, chirping disconsolately from the rafters of a locomotive round-house. Canada's great artists today are Shaughnessy and Mann and Mackenzie and Charlie Hays and those epic-minded workers who are writing a new kind of blank verse in town sites and railway iron and grain routes." Despite such thoughtful homage, the railway heroes got their names in the papers somewhat less frequently than the hockey heroes: Joe Malone and Joe Hall of the world-champion Quebec Bulldogs, and Cyclone Taylor, the already legendary "man who scored goals skating backward," who had just been stolen from Ottawa by the upstart town of Renfrew on the offer of four thousand dollars for ten weeks.

A cynic might have said the eastern respect for railway iron and grain routes reflected nothing deeper than the scent of new profits for the bankers, middlemen, and merchants who provisioned the travelers and dwellers thereon and later bought and sold their produce. But something more exciting was involved too. A new current was in motion within the mainstream of human history. The railways opened up a new caravan trail for the restless, the driven, and the questing and led them to the heartland of Canada. The travelers set forth on many impulses and from many places: some drawn by fear, some by ambition, some by faith, some by gullibility. There were earthy mystics from Russia; heartsick Ukrainians without land and without a country; Cockneys from the crowded East End mews; younger sons of gentry from Surrey and Kent; Ontario farm boys; ranchers from Texas, Oklahoma, and Montana cramped by fences.

The immediate lures had been and were the offer of free homestead land and the persuasiveness of the Dominion Department of the Interior, the Canadian Pacific and Grand Trunk railways, the Hudson's Bay Company, and a few private colonization concerns. For twenty years all these agencies had pooled their resources behind one of the largest, noisiest, and most successful medicine shows of all time. It covered two continents and was conducted in a dozen languages. Its message was simple and direct: Whatever ails you, come to western Canada! In its role as chief barker, the federal government published millions of pamphlets extolling the large stretches of still unsettled land and offering it gratis to anyone who would come and get it. In impressive rounded phrases worthy of a multi-lingual Phineas T. Barnum, its literature cajoled the Swedes in Swedish, harangued the Germans in German, beguiled the French in French, coaxed the Hollanders in Dutch, wheedled the Norse in Norwegian.

A generation before, the white population of the Canadian prairie, from the Red River across a third of the world's third-largest country to the Rockies, had been only sixty thousand. Now it was a million.

In a country of three million square miles, whose total population had grown to only seven million in three hundred years, this was an impressive rate of growth. And its impressiveness was only underlined by the anachronisms and paradoxes. The first gasoline tractors were already appearing, but the last teams of sturdy Doukhobor women, harnessed to a single-furrow plow, could still be seen on the wheat fields of Saskatchewan and Manitoba. In Winnipeg, Regina, and Calgary the wooden mansions of the middlemen were multiplying fast, but in the intervening subcontinents of wheat and prairie grass there were more sod huts and poplar cabins. There were a few hundred miles of roads safe for automobiles, but bull trains still creaked and rumbled up to the new frontier on the Peace River and pack ponies stood bolt upright and stone dead, mired in the muskeg of the Edson Trail.

The Canada of the early 1900s remained, in short, very much a pioneer country. Along with the pioneer's traditional eagerness for new adventures it also inherited his traditional hostility to new ideas. If there was any shifting pattern or augury of change in the news of the world outside, it was almost as hard to perceive from the six-story skyscrapers of Toronto and Montreal as from the poplar cabins of the prairie.

Who could have seen any possible meaning for Canada in the fact that when Czar Nicholas of Russia walked behind the bier of his great-uncle in the snow of St. Petersburg it was thought necessary to line the funeral route with three solid miles of soldiers in order to protect the Czar from terrorists? What homesteader in the West or what tenth-generation tiller of a few score arpents beside the St. Lawrence could be expected to expect that he or his children would be affected in the remotest way by a coming fight between a corporation called U. S. Steel and a man called Samuel Gompers? If Arthur Balfour's warning that Germany was arming at a dangerous rate struck closer to home, it still seemed too outlandish to worry about, particularly in view of the fact that Herbert Asquith and David Lloyd George accused him of trying to catch votes by spreading panic.

Even if they had had the desire to weigh these shadowy portents, Canadians still lacked the means either to weigh them independently or to do anything about them. Though Canada had obtained and was exercising almost complete control over its internal affairs, it still dealt with the world outside as a ward of Great Britain. It discoursed and bargained with foreign governments through British embassies and consulates. Britain negotiated and signed Canada's treaties, and not always to Canada's advantage or with Canada's free consent. British officers commanded and trained the meager Canadian army, and in the absence of a Canadian navy of any sort Britain maintained its own naval bases on both Canadian coasts. For diplomatic intelligence, Canadian statesmen could read the newspapers or wait for such sparse and grudging reports as those appearing in the irregular dispatches from the British Colonial Office to the Governor General.

Although it had led in the recent past to a good deal of unpleasantness over Atlantic fishing rights and the Alaskan boundary, Canada's position of tutelage was by no means universally deplored. Many French Canadians saw in it their surest defense against engulfment by the English-Canadian majority. Many English Canadians saw in it a simple and wise acceptance of two simple and unchallenged precepts: the rightness of everything that was British and the Britishness of everything that was right.

Deep in the heritage of every Canadian boy and girl who had gone to school outside Quebec lay the seeds of his or her personal education for nationhood. For more than a century the basic texts for citizenship in the English-speaking parts of the country had been books either borrowed straight from England or borrowed from England and slightly modified. In their spirit and chief message they found their exemplar and perennial best seller in the Ontario Readers.

The Ontario Fourth Reader of 1910 is perhaps worth a moment's attention, if only for the Talmudic certainty it brought to bear on moral and political questions, as did several generations of its ancestors and cousins.

On the flyleaf, beneath the Union Jack, appeared the motto "One Flag, One Fleet, One Throne." Some verses from Deuteronomy 8 faced the first page of text: "For the Lord thy God bringeth thee into a good land, a land of brooks of water, of fountains and depths, springing forth in valleys and hills; a land of wheat and barley, and vines and fig trees and pomegranates; a land of olive trees and honey; a land wherein thou shalt eat bread without scarceness, thou shalt not lack anything in it; a land whose stones are iron, and out of whose hills thou mayest dig brass.

"And thou shalt eat and be full, and thou shalt bless the Lord thy God for the good land which He hath given thee."

The first page was Kipling: "Oh Motherland, we pledge to thee, Head, heart and hand through years to be." The last page was Kipling too: *Recessional*. The first picture in the volume was a portrait of the late King Edward VII; he looked out approvingly on Shakespeare's verses on ingratitude and the ending of a vignette by George Eliot on life in an English public school. Nor was there a word in the four hundred pages that followed to which the departed monarch could possibly have taken exception.

There were verses from Browning:

> *Oh, to be in England*
> *Now that April's there . . .*

There were verses from Henley:

> *Mother of Ships whose might,*
> *England, my England,*
> *Is the fierce old Sea's delight,*
> *England, my own,*
> *Chosen daughter of the Lord,*
> *Spouse-in-Chief of the ancient Sword,*
> *There's the menace of the Word*
> *In the Song on your bugles blown, England—*
> *Out of Heaven on your bugles blown!*

There was a hymn of empire by the Canadian divine F. G. Scott:

> *Strong are we? Make us stronger yet;*
> *Great? Make us greater far;*

Our feet Antarctic oceans fret,
Our crown the polar star.

There were, of course, Thomson's *Rule, Britannia,* Scott's *Love of Country,* Thomas Campbell's *"Ye Mariners of England,"* Macaulay's *The Armada,* Byron's *The Eve of Waterloo,* Tennyson's *Funeral of Wellington,* Felicia Hemans' *The Homes of England,* and Sir Francis Hastings Doyle's *The Private of the Buffs:*

> *Yes, Honor calls!—with strength like steel*
> *He put the vision by;*
> *Let dusky Indians whine and kneel,*
> *An English lad must die.*

The praise of militarism, Imperialism, and England was by no means confined to the poetry selections. William Howard Russell wrote of Balaclava, Southey of the death of Nelson, and Goldwin Smith of London. Under the title "An Elizabethan Seaman," James Anthony Froude contributed an essay on the special joy it gives God to see a man die with his boots on. And although it was widely believed that the sole criteria for inclusion in the Ontario Readers were literary excellence and the audience's range of comprehension, the Ontario Fourth Reader of 1910 devoted five full pages to an unsigned article from the *Atlantic Monthly* stating that, thanks to her colonial and naval power, Britain could win any conceivable war against any conceivable enemy, including the United States.

There was no compulsion on the children of English Canada—any more than there had been on their parents or their parents' parents—to accept wholly or only the patterns of thought imparted in their public schools. It is equally true that most other nations were bringing up their own young to attitudes at least as jingoistic, unsophisticated, and bloodthirsty. In following the general example, Canada may, nevertheless, have taken extra risks and made itself liable, later, to extra penalties.

For while English Canada's historic faiths and prejudices were being settled and solidified in one direction, French Canada's were being settled and solidified in another. The Canada which solicited the loyalty of the French-Canadian schoolchild took its roots and values from the *ancien régime*. Drake and Nelson and the Thin Red Line were almost wholly foreign to it. The equivalent heroes, who had the considerable virtue of being far closer to home both historically and geographically, were Champlain, the Jesuit Martyrs, and Dollard's heroes of the Long Sault. In the literature classes of French Canada the English classical poets and writers received approximately as much attention as those of Spain and Germany.

The differences in tradition and values seemed, however, at the start of the century's second decade, to be a somewhat less serious irritant than they had been during most earlier decades. Perhaps the "language difficulty," which had so often widened the divisions of race and religion in the past and was very soon to be doing so again, really had in times of natural quiet some of the virtues of a sedative. So long as there was no cause for serious trouble, it sometimes seemed that there was no cause for any trouble at all. What, after all, if *les Anglais* did take as their household gods small silk Union Jacks and enameled sea shells sent over from Blackpool instead of wall crucifixes and portraits of the Pope? What if the French did close their stores and send up fireworks on the feast days of obscure and doubtful saints while virtually ignoring Victoria Day and turning their backs on the Glorious Twelfth? It was a free country and no man was obliged to argue with the misguided in small affairs or defer to them in large ones. Canada's chances of burying the family skeleton within the next twenty-five years— or at least of speeding up the slow and painful process of digging it a decent grave—seemed more promising than they had been in a hundred and fifty years.

But before the year was nicely started the placid climate already began changing for the worse. Sir Wilfrid Laurier's Liberal government proposed to build a Canadian navy.

The navy itself was not to be nearly so far-ranging or important as the decision to build it. The sea of debate it churned up, with its floods and eddies, its suddenly remembered backwaters, and its wild crests, was to surge back and forth across the country's political landscape for at least forty more years. Laurier himself was engulfed by it. So, much later, were his opponents, the Conservatives. Even the sure-footed Mackenzie King came near to being swept away in the third main inundation.

II

The Lauriers of St. Lin—The Bordens of
Nova Scotia—The Bourassas and Papineaus
of Montebello

WILFRID LAURIER'S first Canadian ancestor arrived in New France less than forty years after Champlain, more than a hundred years before the Plains of Abraham. He was one of the tiny band of lay pilgrims who helped Maisonneuve found and hold Montreal against the godless savages who skulked outside the palisades; he died at the hands of the Iroquois.

With such antecedents and others whose sole distinctions were warmth of heart and good sense, the Lauriers of St. Lin, Quebec, had already, by the time of Wilfrid's birth in 1841, achieved a serene though by no means common family philosophy. Their pride in their roots was so calm and sure that they felt no need to proclaim it. Their faith was strong enough for them to have no fear of its being shaken by heretics.

Thus to Laurier's father it had seemed a natural and useful thing to send his son for two years to an English-speaking school in a nearby village. Though he was not yet in his teens, Wilfrid went to live for several months with a family of Scots Presbyterians. The question of attending the Protestant family's nightly prayers was left to him. He attended.

During the almost sixty years since his early schooldays, Laurier's genuine regard for the open mind had been one of the chief instruments in the shaping of an extraordinary human being. He went on to seven more years of classical study at a secondary school controlled by the Church and broke up the school debating society by arguing that Canada would have been better off if the French kings had encouraged the Protestant Huguenots to settle there. He read widely in French, English, Greek, and Latin and later became an admiring student of Lincoln.

As valedictorian of his law class at McGill he made an impressive plea for tolerance between the two races. In his early postgraduate days he twice earned the official displeasure of the hierarchy, and a bishop's ban drove him out of business as editor and proprietor of a small newspaper. Throughout his early and middle life he and the Church continued to send out skirmish parties against each other in the arena of politics; in matters of faith their good relations never faltered.

An early opponent of Confederation, he soon became one of its most eloquent and effective defenders. He combined a great devotion to British institutions and the British concept of liberty with an amiable suspicion of British statesmen and their intentions.

Steeped though it was in its climate of absolutes and either-or's—right or wrong, French or English, Catholic or Protestant, Yankee or redcoat, high tariff or low tariff—Canada for fourteen years had accepted this inconsistent and various man in the spirit in which it had accepted his late opponent, John A. Macdonald. He was clearly the best man to lead the country and therefore it was best to let him lead it.

As the years went on, this pragmatic alliance grew far beyond a marriage of convenience. Perhaps John A., with the help of a few endearing weaknesses, had commanded more of the country's affection, but Laurier did not lack for affection and no Canadian politician had ever had so much respect. In a time when well-turned-out, well-spoken gentlemen were objects not merely of curiosity but of admiration, Laurier might have stood as a living inventory of the ideal: slender, graceful body; patrician face and carefully groomed mane of silver hair; pure, resonant voice; flawlessly cut waistcoats, frock coats, and striped trousers; tall black hats and tall white collars; pince-nez dangling from a silken thread; small jeweled pins nestling in well-arranged cravats.

His opponents might have been tempted to make capital in the backwoods of this almost too perfect figure, but Queen Victoria's Diamond Jubilee, many years earlier, had taught them that he made a very bad target. His triumph at that glittering and cosmopolitan concourse had been second only to Her Majesty's own. She had selected him, alone among the dignitaries from the Empire, to receive his knighthood in the Order of St. Michael and St. George.

When Joseph Chamberlain summoned a meeting of the premiers of the self-governing colonies, it was Laurier who stood at Chamberlain's right in the group photograph. The Canadian Prime Minister was warmly received by the aged Gladstone, then in retirement. During a short visit to the Continent he met the President of France, was made a Grand Officer of the Legion of Honor and had an hour-long interview with the Pope. These gleaming adventures raised Laurier's stock everywhere. In the fuss that London made over him, arch-Imperialists could perceive that he must, per se, be more loyal to the Crown than they had guessed, while ultra-nationalists could mutter grudgingly that at last the English had come up against a Canadian they considered important enough to flatter. Unabashed snobs could rejoice in his knighthood, while democrats of the more belligerent stripe could take solace in the discreetly circulated report—which happened to be true—that Sir Wilfrid hadn't wanted his title and had accepted it only because he had been given no chance to refuse without insulting the Queen. Most of his countrymen were too dazzled and proud for him to notice the condescension in the remark of a London newspaper: "For the first time on record a politician of our New World has been recognized as the equal of the great men of the Old Country."

Now, in 1910, the patina of these glories had faded a little. The administration had spent the last half of the Parliament of 1904–8 answering, with nothing like uniform success, to charges of graft and bribery against its supporters and the civil service. But the electors regarded it as more important that Laurier had attended two more Colonial conferences and showed himself a man of far tougher substance than the social lion of the Jubilee. In the face of much further lionizing and much argument, he had opposed and defeated British proposals for an Imperial Council binding in part on all members, for Imperial free trade as contrasted to Imperial preferences and for a joint and binding Imperial military policy. The English-speaking provinces, for all their cultural and sentimental ties with Drake and the Thin Red Line, conceded that his motive was perhaps no worse than a desire to avoid one-sided bargains. They gave him a majority of four seats in the election of 1908. This, with the now habitual landslide in Quebec, left him with an advantage in the Commons of 134 to 87, and nothing in the visible future seemed likely to upset it.

Nominally the chief threat to Laurier's indefinite continuance in office was the leader of the Conservative party, Robert Laird Borden. The threat did not look formidable. Shaken by scandals and age, the great party of Macdonald, Cartier, and Tupper had fallen on dismal times. In the election of 1900 Sir Charles Tupper had lost his own seat and resigned the leadership. Robert Borden agreed under pressure from fellow Nova Scotians to become acting leader for a year. His only discernible qualifications were that he was a successful lawyer and came of a good and well-regarded family. With his strong head, well anchored to a strong body, his abundant graying hair parted in the middle, his thick no-nonsense mustache, and his kind, mild eyes, he contrasted so remarkably with the picturesque and volatile Laurier that they might have been actors made up for opposite roles in a play.

For a decade they had faced each other across the floor of the Commons and all the good lines had been Laurier's. Laurier's too had been incomparably the more exciting delivery. Borden thus far had generated no more enthusiasm inside his party than outside it. Perhaps he would have given up the leadership long since, in accordance with his original wish, if his pride had not compelled him to stay and put down revolts. After decisive defeats in two general elections his political career appeared to be in danger of permanent stagnation.

But help for Borden and danger for Laurier lay in another quarter.

Henri Bourassa once was described as "the most openly mysterious character in Canadian public life." That was in his own time, when his real shape and meaning were obscured by thickets of passion and stormy incident. He is a little easier to see today, through the filter of years. Physically there never was any mystery. Bourassa was almost theatrically good-looking, with a nearly perfect profile, strong and determined, set in and dramatized by a black well-tended beard that ran into a great shock of dark hair. His eyes were dark and brilliant and the lights did not desert them even after the beard turned white, the hair fell away, and the flesh above the high imperious cheekbones began to droop a little. Like Laurier, he was an elegant dresser, partial to gates-ajar collars and dove-gray vests; he could and often did wear a modernistic bow tie without loss of dignity even in those more formal times.

On the sum of these outer aspects Bourassa's contemporaries

found it perpetually impossible to agree, as they found it impossible to agree on the sum of the man within. To his enemies, who became many and whom he made more than welcome to his enmity, he had the dark and glinting look of Mephistopheles. To his friends, who also were many and wholly welcome, he bore the unflinching iron aspect of a Jesuit martyr.

For Bourassa, a great political orator in the last great days of political oratory, and a great personal journalist in the golden twilight of personal journalism, the first two decades of the twentieth century were made so much to order that they might have been commanded by his private saints. The unaided tongue, the hurrying, urgent pen, the white-hot printing press, were the sturdiest, almost the only, vehicles of human communication. Men of affairs frequently wrote, and they nearly always talked; talked partly for pleasure and partly through duty, in the full expectation of being listened to and, if they talked well enough, of being heeded. The human voice was no mere convenience, no mere electronic nuisance, no mere instrument for selling soap or razor blades. A man who spoke no more than loud and clear could always attract some kind of audience. It was not unusual for a man who talked really well, and on matters of moment, to draw a crowd of ten or fifteen thousand and bring them cheering to their feet at will, like a grandstandful of baseball fans.

Like Laurier, Bourassa was both an exceptional stylist and an exceptional dramatist in either language. Since Bourassa had stalked out of the House of Commons as a protest against Canada's entry into the Boer War, the direct comparison of their oratorical powers had depended on the memory of a constantly receding past; their respective supporters were united on one article of faith at least: one or the other was the finest speaker in the land. Laurier was famous for soft cadences. Bourassa was more robust and usually more strident, but he too was an actor. Once, trying to describe his delivery, a newspaper reporter from Ontario wrote: "How his voice swooped and curved and beat upon the walls! It was like the scream of a war trumpet or the wail of the northeast wind down an old chimney; at times like the whisper of a cobold in a cave—weird and creepily intense."

Bourassa talked so persuasively and so much and wrote so vigorously and so much that inevitably he contradicted himself. Often too—for he carried the blood of rebels—he obviously said more than he meant (though he almost never said less). Thus, to distill his goals and his principles is not much easier than to distill his private nature. Perhaps the only word that encompassed all his complexities and all his inconsistencies was the word that finally settled on him and that he did not challenge—the word "nationalist." He believed that, at least for his time and in his time, nationalism in all its insular, aloof, and proudest senses was the one dependable star by which Canada could hope to set her course amid the chaotic scurrying of other nations. He described this basic nationalism in many ways, depending on the occasion and the mood, and his elaborations, amplifications, and arguments ran into the hundreds and thousands. None was crisper or more specific than this, uttered at the beginning of the century: "What I would wish is that between the old English frigate about to sink and the American corsair preparing to pick up the wreckage we should manoeuvre our barque with prudence and firmness, so that it will not be swallowed up in the vortex of one nor be carried away in the wake of the other. Let us not sever the chain too soon, but let us not rivet the links too closely."

This, for him, was the physical end—or, it might be safer to say, one of the physical ends. The philosophy behind it he once put in three theatrical but precise sentences: "Nations have to choose between British ideals and British domination. I stand for ideals against domination. I may be hanged for it in the name of British liberty but that does not matter."

These were the larger outlines of Bourassa's nationalism as a Canadian. But within the larger frame he came to develop—if he did not always have—a second strain of nationalism, a French-Canadian nationalism. Like a very high proportion of that already high proportion of Canadians whose origins were French, Bourassa knew from birth the instinct to withdraw from the roiled main current of his country's history and seek a haven in the clearer, quieter eddies of its first great tributary. But perhaps even he could not have said, truly and finally, which urge came first with him: to isolate Canada from the dangerous and disreputable turmoils of the outside world or to isolate Quebec from the romantic, bloody, unjust, and generally foolish affairs of Canada. During three wars, when there was no time and little inclination on any side to ponder such distinctions, Bourassa's two kinds of nationalism were to become inseparable. His foes scornfully denied the difference, if they had ever really recognized it. Most of his friends, some of whom had found it only a confusing nuisance anyway, ignored it. Bourassa himself found it simpler to forget. And thus the most passionate and effective of Canada-firsters was to be discovered time without number in attitudes that could be described in equal logic—depending on whose variety of logic was being used—as gloriously Canadian or treacherously un-Canadian.

Like Laurier, Bourassa came from an old *Canadien* family. His grandfather, Louis-Joseph Papineau, had won an important place in Canadian history as French-speaking leader in the revolts of the 1830s against the Family Compact, the cabal of well-to-do dignitaries who governed Canada as concessionaires. Papineau encouraged, then tried to arrest, and finally became the symbol of an uprising in Lower Canada at about the same time that the much more agitated grandfather of William Lyon Mackenzie King was inciting rebellion in Upper Canada.

It is a common notion that Henri Bourassa took his character and his example from Papineau. This is only partly so. It is true that Bourassa spent many of his early years in the old Papineau seigniory near Montebello. It is true that he revered the old man for his independence of mind and his willingness to fight for what he believed. But to his lasting sorrow Bourassa in his later years found it necessary to spend almost as much time apologizing for his late grandfather as in praising him. For Papineau left the Church in his younger days, and to the devout Bourassa, to have had a heretic in the family was a catastrophe, even if the heretic also had happened to be a hero. Once Bourassa wrote: "I thank God every day that I have not submitted to the influence of the ideas of Papineau in religious matters. He lost his faith and ceased to practice his religion at the seminary of Quebec. He lived and he died without practicing his religion." Bourassa was only three years old when Papineau died, but he always claimed to remember him "like yesterday"; to remember walking hand in hand with him through the quiet lanes of rural Quebec, finally to remember stealing into the room where the old rebel lay dead, still wearing, perhaps, the fierce disdainful look of a highborn bandit.

From the other side of his family Bourassa took other things. His grandfather Bourassa had gone from Canada to the United States when in his early teens and had once worked as a servant for a Presbyterian family. There he had learned to read English through a Protestant Bible, and to Henri's eternal shame he never did learn to read French. Ultimately this Protestant Bible was bequeathed to young Henri. He made a point of saying many years later in his autobiography: "In a moment of scruple I threw it into the fire."

Henri's father was a gentle architect and painter who claimed not to understand politics and certainly had no sympathy with his son's tempestuous methods. Once he said pointedly to young Henri: "I don't like bright colors either in painting or in politics."

Like Laurier, Bourassa had been sent to an English school in his youth. There he learned to read and admire Scott, Fenimore Cooper, and other English traditional writers, along with the French classicists. When he burst on the public scene in Canada, as a writer and orator, he was, as young political thinkers went in those days, rather inclined to mildness. His attitude toward *les Anglais* had a fey and twinkling quality. It would have been better expressed by a chuckle than by a roar. So far he was not ready to pay the English the compliment of resentment or of rage. Perhaps in this he was merely reflecting some of the wry indulgence of an uncle of his. The uncle sat in Parliament for forty-two years, the last of these after Confederation as a follower of John A. Macdonald. The uncle neither spoke nor understood a word of English but faithfully sat through every debate in the House of Commons rather than run the risk of being absent when his leader might need his vote on a division. Once Macdonald asked the uncle, in French, why he always attended the debates when he understood not a word of them. Bourassa replied: "That's why I stay here; if I understood them I'd go away." It was a remark that Henri was fond of quoting.

Laurier shared a magnificent jest with Henri in the days when Henri's public career was still very young. Laurier had asked him to join the government, and Bourassa had refused. Laurier then wrote him a letter full of wit, irony, and shared knowledge of the racial struggle. In one place Laurier said: "*Puisque vous êtes un Britisher je puis vous dire* that we can agree to disagree.

This was the third of the three men who now stood on the verge of a struggle far more precarious and complex than any in their country's previous history.

The immediate symbol of the struggle, Laurier's naval service bill, at first found the two strongest of them on substantially the same ground. Laurier and Borden both believed the time had come when Canada, which possessed not a single sailor or a single fighting vessel of her own, must prepare to help Britain maintain mastery of the high seas or at least to help in the defense of her own coastal waters. It seemed less a question of politics than of what a later generation would call enlightened self-interest. The German Kaiser still quite clearly had his shrewd, cold eyes fixed on the goal he had set for Admiral Tirpitz long before: "The trident must be in our fist." How far the goal was from attainment no one now knew. But after nearly two decades of alternately belittling his strength and magnifying it, denouncing him and soothing him by turns, the senior statesmen of England had arrived, in 1909, at a terrifying and unanimous conclusion. The Kaiser was already in sight of naval equality, perhaps even of superiority. At the current rate of building, Herbert Asquith estimated, he would have seventeen dreadnoughts to Britain's twenty by 1912. Arthur Belfour predicted more direly that he would actually be ahead twenty-five to twenty.

These forbidding prophecies brought almost identical reactions from the principal spokesmen of the two main branches of the Canadian family. Laurier declared without hesitation: "The supremacy of the British Empire is absolutely essential, not only to the maintenance of the Empire but to the civilization of the world. . . . If the day should come when the supremacy of Britain on the high seas will be challenged, it will be the duty of all the daughter nations to close around the old Motherland and make a rampart about her to ward off any attack. . . . The salvation of England is the salvation of our own country . . . therein lies the guaranty of our civil and religious freedom and everything we value in this life."

Borden, the Tory custodian of all that lay deepest in the British part of the nation's blood stream, could not have been more staunchly explicit. In the spring of 1909 he had given his full support to a parliamentary resolution calling for a Canadian navy. The resolution had passed the Commons without a dissenting vote.

But it was not until nine months later, after a summer recess and another Imperial Defense Conference, that Laurier was ready to chart the details of his naval bill and bring in the enabling legislation.

In that brief summer, fall, and early winter sleeping dogs began arising, at first almost unnoticed but bristling with baneful augury.

Bourassa had recently been concentrating on provincial politics as co-leader of a loose Nationalist-Conservative alliance in the Quebec provincial legislature. He remained at first silent on the naval proposal, but several of the fiery young journalists he had gathered around him denounced it.

Far more crucial at this stage were the unexpectedly savage attacks on the thought of a Canadian fleet from two opposite wings of Borden's already divided and half-demoralized Conservative party. The Quebec wing was flatly against a Canadian navy or any kind of naval aid to Britain, in cash, in ships, or in men; the people must be consulted first, through an election or a plebiscite. The arch-Imperialist wing, centered in Ontario, stood for more aid than it seemed likely that the government was willing to send. It also endorsed the Admiralty's frequently stated preference for a single Imperial navy with units from the colonies and dominions under direct Imperial command. Canada wasn't ready to build, run, and man her own navy; give Britain the cash and Britain would furnish the tools.

The unhappy and hard-pressed Borden at first had seen in the naval proposals one of the few chances in his political lifetime for a few blessed months to be at peace both with his friends and with his enemies. But now he found himself at the eye of a building cyclone. Frederick Monk, his Quebec lieutenant, told a banquet gathering that the policy Borden had endorsed was "costly and useless"; he spoke darkly of the crushing burden of militarism. At the opposite pole, Sir Rodmond Roblin, the Conservative premier of Manitoba, cried for all-out aid to England, under English control and England's terms, and coined a scornful and durable nickname for the tiny, unborn autonomous Canadian armada: "tin-pot navy."

Laurier, of course, had begun to feel some of the same conflicting pressures within his Liberal party. But he was in much better control of his followers than Borden and he was full of easy confidence when he introduced his naval service bill to the House of Commons. The much discussed fleet was to consist of five cruisers and six destroyers. It was to be manned by a small permanent force, with a reserve and a militia behind it. It was to be under Canadian command, although, in an emergency, Parliament could place it under direct Imperial orders. The capital cost was estimated at eleven million dollars and the annual cost for personnel and maintenance about three million. The annual national budget would thus be increased by about 3 per cent.

Throughout the long debate that followed, Laurier was far more at home than Borden in their common role of man in the middle. It was the kind of issue in which Laurier gloried, one of great principles clearly set forth on a compact stage. He proceeded straight ahead, with unconcealed zest for the passage as well as for the harbor and little visible heed for the shoals on either side.

To the two kinds of opposition, inside his own party and outside, he offered a common greeting: "There sit the two extremes, side by side, cheek by jowl, blowing hot and cold." For those who blew hot, he had words of loyal reassurance ("When Britain is at war Canada is at war"); words of caution, bearing the imprimatur of Kipling himself ("Daughter I am in my mother's house, But Mistress in my own"); and finally words of scorn (they who "carry abroad upon their foreheads the Imperial phylacteries, who boldly walk into the temple and there loudly thank the Lord that they are not like other British subjects, that they give tithes of everything they possess and that in them alone is to be found the true incense of loyalty").

For those who blew cold, Laurier had equal reassurance ("If we do have a navy, that navy will not go to war unless the Parliament of Canada chooses to send it there"); equal words of caution ("Do they forget that Canada is expanding like a young giant? Are we to be told that we do not require a naval service? Why, Sir, you might as well tell the people of Montreal, with their half-million population, that they do not need any police protection"); and derision (if the Canadian navy should be compelled to fight, those who preferred could sit at home and "enjoy the security and comfort procured for them by the self-sacrifice of more generous men").

The more pedestrian Borden possessed neither this joyful vitality of utterance nor, had he possessed it, any immediate occasion to give it rein. For him the seeming choice was narrowed to the least awkward of all impossible worlds. If he stuck by the promise of support for an independent Canadian navy which he had given less than a year before, the credit for the navy would still be Laurier's. The two dissident factions of his own party might be lost to him forever; indeed, they were so far apart from him already that Borden was referring to them in his private papers as "cabals."

Thus, for the harassed leader of the Opposition it had become essential to find something in the Laurier bill that he could oppose, or at least improve upon. Whether he could sell that something to his own party or to the country was a question that could be answered later. He had to take action now.

He found his succor in the politician's traditional wild card—the blessed word "emergency." Laurier did not realize, Borden warned the House of Commons, how desperately close the war might be. He far underestimated the appalling rate of Germany's military growth. There simply was not time enough to build, man, and train the autonomous Canadian navy that both leaders approved of in principle. Let that come later, if the people themselves approved of it. But now, to tide over the emergency, the most effective thing Canada could do was to make a gift to the Admiralty sufficient to build or buy three additional dreadnoughts for the Royal Navy (the sum of thirty-five million dollars was suggested). Later a more lasting and far-reaching naval policy could be settled on, but only after consulting the electorate.

Obviously there was meat in this for Tory Ontario—meat for all those who, in Borden's phrase, were "ready to assume their full share of meeting any peril that shall assail the Empire, come what may." For Quebec there was, if not meat, at least a milder form of poison than in the Laurier scheme. For although Borden's proposed cash gift to Britain had no more real appeal to French Canada than had Laurier's autonomous fleet, it did not invite the nightmare of Canadian boys dying in distant places for distant causes. It did not recall the still recent memory of misguided patriots rushing a third of the way around the world to defend their country by shooting and being shot by Dutch farmers in South Africa. It bore at least a slightly lesser threat of personal and automatic involvement in possible future enterprises of a similar nature. To spend Canadian dollars for someone else's war was, true enough, bad; but it was not quite so bad as spending Canadian lives.

But at first it looked as though Borden was getting nowhere, even with such persuasive, if diametrically opposite, arguments on his side. Laurier's bill passed the Commons without ever being in serious jeopardy. The isolationist Monk continued to oppose both his own Tory leader and the Liberal leader. Borden became so despondent that between second and third readings of the bill he wrote a formal letter to his party's whip announcing that he intended to resign when the session was over. He withdrew the letter before it could be submitted to caucus. But the fact that it was written reflected a conviction most of his fellow M.P.s took home to their constituencies for the summer vacation: if Sir Wilfrid's control of the country was to be disturbed in the discernible future it would take more than a mere parliamentary skirmish to do it.

The extra element was soon provided by Henri Bourassa.

Preoccupied mainly with the smaller stage of the Quebec legislature and with the launching of the new newspaper *Le Devoir*, Bourassa had been, for him, strangely silent during the months before the naval debate. But when the bill came down he surfaced with all the commotion of a long submerged and angry whale.

Laurier's declaration that when Britain was at war Canada was at war, he branded angrily as "the most complete backward step Canada has made in half a century . . . the gravest blow our autonomy has suffered since the origin of responsible government."

In *Le Devoir* he pictured the consequences: "Let the notion occur to a Chamberlain, a Rhodes, a Beers, to gold-seekers or opium merchants, of causing a conflict in South Africa or India, in the Mediterranean or the Persian Gulf, on the shores of the Baltic or the banks of the Black Sea or in the China seas, we are involved, always and regardless, with our money and our blood."

He took to the public platform to drive the point home again and again. For a packed meeting in Montreal he listed more than twenty British wars since 1812. He asked with telling sarcasm how Canada had been saved thereby from invasion by the Boers, the Russians, the Afghans, the Sepoys, or the Sudanese.

He returned with new vehemence to an old point of contention —Laurier's coolness toward the fight for separate Catholic schools in the West, an end approved of and sought by most Catholics except the Prime Minister. Laurier remained firm in his conviction that, since education was a provincial matter under the Constitution, federal interference would be folly. Moreover, it might lead to the loss in Quebec of the Catholic rights which the Constitution now protected. He struck back heatedly against "the Pharisee end of Canadian Catholicism; those who have constituted themselves the defenders of a religion which no one has attacked; those who handle the holy-water sprinkler as though it were a club; those who have arrogated to themselves the monoply of orthodoxy; those who excommunicate right and left and whose stature is little greater than theirs; those who seem to have only hatred and envy for their motive and instinct." The Church officially supported neither the Prime Minister nor Bourassa, but among the clergy, high and low, Bourassa's strength grew by the day as Laurier's diminished.

Still, as Laurier knew full well, Bourassa himself had been heard to repeat Daniel O'Connell's firm declaration: "I take my religion from Rome, but my politics from home." Many a habitant quite as devout as either Bourassa or Laurier felt the same, had proved it in the past, and was quite capable of proving it again. Moreover, in the general election that everyone now saw could hardly be postponed beyond another year, the schools would be a minor issue. On the more pressing naval question it seemed unlikely that Bourassa could throw himself wholly behind the Tories. If Laurier's plan to build a Canadian navy to help Britain could be said to represent a surrender of independence, Borden's defeated amendment proposing a cash grant to Britain must surely be considered a greater surrender.

Thus, as he prepared to face Parliament again in the fall, Sir Wilfrid's composure was still relatively intact. So much so that he was led into one of the greatest tactical blunders of his career.

Since the death of a sitting member in February, there had been a Quebec vacancy in the Senate. Now, in October, Laurier filled the vacancy with the M.P. from Drummond-Arthabaska, thus in turn creating a Commons vacancy and calling for a by-election. By clear implication this dared Bourassa to nominate a candidate of his own and submit his quarrels with Laurier to the decision of their fellow French Canadians.

As both men knew, the challenge was heavily loaded in Laurier's favor. Drummond-Arthabaska was Laurier's own old riding; he had practiced law there as a young man and still made his summer home there.

Though Bourassa rose to the bait, it was only because to have done less would have involved a confession of defeat or timidity. He fully expected his man to lose. Indeed, he had already written, before the ballots were counted, an editorial intended for *Le Devoir* in which he attributed the victory of his opponent to "drunkeness, debauchery, tumult . . . appeal to the lowest passions under the serene eye and with the tacit and complacent connivance of the

Right Honorable Sir Wilfrid Laurier, P.C., G.C.M.G., K.C., D.C.F., LL.D., etc."

At the nominating convention to choose the Liberal candidate Laurier himself was in the chair. The man chosen by his party had an impeccable background and connections. Bourassa's Nationalist candidate was a young farmer.

Bourassa, despite his gloomy expectations, took to the stump with style and vigor. He painted a painful picture of draft officers "scouring the country and compelling young men to enlist in the navy or in the army, to go to foreign lands and fight the battles of Great Britain, to co-operate with Downing Street in the oppression of weak countries, and to maintain, at the price of their blood, the supremacy of the British flag in Asia or Africa." His lieutenants outdid him: "Those who disemboweled your fathers on the Plains of Abraham are asking you today to go and get killed for them"; "I come from a parish where the church still bears the mark of English bullets."

Officially the Conservatives were on the sidelines, although Monk and other Quebec Tories supported Bourassa's Nationalist candidate with enthusiasm. When the ballots were counted Laurier's certain victory emerged as a 200-vote defeat—and as a disaster of two dimensions. In the first and simplest dimension, it was a serious blow to the Prime Minister's personal prestige. In the second and perhaps more important one, it represented a transferal of images and of targets. Through two months of high passion and unbridled invective between Laurier's Liberals and Bourassa's Nationalists, the traditionally pro-British Tories had achieved the advantage of being almost unnoticed. To many of his compatriots, Laurier was at the same time becoming, through one of the most grotesque cases of mistaken identity ever to confuse the passage of history, a stranger in a hand-me-down red coat. Many years later Laurier's official biographer, the brilliant historian O. D. Skelton, called this "the most important by-election in Canada's history."

III

The strange, voluptuous fascination of the tariff—The Conservatives take over with help from abroad

OTHER clouds were gathering above the scene of federal politics. They were older than those above the still non-existent navy. The name for them was "the tariff."

Put by itself, "tariff" may well be one of the most opaque and lifeless words in the English language. But in its peculiar Canadian context it soars and breathes with a sensuousness worthy of Hindu poets. Sometimes it crashes forth like the curse of Baal.

Sir John A. Macdonald girded himself with the tariff like a warrior girding against lions. For him and the country he helped to create, the flaccid, bookkeeper's word dripped with emotion and cried out loud with mighty promises and desperate warnings. It had its own associations, quite as vivid as "woman" and "man," "salvation" and "doom," "victory" and "defeat," "love" and "hate."

Considering the rages and paeans it had inspired throughout the country's lifetime, the principle of the tariff was simple. Canada was a big and easy market for manufacturers from abroad, particularly from the United States. Canada was a big and easy source of raw materials. The essential and eternal Canadian dilemma was this:

Low tariff or no tariff: Canadian wheat, pulp, timber, and other natural products would pour across the border to the States. American cars, clothes, and canned food would pour back, because they could be made more cheaply in the United States than at home.

High tariff: Raw products would be harder to sell abroad. Manufactured products would rise in price, but more of them would be made at home and there would be more industry and employment at home.

But nothing so mundane as goods and prices could have planted the tariff so deep in the Canadian mystique. For nearly a century it had been a catchword for patriots, a rallying cry for radicals, and an object of hope, suspicion, and fear for thousands of ordinary people who barely understood its workings. In the still recent days of almost undiluted colonialism Britain had more than once used Canada's trading position, carelessly and without any real regard for Canada's interests, to obtain concessions of one kind or other for herself from the United States. Yet it was possible for a Canadian to be in a fury about this and still feel in his bones that Canada must use the tariff to shore up her ties with Britain and to avoid complete engulfment by the United States.

The tariff invited passion and national schizophrenia in other forms. High tariffs played into the hands of the rich eastern manufacturers and the financiers behind them. They made the average Canadian a captive consumer and made him pay artificially high prices to inefficient manufacturers. They hurt the farmer, who was, or until recently had been, the backbone of the nation.

But the coin had another side. To many Canadians the tariff wall was not an economic device, but an instrument of their very being. To eradicate the wall might be to eradicate Canada. Low tariffs encouraged domination by the United States—economic domination, political domination, and then perhaps outright annexation. It was no accident that the tariff was the real subject of Canada's closest approximation to a Gettysburg Address. When John A. Macdonald cried the immortal words "A British subject I was born, a British subject I will die!" he was thinking in the immediate and specific sense not of Raleigh, Wolfe, or Nelson, but of the tax on ladies' dresses from New York.

In point of fact, it would have been difficult in this later time of Laurier and Borden to find any hard evidence that the United States had the slightest desire to devour Canada under the cloak of free trade. Indeed, so far as the voting record showed, everything pointed in an opposite direction. Each of the countries had had a general election in each of the years 1896, 1900, 1904, and 1908. In each case the party that favored lower tariffs had been elected in Canada and the party that favored higher tariffs had been elected in the United States.

However, through an apparently modest temblor of U.S. history the Republican party was now beginning to have second thoughts about the benefits of economic isolationism. The Taft administration had made relatively liberal trade agreements with half a dozen countries in Western Europe and South America. When Canada proved somewhat more difficult to deal with, Taft became surprisingly conciliatory. Hitherto he had taken the position that so long as Canada granted preferences to British imports, Canadian exports to the United States must be charged penalty taxes. But now he changed his mind. In the friendly climate that ensued as the year turned into 1911 the two governments completed a new reciprocity agreement, which, although it was not free trade, offered lower and in some cases no duties on raw Canadian exports to the United States. In return there were to be lower duties on a number of American manufactured products coming into Canada.

The agreement, negotiated in a secrecy that added to the indignation of its opponents, still had to be ratified in both legislatures. Taft won approval of both the House of Representatives and the Senate by the middle of the summer. Laurier had not expected to take so long to gain ratification from Parliament, for he was sure the country was behind him. Borden was of a similar mind. The day after Laurier's Finance Minister put the reciprocity proposals to the House of Commons, Borden called a party caucus. "The atmosphere that confronted me was not invigorating," he wrote later. "There was the deepest dejection in our Party, and many of our members were confident that the government's proposals would appeal to the country and would give it another term of office. Foster [George E. Foster, a leading Tory financier] was greatly impressed by the proposals and said that when they were presented his heart had gone down into his boots. The western members were emphatic in their statements that not one of them would be elected in opposition to reciprocity. One of them declared that he dare not vote against the government's proposals. I stemmed the tide as best I could, although I was under great discouragement. . . . I had the support of many of our members, although the difference of opinion which had developed seemed in itself to be a forerunner of disaster."

But again Borden's pessimism, nourished as it had been for so long by his rejection by the electorate and his only partial acceptance by his own party, proved deeper than it need have been. Almost overnight a group of Laurier's wealthiest and most influential followers sprang into open rebellion against the Prime Minister. The Toronto Board of Trade called a protest meeting against his proposed hospitality to Yankee textiles and threshing machines. Sir Edmund Walker, president of the Bank of Commerce, declared to a cheering assemblage: "Although I am a Liberal, I am a Canadian first of all, and I can see that this is much more than a trade question. Our alliance with the Mother Country must not be threatened. We must assimilate our immigrants and make out of them good Canadians, and this reciprocity agreement is the most deadly danger tending to make this problem more difficult. The question is between British connection and what has been well called 'continentalism.'" Sir William Van Horne, of the Canadian Pacific Railway, roared at reciprocity that "he was out to bust the damn thing." And finally the western newspaper baron Clifford Sifton—still, next to Laurier himself, perhaps the best-known Liberal in Canada—led seventeen other prominent members of the party in signing a manifesto against reciprocity.

How much of this quick and stunning antagonism was due to the tug of special interest and how much to genuine uneasiness about the independence of the nation will never, of course, be established in mathematical terms. Without doubt the heartstring that Macdonald had struck so resonantly in the earlier tariff disputes had been truly struck again, and in the echoing notes there was much that was strong and genuine. And also without doubt the plain suspicion and perversity of a small country growing up in the shadow of a larger one began working among people who had no personal stake in the tariff or the lack of one. Having denied Canada reciprocity for so long, why was the United States so eager now to grant it? What did President Taft have up his sleeve anyway?

Soon Sifton, the disaffected Liberal, was conferring with Borden in secret. But Borden's elation over a break in his rival's inner guard was short-lived. His old enemies within the Tory party professed horror at the impending alliance with the dissident Grits. If they submitted to it, they contended, the embrace of the Sifton group would suffocate them all in the end.

Again the much bruised Borden was plunged in despondency. He tried to rally the Tory party at a caucus but soon concluded that his opponents could not be won over. Again he tendered his resignation and consented to reconsider only after a delegation

came to him late at night "almost with tears" and fifty-nine of the
Conservative M.P.s signed a round robin pledging him their loyal
and undivided support.

Thus heartened, Borden fought the reciprocity bill with mounting resolution and hope. In the House of Commons his party
carried the debate deep into the spring and forced an adjournment
while Laurier attended the coronation of King George V and
another Imperial Conference. When Parliament reassembled in July,
the Tories were still half fighting and half waffling. A Tory backbencher proposed adjournment of the reciprocity debate to discuss
pensions for veterans of the Fenian raids, and it became obvious
that Laurier had two choices: to push his bill through by force
of numbers and remain in office or to call an election while he
still had reasonable control of Parliament, of his party, and presumably of the electorate. He chose the latter course.

The election date was September 21, 1911. The campaign that
preceded it may well have marked the end of an age in Canadian
politics, the age of joyful innocence. Never again would the torch
of truth burn so high and pure, in all its shades and degrees of
heat. Never again would the nation's heart swell to so many and
such sure and eager hymns. Never again would so many noble
readings of the gospel resound in so many splendid accents. It
was a passionate campaign, drawing wellsprings from many sources.
It was full of the round Victorian rhetoric that, as any well-
cultivated flower should, had reached its finest bloom just before
its time to die. And if it had an overlay of bitterness, it was not the
savage, very nearly homicidal bitterness that was to becloud and
besmirch another campaign six years ahead. Often, indeed, the
bitterness had a leaven of something vaguely like good humor. As
elections go today, when stump oratory is almost gone and a few
careful dignitaries read antiseptic speeches before microphones
and cameras, it would be considered a dirty election. By the standards of any time it was a robust and fascinating one.

Throughout the parliamentary debate over reciprocity Henri
Bourassa, content with his victory over Laurier in the naval by-
election in Arthabaska, had enjoyed a rest from the national scene.
His early pronouncements on the tariff issue were perfunctory,
almost bored. At first he expressed approval of reciprocity, then
indifference, and finally—like a man doing a double take—he ap-

peared to remember that he was at loggerheads with Laurier over the navy and began attacking him on reciprocity too.

Whether Bourassa's switch to the high-tariff side was a cause or an effect, it coincided with the emergence of a remarkable alliance. The ultra-nationalist *Le Devoir* and its ultra-nationalist editor suddenly found a staunch friend in the ultra-Imperialist Montreal *Star* and its ultra-Imperialist proprietor, Sir Hugh Graham. Other strange companions flocked to Bourassa's side. One of his own lieutenants was later to boast that an English Conservative who had once called the nationalists "rebels and disloyal traitors" bought forty subscriptions to *Le Devoir*. The Conservative Toronto *World* eulogized him as a man "of stainless reputation, of great moral energy, a sincere admirer of English institutions." Some of the biggest manufacturers and financiers on St. James Street supplied him with money and encouragement.

Laurier contemplated all this with worldly amusement and summed up his own predicament thus: "I am branded in Quebec as a traitor to the French, and in Ontario as a traitor to the English. In Quebec I am branded as a Jingo, and in Ontario as a Separatist. In Quebec I am attacked as an Imperialist, and in Ontario as an anti-Imperialist." Although he was now almost seventy, Sir Wilfrid entered the lists shaking his noble mane and shouting forth the rallying cry he had borrowed from Henry of Navarre: "Follow my white plume!"

During the last month of the campaign Laurier made more than fifty speeches. They were not all easy, for winds of adversity had begun to threaten from abroad as well as at home. President Taft, his co-sponsor of reciprocity, had publicly described Canada as being "at the parting of the ways." Protectionists quickly and gleefully ushered the phrase into the demonology of the times along with the still more painful utterance of Champ Clark, Speaker of the U. S. House of Representatives: "I hope to see the day when the American flag will float over every square foot of the British North American possessions clear to the North Pole. . . . I have no doubt whatever that the day is not far distant when Great Britain will joyfully see all her North American possessions become part of this republic."

A U.S. senator was heard to cry: "Canadian annexation is the logical conclusion of reciprocity with Canada." And Champ Clark spoke again: "We are preparing to annex Canada." Another congressman said candidly: "Be not deceived. When we go into a country and get control of it, we take it."

The Hearst papers applauded reciprocity. One of them, the New York *American*, announced comfortably: "Eventually, of course, Canada will come in. That will be when we want her." Each such utterance, intended to comfort and applaud Laurier, helped to ruin him.

Even in the West, where there had been no serious doubts about the benefits of reciprocity, a few people began to have second thoughts. J. J. Hill, the American railway magnate, suddenly loomed to some as the probable chief beneficiary. If there were no tariff on grain Hill would drain Canada's export wheat into a labyrinth of U.S. rail lines to the eastern U.S. seaboard for shipment across the Atlantic. Canadian railwaymen would be thrown out of work, Canadian steel would rust, the great Canadian terminal elevators at Port Arthur and Fort William would empty and fall into decay. An alarmed legislator from Port Arthur cried: "Under the new agreement, if it is carried, all the wheat will be shipped to Minneapolis and St. Paul or to the United States markets by way of Duluth, which means that we might as well take our elevators and dump them in the lake."

The Buffalo *Courier* predicted happily that there would be an increase in receipts of two hundred million bushels of grain "at this port if the reciprocity treaty is adopted and the Buffalo elevator interests act in concert."

The American Association of Railways itself passed a resolution in support of reciprocity, and the *Wall Street Journal* published a chilling report in support of the fear that J. J. Hill had been developing his Great Northern Railway in the expectation of grabbing business from Canada. The *Financial Review*, of New York, said flatly: "It is evident . . . that if it goes into effect practically all the wheat of Western Canada will be drained into the American mills in adjacent territory."

Unwelcome applause for reciprocity came also from the president of the United States Holstein Association, who hurried to Toronto with "the greetings of one hundred million people who are overjoyed to know that an imaginary tariff line between people of the same blood, the same fathers, whose every interests are identical, is about to be obliterated and torn down."

Those who opposed the new treaty were just as emphatic.

Rudyard Kipling cabled from London as the polls opened: "It is her own soul that Canada risks today." A speaker at a meeting of the Canadian Defence League cried: "I feel prepared to do almost anything, even to fighting in the streets, to prevent reciprocity going through." Leading clubwomen of Montreal organized a Woman's Branch of the Anti-Reciprocity League and sent a petition to the government saying that reciprocity meant: "Annexation, injury to home life and the marriage tie, a lessening of national religion, morals and patriotism." The Tories circulated a new campaign song to the tune of "Yankee Doodle":

> President Taft he made a pact
> With Laurier and Fielding
> And in the trade that Tafty made
> He found them very yielding.

Chorus: *Yankee Doodle Laurier,*
> Crafty Taft's a dandy,
> Fielding bust the Farmers' Bank,
> Railroad Hill's the candy.

> We'll take our stand throughout the land
> And preach to you this story
> That ancient rag, the British flag,
> Must float below Old Glory.

An age of political polemic was dying to the last sound of drums, the wail of fifes, and the flicker of torches. Another example of the splendid, fading art of campaign poetry was introduced by one of Borden's most powerful supporters, the Honorable Robert Rogers, of Manitoba:

> Lord God of our Fathers be with us, rise up
>   at Thy people's cry
> For blindness has stricken the nation and the
>   doom of our land draws nigh.
> Rise, rise up ere it falls, Lord, and save us,
>   and blast with the fire of Thy mouth
> The treason that barters our birthright for
>   the gold of the Kings of the South.

Election day was the first day of fall, crisp and clear in nearly all parts of the country. Long before dusk closed in on the autumn evening, crowds began gathering before the newspaper bulletin boards, confident Grits before the Toronto *Globe*, the Winnipeg *Free Press*, and the other Liberal papers, hopeful Tories before the *Mail and Empire* and the Montreal *Star*. The suspense was not long-lived. A hundred thousand people poured through the streets of Toronto by ten o'clock, and those who held their torchlights highest and shouted loudest were those who had heard the returns at the *Mail and Empire*. Before the night was through someone threw a brick through the front window of the Liberal *Globe*. The Tories had won, won overwhelmingly. If the Quebec Nationalists were to be counted as Conservatives—as for all early and practical purposes they assuredly were—the standing in the Commons had been exactly reversed. At the closing of the polls it was: Laurier 133, Borden 88. When the returns were completed it was: Borden 133, Laurier 88.

In the debacle seven Liberal ministers lost their seats, including the promising young Labor Minister, Mackenzie King, as well as Finance Minister Fielding, who had negotiated the reciprocity agreement with Washington. Most of the Grit casualties were in Ontario. Here the Tories had won 72 seats to 14. Quebec still remained Liberal, but the uneasy alliance of Monk and Bourassa had cut Laurier's majority there from 43 seats to 11.

If Canada was mildly stunned by the result, the effect on the United States was of stuttering and choleric incomprehension. The outraged speaker Clark blamed the whole thing on "corruption funds sent from this country and Great Britain to Canada," threatened to run for President on a program of annexation, and boasted that if he did he'd "carry every state in the nation." The abandoned and embarrassed President Taft muttered aggrievedly: "I think we know a little more on this side than they do on theirs, because we are an older country, and after some years of experience it is possible they will come to take the right view." A Buffalo paper blamed the result on "every imaginable form of misrepresentation, intimidation of the work-people, appeals to passion, to prejudice, to cupidity." The St. Louis *Republic* gave the credit to "Cockney and hooligan Jingoism" and warned Borden, whom it called "the chief Imperial hypocrite," that unless his country came to its senses it might be necessary to accept "annexation in all its phases." Hearst's

New York *American* harumphed acidly that Laurier had over-estimated the intelligence of the Canadian people. The New York *World* stood aghast at such a display of "popular stupidity." The *Times*, which was less noted for its temperance in those days, found in it an example of "prejudice, delusion, reaction and ignorance." The Chicago *Tribune*, while also deploring the Canadian people's decision, chivalrously confessed to seeing in it "a certain splendor."

For the time being Borden's American enemies remained far more valuable to him than his friends. In a few months Taft himself was to supply the finest testimonial he could have asked for. This he did when he made public a letter that he had written to Teddy Roosevelt before the reciprocity campaign. In this letter Taft, then hard pressed in his own country, had urged upon T.R. the argument that reciprocity would produce "a current of business between Western Canada and the United States that would make Canada only an adjunct of the United States." It would transfer all their important business to Chicago and New York, "with their bank credits and everything else." It would increase greatly the demand in Canada for American manufactures. "I see this is an argument against reciprocity made in Canada, and I think it is a good one," Taft concluded.

Thus Borden, who had not in his wildest dreams hoped to do better than back into a narrow and insecure victory, rode to triumph to the sweetest music a politician can ever hear: the astonished voices of his routed foes.

IV

The incomparable Sam Hughes

BORDEN heard the news of his victory in Halifax. For a dozen years he had scarcely dared turn his back on his impatient and frustrated followers. And now it must have given him a certain gentle satisfaction—and it would have been a gentle kind, for he was not a malicious man—to disappear alone and unavailable to his old home at Grand Pré beside the Bay of Fundy. Eight hundred miles away in Ottawa there grew and swelled to the edge of bursting a cloudhead of public rumor and speculation and private hope and anxiety that had hardly seen an equal since Confederation.

When Borden returned to the capital five days after the returns had been counted, it was not only the minor lobbyists and office seekers who were crowded in the corridors and anterooms leading to the country's new inner sanctum. The Prime Minister-designate heard directly from or soon heard urgently on behalf of scores of men who believed themselves deserving of cabinet or other high rank in the public service. Letters and telegrams, not all of selfless congratulation, were coming in at the rate of three or four hundred a day.

The Cabinet, of course, was the first order of business, and here there were many nice points to consider. Priority of numbers would go automatically to the true-blue Tories, but the Quebec Tories, even though everyone knew them to be anti-Laurier and Nationalist rather than pro-Borden and Conservative, had to be well represented in common equity and sense. And the rebel Grit bankers and manufacturers whose flight to the protectionist banner had so clearly contributed to Laurier's demise in Ontario must have their spokesman in the Cabinet too. Then there were wheels within the wheels. At least a token caning was required for the most persistently difficult of the older Tories. The usual individual rivalries and jealousies had to be considered.

Mercifully Borden was limited in the time for soul searching. Less than three weeks hence a new Governor General, the Duke of Connaught, would arrive at Quebec. It was imperative that the new Cabinet be sworn in before the Prime Minister left to meet him at the dockside. Within a few days Borden appointed seventeen ministers. His long-time chief lieutenant in the Tory councils, George E. Foster, reluctantly took the Ministry of Trade and Commerce. Finance, the post that Foster really wanted, went to the Liberal apostate Thomas White. Monk became Minister of Public Works and was joined in the Cabinet by two other Nationalists.

But none of the decisions Borden made in that October 1911 and perhaps no decision of his lifetime had anything like the bravura, the splendid derring-do, of his choice for the apparently secondary Ministry of Militia and National Defence. For that portfolio Borden selected Colonel Sam Hughes. In Hughes he chose and prepared for fulfillment one of the most bizarre and unlikely figures in all of Canadian history.

Sam Hughes was born in 1853 in the pastoral Ontario county of Durham. A Huguenot great-grandfather on his mother's side had died at Waterloo fighting for Napoleon. On the same field blood from the other side of the family had been shed for Wellington. The mixed and storm-tossed tribe put out its Canadian roots during one of the Irish potato famines and soon took on the very bloom and texture of Ontario: in blood, mainly Irish and Scots; in religion, Methodist by way of Presbyterianism.

Sam grew up a non-smoker and a non-drinker. He had the solid build of a lacrosse player and the square jaw and unswerving, humorless blue eyes of a man destined to live and die without a single doubt. At seventeen he had taken up arms in the Fenian raids. Soon after that he was teaching school in eastern Ontario. From there he went to Toronto as a high school instructor in English, and shortly after his thirtieth birthday he had saved enough money to buy a weekly newspaper, the Lindsay *Warder*.

Lindsay nestled at the very heart of what was then a kind of subprovince of Ontario—the Loyal Orange Lodge—and as an Orangeman, an Irishman, an editor, and a teetotaler, Hughes soon became one of its leading figures. Within a few years he was Conservative member of Parliament for Victoria North and—a source of almost equal satisfaction—officer commanding the 45th Victoria Regiment of the Canadian militia.

In spite of the Irish strain Hughes was a devoted—though by no means an inflexible or uncritical—Imperialist. He saw in the South African War at the turn of the century a clear call to duty. Canada then had no regular army. Its few permanent garrisons were manned by British redcoats, and the senior staff officer of the Canadian militia was a British regular army officer.

Partly because it had no army to send and partly because there was no popular enthusiasm for the British excursion to the far-off veld, the Liberal government of the day showed no tendency to rush to the mother country's aid. Colonel Sam chafed briefly under what he considered his country's humiliating inertia and then acted unilaterally. To the then Canadian Militia Minister, Sir Frederick Borden (a cousin of Sir Robert), he dispatched an offer to raise and personally command a Canadian battalion to aid the British Expeditionary Force. Without waiting for his own government's reply he sent the same offer to Joseph Chamberlain, then Secretary of State for the Colonies.

Chamberlain interpreted this message from the Canadian member of Parliament and officer as an earnest of Canada's intentions and indicated his and the Empire's gratitude. The Canadian government, which very probably would have matched or bettered Colonel Sam's private and unsanctioned offer in its own good time, was only moderately embarrassed. But Major General Hutton, the British army officer in command of the Canadian forces, could not contain his rage or even bring himself to the attempt. Hutton had been in the habit of going over the Canadian Cabinet's head to communicate directly with the War Office and with the Governor General, Lord Minto, in matters of defense. He now found the idea of a civilian colonel going over his, Hutton's, head quite insupportable. There ensued between the two men a duel that would have enriched the pages of Cervantes, although on occasion it became difficult to tell which was Quixote and which was the windmill.

Hutton vowed that the upstart militia colonel from Lindsay not only would get no command in South Africa but would not get to South Africa at all. In one of the many exchanges of view and ukase about military affairs which he conducted with Lord Minto and the War Office without troubling to inform the Canadian government, the general wired London in cipher: "I regret that I must decline to recommend Colonel S. Hughes for employment with our troops proceeding Transvaal in any capacity whatever. This officer's want of judgment and insubordinate self-assertion would seriously compromise success of Canadians when acting with Imperial troops. His insubordinate and improper correspondence, official and unofficial, renders his appointment moreover impossible on military grounds."

And that, the general was happy to suppose as he reported the message to his sympathetic confidant the Governor General, was that.

But Colonel Sam still intended to march against the Boers whatever Hutton said. As an M.P., of course, he had ready access to the ears of members of the Cabinet, and as an Opposition M.P., he had a special nuisance value. No doubt, too, there was a certain grudging sympathy in the highest circles for the well-meaning Canadian civilian in collision with the autocratic British officer.

At any rate, when Hutton's opposition to Hughes became public and apparent, the Cabinet insisted on Hutton's appearing three different times to explain why Hughes should not be allowed to go to South Africa at least as a captain. Hutton remained unyielding and within ten days he was able to report to his ally Lord Minto, the Governor General: "Have carried all my points." He added: "Poor Hughes is almost heartbroken and has been to see me twice full of tears and contrition. The struggle is over. No one but Your Excellency and I will ever realize the magnitude of what has been achieved by the overthrow of Hughes, the Conservative Insurgent."

Hughes compounded his humiliation by writing two extremely docile letters to Hutton and as a reward he was now given permission to accompany the first Canadian contingent to South Africa as a civilian. But he was specifically forbidden to wear a uniform.

This posed no serious problem for the indomitable Hughes. When he disembarked at Cape Town he took a good room in the Grand Hotel and began looking around. Soon he discovered a number of high-ranking British staff officers he had met at the Diamond Jubilee celebrations in London two years before. Soon he was in uniform as a transport officer. And soon he was writing letters home to his paper in Lindsay recounting his military exploits in vivid detail. Actually, as nearly as can be ascertained through the fragmentary official accounts and the purple fog of Sam's own narratives, he did conduct himself well as a supply officer and as a combat officer in a small handful of minor skirmishes. Certainly in his activities as a belligerent against the Boers there was nothing that was not to his credit. On the other hand, there was nothing so spectacularly heroic as to protect him from the consequences of his bombast. In newspaper dispatches in praise of himself and his ever faithful batman, a soldier named Turley, Hughes had directly or indirectly made comparisons to his and Turley's credit with a number of other soldiers, including a few of considerably higher rank than his own. After some eight months in the field he was quietly ordered to return to Canada. Hughes received no reprimand and was indeed made officer commanding troops on the ship that bore him to England on the way back home.

Sam now thought he had scored at least a partial victory over Hutton, but its incompleteness and the lack of public acknowledgement of it was to rankle until his death. When the Boer War ended, Hughes received his service ribbons. But there were no decorations to show for what he clearly regarded as an exceptional combat record; he hadn't even received his war gratuity.

He appealed for justice first to the Liberal government and finally, failing to find satisfaction there, directly to the Governor General. The Army Council of Britain notified the Governor General in 1904 that Hughes's services in South Africa "were not such as to warrant the issue to him of the war gratuity." But either through charity or prudence the Governor General did not pass this message on to Hughes, whose assessment of his exploits in Bechuanaland and the magnitude of whose slights thus grew year by year.

By 1908, eight years after his return from the wars, he wrote Prime Minister Laurier again demanding what he called recognition. By now he was convinced, and so intimated to Laurier, that he was entitled to at least one Victoria Cross and perhaps two. He said this estimate had been made to him by his divisional commander in South Africa, General Sir Charles Warren. Warren, he assured Laurier, had promised to recommend him for this highest of all British military decorations on two distinct occasions.

This much at least of Hughes's background and temperament was well known to Borden when he took Hughes into his Cabinet. Perhaps the new Prime Minister had no certain way of knowing that Sam's difficult streak was widening rather than narrowing. The fact was that it already bore symptoms of paranoia.

Six months before the election Hughes had begun to wonder seriously whether Borden himself was to be trusted. Throughout the party intrigues preceding the election victory Hughes had remained steadfastly a Borden man and he had confidently expected, after the abortive uprising of 1910, that he would be appointed either party whip or chief organizer. Instead the key posts went to George Perley and Herbert Ames. In a letter to a friend Sam poured out his misery and fury.

"Mr. Borden," he began under taut control, "is a most lovely fellow; very capable but not a very good judge of men or of tactics." But in a paragraph or two Hughes was claiming that he had almost singlehandedly saved Borden against a conspiracy led by the selfsame Perley and Ames. "You may imagine my horror this session to find Mr. Borden honoring and putting to the front, not the men who were loyal to him, but the men responsible for the agitation which caused and gave reason for the conspiracy." "Ames," he said reasonably, "has a nice mild appearance." But he added, "He is absolutely vain and egotistical; a man of no depth or foresight. Indeed he would have made a marvellous main floorwalker for some large establishment such as Eaton's but he has no political sagacity. The businessmen of Montreal will positively not have anything to do with him. . . . He is despised by the big men there."

As for the other new favorite, "Perley is cold, tyrannical and very egotistic." In a moment Hughes returned to the despised Ames, his orange banners flying. "He is from Quebec. He fought us on the autonomy bills; is under the control of the ecclesiastics of Rome. . . . The Orange Order, with its tens, aye, hundreds of thousands of friends will not put up with this sort of thing."

Faced with such monstrous buffetings, Sam changed, almost between sentence and sentence, from stoic imperviousness to black despair. "As you know, my strength is that I am powerful where I am longest and best known. I am loved by my friends, and feared but not despised by my opponents. These fellows are despised by both sides. . . . In my own case these d——d noodles, with one or two other nonentities, have for years whispered privately to suppress me. I have dozens of examples where these fellows over and over again prejudiced me by a word, a shrug of the shoulder, a grin or a direct condemnation."

Hughes's remarkable outcry, much more remarkable because it was utterly uninhibited by any official or semi-official purpose, ended thus: "Personally I want no recognition. I fought almost singlehanded for Borden last year and completely overthrew the conspiracy; yet my reward was to be put under the very men primarily responsible for the trouble. They were promoted leaders. It will not do. I incurred more enmity over that than over anything I ever did, and yet see my reward. As you know, I was never surpassed in organization yet or in getting work out of the fellows whether they were orange or green, but I would not care to give my time any longer towards organizing the whole country. That day has gone by. But a man likes to be trusted."

This letter was written in March 1911. It produced no result of course, but by the winter of the following year Hughes had a new avenue of appeal. The stately, soldierly, and stuffy Duke of Connaught—third son of Queen Victoria—was now installed as Governor General. Hughes, again overlooking the niceties of rank and procedure, wrote him personally. On this occasion he discussed himself in the third person. In the now ancient South African campaigns participated in by the third-person Hughes, the Governor General was told, "there were very many pretty 'scraps' and some pretty heavy fighting." He went on to localize these engagements. "In each and every one," he said, "it fell to the lot of Hughes to direct the British forces, and in each and every instance victory fell to their lot, although the numbers and positions were invariably in favor of the Boers."

He told Connaught of his two missing Victoria Crosses. His decision to leave the South African front, he went on, had been entirely his own, made on the advice of his commander in chief, Lord Roberts, that the war was as good as ended and in the conviction that he would be needed back in Canada during a forthcoming election campaign.

"General Warren," Hughes wrote the Duke of Connaught, "begged and implored Hughes to remain. He assured Hughes that he had no officer left on whom he could rely. On the night of the 25th June, sobbing like a child, General Warren went over the same story, and again begged Hughes to remain, but the return fever had seized him, so he insisted on going." Hughes recollected his ancient feud with the now long vanished General Hutton, whom he called "a madman." He demanded that Connaught, having been informed of all these matters, now arrange that he, Sam Hughes, receive the "recognition" still owing to him because of his record in South Africa.

Connaught was almost stunned, partly by the nature of Hughes's communication and partly by its mere submission. He had, without doubt, been warned to look out for this strange, untrained, and ignorant member of Parliament and militia colonel, but he had not expected to hear from him with so little ceremony. If Hughes had been a genuine officer or a genuine gentleman, Connaught would have disposed of him as easily as he'd have stared down an erring footman. But Sam was only a part-time officer and he made no pretense to being a gentleman; when Connaught fired a whiff of regal grape across his granite prow, he not only failed to cower—he almost failed to notice. Connaught urged him sternly to remember that he had long ago promised to bury the hatchet over the Hutton affair. Hughes urged Connaught just as sternly to get him justice—"justice meaning full recognition by Imperial authorities of all my South African services, my many times being named in despatches, the gratuity and any honors given to any Canadian." Connaught's ultimate reply was to scribble an angry note to Borden suggesting he get rid of Hughes at once and for good.

But the remarkable Colonel Hughes was already beyond the reach of viceroys and barely within the reach of premiers. Borden was scared stiff of him—and so remained for five years—and was also impressed by his performance.

Hughes threw himself into his job at the comatose Department of Militia with high heart and high energy. He went to work at once on new armories, on a master plan of military training under which all male citizens would be trained for combat by the age of twelve. It was his aim to have in five years "some hundreds of thousands of our youths trained to shoot and march." As his plan took shape he was able to condense it to a sentence: "Give me one million men who can hit a target at five hundred yards and we would not have a foe who could invade our country."

In most quarters he was heard attentively and politely. But the cynical Henri Bourassa still had no respect. *Le Devoir* interpreted Hughes's military blueprint in a different way: "He has invited twenty-five thousand schoolboys to go and make exercises in the fields and learn to become debauchees and play the fool at the expense of the state. He has drawn a map of the country as a vast field for maneuvers where he proposes to enroll the nation and teach them, democratically, the art of shooting human game at a convenient distance."

V

An obnoxious young man named Winston Churchill—The defeat of the naval bill

SIR WILFRID LAURIER on the morrow of the 1911 election looked a tragic figure—frail, just two months short of seventy, not quite so erect as he once had been, a badly beaten old man. But his own assessment of his position was far more cheerful. He made a perfunctory attempt to resign as leader of the Liberal party but yielded to the overwhelming and partly desperate demands of his supporters that he stay. Very shortly he was boasting to a banquet audience: "I don't feel ripe for heaven, and at all events I want another tussle with the Tories."

In this tussle he now had the advantage of being able to choose his weapons. Of the government's program he could accept what he chose to accept and oppose what he chose to oppose. The selection gave him little trouble. He was far too good a politician not to acknowledge that he had been trounced, and soundly trounced, on reciprocity, and the less said about that for the time being, the better. On the second big issue, the naval service bill, he had been trounced too, but now the very flail that bore his bloodstains lay at his feet, ready for picking up. His late tormentor stood before him, as naked to attack as he himself so recently had been.

For the first time in fifteen years Laurier had the advantages of opposition. He was unencumbered by the grotesquely impossible task of putting into effect a naval policy that could be acceptable to both the Quebec Nationalists and the Ontario Imperialists. He barely waited until the new king was seated before he gave the Damoclean sword a joyful twang. When he rose to reply to the Speech from the Throne, after Parliament had reassembled, Sir Wilfrid wondered wistfully why the speech had made no mention whatever of naval policy. As far back as 1909 the new Prime Minister and his followers had unanimously supported a resolution calling for naval assistance to Great Britain. In 1910 they had proposed to give Britain ships rather than train and equip an autonomous Canadian navy; then they had seen a dire emergency. But now, alas, although the previous government's naval bill remained on the statutes, it was proposed to do nothing to implement it. What, if anything, was proposed to replace it?

Borden's task in replying to such untimely questions was not easy. On the very day after his election triumph his uncertain but essential ally, Henri Bourassa, had trumpeted publicly: "We [meaning the Quebec Nationalists] have destroyed one government and we shall destroy yet another unless our principles are respected." The chill these words had laid upon the first glow of Borden's triumph was not relieved when, a few days later, he sent Monk to offer Bourassa a seat in the Cabinet and Bourassa politely declined.

At first, in the resumed navy debate, Borden contented himself with repeating the old attacks on the existing Liberal bill without pressing any substitute of his own. Henri Bourassa's locum tenens, Monk, reminded the House of Commons that Quebec would not accept any kind of naval aid without a plebiscite. On this uneasy note the government shoved the whole navy issue back into its cluttered and faintly noisome pigeonhole.

Borden took part of the summer to go to London to try finding out the real state of the race for sea power. Also he made a systematic attempt to explain to various members of the British Cabinet that the blank-check, my-England-right-or-wrong concept of Ottawa's duty to London was nearly finished.

In interviews with all the leading politicians of the mother country Borden stressed this new truth again and again. During that 1912 July in London he heard it at last acknowledged when Prime Minister Asquith rose in the House of Commons and said: "Side by side with this growing participation in the active burdens of the Empire on the part of our dominions, there rests with us undoubtedly the duty of making such response as we can to their obviously reasonable appeal that they should be entitled to be heard in the determination of the policy and the direction of Imperial affairs."

Today the words sound as tame, obvious, and unexciting as the leftover notes of a visiting Rotarian. But they had real meaning in their time and place, and even a certain drama. Only a year before, at the Imperial Conference of 1911, Asquith had unequivocally restated the principle that Britain and Britain alone determined the Empire's courses in world affairs; it was for the colonies and do- minions to follow without asking questions. With Britain's official renunciation of divine right, Borden now had a practical basis on which to return home and discuss Canadian naval aid in practical terms with his countrymen.

And thereupon, from the strange grab bag of villains and whip- ping boys who bestrewed and bedeviled the path of Canadian for- eign policy, there spilled a new and startling figure. For the next few months he was to loom even larger in the country's public debates and to arouse at least as much suspicion and displeasure— though not quite so much hatred—as even Taft and Bourassa.

Although still in his thirties, Winston Churchill was already a considerable figure in British politics. As First Lord of the Admi- ralty, he had naturally been the man Borden consulted most fre- quently in London about the details of Canada's contribution to the common naval defense.

Churchill had warned the Canadian Prime Minister that Ger- many meant "to strike at the first favorable opportunity," and added that any help for Britain would be welcome, and the sooner and the more, the better. By the time Borden returned to Canada the two men were agreed on two things. Canada would not attempt to build a navy of its own, but would supply Britain with money to build ships for Imperial defense under the Royal Navy. To help Borden sell this policy to his Cabinet and to the public, Churchill would send him two messages—one confidential and outlining all the relevant military facts, the other edited for public comsumption.

In late September the promised Churchill memoranda arrived in Ottawa. Borden prepared a naval aid bill under which Canada would spend thirty-five million dollars to build three dread- noughts for the Royal Navy. Frederick Monk, Borden's chief aide and representative in Quebec, promptly resigned from the Cabinet. He did so to the public applause of Bourassa. In the House of Com- mons, Laurier paid his last respects to what he called the unholy alliance between the Nationalists and the Conservatives and then pressed to the attack. In essence he stood behind his own now comatose naval bill of 1910, which had resulted only in the purchase of two elderly British cruisers, the *Rainbow* and the *Niobe*, for training purposes.

Canada should and could build its own navy, Laurier persisted. Canada should man this navy with its own men and send it to the defense of Britain and the Empire at its own discretion. The Borden plan was "a hybrid policy, a cross between jingoism and nationalism."

To justify vesting the control of Canadian warships in the Imperial government, Borden proposed to demand a voice in the making of Imperial foreign policy. But was this really possible? Was it really desirable? The British Foreign Office was repeatedly involved in matters of high moment affecting the Afghan boundary, the division of Persia, and alien warships cruising off the coast of Africa. Did Canada want to be consulted on what was to be done about these recondite, far-off matters and thus by inference to become a party to what was done? Was Canada to embark on the whirlpool of European politics?

With something close to savagery the usually suave, self-contained Laurier hurled a special taunt across the floor in reply to the hard-pressed Borden's reassurance that, although the Canadian ships would be under British control, Canadian officers, but not Canadian men, would be permitted to serve aboard them. "Oh, ye Tory jingoes," Laurier cried, "is that the amount of the sacrifice you are prepared to make? You are ready to furnish admirals, rear admirals, commodores, captains, officers of all grades, plumes, feathers, and gold lace; but you leave it to England to supply the bone and sinews on board those ships. You say that these ships shall bear Canadian names. That will be the only thing Canadian about them. You hire somebody to do your work; in other words, you are ready to do anything except the fighting. Is that, sir, the true policy?"

The harassed Borden, threatened with further defections among his supporters, appealed to Winston Churchill for support again. Churchill, who already had a highly developed confidence in his ability to bring lesser men to their senses with a few well-chosen words, sent two crisp messages late in January, which Borden quickly made public. In them Churchill proved with a maddeningly simple recital of the facts that Canada was incapable of building its own fleet. He proved that Canada was incapable of sailing such a fleet in battle even if built; probably incapable, so far as that went, of preventing it from rusting away in harbor through sheer incompetence and neglect. He added also that for good military reasons Britain wouldn't be "able to co-operate to any great extent" in managing and sailing Canadian ships in the event that the foolhardy and presumptuous Canadians went ahead and built them anyway instead of giving the money to Britain.

Churchill, of course, was right—dangerously and recklessly right, altogether too right to carry the judgment of a Canada grown touchy to the brink of neurosis by the wild animosities and wilder love affairs of nationalist and Imperialist, Canadian and Yankee, Canadian and Briton.

One loyal Liberal, H. R. Emerson, read part of the American Declaration of Independence in the Canadian House of Commons. And he pronounced an awful judgment on Churchill's latest memorandum: "That document is calculated to cause more irritation, to undermine more seriously our constitutional freedom, than any document that has come from authority in Great Britain to any colony since the days of Lord North." Another member of Parliament called it "the first step in the direction that will ultimately mean the separation of the Dominion from the great Empire of which we are very proud to form a part." The Ottawa *Free Press* rumbled: "If Winston Churchill's special pleading does not have the effect of awakening Canadians to the tremendous assault which the Borden naval policy is making upon Canada's most cherished possessions—freedom, liberty, absolute autonomy within the Empire—then we do not know our Canada. To us it seems to provide the concrete example up to date of the fatal dangers awaiting a confusing of the interests of Downing Street with those of Canada."

Dr. Michael Clark, a highly respected Liberal, who was "named" and barely escaped expulsion from the House during the debate, managed to link the naval bill and the tariff by an ingenious feat of guilt by association: "I was brought up under the British flag, which, if it taught me anything, taught me to believe in courage and freedom. There is no courage in sending empty boats to Britain; there is no freedom in saying that we cannot trade with the United States without being annexed." From the wings the saturnine Bourassa reminded French Canada that the proposed contribution to Great Britain would cost every man, woman, and child five dollars for the relief of the "English lords who are share-holders in the Krupp-Maxim-Vickers trust."

A Liberal M.P. rose to quote the Liberal Churchill as a witness against himself: "Above all, I think a Liberal is a man who should keep a sour look for scaremongers of every kind and every size, however distinguished, however ridiculous—and sometimes the most distinguished are the most ridiculous—a cold, chilling, sour look for all of them."

For the British cabinet minister who had inspired these remarks, there were cold, chilling, sour looks in profusion. The Ottawa *Free Press* returned to the fray to dispose of him once and for all: "Winston Churchill expects the eyes of Canadians to bulge at the idea of 150-ton cranes and a dockyard costing the appalling sum of four million dollars! How could expert workers in steel be found in a country whose sole inhabitants are either trappers or plowmen? Canadians build anything bigger than a harrow or a binder—monstrous dream! What can we wild and woolly western-ers, clad in blanket coats and tramping around the bush on snow-shoes, possibly know about intricate electric machinery?"

Finding themselves on a far better wicket than they had dreamed, the Liberals decided to stay in until the bitter end. On second reading of the Borden naval bill they stalled. On third read-ing they launched the longest and most memorable filibuster in Canadian parliamentary history. Through early March 1912 they kept the House in constant session for twenty-four hours a day, two weeks in a row, with only one Sunday off to revive the ex-hausted.

Like miners working around the clock, the M.P.s, both on the Government and Opposition benches, were detailed to eight-hour shifts. Considering that the navy had now been under fairly regu-lar debate in the House for three years, considering that there was still no sign of a navy (except the two elderly training cruisers), and considering that there was still no money for a navy and no sailors for a navy, it might have seemed inevitable that a truce of boredom and frustration would set in. But this was far from the case. Both parties had been guilty of their full share of cynicism and opportunism in their incursions against and in behalf of the phantom fleet. But now both parties saw themselves as the cham-pions of a sacred cause. Liberals who hadn't been heard on the floor in years staggered to their feet to mumble phrases from the

Bible, the British North America Act, *Jane's Fighting Ships* or any other remotely relevant document, to pass the torch to the next bleary-eyed backbencher and totter off to their hotels and rooming houses for a few hours of sleep.

The Conservatives were equally stoic in their silences; after the early stages of the debate hardly a Tory rose at all, no matter how unspeakable the provocation, except to pound a desk or shake a fist or shout "Shame!" The Tory strategy, of course, was to wait until the Liberals dropped of exhaustion. The normally sedate Canadian Commons dozed off, sprang to life with thumping desks, dozed off again, awoke to forests of waving arms and ferocious cries, staggered home for Easter, and came back after the brief respite still groggy, and stalemated.

Laurier now made no attempt to conceal the fact that he was deliberately obstructing. It was his avowed aim to prolong the naval debate so impossibly that Borden would have to dissolve the House and call an election. By now it was apparent both to their deadlocked colleagues and to the waiting nation that if neither man's will was to crack someone's body had to. Oddly it was Borden, thirteen years the younger, who first came under a doctor's care. Through March and early April he had been intermittently forced to take to his bed with a severe outbreak of carbuncles, and in at least two of the recurrent emergencies he had to make his way to the House with his neck heavily bandaged and once with a physician in attendance. Whether he thought that he might be coming close to the end of his tether is doubtful—if so, Borden never admitted it—but in early April he made a drastic, unusual, and mildly distasteful decision. He would invoke closure. To do so involved a not wholly dignified trick of debate for which Borden had little taste. Before he took the fateful step, he read to the House from the twenty-first volume of Carlyle's *Life of Frederick the Great:*

"In 1652, the incredible Law of Liberum Veto had been introduced, in spite of John and his endeavors. Liberum Veto; the power of one man to stop the proceedings of Polish Parliament by pronouncing audibly: 'Nie pozwalam—I don't permit.' Never before or since among mortals was so incredible a law. Law standing indisputable, nevertheless, on the Polish Statute Book for above two hundred years; like an ever-flowing fountain of anarchy, joyful to the Polish nation. How they got any business done at all under such a law? Truly they did but little; and for the last thirty years as good as none. But if Polish Parliament was universally in earnest to do some business, and Veto came upon it, honorable members, I observe, gathered passionately round the vetoing Brother; conjured, obtested, menaced, wept, prayed; and if the case was too urgent and insoluble otherwise, the Nie Pozwalam gentleman still obstinate, they plunged their swords through him, and in that way brought consent. The commoner course was to go home again, in a tempest of shrieks and curses."

And so, having conjured, obtested, menaced, wept, and prayed over Laurier, Borden plunged the sword through him. It happened very quickly. When Laurier next rose to speak on one of his party's unending amendments to the Borden naval bill, a carefully coached Tory member sprang up to contest the floor with him. Another Tory member, also by prearrangement, then moved that the first Tory and not Sir Wilfrid be heard. Under the rules of Parliament, as mysterious to ordinary mortals as the mating dance of the whooping crane, the subsequent vote—which of course went against Laurier—meant the debate was virtually over. Borden at last rushed his bill through the Commons.

But the mythical though much-quarreled-over navy was still far from a safe harbor. The Borden bill still had to go through the Senate, and thanks to fifteen years of Liberal rule that elderly and appointive body was top-heavy with Liberals. At first Borden held hopes that in spite of this the Senate would see in the Commons's acceptance of the Naval Assistance Act a reflection of the genuine and proper will of the nation. Not so. With Laurier briefing him from the sidelines, Sir George Ross, leader of the upper house, disdainfully announced that Mr. Borden's bill was "empty as an exploded cartridge, soulless as its plated sides." He would have none of it. And neither would his followers. The Senate vote was 51 to 27 against, and the bill was dead after all.

The date was May 30, 1913. A little more than a year later the first great war was to begin. A little more than a year earlier naval news had been building in other parts of the British Empire. Australia was halfway through a sixty-five-million-dollar three-year plan which was intended, with extensions, to produce twenty-three warships by 1918. Even South Africa, though still bearing

the fresh scars of the Boer War, was offering aid to the Royal
Navy. The Federated Malay States—represented by dark-skinned
subject men with such bizarre titles as the Sultan of Selangor and
Yam Tuan of Negri Sembilan—had freely offered the mother
country a first-class battleship to cost eleven million dollars. Among
Canada's major public men only Henri Bourassa heard the long
bleak episode of the Canadian naval debate with unmixed feelings.
He quickly claimed for himself "a moral triumph without precedent."

VI

The Stringency and the collapse of the land boom—Farewell to Eureka Park

FOR all the *Sturm und Drang* over Parliament Hill, for all the confusing and contradictory reports from abroad about the imminence or impossibility of war, the country had other things to think about. During the previous twelve months Stephen Leacock had published his delightful *Sunshine Sketches of a Little Town*. Robert Service had written *Rhymes of a Rolling Stone*, and the new verses of a wide-eyed Indian maiden named Pauline Johnson had caught the country's imagination more vividly than either Leacock or Service.

But it was not Parliament, not culture, not even the Kaiser, that bulked most prominently in the ken of most Canadians in the year 1913. The biggest and certainly the most intimate news was the Stringency. A few editors of the less responsible kind came right out and used the word "depression." But "stringency" was the accepted euphemism.

Whatever the name, the reality was felt everywhere. During the year ninety-eight leading stocks dropped an average of 17 per cent. C.P.R. slumped from a high of $2.66 to a low of $2.15, and even bank stocks were down an average of seven points. New building was down by a quarter.

No two people agreed exactly on all the causes. That most of the world was undergoing a minor recession was apparent; it was equally apparent that Canada's was a major one. The more or less universal factors affecting most nations were wars and threats of wars in the Balkans, revolutions and threats of revolutions in China and Mexico, and a nervous tendency to hoard gold almost everywhere.

All this made money hard to come by, and Canada, with an adverse trade balance of $300,000,000 and a record intake during the year of 412,000 immigrants, most of them with no visible resources but their health, stood in particularly pressing need of money. The swift mushrooming of the West left scores of towns and cities without adequate streets, waterworks, and sewers; many of them, convinced there was no end to their growth, not only borrowed to meet their current needs but tried to borrow to meet the needs of a boundless future. Other causes, symptoms, and effects, real and imagined, met and reinforced one another at a dozen other points; the recklessness of the banks, the cowardice of the banks, the rapacity of the railroads, profiteering in farm machinery, the inefficiency and laziness of labor, general extravagance.

The most memorable outcome of the Stringency was the collapse of the land boom. Since 1897 a million people from the British Isles, nine hundred thousand from the United States, and seven hundred thousand from other parts of the world had come to live in Canada, most of them in the booming West. For forty years the government had been offering a free homestead of 160 acres to anyone who would keep it under the plow for three years. With this went an option to buy the adjoining quarter section at giveaway prices. The railways, which had been given millions of acres of farmland along with their franchises, had been hawking prairie wheatland at bargain rates all over the world; to them empty land was worse than useless along their rights of way and every settler was an asset. In the intermediate stages of the land rush private colonization companies had been paid up to five dollars for every person they could set down in the West. Now the best of the cheap land and the free land were beginning to run out. About the same time a vision caught fire—the vision of five, ten, fifty million people transforming the Canadian West into a kind of agrarian World of Oz, with seas of gleaming, unfailing wheat stretching interminably from one vast spired city to another.

In 1901 the village of Saskatoon had a population of 113. Ten years later its residents were investing their savings in a projected industrial suburb to be called Factoria, which was expected to be as large and important as Detroit or Pittsburgh in a very short time. In the wake and sometimes in the van of hopes like these, real estate speculators became as thick in the West as the whisky traders of forty years before. Get-Rich-Quick Wallingfords fanned across the lonely plains with wondrous stories, and some of their stories were partly true. Land jumped ten and twenty times in price if not in value almost overnight. When word went around that a new block of the diminishing reserves of homestead land was being opened up, the eager takers sometimes lined up for as much as two weeks in front of the government offices. The fever of land speculation spread to the East, to Montreal and Toronto. Every big city was encircled by its own nimbus of subdivisions, identifiable only on the maps of the real estate agents, distinguishable from the two million square miles of still unsettled Canada only by the fancy and artificial price tags.

Then, when money started to grow scarce, everybody began to unload land at once. Some of the dream subdivisions were to be revived and become real years and decades later, but for the time being the Eureka Parks, the Grand View Heightses, the Lakeshore Gardenses, the Maple Vales, the Dunvegan Terraces, the Inglewoods, and the Cobble Hills lay forgotten among their hillsides, ravines, poplar bluffs, and sweeps of naked prairie.

Thus the nation's preoccupations, although not altogether pleasant, were on an intimate and domestic scale as the year turned into 1914. On Christmas Eve of that year it would be a hundred years since the end of the War of 1812. The accusations and insults of the last election had now had two years of cooling out, and everyone was looking forward to celebrating a century of peace along the famous undefended border.

VII

*The king and the duke—The strange saga
of Mackenzie and Mann and the Canadian
Northern Railway*

WELL, *the first I knowed the king got a-going, and you could
hear him over everybody; and next he went a-charging up onto
the platform, and the preacher he begged him to speak to the
people, and he done it. He told them he was a pirate—been a pirate for thirty years out in the Indian Ocean—and his crew was
thinned out considerable last spring in a fight, and he was home
now to take out some fresh men, and thanks to goodness he'd
been robbed last night and put ashore off of a steamboat without
a cent, and he was glad of it; it was the blessedest thing that ever
happened to him, because he was a changed man now, and happy
for the first time in his life; and, poor as he was, he was going to
start right off and work his way back to the Indian Ocean, and put
in the rest of his life trying to turn the pirates into the true path; for
he could do it better than anybody else, being acquainted with all
pirate crews in that ocean; and though it would take him a long
time to get there without money, he would get there anyway, and
every time he convinced a pirate he would say to him, "Don't you
thank me, don't you give me no credit; it all belongs to them dear
people in Pokeville camp-meeting, natural brothers and benefactors
of the race, and that dear preacher there, the truest friend a pirate
ever had!"*

*And then he busted into tears, and so did everybody. Then
somebody sings out, "Take up a collection for him, take up a
collection!" Well, a half-a-dozen made a jump to do it, but somebody sings out, "Let him pass the hat around!" Then everybody
said it, the preacher too.*

So the king went all through the crowd with his hat, swabbing his eyes, and blessing the people and praising them and thanking them for being so good to the poor pirates away off there; and every little while the prettiest kind of girls, with the tears running down their cheeks, would up and ask him would he let them kiss him for to remember him by; and he always done it; and some of them he hugged and kissed as many as five or six times—and he was invited to stay a week; and everybody wanted him to live in their houses, and said they'd think it was an honor; but he said as this was the last day of the camp-meeting he couldn't do no good, and besides he was in a sweat to get to the Indian Ocean right off and go to work on the pirates.

When we got back to the raft and he come to count up he found he had collected eighty-seven dollars and seventy-five cents. And then he had fetched away a three-gallon jug of whisky, too, that he found under a wagon when he was starting home through the woods. The king said, take it all around, it laid over any day he'd ever put in in the missionarying line.

In its heyday of business adventure Canada never quite produced a pair of entrepreneurs to match the king and the duke of Mark Twain. But in William Mackenzie and Donald Mann—each to be knighted in the fullness of time—it did create two of the most engaging dreamers who ever pursuaded their country that what was good for them was good for the country too. They were a rare and able pair, both sprung from good Ontario stock, of the best Scots Presbyterian blood and persuasion. They met first in western Canada, following the golden trail of the C.P.R. By this year, 1914, they loomed as mightily on the stage of current events as Borden and Laurier; compared with their granite Scots-Canadian figures, the German Kaiser and even the British Prime Minister were distant and indistinct.

With their Canadian Northern Railway, Mackenzie and Mann had by now achieved prodigies of promotion that made such other giants in their field as Van Horne, Lord Shaughnessy, Charlie Hays, and J. J. Hill appear as rather stodgy and timid. They had begun with a chaotic and insignificant little complex of feeder lines on the sparse and unprofitable prairies. But they had expanded quickly with government help of various kinds.

All governments, municipal, provincial, and federal, had recognized since the last half of the nineteenth century that only steel rails could galvanize the great mass of Canada to life and prevent it from sinking into paralysis like a lumpish giant. And in those times the notion of public ownership, public utility, and public building was relatively strange and even vaguely terrifying—more so by far than the well-accepted practice of putting public money into private business. Allying their own instincts to the popular philosophy of government, Mackenzie and Mann stretched out eagerly across the country, devouring public money by the sackful.

Mackenzie, the small-town teacher and occasional storekeeper, had become gifted in the ways of high finance. Mann, the student for the ministry and lumber-camp foreman, had become a highly competent construction boss, perfectly willing and able to beat up the average lumberjack with one hand tied behind his back. They had reached their zenith together at a highly favorable time.

The gigantic C.P.R., despite its scandals and its skeletons, was working to the manifest advantage of the country as well as that of its proprietors. All but a few socialists—and socialists were then very few—accepted it as an example of how public help to private enterprise could end in public good. On the other hand, other railroads, notably the Grand Trunk, were in deep trouble even with the substantial aid they had had from the privy purse. As the confident and plausible Mackenzie and Mann continued to expand their Canadian Northern, Laurier and most other Canadians were staunchly in favor of what was to be—depending on the ultimate fate of the Grand Trunk—either the country's third or its second transcontinental line.

The king and the duke carried through a bewildering array of schemes for finding money. Behind an impenetrable fog of debentures, mortgages, bond flotations, loans, subsidies, and guarantees, they disappeared from the ken of the ordinary Canadian and went on with the exciting business of putting up their railroad. They built hotels, created telegraph companies, express companies, and grain elevators, acquired coal and iron mines, halibut fisheries, and whaling stations. They gave business to subcontractors who were frequently their own creators. They created trust companies and bought and sold a street railway. In time they found themselves so much in debt to the state in its various forms that the state was faced with a difficult decision: either cut off the subsidies and guarantees, force Mackenzie and Mann into bankruptcy, and admit that the state had been grotesquely careless with the taxpayers' money, or continue the guarantees and subsidies in the hope that Mackenzie and Mann would succeed as the C.P.R. had done in not dissimilar circumstances before.

As outright grants and gifts, the Canadian Northern had by 1913 received more than seven million acres of government land, as much as the area of Belgium or Holland. In addition to these grants of property from the Dominion and the friendlier of the provinces, the promoters had been given about $30,000,000 in cash. For their services as launchers and managers, their creditors had allowed them to keep almost all the common stock of the railroad, now valued at $100,000,000.

The handouts of land and money were only a part of the railway's benefices from the public purse. In its last ten years the Laurier administration had guaranteed the Canadian Northern's bonds for more than $50,000,000. In its first three years Borden's government guaranteed them for almost as much more. The provinces had guaranteed an additional $100,000,000. Thus, in subsidies of cash and land and the underwriting of their credit, more than a quarter of a billion dollars of public money stood behind the empire the king and the duke had built from virtually nothing except their magnificent energy, ability, nerve, and powers of persuasion.

But a quarter of a billion still wasn't enough. Mackenzie and Mann were now more gloriously and heroically broke than any two men in Canada's history. Yet so adept had they become at using other people's money that they were both immensely rich. In a confidential letter to Borden, the Tory banker E. B. Osler said Mackenzie's closest friends estimated his personal and untouchable fortune at between fifteen and forty million dollars. But his and his partner's railroad continued to totter on the verge of bankruptcy.

The proprietors now announced to Borden that they needed another $45,000,000 if they were to finish their line to the Pacific coast. This demand was accompanied by the now familiar promise that it was to be positively the last. Borden, to whom the alternatives of abandoning the railroad to ruin and defeat and taking it over as a public property were equally unpalatable, conceived the revolutionary notion that it was time the government safeguarded its equity by taking over some of the common stock. Mackenzie and Mann and their closest associates held $100,000,000 of this, and Borden proposed that they surrender $40,000,000 worth to the nation in return for the new bond guarantee and past obligations.

During the late spring and early summer, debate about the railway question pushed the aborted navy, the Kaiser and Winston Churchill, and even the happily relaxing Stringency well down into the second layer of the nation's consciousness. The chief entertainment of the debate was provided by two young Tory lawyers—each to become in his own time a Prime Minister. The newest resolution for the relief of Mackenzie and Mann had been framed by Borden's Solicitor General, Arthur Meighen, and Meighen pressed the case for it with unremitting vigor. This enraged a somewhat older but equally rising Conservative named Richard Bedford Bennett. Bennett assailed the "shameless mendicancy" of the only mildly embarrassed king and duke, whose aides were busy lining up support in the lobbies. His demand was simple and, as events were to prove, prophetic. Let the country take over the railroad at once. When Bennett's young colleague arose to challenge him he berated Meighen for his "impertinent interruptions" and dismissed him as the gramophone of Mackenzie and Mann.

Bennett, who partly through a mishap of history was to win a place in his country's memory as a mere defender of wealth and orthodoxy, continued his attack on wealth and orthodoxy for hour after hour. Borden for the most part kept to the sidelines and let the young and confident Meighen take the brunt of Bennett's attack.

Bennett's main argument was simple enough. Mackenzie and Mann had assets of their own and they refused to use their own assets either to build the railroad that was making them rich or to rescue it from its difficulties. They wanted the country to pay their debts. Mackenzie and Mann were not even paying the men who worked for them, Bennett said. "Look at the contractors who have been swarming around the hotel corridors in Ottawa. Why have these contractors come here? Because these men would not pay them." Among the charges he made against Mackenzie and Mann were "boundless ambition," "greed for wealth," "falsifications and subterfuge." And the railroad, he contended angrily, was as bad as the men behind it. In some respects it was unworthy of being called a railroad. It had so much dirt ballast, dirt track, poor ties, light steel, and so many sharp curves and heavy grades that a real railroader would call it at best a "minimum-cost road." He cried that they had laid a trail of corruption extending from

Victoria to Halifax. Of Meighen he demanded again: "Since when did bogus surpluses and false accounts constitute a groundwork and foundation on which to lay a claim for the use of the collective credit of the people of the country?" "Are they [Mackenzie and Mann] insolvent or solvent? There is their annual report sent to investors in England. Here is the report made to the Parliament of Canada. Here is the report you make to those you get money from; here is the report to those you want money from. Here is the mendicant, there is the promoter."

An exasperated backbencher tried to summarize the operations of Mackenzie and Mann during one of the silences permitted by the outraged Bennett, and this was what he said:

"Who is the Canadian Northern Railway Company? Messrs. Mackenzie and Mann. In order to get aid from this country they form eighteen or more companies, called subsidiary companies, and who are the principal stockholders in the subsidiary companies? Messrs. Mackenzie and Mann. They come to the Canadian Parliament, they go to the different legislatures, and they get money for these different companies; and in getting this money they are getting money for Mackenzie and Mann. They thus form a construction company under the name of Mackenzie, Mann and Company Ltd. and the money they have received from the federal government and the governments of the provinces for Mackenzie and Mann acting as the Canadian Northern Railway Company they pay over to Messrs. Mackenzie and Mann acting as Mackenzie, Mann and Company Ltd., construction agents. So that all the money that is paid out still remains in the pockets of Messrs. Mackenzie and Mann.

"Of course Messrs. Mackenzie and Mann, construction agents, get rich and make money, but the Canadian Northern Railway Company gets poor because it gives all its money to Messrs. Mackenzie and Mann. Messrs. Mackenzie and Mann, as the Canadian Northern Railway Company, come back to Parliament and ask for more aid. They should tell us, if they want to be absolutely fair: we have two moneybags at home; one belongs to the Canadian Northern Railway Company, the other to Messrs. Mackenzie, Mann and Company Ltd. We have taken all the money out of the moneybag belonging to the Canadian Northern Railway Company and we have placed it in the moneybag belonging to Mackenzie, Mann and Company Ltd. There is no more money in the first bag, it is all in the second; kindly fill up the first."

Laurier, perhaps because he was enjoying the sounds of internal strife in the Tory ranks, perhaps because his own earlier record in the matter was beginning to look increasingly unfortunate, offered little more than perfunctory opposition to the new Borden-Meighen plan for the relief of the railway promoters. He expressed admiration for Mackenzie and Mann, but said that if the country had to go into partnership with them the country should be the senior, not the junior, partner.

The bill giving them another forty-five million passed without much real difficulty. The king and the duke had reason once again to count their blessings and praise their brothers and benefactors.

VIII

Colonel Hughes creates the first contingent—
"There is only one feeling as to Sam, that
he is crazy."

IT was now well into June of 1914. Parliament was prorogued on the twelfth. On the twenty-eighth the Archduke Franz Ferdinand of Austria was assassinated at Sarejevo. On the twenty-ninth Borden's memoirs record: "I left for Nova Scotia, arriving at Halifax late the following evening. Here I received various delegations, chiefly respecting patronage." This now seemingly incredible serenity reflected not irresponsibility but sheer innocence. Borden had concluded at least two years earlier that war—sometime, somewhere—was inevitable, but he still had no suspicion that it was imminent. Nor was this surprising. For his knowledge of what was about to happen in Europe, he remained dependent on the press, on his intuition, and on the vague and irregular dispatches relayed to him at the pleasure of the British government through the Governor General.

As late as July 23—barely two weeks before war was to begin—the only Canadian military units in an attitude of belligerency were poised to repel, not an armed invasion from Europe, but a shipload of 376 would-be East Indian immigrants. The unfortunate party had sailed from Hong Kong on a Japanese vessel in the full but unwarranted expectation of being allowed to enter Canada at Vancouver. Ever since coolie labor finished the C.P.R. and filled the country with leftover laundrymen and café owners, Canada's imigration policy had been distinctly hostile to Orientals and there was no change now. On Borden's orders the H.M.C.S. *Rainbow*, the dubious pride of the hapless Canadian navy, had rushed to the Vancouver dock area, as had a detachment of militiamen. Ultimately the unhappy Indians sailed back home after the equally unhappy Canadian government had restocked their ship with food. On the same day Winston Churchill cabled that Admiral Jellicoe would soon arrive to reopen discussions about Canadian naval aid. The admiral could be expected either in August or October.

Borden thereupon took off for what he expected to be a month's golfing and swimming in Muskoka. In the meantime the Governor General was relaxing at Banff, half the width of the country away. The Prime Minister did not return to Ottawa until the last week of peace; the Governor General, not until the first day of war.

Borden had officially volunteered military help to the British government two days before the war began. On August 6, two days after it had begun, he was informed: "His Majesty's Government gratefully accept your offer to send expeditionary force to this country and would be glad if it could be dispatched as soon as possible."

No such force was ready or in sight. But if Canada as a nation was not well prepared for the onrush of history, there was one Canadian who was more than ready. This was Borden's Minister of Militia and National Defence, Colonel Sam Hughes. Hughes was soon to become—next to Borden himself and not infrequently above Borden himself—the best known and most influential of all Canadians. In the first days of August 1914, the role had already begun to fit him as snugly as the red-tabbed khaki twill for which he happily discarded his mufti.

Hughes had been at his desk in Ottawa throughout the mysterious, ill-comprehended days before the mysterious, ill-comprehended decision that there must be a war. If there was going to be a war he, at least, was set for it, spiritually and psychologically. Indeed, as late as August 3, the martial spirit of Grey and Asquith was far too tame for his liking.

On the morning of that fateful day, Hughes's military secretary, who was later to become his biographer, found Colonel Sam pondering his morning paper with growing distaste. Although Germany and Austria were already at war with France, Russia, and Serbia, Britain's course still lay before Parliament. Suddenly, according to his secretary, "Colonel Hughes rose from his desk, banged the paper with his fist and said: 'They are going to skunk it. England is going to skunk it; Morley and Burns have resigned from the cabinet as a protest against participation in the war, and they seem to be looking for an excuse to get out of helping France.

Oh! What a shameful state of things! By God, I don't want to be a Britisher under such conditions; to think that they would want to go back on France!'"

Then Hughes, by now thoroughly worked up, ordered the flag lowered from its masthead above his headquarters. And down it came and remained down for fully an hour before the Minister of Militia was persuaded by cooler heads that the honor of the Empire was not, in truth, in jeopardy. A day later Hughes's fears were fully at rest and he was fully embarked on the job of raising, equipping, and sending into battle one of the finest groups of fighting men of its size in modern history.

On the surface he had not much to build on. In his three years of office, Colonel Sam had been able to enlarge the military budget only from seven million dollars to eleven million. His regular army stood at three thousand men and it had no reserves. The militia had a paper strength of seventy-five thousand, but by no means all of these took part in the brief annual course of training, which consisted mainly of two weeks of foot and rifle drill, field skirmishes, physical training, and community singing. (The teetotaling Hughes had imposed an absolute ban on wet canteens in the militia camps.)

Field Marshal Sir John French had inspected the Canadian militia a few years earlier and reported that it was "only a large collection of troops without any organization." A German general had said it could be completely ignored insofar as any effect it might have on any war in Europe. A Canadian officer, Colonel Hamilton Merritt, credited his country with "perhaps the most expensive and ineffective military system of any civilized community in the world."

Hughes set out to correct these conditions with the erratic energy that he soon made his trademark and finally left as his monument. The country had about two million men of military age to draw upon. The terms of service in the Army were compatible with the general standards of the time. Pay ranged from a dollar a day for privates to twenty dollars a day for major generals. A private who came back from the war totally disabled could expect a pension of twelve dollars and fifty cents a month. One who left a widow would leave her thirty cents a day, plus a dime for each of the first two children only. If, after his enlistment, his father or mother or his wife wanted him discharged and could give a good reason, any soldier could be bought back into civilian life for fifteen dollars or less.

Sam Hughes, seeing in the profile of his country a strong trace of his own granite, true-blue cast of jaw, rightly estimated that the immediate problem was not how to raise recruits but what to do with them. He wired his two hundred militia units instructing them to recruit to war strength. But, he said emphatically again and again, only volunteers would be accepted now, and only volunteers would be accepted in the future.

Borden had asked for a first contingent of twenty thousand. As a place in which to assemble, house, partly train, and sort out so considerable and—for Canada—so unprecedented a community Hughes selected the valley of the Jacques Cartier River near Quebec City. There, amid Plantagenet swirlings and clankings, oceans of dust, mud, oaths of humans, groans of horses, and the creaking of wagon wheels and harness, he built a great tented camp almost overnight. Valcartier was one of Sam Hughes's authentic triumphs. Out of its pastoral slopes and fields he created, in the late August and early September of 1914, four miles of bell tents, a maze of rope corrals and canvas mangers, and an artillery range the size of the townsite of Montreal. As its first settlers began converging on it in response to the first calls for volunteers, he treated the growing settlement as a personal empire.

Its management, he shortly told Borden in a memorandum, compelled him to deal with "thousands upon thousands of cranks, contractors, grafters, self-seekers and interlopers, as well as with thousands of decent men." But neither then nor in the more complex future awaiting him did Hughes's willingness to cope with these problems waver in the least degree. On more than one occasion he hinted that he personally would lead the first contingent overseas and command it in battle, as there was no one so well qualified. He made frequent tours of inspection at Valcartier, sometimes augmenting his weekday colonel's uniform with a sword and a feathered hat. Occasionally he appeared on horseback.

He took a special delight in handing out promotions on the spot. "A fine unit you have here, major," he would say. "Pardon me, sir," an embarrassed officer would say, "I'm only a captain." "You're a major now," Hughes would say, moving grandly down the parade lines or tent rows.

Although it was of undoubted advantage to the country and to the government to have so vigorous and forthright a man in command of the war effort, there were also some serious disadvantages. On the relatively small stage of the Boer War and during its long but narrow epilogue, Hughes had aroused the choler of none but men of eminence—two Governors General, a British War Minister, three or four British generals. But now he began to antagonize people of no greater stature than his own, and this, in time, proved more serious.

The Anglican bishop of Montreal came to see him, complaining that there weren't enough Anglican chaplains to serve the first overseas contingent. Hughes used so many swear words in rebuttal that the bishop was moved to complain to Borden. The secretary of the Toronto Humane Society visited Hughes to complain about the mistreatment of military horses. Hughes at first called him a liar, then amended it to a damned liar, and according to the official objection of the distraught friend of animals, "finally pushed me out of the room."

But Hughes had already made an assessment of Borden that was to stand him in good stead for some five years. Shortly after taking office he had written a friend: "Mr. Borden is a most lovely fellow; gentle-hearted as a girl." After the war began, his attitude toward the Prime Minister ranged from obsequiousness to outright bullying. A journalist of the day summed up their relation like this: "The trouble between Sir Sam and the Prime Minister is that the Prime Minister has never been able to lassoo him and keep him lassooed. Sir Sam is a bronco of broncos and will ever be." The gentle and gentlemanly Borden's acquiescence in Hughes's conduct is not easy to understand over the distance of the years. But the vast if somewhat awkward drive with which Sam had raised the first contingent, assembled it at Valcartier, and got it to the front had commanded the Prime Minister's genuine respect. And there is also no doubt that Borden was afraid of him—not because Sam knew of any hidden bodies, but just because Borden had a quiet and peaceable nature and to avoid a public collision with the unquiet and unpeaceable Minister of Militia meant a good deal to him.

In Hughes's two years as a wartime minister he picked on Borden outrageously and sometimes deceived him. Once Borden, who customarily detached himself from the troublesome business of procurement, ventured to question an order of Hughes's to fit out a

Canadian brigade with kilts. Hughes was on one of his numerous trips abroad and Borden cabled him timidly: "We decided last winter against large additional expense necessary for kilts." Hughes sternly cabled him back: "You are entirely in error regarding kilts. They are less than half the cost of trousers. One kilt outwears four to six pair trousers."

When Borden wondered whether an unsuccessful contractor mightn't have been given more consideration Sam dismissed the man as "an ordinary, Yankee, boozing agitator." Hughes, who quickly arranged his own promotions from colonel to major general to lieutenant general and also acquired a knighthood in the process—needed Borden's acquiescence in these ventures. On his first trip to England he found it necessary to cable Borden nervously: "No report rank from you." Borden cabled back timidly: "Are you specially desirous that your promotion should be made in meantime?" Hughes then replied firmly: "Re promotion my deputy or others announced long ago it seeming everyone wondering what wrong." (To a Canadian wit, Hughes's knighthood provided the opening for the war's most ingenious pun: "Le roi Sam Hughes.")

General Alderson, the commander of Sam's First Division, was soon complaining behind the minister's back to the Governor General. Guns, horses, and men had been loaded indiscriminately on the troop transports from Quebec and it took weeks to sort them out after the disembarkation in England. Moreover, Alderson complained, Hughes's prejudices as a teetotaler were injuring morale. He had personally decreed that there would be no wet canteens, and so when they had a chance to leave the dismal Salisbury Plain encampment in England, the Canadian troops were under a strong compulsion to drink as much as they could as quickly as they could. In one of his rare retreats, Hughes authorized wet canteens, but to his growing list of enemies the name of the First Division commander had been added.

Alderson had further infuriated Sam by predicting that the Ross rifle, the Canadians' basic infantry weapon, would not stand hard usage. The Ross rifle was not of Hughes's devising. The first contract for it had been let by Frederick Borden, his predecessor in the Liberal government of Laurier. The manufacturer, the Scottish industrialist Sir Charles Ross, undertook to make twelve thousand rifles a year at twenty-five dollars each. Hughes had supported the contract himself even when he was a member of the parliamentary opposition. He tried it on the ranges and was impressed by its accuracy, and thus when he inherited it from Frederick Borden he also inherited his own blessing. From that point on his pathological inability to revise his first judgments held him a prisoner. By the time the first Canadian division went into the trenches at St.-Julien and Ypres, Canada had acquired 150,000 of the Ross rifles and Hughes was incapable of entertaining criticism of them.

Many of his other activities were, to put it mildly, provocative. He abused senior officers in front of junior officers and junior officers in front of their men, and he made no bones about it. He made many speeches holding the regular army up to ridicule and contempt; in one he lumped all the permanent officers together as barroom loafers. One junior commander, born and grown to a tradition in which such conduct was both unspeakable and unthinkable, was himself shocked into an unspeakable and unthinkable breach of discipline. He wrote the Prime Minister direct urging him to "get rid of this objectionable cad." Sam Hughes, he said, insulted officers and men by the score, using the vilest language "whether ladies are present or not, indiscriminately cursing all and several." When the city of Toronto conducted a mobilization test under the auspices of all the leading officials and local military officers, Sam described it publicly as "ridiculous nonsense."

Within weeks Hughes was the most newsworthy and the most debated figure in the Dominion. Sir George Foster, Deputy Prime Minister and a senior to Hughes in the Borden Cabinet, scribbled in his diary: "There is only one feeling as to Sam, that he is crazy." Even Sir William Mackenzie, the railway baron, whom Sam had befriended in the earlier debates about the Canadian Northern, began to wonder about him.

Hughes looked all critics and doubters squarely in the eye. To Mackenzie he wrote: "In short, Sir William, my character is unique, my ways are unique, and I purpose following the old road to the end." When the Toronto Board of Trade passed a motion in censure of him he replied: "My critics will stop their yelping as a puppydog chasing an express train gives up its job as a useless task."

To Borden he wrote: "It is my intention to stop all this backbiting, intriguing, whispering and all this premeditated plan of 'suppression.' They forget that half-a-dozen grasshoppers in a meadow make more noise than one thousand fat oxen grazing."

As for the charge of abusing officers, his only answer to that was to recall wistfully that Wellington used to order unsatisfactory subordinates shot on the spot and that Edward VII once, "in the presence of tens of thousands of soldiers and spectators," publicly dismissed a major general because he had forgotten to wear one of his decorations.

As the Valcartier encampment grew, Hughes's sense of mastery grew with it. When one of his lady secretaries invented a spade with a hole in the middle which was supposed to serve as combination trenching tool and bulletproof shield for snipers, Hughes promptly ordered twenty-five thousand of them at $1.35 each. (When they received their brief baptism of fire many months later, they proved so useless that the government sold them all off as scrap for a total of fourteen hundred dollars.) He dispensed procurement contracts in wholesale lots with reference to no one but himself. He bestowed honorary colonelcies on his most trusted purchasing agents. Only in the choice of a commander for the Canadian contingent did his self-assertiveness desert him. It had been taken for granted that the British War Office would make the appointment, with or without consultation with the Canadian government. Hughes took this for granted too, but put forward three nominees of his own, all of them Imperial officers. All were rejected. Ultimately Lord Kitchener announced that the Canadians would be led into battle by Lieutenant General Edwin Alfred H. Alderson, whose thirty years of soldiering with the British Army had taken him to the Nile, Poona, and South Africa. Hughes cabled Kitchener accepting the appointment with grateful thanks.

But not to Alderson, to Kitchener, or to anyone else would Hughes entrust the embarkation and safe conduct of his first contingent. There were believed to have been at least a dozen armed German liners in or close to the neutral and nearby harbors of Boston and New York when war broke out. When the time came for the contingent to sail from Quebec City, Hughes personally took charge of the embarkation. It probably wasn't his fault that some ships were overloaded and some underloaded—at least one so underloaded that it had to get the Quebec fire brigade to pump water ballast into its bilges before it could be considered stable enough to sail. Nor would it be fair to say it was Hughes's fault that when the last ship of the convoy departed from Quebec City it left behind on the docks a handful of men, eight hundred horses, and nearly five thousand tons of wagons, ammunition, and other stores and supplies. Of the force that embarked, every man, every horse, and every pound of supplies arrived in England safely. Some weeks later in a speech at London, Ontario, Hughes declared that, but for him, the entire convoy of more than thirty ships might have been sunk by the German submarines. He said he had refused to accept Lord Kitchener's advice that the transport ships were properly protected. "As a result of the continual hammering away," he said somewhat cryptically, "the people of England came to know that German submarines were hovering in the English Channel."

Once he had the first troops safely embarked, Hughes sped on ahead of them aboard a fast liner to prepare for their coming. He was in uniform when he called to see Lord Kitchener at the British War Office. According to the official history of the Canadian Army in the First World War, the following scene ensued: Colonel Sam marched up to Kitchener's desk. When he arrived at the desk, Kitchener spoke up quickly and in a very stern voice said: "Hughes, I see you have brought over a number of men from Canada; they are of course without training and this would apply to their officers; I have decided to divide them up among the British regiments; they will be of very little use to us as they are."

Hughes replied: "Sir, do I understand you to say that you are going to break up these Canadian regiments that came over? Why, it will kill recruiting in Canada."

Kitchener answered: "You have your orders, carry them out."

Hughes replied: "I'll be damned if I will," turned on his heel, and marched out.

As Kitchener and many other eminent persons had discovered and were still to discover, Sam Hughes might have been moderately crazy but he was also very tough. He saw Asquith, the British Prime Minister, and Lloyd George, the Chancellor of the Exchequer. He exchanged cables with Borden. Kitchener's plan to break up the Canadian contingent was dropped and Hughes went back to Ottawa.

IX

Life and death in the trenches—The gas
attack at Ypres

WHILE all these hidden dramas were being conducted by men of
fame and influence, a much greater drama was in preparation. Its
cast was largely faceless and ill assorted to the verge of untidiness.
The Cabinet's first decision had been to send twenty thousand men
overseas. This, considering the puny state of the country's existing
military sinews, seemed like a sizable enough undertaking. But
before the war was over more than thirty times that number, nearly
three quarters of a million Canadians, were to serve in uniform.
Sixty thousand were to die and three times that many to be
wounded. Of all the Canadians of military age one in every eight
was to become a casualty.

The first volunteers in 1914 came for the disorderly maze of
reasons that usually send men to war: some because it was the thing
to do, some because it offered their lives a prospect of new scope
and meaning, some because of old-fashioned chivalry and knight-
errantry enriched by the blood and thunder and the vision of their
Empire that they had acquired with their ABCs. Early in 1915 Sam
Hughes was able to proclaim: "Canada has sent one contingent, a
second is on the way, and if necessary we will send a fifth, a sixth
or a twentieth." If his mathematics were to prove somewhat at
fault, his sense of the country's heart spring was unerring. By early
September thirty-two thousand men had crowded into Sam's camp
at Valcartier, far more than were wanted.

Parliament had already voted fifty million dollars as an immediate
war appropriation and passed a sweeping War Measures Act which
conferred on the government the powers of a dictatorship. Within
two weeks various of the provinces heaped. oats, potatoes, flour,

horses, and canned salmon on the mother country by the shipload. For most of August, British Columbia was loyally in the grip of an invasion scare. Two German warships had been seen off the west coast. Banks in Vancouver sent their gold reserves to Winnipeg and Seattle and made plans to burn their paper money in the event of a German landing. A few civilians fled inland, but thanks to two submarines bought hurriedly in Seattle, confidence soon returned.

For the first overseas contingent the first three and a half months on the bare plain of Salisbury were a winter of mud and misery on a heroic scale. The sparse grass of the plain soon dissolved under weeks of rain and the traffic of infantrymen's boots, horses, cannons, and wagon wheels. Tent ropes tightened and pulled loose, canvas collapsed, oil stoves went out or gave enough thin heat to turn the surrounding accumulation of blankets, kit bags, packs, palliasses, and overcoats into reeking bogs and backlashes of web equipment and unwashed socks. Lice were epidemic.

By the time they began moving across the Channel to France early in 1915, most of the Canadian troops were sure that whatever they were about to meet was certain to be better than what they had left. In this they were pathetically mistaken.

Having been thrown at each other's throats by the ineptitude of emperors and statesmen, the marshals and generals were now just beginning to recover from their own ineptitude and to sort the war into some manageable and predictable pattern. Rather like two nearsighted men caught in a revolving door, the German and French general staffs had both groped and pawed for direction during the first two weeks of the fighting. Both had thrown away any immediate chance of advantage. Germany's hoped-for breakthrough from the northwestern plains of Belgium had been based on the hope of enticing France to attack in the south and east in Lorraine. But Rupprecht, the vain Crown Prince of Bavaria, who was in command of the Germans in Lorraine, could not bring himself to retreat when the French, as anticipated, attacked. The expectation had been that if he merely held or gave ground slowly, the thus hopeful French would concentrate their strength on that front. Thereupon Germany would mass in the north and break through to seize the Channel ports. But Rupprecht could not bear to accept a passive role. He attacked. In so doing he threw away his chance of drawing the French in on the southern hinge and left them free to maneuver on the Belgian front.

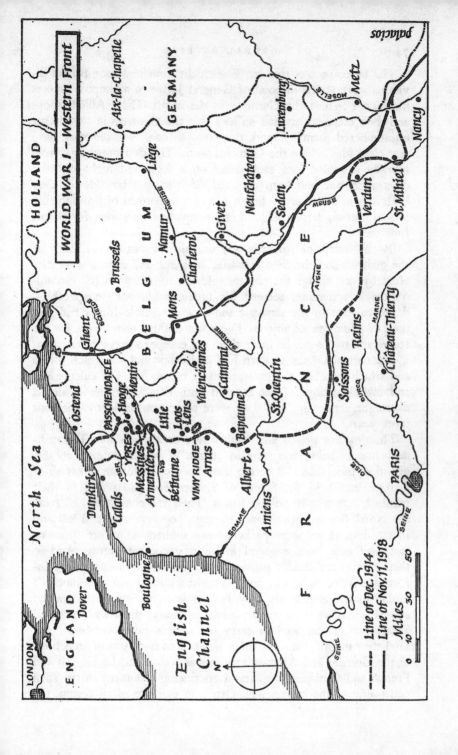

WORLD WAR I – Western Front

HOLLAND

GERMANY

BELGIUM

FRANCE

ENGLAND

North Sea

English Channel

LONDON

Dover

Calais

Dunkirk

Boulogne

Ostend

Ghent

SCHELDT

Brussels

Aix-la-Chapelle

Liège

MEUSE

Namur

Givet

Charleroi

Mons

Menin

Hooge

PASSCHENDAELE

YPRES

YSER

Messines

Armentières

LYS

Lille

Loos

Lens

Béthune

VIMY RIDGE

Arras

Valenciennes

Cambrai

Bapaume

Albert

Amiens

SOMME

St. Quentin

SAMBRE

Luxemburg

MOSELLE

Metz

Neufchâteau

Sedan

MEUSE

Verdun

St. Mihiel

Nancy

AISNE

Reims

MARNE

Soissons

OISE

AISNE

Château-Thierry

OURCQ

PARIS

SEINE

SEINE

N

Line of Dec. 1914
Line of Nov. 11, 1918

Miles

0   10   30   50

palacios

The outcome was that ten French divisions and four British divisions were at the disposal of General Joffre to attempt a pincers movement against the Germans in the north. These Allied troops and their commanders had no idea that the Germans in that sector outnumbered them by more than two to one. Nor did they have any clear idea where the Germans were. The two opposing forces literally stumbled into each other on a fogbound night eighteen days after war had been declared. Startled and bewildered, they both dug in and thereby began to create a pattern of fighting that was to prevail, despite all local and temporary variations, for almost four years.

By the winter of 1914 the war was already out of the hands of the generals and the field marshals. Its shape and nature were dictated by one thing: the private soldier's stubborn—in the circumstances it sometimes seemed his unreasonable and inexplicable—desire to live. In the strategic sense two resistible forces had met their two immovable objects. There was nothing now to do, for the forces and the men who made them up, except to carve two systems of trenches along the western half of Europe and see which forces and which men had the greater power to survive. The calculations and miscalculations of the men of authority had become, almost overnight, irrelevant, and they were to remain irrelevant for four more years.

The time for genius and mighty utterance was done. The ordinary human being was now in charge of human fate. Wet, disgruntled, miserable, and heroic men faced one another across all of Europe, and held the future of Europe and the world in their numbed, not wholly willing hands. Their trenches stretched from the North Sea to Switzerland, through bog and mire and hill and forest. Into them were packed more soldiers, at closer quarters, than had ever been engaged in military combat before. And in their painful and deadly proximity this multitude of strangers reinforced and fed upon one another's virtues and upon one another's faults. In the animal life they had to learn to live, there was an animal brutality; there was an animal stupidity; there was an animal acceptance of the need to carry out orders, however absurd and fatal they might seem. But there was too, in both sets of trenches— in the German and Austrian trenches as well as in the English and French and Canadian trenches—a continuing testament to the spell and magic of the human will. Often, in defiance of all reason, the muddy beaten soldier of the front-line trenches, half drunk with noise and fear and mud and cold and insects and the approach of a tomorrow that could only be more uncomfortable and menacing than today, rose to acts of exaltation, courage, and endurance that had never been surpassed in any place or any time.

During the three years between early 1915 and mid-1917 the whole of the Canadian ground forces fought and died, and if fortunate lived, in an area hardly bigger than three or four Saskatchewan townships. Their every value and perspective had to be adjusted accordingly. From one small piece of quagmire another piece of quagmire fifty yards away could look as enticing as the towers of Cathay. The slightest bulge on the flat, sodden, dangerous plains they contested for became a hill or a mountain. On a reverse slope a company or a battalion could buy respite from the incessant artillery barrages. On a forward slope it could be wiped out. In the desperate lore of the front, hummocks not large enough to make a toboggan slide became as high and famous as Everest or the Matterhorn.

The exact nature of the trench war varied from time to time and from place to place. In the flat northern plains the depth of the fortifications—which were also the living quarters—was often limited by local drainage conditions. Usually the troops dug until they struck water. This might mean a trench only two feet deep. To the front and to the rear there were parapets of sandbags, often wired together and fixed to wooden stakes. Along the top of the parapets there was a series of snipers' plates of thick steel, with holes just big enough to accommodate a rifle barrel and a human eye. At the back of the trenches there was usually a row of dugouts, also protected by sandbags. It was there that the soldiers off duty slept when they could. Communications trenches zigzagged toward two or three lines of reserve trenches between a quarter and a half mile to the rear of the main trench. Both sides used the same basic scheme of fortifications and in many places the front lines were only thirty or forty yards apart. Along the whole of Western Europe there was hardly a single front-line soldier of either side who could not make himself personally acquainted with his opposite number merely by waiting for a lull in the barrage and slightly raising his voice.

Both sides thrust out narrow trenches into No Man's Land, or the

Devil Strip. Both sides maintained listening posts there amid the tangles of shell craters and barbed wire. A primitive and sardonic humor surrounded all these hazardous enterprises. New place names sprang up: Plug Street, Wipers, the Piggery, Goldfish Farm, the Devil's Elbow, the Doll's House, Rats' Paradise, the Barbary Coast, and Lover's Walk. In the wettest, coldest trenches the infantrymen not infrequently got what sleep they could standing up and leaning against the sodden sandbags. For amusement they filled old jam tins with clay and odds and ends of metal, put fuses and guncotton in them, and hurled them at the neighboring trenches. The standard front-line tour was four days, but often it was much less. After that, exhaustion or despondency became a threat to morale.

When the Canadian First Division left the dank plain of Salisbury for the danker and far more dangerous plain of Belgium, it was with a feeling of relief and anticipation. The division had an important job to do and the job was easily understood. Although they had been thwarted in their first attempt at an encircling breakthrough, the Germans had taken virtually all of Belgium except the old cloth city of Ypres. The reluctance of the Allied command to abandon the city, while it was to create endless debate in the years to come, had a strategic purpose behind it. Ypres commanded a canal that entered the North Sea about halfway between Dunkirk and Ostend. Far more important, it stood directly in the path of St.-Omer, and St.-Omer in turn was the crossroads to the Channel ports of Dunkirk, Calais, and Boulogne. Since wars do not have control groups, it cannot be said what might have happened if Ypres had been lost in the first German surge to the northwest in 1914. At the very least it would have become more difficult for Britain and the British dominions to send reinforcements to France and to supply them properly. But in any case, the Allies were still holding the bulge in front of Ypres in the spring of 1915 and a key part of the bulge was held by the Canadians.

In front of the city there lay a wallow of sunken roads, soggy fields, tiny woods, and trenches. In mid-April 1915 the Canadian division took over a frontage of four thousand yards from the French Eleventh Division. Nothing in their training and indoctrination had prepared them for what they found. Through a tacit semitruce the French and Germans on that part of the front had spent most of the winter avoiding anything but the most perfunctory show of hostility. The forward trenches had been manned lightly and given up and retaken repeatedly by both sides, often without much fighting. The French were rich in artillery, where the British were lamentably poor. With their abundance of shells the French could yield their trenches briefly to an advancing wave of German infantry, fall back on their reserve trenches and their guns, and then shell the Germans out again.

As a consequence of this kind of warfare the front-line defenses that the Canadians took over and were ordered not to yield were primitive and insecure even by the prevailing general standards. They found no continuous trench, but only a series of unconnected ditches two or three feet deep. The customary breastwork of sandbags was extraordinarily flimsy. In many places it was not even thick enough to stop a sniper's bullet.

The rear part of the trenches—called the *parados*—did not have the customary reverse breastwork to offer protection from shrapnel breaking behind them. A captain of the Canadian Engineers, making an official report on the condition of a section of the trenches, described "the ground where the men stand in the firing position" as being "paved with rotting bodies and human excreta." In places the parapet was only six inches thick and two feet high and almost everywhere it was open to enfilading fire.

To the French, well versed in and well equipped for artillery fighting, these muddy scars on the face of the Ypres salient had been hardly more than observation posts to be abandoned and repossessed at their convenience. But when the Canadian division took over the left of the line of the British Second Army, its assignment had far less flexibility.

Near the battered little village of St.-Julien there was one of those precious little wrinkles in the ground, called the Gravenstafel Ridge. There was also a little stand of oak trees, hardly as large as an Ontario farmer's back maple lot, called the St.-Julien Wood. The Canadians' chief assignment was to deny these two tiny fragments of Belgium to the enemy.

According to their training and instruction, the way to do so was to hold their trenches. For any unit that lost a section of its forward fortifications the standing order was to counterattack at once and take it back. To give up a trench was to lose honor, hope, and the bare expectancy of life.

By modern standards the Canadian division that held this assignment was a big and deep division, with each of its three infantry brigades four battalions strong. From the seventeenth of April to the twenty-second they spent much of their time trying to deepen and strengthen their flimsy and reeking trench positions, but for the bitter ordeal that was to give them their baptism of fire they were prepared only by their own inner resources of courage and instinct.

Two French divisions stood at the Canadians' left, one a territorial unit, the other made up of Algerian conscripts. On this part of the front German prisoners taken as early as the middle of March had told their captors that cylinders of poison gas were being stored in the trenches opposite Ypres. On April 13 a German deserter actually showed up with a primitive gas mask consisting of a wad of cloth soaked in protective chemicals. To intelligence officers of the French Eleventh Division, soon to be relieved by the Canadians, he reported that the Germans had prepared twenty cylinders of gas for every forty meters of front.

On April 14 the Germans accused the French of using gas at Verdun. Although the accusation was false, the fact that it was made might have suggested the Germans were getting ready to "retaliate."

When Ferry, the local French commander, handed over his trenches to the Canadians he told them they might soon be attacked by gas. He had already passed on the same opinion to his corps commander, along with a proposal to shell the German trenches in the hope of destroying the gas cylinders. His corps commander not only overruled him but caused him to be dismissed for passing on the frightening reports of impending gas warfare to the British troops on his flank.

By the time the Canadian division actually reached the trenches, the talk of gas had become a little stale, a story for frightening newcomers to the foul, weird land of Flanders. The British corps sent a few reconnaissance planes over the German trenches to look for gas cylinders, but spotted none. The corps commander, Sir Herbert Plumer, finally relayed the reports of an impending gas attack to his divisional commanders with the warning that he did so only "for what it was worth."

If the Allies' assessment of the imminence and effectiveness of gas as a major weapon of war was at fault, it was no more so than that of their enemy. To the German high command, steeped in orthodoxy, the slender canisters of chlorine had never appeared to be a major instrument of war. Rather they were a new toy, one that might or might not work. Certainly the German commanders were not ready to make heavy investments in them. So, although the enemy had a strong striking force of four divisions ready, only one division was in reserve when the first gas attack began. Neither the individual German infantryman, clutching his strange wad of a respirator, nor the high command was prepared to exploit success, for no decisive success was expected.

But none of this was known to the Canadian soldiers who brewed their tea and munched on their bully beef and hardtack in the trenches before St.-Julien on the morning of April 22, 1915. It soon turned to a fine fresh day, too calm for the Germans to spill forth their chlorine as it had been planned for them to do shortly after dawn. But they kept up their shelling and lobbed at least one of their high-explosive coalboxes, five feet long and a ton in weight, into Ypres. Early in the morning they mounted a brisker than usual artillery attack on the forward trenches and dropped in a few gas shells. But on balance the day seemed like almost any other —that is, a day to be endured and, if possible, survived and if not the hell with it.

Early in the afternoon the Canadian Third Infantry Brigade asked its divisional headquarters to send up some mouth organs and playing cards. It was informed that cards were out of stock but a hundred mouth organs were available. The long day went on. In the nearby German trenches they tested the wind again, and again found it wanting. But by late afternoon a little breeze had risen and the Germans at last released their gas.

It came across the low-lying fields as a drifting fog that some men saw as gray, some as yellow, some as green.

When the cloud of gas struck the Algerian conscripts on the left of the Allied line they simply broke and ran. This had not been their war to begin with. They were only there because they had been made to come, and now, as the choking fumes enveloped them, their only thought was to get away. They threw away their rifles and raced, crying, ahead of the deadly cloud. Many, overtaken, clutched their throats and fell into the canals and roadside ditches. Some cut artillery horses loose from their stakes, mounted them, and raced for Ypres. The gas was moving at almost six miles per hour, which was nearly as fast as a fit man could run.

Soon the civilians who had remained near the front were fleeing too, with their dog-drawn carts, and with their bundles of bedding, clothing, and food piled grotesquely on the stooped backs of old men. All around, the scenes were apocalyptic, some of them noble, some ignoble. *"Pauvre France! Pauvre Paris!"* a group of stragglers sobbed as they streamed through St.-Julien. A Canadian sergeant who had not yet seen or tasted the gas reported in bewilderment to his headquarters that the streets were "full of runnin' niggers."

In their sum all these personal disasters could well have dealt an important—perhaps even a fatal—blow to the Allied cause. The two French divisions at the left of the Allied line had virtually ceased to exist. Where they had stood there was now a beckoning gap three miles wide. The Germans came storming across the fields with bayonets high and no one to resist them and soon were within four miles of Ypres itself. On reaching there they completely turned the flank of the Canadian division and left it naked and un-tended. Had they pushed on to take the city, more than fifty thousand British troops and nearly two hundred cannon would have been enveloped. But three things stopped the Germans: their lack of any master plan at the level of high command; the terror and discomfort the advancing soldiers met as they themselves stum-bled over their writhing enemies into the gas cloud they had created; and perhaps above everything else the unreckoning and unreckon-able valor of the Canadian division. Entirely aside from the advan-tage their gas attack had given them, the Germans held an advantage on the main approaches to Ypres of more than two men to every one.

Twenty-one British battalions confronted forty-two German battalions, and twelve of the British battalions belonged to the oversized Canadian division. To make matters far worse, an already scandalous shortage of ammunition on the British front had been worsened by the demands of the campaign at Gallipoli, then be-ginning. In the last half of April the British in France had been driven to a cruel scale of artillery rationing: an 18-pounder was allowed to fire two rounds of ammunition a day; a field howitzer could fire three and a medium howitzer six.

With gas ahead and overwhelming artillery superiority behind, the German infantry came across the fields like an ancient Saxon horde, with standard-bearers racing in front to mark the captured trenches.

The little oak forest near St.-Julien—soon to be renamed Kitchener's Wood—was one of the tiny bits of ground where the question of ownership was particularly vital. In the main breakthrough a battery of 4.7-inch guns attached to the French by a London division was overrun in the wood and captured. The Germans kept it in action and turned the guns on the half-encircled Canadian division's rear.

As midnight settled over the battlefield two battalions of the Canadian division set out to recapture the wood. Their method was grotesquely valiant and grotesquely outdated: eight little waves of men marching through the dark fields and craters with their bayonets high. They had almost no artillery support, for, besides the chronic shortage of ammunition, the guns that would ordinarily have tried to clear a way for them were either in enemy hands or groping in the darkness to establish new lines.

While still a quarter of a mile away from the wood the desperate little crest of infantrymen ran into a fence and betrayed its approach. Instantly the black sky became a white nightmare of flares and the entrenched Germans opened up with their rifles and machine guns. But the attacking force plunged on, reached the wood, and finally recaptured the British guns. Before dawn the Germans counterattacked and won back most of the wood in their turn, but another Canadian assault once more carried a fringe of the wood.

Ordinarily it is the attacking force which suffers the heavier casualties in ground warfare. But with the advantage of gas and the breach of the Allied flank the Germans were inflicting greater losses than they sustained. Altogether the Allies were to lose sixty thousand in killed, wounded, and missing in this brief and furious battle. The most damaging blows of all, proportionally, were felt by the Canadian division. Within twelve hours one of its battalions, the 10th, had been reduced in effective strength from more than 800 to 193. Another, the 16th, could muster only 250 men. But the ordeal of Ypres was far from ended in the first eruption. The two crushed French divisions on the left rallied slightly, British reinforcements arrived, and the sorely weakened Canadians still held a line of trenches when dawn broke on April 23, less than twelve hours after they had seen the first wave of chlorine.

Through that second day the Third Infantry Brigade withstood repeated attacks. All along the regrouping British and Canadian front, battalions, companies, and platoons jabbed at the Germans in a series of suicidal attacks whose only but essential purpose was to persuade the enemy he was facing resolute and organized opposition. At least four times the Germans opposite the Canadian positions tried to sweep from their trenches and add more ground to the seven square miles they had already won. But each time they were driven back.

There was, providentially, no optimism. The survival of the Canadian division and indeed of the whole of the Allies' northwestern position was still in the direst jeopardy. The fact that after twenty-four hours it had not collapsed but had even shown some sign of strength was not taken by those on the ground as a sign of hope. As the second night set in, local commanders began grimly passing out cotton bandoleers and ordering kettles of water to be placed on the ground immediately behind the parapets of the trenches they still held. The instinct of every good battalion commander told him that gas would come again with the first favorable breeze. By now most of the waiting men knew there was some chance of living through another gas attack by breathing through wet cloth. So they worked and waited through the night, repairing their trenches as best they could and looking anxiously toward the slowly filling emptiness on their left.

At stand-to on the early morning of the twenty-fourth a few signal rockets soared overhead. Two German airplanes chugged across the Canadian trenches and then chugged back home. In a minute the whole array of German artillery opened up, and the Canadian sentries peering across the scarred and flickering strip of No Man's Land saw what they had been half expecting. Above the German parapets a few knots of men in miner's helmets appeared. They thrust forth long dark hoses and in the interstices in the crump of falling shells the waiting Canadians heard a vast hissing. Then, almost at once, they saw the green-gray-yellow fog of chlorine rolling toward them again. And now once more the German infantry came storming across the black, cratered, city-block-long stretch of No Man's Land. And now another unpredictable disaster fell on the holders of the trenches.

Their basic infantry weapon was the already controversial Ross rifle. It was, by common agreement, a superb rifle for target shooting, and Sam Hughes, himself a target shooter of nearly championship caliber, was one of the many experts who vouched for it.

But for all its accuracy the Ross was subject to jamming in heavy action. It was not an effective weapon in the rough-and-tumble of a war where men often did not begin shooting until they were no further apart than the width of a good-sized sitting room. In this fighting the Ross rifle failed. Its too delicately tooled bolts and cartridge chambers seized against each other in the heat generated by quick fire. Without warning hundreds of Canadian infantrymen found they could do nothing but weep, curse, or pray in the face of the advancing Germans and attempt to pry loose their jammed rifle bolts with trenching shovels or the heels of their big army boots.

The gas too proved more damaging than had been expected. On the first day of the attack its power to destroy the human body had been established. But now, as became apparent, it could destroy the human will. In the last minutes of a fatal exposure the victim lost all desire to live. Many a victim of chlorine in the great battle of Ypres greeted his fate with words no more memorable than the plea: "Go away and let me die!"

As the Germans clawed and hammered their way into the forward trenches behind the pall of gas, the disorder and lack of communication became so great that companies, battalions, and even brigades found themselves isolated and apparently fighting alone. Gradually the front was forced back another half mile. Except for the handful of men who were trapped there and went on fighting, the vital village of St.-Julien itself was abandoned. But against the threat of a complete collapse in the Allied position, the Canadian 8th Battalion clung implacably to the equally vital welt of land called the Gravenstafel Ridge. The Third Infantry Brigade attacked and closed the gap to the Second Brigade. The Germans attacked again with gas toward Ypres on May 2, ten days after the first assault. Another attack came in on May 4, but by then the Ypres salient, although almost wholly flattened out, was again firmly held.

Of the little Canadian contingent raised so quickly and rushed so quickly into battle, over six thousand men—one in every five—were now killed, wounded, or missing. In the first respite one officer of the 15th Battalion tried to remember what those days were like: "Awful days they were, and if hell was ever let loose it was around that spot. We were gassed, we were charged, we were bayoneted and shelled most unmercifully. We were blown from out of our positions by high-explosive shells, many buried alive, many torn and wounded . . . many blown to eternity."

The individual Canadian soldier and the individual Canadian commander had no idea, of course, what part his deeds of desperate resolve were playing in the grand plan. This was continually being debated far to the rear. General Smith-Dorrien, who had originally been in charge of the British corps on the left, was fired because he kept insisting that it was up to the French to restore the left flank. On a higher plane General Foch, the French commander in the north, and Sir John French, the British Chief of Staff, had been continually wrangling about what to do with Ypres in the total design. French wanted to abandon the salient, but Foch persuaded him not to do so. A week after the first German attack French won an admission from Foch that, far from reinforcing, he intended to draw off troops to mount an attack from Arras. French thereupon decided to shrink the salient within the boundaries which, in fact, had already been settled by the battalions on the ground. Though the blunt thumb of earth reaching out into enemy territory was thus shortened, it still could be attacked from three sides.

Whether the redoubt at Ypres had ever made sense was a question still to be debated for decades. The British military writer Liddell Hart offered this judgment twenty years later: "Having forfeited sixty thousand men for the privilege of acting as midwife, the British were then left to hold the most uncomfortably cramped new salient, or target, at continued expense, for over two years."

X

Pacifism and isolationism—The battles
of Loos and the Mound

WHILE these enterprises were being carried out in distant places, Canada was adjusting its bearings closer to home. It was already apparent that the task of preserving friendship with the United States of America might become more difficult than anyone would have thought. More than one resident of the United States out of every ten was of German extraction. Their total number was nearly as great as the number of Americans of British ancestry.

And, leaving these loyalties aside, there was always the point about war itself. William Jennings Bryan, the U. S. Secretary of State, spoke with maddening logic for millions of isolationists: "If the dogs of war have got to fight it out in Europe, let us avoid hydrophobia at home."

From Los Angeles to Cape Cod good and earnest American women were singing a good and earnest song:

> I didn't raise my boy to be a soldier,
> I brought him up to be my pride and joy,
> Who dares to put a musket on his shoulder
> To kill some other mother's darling boy?

> The nations ought to arbitrate their quarrels,
> It's time to put the sword and gun away,
> There'd be no war today, if mothers all would say.
> "I didn't raise my son to be a soldier."

Woodrow Wilson and Henry Ford were against the war. So was William Howard Taft, who accepted the presidency of a League to Enforce Peace and came to Toronto to deliver a lecture on the blessings of the Monroe Doctrine. Henri Bourassa, ironically, had been almost trapped during a walking tour of Europe when war broke out, but he returned to take over his role as the leading Canadian isolationist. He was as yet, for him, in a subdued and tentative mood, but he soon deplored "the grotesque and stupid intolerance manifested in Canada against everyone who dares think and say that there are many aspects to the struggle in Europe."

Long before the Canadian contingent's arrival in France, Bourassa was being called at home a pro-German. The respected journal of opinion *Saturday Night* said: "Every day in Europe men who have done no more harm are hung as traitors." Some of the most widely circulated French-language papers hastened to disown him. *La Patrie* declared the government would be justified in trying him for high treason. *Le Soleil* asserted angrily that he had "done more harm to the French-Canadian people than its worst enemies have ever been able to do."

Even some of Bourassa's most ardent disciples began to question his judgment. One of them, Olivar Asselin, complained lugubriously that his leader had "once more fallen into his customary air of being erudite when it would have sufficed to entrench himself in plain common sense." But Bourassa's wrath and resentment only mounted. When Sir Wilfrid Laurier spoke in favor of recruiting he denounced the speech as "an explosion of empty and sterile chauvinism." And leaving abstract principles aside, he got down to cases. The war effort was surmounted by "boodlers, vampires, the furnishers of bribes and electoral funds." The soldiers being sent abroad were "badly clad, badly shod, and undisciplined."

The Montreal *Star* began calling him "von Bourassa." Bourassa stubbornly demanded that war contracts be investigated, and when funds were asked for the suffering of Belgium he countered by demanding charity for "the wounded of Ontario"—by whom he meant the Catholics who had been denied their separate schools.

The military forces in France heard nothing of these domestic quarrels. In their part of the world other matters were under way. With the Channel flank secured by the bloody stalemate at Ypres, the Allied generals persuaded themselves that they were in a position to attack. They debated where to begin. It was decided that Sir Douglas Haig's First British Army should strike into the plain around Loos and Lens, a little south of Ypres.

Haig did not want the assignment. He protested that he had neither enough guns nor enough ammunition. But after a long wrangle that ultimately involved Joffre, Sir John French, and Foch as well as Kitchener and Poincaré at the political level, he was ordered to go ahead.

He made up his mind to use gas. The chlorine that had given the Germans so great a temporary advantage at Ypres appeared to be a useful weapon and now it needed no apologizing for.

Haig brought up a hundred and fifty tons of gas in five thousand cylinders, but his attempt to use it turned into a fiasco. There was almost no wind. At dawn just before the attack he left his headquarters to test the wind in person. He told an aide to light a cigarette. The smoke sat still in the stagnant air.

The British commander nevertheless had been waiting a week and he gave the order that the attack must go ahead. The gas was released. Instead of drifting toward the German defenders according to the week-old battle plan, it behaved according to the laws of nature. It hung above the British attackers and hundreds of them stumbled through it, half blind and half paralyzed, to be mowed down helplessly when they emerged at the brink of the German trenches. The offensive halted with a quarter of a million Allied casualties and half that number to the enemy.

The Canadians took no part in the offensive at Loos. After Ypres they spent most of 1915 in a holding action on the left flank, building up their casualty lists in a deadlock of attrition and also building up their total strength as fresh contingents poured across from Canada.

As even Ypres had not done, the nature of the fighting almost perfectly demonstrated one great fact, now half forgotten in an age of atoms and missiles. No matter with what majesty of design and purpose wars begin, they nearly always end with multitudes of half-drugged people scrambling for goals of insignificance and squalor.

At first the only prizes visible to the soldiers fighting over them had been the same slopes and rises and clumps of wood that emperors, dukes, and princes had been fighting over since long before the days of gunpowder. Around these natural features there grew artificial features: the trenches, the sandbags, the wire, the craters. The shallowest of the craters were made by heavy shells, the deepest by sappers burrowing under No Man's Land to blow up the trenches of their enemies.

In this churned-up but immovable battleground no commander, however small and local, had any choice but the choice of mistakes. Inaction repeatedly proved less dangerous than action; yet inaction was a military sin and, above all, it was no way to promotion. The need to do something—to do anything, however vain and futile— haunted every soldier in any kind of command, from sergeant to field marshal.

Under these barren and suicidal laws the front of the thickening Canadian Corps strained and struggled back and forth a few yards at a time for nearly a year. There was no discernible result except the mounting stream of casualties.

In early 1916 the monotony was relieved by several savage battles with enough shape and direction at least to earn their own identities.

Before the Canadian Corps there lay one of those gigantically puny, grotesquely treasured swellings in the ground. This one bore the name "the Mound." Near by lay the battered village of St.-Eloi, and as the climax to a spectacular orgy of tunneling and mining, seven great craters were blown in the Mound and its flat approaches on March 27, 1916.

The British Third Division had been assigned to seize the craters and the Mound, but was cut to pieces before it got there and was relieved by the Second Canadian Division. St.-Eloi spilled over into other battles—Hooge, Sanctuary Wood, Mount Sorrel—and another ten thousand Canadian casualties. A minor by-product was the dismissal of General Alderson. Sam Hughes's enemy was replaced as the commander of the Canadian Corps by Lieutenant General Sir Julian Byng.

The Canadians who stayed at home had expected to share, at least in some degree, the hardships of those who went overseas. In fact, they did not. In spite of the country's heavy spending on the war, their economic condition was relatively good.

It could not, of course, be compared with the opulence of the United States which was described, accurately but with infuriating self-righteousness, by the president of the National City Bank:

"We have always known that nature had been lavish, that in a material way everything was ready at hand and it needed but industry, thrift and right-living to bring material success to the country and to all of its people. But on top of that comes what seems almost a conspiracy of events to test our moral fibre—a flood-tide of wealth, of opportunity, which, added to our resources, puts upon the people of this country a responsibility of trusteeship to the world. We are like the heir of an enormously wealthy father. None too well trained, none too experienced, with the pleasure-loving qualities of youth, we have suddenly, by a world tragedy, been made heir to the greatest estate of opportunity that imagination ever pictured."

The United States was showing a favorable trade balance of nearly $3,000,000,000 a year. (Canada alone had increased its buying from the United States by $165,000,000.)

Bethlehem Steel declared profits in 1916 of nearly $50,000,000, and Du Pont sales of gunpowder and other explosives gave it a fantastic profit margin of 200 per cent. But for all its prosperity, the United States was not oblivious to the fact that, indistinct though they might appear, certain other issues were at stake in the far-off mud of Flanders and the United States might eventually be called on for hard decisions of its own.

Although neither Canada nor Britain had yet adopted conscription, more than nine Americans in ten, in an informal plebiscite, declared themselves in favor of it. Henry Ford had sailed his famous peace ship across the ocean and was asserting that America had three duties: to keep out of the war, no matter what the "Wall Street Tories and patriots tell us"; to strive for peace among the nations already at war; and to seek disarmament. President Wilson was firmly on the side of abstinence and peace. Norman Angell put the country's orientation thus: "America is not interested in its foreign problems. It is far more interested in baseball."

"This is a peace-loving nation," Wilson said. "Everything we hold most dear depends upon peace."

To the chairman of the Senate's Foreign Relations Committee the President wrote officially: "You are right in assuming that I shall do everything in my power to keep the United States out of war. I think the country will feel no uneasiness about my course in that respect."

Applauding Wilson when he was renominated at the Democratic National Convention, Martin H. Glynn, temporary chairman of the convention, announced that as a result of Wilson's policy "Ameriica stands serene and confident, mighty and proud, a temple of peace and liberty in a world of flame, a sanctuary where the lamp of civilization burns clear and strong, a living, breathing monument to the statesmanship of the great American who kept it free from menace of European war. Wealth has come to us, power has come to us, but better than wealth or power we have maintained for ourselves and for our children a nation dedicated to the ideals of peace rather than to the ideals of peace and slaughter."

These lofty utterances and many others like them made a strong impact, but they could not change the fact that for better or for worse Canada was at war.

XI

The remarkable adventures of Colonel J. Wesley Allison

VERY little information came back from the front and most of that was half hidden behind censorship and communiqués. One unfailing, fully visible source of news was Sam Hughes.

In the early months of the war Hughes had created a munitions buying and manufacturing complex called the Shell Committee. Characteristically he put it under the direction of a handful of honorary colonels.

Hughes's most favored honorary colonel was not a member of the Shell Committee but a sort of free-lance commission agent. J. Wesley Allison had come to Canada from Ohio as a contractor. He had done well in many things, but in none so well as in making a friend of the editor from Lindsay, Ontario. With Sam's sponsorship behind him, Allison went into the buying of arms with a status resembling that of a Chosen Instrument.

The Shell Committee's chief job was to obtain munitions, mostly from Britain, in Canada and the United States. On some, if not all, of the half billion dollars' worth of orders he placed, Allison collected commissions. Everything he did was within the law, and was made much simpler by the prevailing air of confusion and subterranean haste.

Finally, in the second year of the war, the Liberal opposition got wind of Allison's activities and launched a massive assault against him.

The ground was well prepared by a former Laurier cabinet minister, William Pugsley, and two fellow M.P.s, Frank B. Carvell and G. W. Kyte. They had not only found out where the body was buried; they had seen it. Carvell accomplished this by going to

New York and hiring a lawyer and a private detective. The detective, in the best cloak-and-dagger tradition, broke into the offices of the New York commission broker through whom Colonel Allison and the Shell Committee placed some of their largest Americian orders. Reinforced by the resulting evidence, William Pugsley read the main indictment to the House of Commons. Carvell and Kyte spelled him in reciting the particulars. The indictment was this: Members of the Shell Committee had made money from munitions contracts; on many contracts there was no competitive bidding; huge orders were placed in the United States when they could have been filled more cheaply and quickly in Canada; finally, and most flagrantly, Sam Hughes's friend and protégé, J. Wesley Allison, was turning these practices to his own excessive profit.

Assertions as harsh as these would have embarrassed any government, at any time. At this juncture the administration found them especially painful. During much of the previous year—the first full year of the war—it had been explaining and correcting a whole mare's-nest of lesser scandals. The first contingents were equipped with shoddy, substandard boots and it had taken a special committee of the House of Commons to get to the root of the matter and start setting it right. Of the first 8500 horses bought by the Army, nearly one out of four had been proved unfit for use. There had been public charges of profiteering in drugs, in binoculars, in trucks, in field dressings, in bicycles, and even in jam. Two Conservative M.P.s were among those caught simultaneously robbing the public purse and endangering the war effort, and the outraged Borden had forced them to resign their seats.

For the most part, the public was ready to attribute these early derelictions to a combination of rush and human nature. So far there was no widespread inclination to blame the government. But the accusations against Colonel Allison and the colonels of the Shell Committee were a different matter. If there was the slightest doubt that the colonels were a government responsibility, Sam Hughes put it right. He had been associated with Colonel Allison, he told the House of Commons staunchly and definitely, for twenty-five or thirty years. Among other things he described his lifelong friend as "an absolutely disinterested and straightforward businessman, the soul of honor and kindness." Moreover, Sam told the House indignantly, Allison constantly refused to take his legitimate commission on arms he bought for Canada. On purchases for the Allies he had refused to accept "more than 50 per cent of what was offered him for his services by those countries." Through his wisdom and integrity, the much abused Allison had "saved upwards of fifty millions to Great Britain and Canada."

How much of this was Hughes's instinctive bluster in the face of criticism, how much loyalty to a friend under duress, how much the flame of full and honest belief, even Borden could not be sure. But the Prime Minister wanted desperately to think the best or a sufficient portion of the best to refuse the full parliamentary inquiry the Liberals were asking for. For the time being he took refuge in the reminder that the Shell Committee had done all its buying for Great Britain and therefore if anyone was robbed it wasn't Canada.

"If any investigation is sanctioned or approved by the British government," Borden assured the House, "we shall not have the slightest objection, and we will assist and co-operate in every way. So far as our own affairs are concerned, so far as the actions of the government are concerned, these stand upon a different basis."

Any relief that this evasion might have given the government was dissipated by another act of evasion on the part of Hughes. Having declared his confidence in Allison, the Minister of Militia almost immediately took another ship for England. Borden pleaded with him to stay in Canada at least until the end of the defense debate (but inexplicably did not order him to do so). Hughes in turn pleaded that he needed a rest, needed a change of scene, that his health was failing, that he couldn't sleep. Finally he wrung Borden's reluctant consent to the journey after telling the Prime Minister he had been secretly in touch with the Opposition and won their promise not to insist on an inquiry. No such pledge, as Hughes well knew and as Borden had a ready means of finding out, had been given. The Liberal onslaught continued as Hughes sped across the Atlantic to attend to what he insisted were more pressing duties.

In the early stages of the debate the nation, while fascinated, had found it difficult to follow all the details. But on March 28, G. W. Kyte produced a case history that had all the lucid symmetry of a short story by O. Henry.

This involved three New York entrepreneurs, who took as their corporate name the American Ammunition Company. Beginning with a total capitalization of $3000, the neophyte concern—with Allison as the go-between and the Canadian Shell Committee as backer and ultimate buyer—was given about $10,000,000 in orders for artillery fuses. Since it had neither a factory nor the money to build a factory, Allison arranged for the Shell Committee to advance the company $1,500,000. Ultimately the orders were filled under this arrangement. The three primary partners, one of them the already legendary railway promoter Benjamin Yoakum, thereupon received a cash commission of $1,000,000. Of this sum $220,000 was kicked back to Colonel Allison.

These astonishing revelations could not be met by mere adroitness. Old Sir George Foster, Deputy Prime Minister to Borden, went home that night from the Commons to scribble a lament in his diary: "To this point of great danger the foolish tolerance of the Hughes-Allison alliance carried us. The Prime Minister knew the connection, was warned by all his Ministers of the probable results, but did nothing." But Borden at last did three things: he appointed a Royal Commission; he asked Hughes to come home from London; and he cabled the apologetic suggestion: "Hope you will take into consideration desirability of placing your resignation in my hands while inquiry is pending." George Foster was still uneasy: "The danger ahead is the premier's lack of will when Sam sits opposite. What he will do no one can tell. What he will not do, we all fear."

Hughes arrived in Ottawa in mid-April and proceeded to Borden's office. The latter's diary described the meeting thus: "Hughes came at four and was as eccentric as ever. Wept at one time and laughed at another. He is confident that he will come through inquiry with flying colors, which I doubt considerably. Discussed with him my proposal that during the inquiry I should administer his department. He objects, thinking it will humiliate him. I told him it would strengthen him and that in making his statement on Tuesday he should say that he had asked me to relieve him of administration during progress of inquiry. We finally left it open after I had impressed upon him its importance."

Though he might show signs of weakness in the privacy of the Prime Minister's office, the Minister of Militia still confronted his enemies with unwavering self-righteousness. On his first day back in Parliament he gave a lecture to the entire House of Commons. After painting a picture of the rigors of the war from which he had just returned, he thundered: "Yet, after an absence of four or five weeks I find, on my return to Canada, that two hundred of the ablest men in this country, members of the House of Commons, instead of being out helping in the cause, are sitting here listening to piffle."

He returned to his championship of Allison: "A gentleman who today stands high in the estimation of the people of the country." When, during the proceedings of the Royal Commission, the Auditor General asked some suggestive questions about Allison's operations, Hughes rose to charge in Parliament that he "makes reflections on a gentleman who has more honor in his little finger than the Auditor General has in his whole carcass." Although the new object of his wrath, the Auditor General, held an office nominally outside politics, Hughes promised darkly: "I will find means of reaching him."

The length to which he was willing to go to reach an enemy or a fancied enemy was illustrated during the same month in a stormy contretemps with P. D. Ross, president of the Ottawa *Journal*. The *Journal* happened to be among the many papers that were now calling for Hughes's resignation. The brother of the paper's publisher happened to be the Canadian Paymaster General in France. Hughes telephoned Ross, the publisher, one night and in effect ordered him to have the paper stop its criticism. Ross told Hughes—in exactly those words—to go to hell. Hughes thereupon telephoned a note to the press gallery at Parliament with the request that it be circulated to "all the boys." The note read: "It is rumored that Colonel Ross of Montreal, Paymaster-General at the front, is being recalled. No reason is assigned. No confirmation can be got here." The attempted plant and the insinuation behind it were treated by the press with the suspicion they deserved; one of the first men to see Hughes's message was a *Journal* reporter, who passed it on to his employer, who passed it on to Borden.

The hearings of the Royal Commission did nothing to ease the government's discomfort. Big Ben Yoakum came up from New York, eased his burly frame into the witness chair, and blandly corroborated every detail of the American Ammunition Company transaction, including the kickback of a quarter of a million dollars to Allison. Allison made the same admission during a wearing two-day appearance, but attempts to pin him down on his other ventures in the buying of arms ended in a blind alley of I-don't-remember's. Toward the end of his second afternoon on the stand Allison collapsed, and his lawyer demanded that he be excused on grounds of health.

The Commission's ultimate findings, as the findings of Royal Commissions occasionally do, bore faint echoes of Lewis Carroll. Everyone was guilty, so in fairness to all everyone was acquitted. The Shell Committee had discriminated among manufacturers, notably in favor of Americans against Canadians. It had paid more than four dollars a fuse for twenty million dollars' worth of fuses when even the most perfunctory investigation would have shown the going price to be three dollars a fuse.

Hughes had known nothing of his friend Allison's rake-off on the American Ammunition Company contract and certainly had not partaken of it. Hughes had, however, successfully urged the Shell Committee to award contracts to certain of his own constituents, including his own son-in-law. As for Allison, he had practiced deception. From these premises the Commission proceeded to three main conclusions: (1) the members of the Shell Committee had been overworked and deserved the nation's sympathy; (2) Hughes was exonerated of complicity with Allison and of using undue influence in the awarding of contracts; (3) Allison's conduct in the American Ammunition purchase "could not be either justified or excused."

The sole visible outcome was that Allison was stripped of his honorary colonelcy. Hughes tried to soften the blow by complaining privately to Borden that his friend deserved better in view of his "services to the Empire" and publicly that he was "the biggest and best man in Canada—and the cleanest too."

XII

The most loved, hated, and debated military
weapon of its time: the Ross rifle

ALMOST simultaneously another confusing drama was approaching another conclusion of sorts. Again Sam Hughes was the most vociferous if not the most convincing figure on the stage.

The Ross rifle was a mere thing of wood and steel (and possibly of tin, some of its adversaries were known to cry), but during the quarter of a century covering its gestation, birth, rise, decline, and fall it became almost a part of the country's animate being. This would have been true of any basic infantry weapon in a war of infantry.

But more than ten years before 1914, in a time of peace and peaceful prospects, the Ross rifle had already begun to excite feelings of special depth and complexity. If it had come into being fifty years earlier or fifty years later, it would have stood a good chance of being judged solely on its performance as a machine; arriving when it did, it could not escape becoming a symbol.

Until well after the Boer War, Canada, like the other dominions and colonies, was absolutely dependent on Great Britain for weapons and most other military supplies. The feeble militia forces got only what the mother country chose to let them have, sometimes by sale, very frequently as handouts. During most of the nineteenth century Canada had not only acquiesced in this arrangement but basked in it.

But immediately before and during the Boer War, the Laurier government was rudely reminded of the drawbacks. Britain helped to equip the Canadian contingents sent to South Africa, but when Laurier's militia department tried to order 15,000 Lee-Enfield rifles in England for direct delivery to Canada, it found it couldn't buy a single one. The British Army, quite naturally, was exercising its priority on all arms production.

An earlier attempt to persuade the Birmingham Small Arms Company to establish a branch plant in Canada for the manufacture of the Lee-Enfield had been rebuffed. Accordingly, Laurier's Militia Minister, Sir Frederick Borden, persuaded his leader that Canada would have to make its own rifles.

This, it soon developed, would not be so formidable an undertaking as might at first have been supposed. It happened that an exciting new sporting rifle, incorporating several features of design and performance more advanced than the Lee-Enfield, was just being put on the market in Great Britain and the United States. Its sponsor was Sir Charles Ross, ninth baronet of Balnagown and an inventor of promise, a soldier of excellent record, and a businessman of good reputation. Ross expressed the conviction that, with a very little modifying, his rifle—which had been patterned after a military weapon, the Austrian Mannlicher—would make a first-class infantry rifle. He brought several of them to Ottawa from his American factory in Connecticut. Sir Frederick Borden was so impressed by what he saw and heard that in the early summer of 1901 he drafted, but did not sign, an agreement to buy sixty-two thousand of them for the Canadian militia during the next six years. At the same time he appointed a five-man committee to prepare a report on the Ross invention and suggest changes. One of the members of the committee was Sam Hughes, then a private M.P. on the Opposition benches, a battalion commander in the militia, and a well-known amateur marksman.

Hughes, in common with most of his fellow committee members, liked the look and feel of the Ross. It was an unusually long rifle, but it was light and well balanced. These things could have been perceived by any tyro. What particularly appealed to the experts was its simple, straight-back-and-forth bolt action (two motions to unload and load, compared with four motions for the Lee-Enfield). They liked its strong breech mechanism, with its certain promise of standing up to higher chamber pressures, hence greater muzzle velocities, longer ranges, and greater accuracy. Sam Hughes, as always the man of impulse, fell in love with it on the spot. But before they would consent to begin the tests, he and his colleagues insisted that Ross make half a dozen changes in the sights, magazine, breech, and bolt.

No inventor ever had a more sympathetic audience than had the baronet of Balnagown when he came back to Canada to subject his new Ross Mark 1 to a trial of accuracy and endurance against the veteran Lee-Enfield Mark 1. The government's desire to make the Canadian foot soldier independent of the whims of the British Ordnance Corps had already been communicated to the nation, and the nation, generally speaking, had applauded. What a poetic thing if Canada, which only a year or so ago had not been able to buy or beg a rifle from Whitehall, should now be on the brink of making rifles of her own of such incomparable merit that Whitehall might in time be coming, brass hat in hand, to Ottawa to buy others like it! Though all Hughes's colleagues on the jury were, like him, loyal officers of the Crown and unswerving admirers of the Empire, it would have been strange if each of them had not felt some tiny bias against the Imperial Lee-Enfield and in favor of the "Canadian" Ross.

Had it been otherwise the history of the Ross rifle might have ended then and there, on a rifle range near Quebec City on an August day in 1901. Twelve different tests had been agreed upon. Reporting on one of them, the dust test, the jury was obliged to observe politely: "Both rifles were heavily sanded. . . . Sir Charles Ross oiled Lee-Enfield bolt under cover, but this was objected to by the committee, and both rifles were fired dry." The two rifles were rated about even by the committee in this particular test and in nine others.

But in two of the most critical ones, the Ross came off very badly. One was designed to show how the two rifles would react to overheavy charges of powder. The Lee-Enfield passed without incident. On the first round the Ross jammed and had to be kicked open with the heel of a boot. After the second round Sir Charles refused to let his rifle continue the excessive-charge test.

Perhaps the most important of the dozen tests was that intended to show how well each weapon would stand up under steady and prolonged action. They were to fire a thousand rounds each. The Lee-Enfield performed perfectly. The Ross jammed and misfired constantly. After fifty rounds the bolt worked stiffly, if at all. After three hundred rounds the barrel was so hot that it melted away the soldered foresight.

For the Canadian militia the Ross remained, however disappointing its first trial had been, the only rifle Canada could make for itself. Thus, when the inventor put forward a ready explanation for its failings he found in the testing committee a ready audience. All the tests, he pointed out, had been made with British .303 shells made in Canada. All his earlier private trials and hence all his niceties of tooling had been based on experiments with American and Austrian shells. The British-Canadian shells he had been compelled to use in the tests were inferior to these both in precision and quality, he informed the jury, and no one called on him to prove it. Now that he knew more about the ammunition his rifles would have to use, he would make the needed adjustment, which involved "only a small detail of manufacturing."

Thus reassured, all five members of the testing committee recommended that Canada switch to the Ross. One of them had brief second thoughts and wrote a letter for the committee's records pointing out an ominous coincidence: everyone had observed that the bolt action of the Ross grew stiff under heat; nine years earlier the United States Army had tested the Austrian Mannlicher, which had the same breech and bolt mechanism and which had shown the same weakness.

There were other belated protests at more exalted levels. A month after the contract was signed the major general commanding the militia, R. H. O'Grady-Haly, received a report on the tests. He raised several objections to the tests themselves and to the rifle which passed them. Still a month after that, the British War and Colonial offices joined in an alarmed plea that Canada abandon the Ross in the interests of uniformity and efficiency. When this warning was ignored, the War Office began issuing statements to the effect that it too had tested the Ross against the Lee-Enfield and established that "the inferiority of the Ross was very marked."

Nothing further was needed to remove the issue forever from the realm of cool and logical discussion. The Ross rifle was now in politics—in Empire politics and Canadian politics. In the next dozen years the original Ross Mark 1 underwent more than eighty changes, and created at least as many headlines. Australia was about to buy 100,000 Ross rifles; Australia was about to do nothing of the kind. The peerless and discriminating Royal North West Mounted Police switched to the Ross in 1904; the disgruntled Royal North West Mounted Police switched back to Winchesters, Lee-Enfields, and Lee-Metfords in 1906. The newly formed Department of Naval Service found 350 Mark 1 Rosses in its stores in 1911 and tried to give them to the militia; the militia would not have them.

A Ross Mark 1 blew up in a militiaman's face, mortally wounding him. A Liberal M.P. thereupon charged in the Commons that the Ross killed "as much behind as in the front." Sam Hughes rose fiercely and declared his willingness to *swallow* any Lee-Enfield rifle that did not jam when he fired it. By 1907 Hughes wrote that with just a few more changes the Ross would be "the most perfect military rifle in every sense in the world today." "I condemn the Lee-Enfield from start to finish," he added with finality.

The facts, rumors, pronouncements, and contradictions about the Ross piled up endlessly. There was not a saloon, hotel lobby, or barbershop across the whole Dominion whose rafters had not rung at the merest whisper of that name.

After the 1911 election, which made Hughes the new Minister of Militia and National Defence, it seemed likely that the argument was settled for good. As though to emphasize his own expectations, Sam included Sir Charles Ross among his first wave of honorary colonels and gave him the title "Consulting Officer, Small Arms, Ammunition and Ballistics." By the time war broke out, the baronet had manufactured 112,000 rifles of various marks at his factory near Quebec.

Without correcting all its defects, the endless revisions had lengthened the rifle's barrel by more than two inches and increased its weight by more than two pounds. No one disputed that it was still an excellent target rifle—it had, indeed, won the King's Prize at Bisley in 1911 and again in 1913—but it was now more than a pound heavier and seven inches longer than the Lee-Enfield. When the first contingent went into the trenches at Ypres, thousands of men who had experienced or heard of epidemic jamming and faulty cartridge ejection on the ranges of Salisbury and Valcartier had begun to regard the traditional "soldier's best friend" with suspicion and alarm.

In the First Division's memorable stand at Ypres against gas, artillery, small arms, and an empty flank, the Ross's already shaky reputation among the men who had to use it was all but obliterated. The battle ended with about five thousand Canadian infantry survivors, and an official arms census showed that 1452 of them had thrown away their Rosses and armed themselves with Lee-Enfields, picked up on the battlefield beside dead Englishmen or acquired in trades with adjoining units moving out of the line into relief. If men could judge dispassionately when their own lives hang upon the judgment, it might have been said that this soldier's verdict against the Ross was more harsh and sweeping than it deserved. Just as there were infinitesimal differences in the chamber measurements of the Canadian-manufactured Ross and the British-manufactured Lee-Enfield, so were there infinitesimal differences in the Canadian-made and British-made .303 shells used by both. Since they were part of a British army and were in a British chain of supply, a high proportion of the Canadian rifles were supplied by British shells; their rate of failure was greater than that of the rifles which had been supplied by Canadian shells.

But none of this had the slightest meaning to the Canadian infantryman who, fighting for breath itself as he peered across his parapet into the gray-green fogs of Ypres and the gray-green Germans marching through them, suddenly found himself with a seized-up rifle. There was, of course, no way of telling what loss of life was directly entailed while the desperate forward battalions tried to kick back their frozen bolts with muddy boots or hammer them loose with trenching spades. But Alderson, the divisional commander, determined to get as much precise information as he could. As soon as the battle ended he asked his brigade and battalion commanders to report on their experiences with the Ross and the feeling toward it in their units. A few officers reported favorably and a few noncommittally. The majority reaction ranged from one officer's terse "The men have lost confidence in the Ross as a service arm" to another's angry "It is nothing short of murder to send our men against the enemy with such a weapon."

Alderson forwarded the reports to the British commander in chief, Sir John French, along with a warning: "This matter is as delicate as it is important. . . . Canada will no doubt be extremely annoyed if fault is found with the rifle; this, however, cannot be allowed to stand in the way when the question may be of life and death, and of victory and defeat." French appointed another committee to test the Ross against the Lee-Enfield. The report he sent to the War Office in London was a model of tact. The Ross worked smoothly and well with Canadian ammunition. But it was still impossible to guarantee a continuous supply of Canadian ammunition to the front line. Therefore French had ordered the entire First Division to be rearmed with the Lee-Enfield.

No amount of polite dissembling could alter the shocking truth: the Ross, endorsed by two successive Canadian governments and a personal favorite of a strong-willed and notoriously difficult Canadian Minister of Militia, stood repudiated. The British Army Council nervously admonished French that he had condemned the Ross on insufficient evidence. "In view of the very favorable character attached to the Ross rifle by the Canadian government the Army Council would be glad to have some independent opinion of a few selected Canadian officers on the general serviceability of this rifle as compared with the Lee-Enfield."

But French was on unassailable ground and he knew it. "This is a difficult and complicated question, which can only be satisfactorily settled by the best expert opinion," he replied carefully. "The views of a few selected Canadian officers, who may or may not be prejudiced in the matter, will not be of any material assistance." And it was a matter not of opinion but of cold fact that the number of Canadian infantrymen who had thrown away or traded their Ross rifles for Lee-Enfields had by now risen from 1452 to about 3000. French conceded that there was as yet no need to switch the Second Division, then in England, from the Ross to the Lee-Enfield. If it could be guaranteed a steady supply of Canadian ammunition, it might fight with the Ross indefinitely; ultimately, indeed, if the cartridge chambers were slightly enlarged, the First Division's old rifles might be reclaimed for useful duty. But the First was already poised for another hard battle, and French, in effect, dared his superiors to issue "an authoritative statement which will carry conviction to the men that their apprehensions are unfounded." The Army Council hastily backed down and accepted the switch-over to Lee-Enfields.

During the next few months all the Ross rifles of the Second Division were rechambered, as were those returned to stores by the First Division in exchange for Lee-Enfields. But almost at once and in every main particular, history began to repeat itself. Despite Sir Sam Hughes's personal order that its members should be told "the Lee-Enfield jams even worse with bad ammunition than does ours," the Second Division, equipped with the Ross, was full of foreboding when it arrived in France. No amount of reasoning could dissuade the soldier who carried it from the notion that the Ross was heavy and ill balanced; that the long barrel took a long time to bring on a target and was forever knocking against the parapets and other abutments in the trenches; above all, that it had been disowned and cast away by the men who had passed that way before.

In the confused, costly, and futile fighting around the craters and Mound of St.-Eloi in early 1916, Canadian soldiers again found themselves defending themselves with rifles that had ceased to work. Those who had a chance followed the example of the First Division and acquired British weapons in whatever way they could. The exact number was never established, but there were enough to make the Second Division think it necessary to issue a special order threatening to court-martial any company commander who allowed his men to use the Lee-Enfield or to keep the Lee-Enfields they had already obtained.

As for the Third Division, which also fought its first main engagement at St.-Eloi, so many of its infantrymen threw away their Ross rifles that Hughes sent a personal emissary to demand an explanation from the divisional commander in the field. Major General M. S. Mercer—who as a brigadier a year earlier had declared the Ross "a satisfactory weapon"—made a devastatingly unapologetic reply. His men had little or no confidence in the Ross. His officers had reported overwhelmingly against it. It jammed whether the ammunition was Canadian or British, good or bad. He stated his conclusion in the same clear terms as he had in presenting the evidence: "To longer withhold the issue of the L. E. rifle and compel the men of this Division to use the Ross rifle would be criminal in the extreme."

General Alderson, now promoted to commander of the Canadian Corps and apparently less impressed by the political delicacy of the issue than he had been during the previous round, had in the meantime launched his own attack against the Ross. In another of the interminable tests between the two rifles he had invited two of Hughes's closest friends and confidants to attend as observers. One of these was Major General J. W. Carson, Hughes's special representative in London. The other was Sir Max Aitken, the Canadian-born newspaper publisher whom the Militia Minister had appointed to his roster of honorary colonels and given the title of Special Representative at the Front.

The report Carson and Aitken signed was similar in tone to a dozen others that had gone into the record during the previous fifteen years. Three different marks of ammunition were used in this latest test. The Lee-Enfield fired from 100 to 125 rounds "as rapidly as possible." The Ross jammed from the twenty-fifth to the fiftieth round.

Alderson summarized this information and some other unflattering observations about the Ross in a letter to the Chief of the General Staff at Ottawa, Major General W. G. Gwatkin. Actually, he added, the official report had flattered the Ross. "It does not state, as it should, that the Lee-Enfield, although handled by men not trained to it, fired (owing to it being, as I have before said, much easier to charge the magazine) its 100 rounds in about one-third less time than the Ross. Nor does the report state, as was the case, that the hands of the men using the Ross were cut and bleeding owing to the difficulty they had in knocking back the bolt."

Alderson ended his letter to headquarters in Ottawa with a pointed hint that Gwatkin show it to Hughes. This he did, whereupon Sir Sam replied directly to his corps commander with a torrent of insults. "I am well aware that very few officers, British or Canadian, know much about any rifle, especially a new one like the Ross," he said by way of preamble. "You seem to be strangely familiar, judging from your letter, with the list of ten suggestions intended to prejudice the Ross rifle in the minds of the Canadians. . . . It is not worth while, with men who know little or nothing about rifles, to take up these ten points in detail, but some of them are so absolutely absurd and ridiculous that no one excepting a novice, or for an excuse, would be found seriously advancing them. . . . Each and every one, to anyone informed on the expert aspect of rifles, carries its own condemnation on the face."

Sir Sam could not forgo a few words of reproach for the misguided friends who had given comfort and support to Alderson: "So far as concerns your amateur test with experts like yourself, Sir Max Aitken, Sir George Perley and General Carson . . ." Nor could he resist the old temptation to a bit of straight romancing: "I shall not . . . produce hundreds of documents in the form of letters, etc., to show that, from the very outset, the expert British soldier, whenever he found an opportunity, invariably slipped off with the Ross rifle leaving the L. E. instead."

The crux of the matter was not rifles, Hughes persisted, but ammunition. "With good ammunition the Ross has never been known to jam. . . . The aspect which borders on criminality is the permitting of bad ammunition being placed in the hands of soldiers who are risking their lives in defence of the liberties we all hold so dear. There might have been an excuse at the beginning that some routine officer had passed the ammunition without detecting its faults, but over and over again, in spite of the loss of thousands of the boys, this defective ammunition was placed in their hands."

Sir Sam ended his letter to his corps commander with the menacing injunction: "Your emphatic energy concerning what your intentions are, if you will pardon me, might better be directed to having your officers of every grade responsible in the premises to make sure that none of the defective ammunition again finds its way into the Canadian ranks." He took the extraordinary step of sending a copy of this communication to every Canadian unit commander, brigadier general, and major general stationed anywhere overseas.

Alderson's reply was to order still another pre-Gallup poll of the officers of the Second and Third divisions. Before the returns were in he was relieved of his command and returned to England as Inspector General of the Canadian forces. Like General Hutton, Hughes's adversary of the now distant Boer War days, Alderson suddenly found himself face to face with a bewildering and painful discovery. To win an argument with Sam Hughes, all you needed was a resolute will, a clear mind, a thick skin, and a detachable head.

But he and the other critics of the Ross did, at last, prevail. Hughes was still good for another six weeks of rearguard action and he fought it out so doggedly that a final decision was reached only after the intervention of Sir Douglas Haig, the new British commander in chief in the field; the Governor General; Prime Minister Borden; Sir Max Aitken; the Privy Council; and the Colonial Secretary, Bonar Law.

On the same day that Alderson was fired, Haig informed the War Office that "the Ross is less trustworthy than the Lee-Enfield," and recommended that the Canadian Second and Third divisions be rearmed with the British weapon. Hughes immediately demanded yet another round of tests. Almost simultaneously, Borden, who had played a largely passive role throughout the earlier years of argument and invective, demanded yet another poll. When the returns were tabulated the senior officers of the Second Division were exactly divided in their recorded opinions of the Ross: 25 for, 25 against, 13 undecided. But the Third Division was unanimously against. Haig repeated his recommendation that the Ross be abandoned "without delay," and his recommendation was accepted in July 1916 and put into force in August.

Altogether the Canadian government bought 342,000 Ross rifles. The prices, at various stages of the contract, ran up to twenty-eight dollars each. In general they were between a quarter and a third higher than the cost of Lee-Enfields to the British Army.

The government expropriated Ross's factory in 1917 and paid him a settlement of $2,000,000 in 1920. Ross had financed the venture privately on an initial capitalization of $1,000,000 and declared himself to be the sole proprietor. His statement of 1906 that no one in Canada had any interest in the company was never in dispute. Nor was corruption or profiteering ever seriously charged against the inventor or his supporters. The only real issue was whether the Ross was a good service rifle.

XIII

Exit Sam Hughes—"Tell 'em to go like blazes!"

THE demise of the Ross rifle coincided almost exactly with the exposure of Sam Hughes's proudly acknowledged "guide and counselor," J. Wesley Allison. A man of more flexible temper might have been crushed by two such blows. But Sir Sam, though he was hurt and indignant, was not even mildly deflated, much less apprehensive of his future. He had as yet seen no reason to revise his old estimate of Borden, carefully pondered and written out in the days just after the party came into office: "A most lovely fellow . . . gentle-hearted as a girl." Acting on that estimate and fully aware that many of his colleagues in the Cabinet were imploring Borden to get rid of him at once, he coolly wrote Borden: "The general opinion is that Sir Thomas [White] bores you until, out of patience, you finally accede to his plans. I can assure you the effect on the country or the party is not beneficial." And in another message, sent from England, Sir Sam comforted the Prime Minister on the burdens imposed on him by the men in his Cabinet: "Your road is more or less a hard one. It is generally understood that White and Foster seek to impose their influence, adverse to me, upon you. But I know you are capable of seeing through them."

But after five tempestuous years, Borden had begun to develop some resistance to Hughes's blandishments and bullying. He had written in his diary, in the aftermath of the Ross-rifle and Allison revelations: "It is quite evident that Hughes cannot remain in the government." Nevertheless, it required another four months and another first-class public row before the two men made their parting.

The Cabinet's liaison with the overseas forces had been chancy and sporadic from the outset. For information about higher strategy and higher statesmanship, Borden was wholly dependent on the occasional confidences of the British Cabinet and the War Office, who told him very little, usually very late. And for information on the interior housekeeping of the Canadian Corps, its welfare, armament, and state of mind, he was largely dependent on Hughes. Through General Carson, his special representative in London, various other plenipotentiaries, and his own frequent voyages abroad, the Militia Minister had established a highly efficient intelligence system of his own. But Borden had begun to feel the need of an overseas agent or agency whose first loyalty was not to Sam Hughes but to the government.

With that in view he instructed Hughes to study the whole overseas organization of the Canadian forces—excluding their actual combat role within the British Army—and cable recommendations for a change back to Ottawa. The risks he took in thus asking Hughes to preside over the liquidation of his own powers must have preyed on the Prime Minister's mind. For within a few days of Sir Sam's arrival in England, Borden cabled him: "When you have reached conclusions respecting your proposals for reorganization, please cable fully, as they should be definitely embodied in order-in-council and it would be desirable to consider them before they are actually put in operation." Two weeks later Borden cabled again asking for Hughes's proposals. Finally, after three more weeks, the Prime Minister learned through an announcement to the London newspapers that his Militia Minister had appointed a Canadian Militia Subcouncil in England and given it major responsibilities in liaison and administration. A son-in-law of Hughes was to act as secretary to the council. Borden cabled Sir Sam to come home at once.

At their meeting in Ottawa in October, it was Borden who had disquieting news to convey. He had decided to appoint a Minister of Overseas Forces. As the holder of cabinet rank, the Overseas Minister would, of course, report directly to the government. Moreover, the man proposed for the job, Sir George Perley, was one of Hughes's oldest and bitterest enemies. Sir Sam, Borden recorded in his diary, "objected strongly and argued against it, saying there would be nothing left for him, that he would be humiliated and that he would have to leave the Government. He gave a tirade against Perley and decried his ability. Said that everything he had done was perfect, etc. Complained that White was conspiring against him."

A week or so later Hughes attempted a compromise. He would support the new Overseas Ministry if Borden would drop the idea of appointing Sir George Perley and offer the position to Sir Max Aitken. The Prime Minister's refusal did not deter Sir Sam from cabling Aitken and offering him the appointment anyway; Aitken fortunately declined, on the ground that he wasn't qualified.

A few days later Borden carried out his intention. Sir Sam put his last sulphurous and mutinous protests into a letter, and Borden, to his own vast relief, now had no possible choice but to demand his resignation. This was duly provided on November 11, 1916. Sir Sam's valedictory as minister contained few surprises. It was liberally peppered with complaints about meddling and intrigue and it roundly taunted Borden for the very quality, or lack of quality, which had permitted him to put up with Hughes so long. "Well, Sir Robert," his departing colleague wrote, "each one's manner is his own. It might be well if we could all possess your soft manner-isms, but I'm very much afraid, judging by all periods of history, that human liberty and human progress would not make much advance, as they never have made much advance, under such dip-lomatic forms and utterances."

And thus, except for a few minor postscripts, there ended one of the most bizarre and astounding public careers in all of Canadian history. For three of its most momentous and critical years the country's energy and resources had lain to a very considerable degree under the command of a man who would have had the utmost difficulty in passing a standard medical test for sanity. Al-most as remarkably, the hypersane Borden was aware of Sam Hughes's infirmities—or later said he was—before he took him into his Cabinet, and often reflected on them during the five years before discharging him. Borden, who arranged his memoirs in 1928, then remembered the man he made Militia Minister in 1911 in these terms: "While he was a man of marked ability and sound judgment in many respects, his temperament was so peculiar, and his actions and language so unusual on many important occasions, that one was inclined to doubt his usefulness as a Minister. There was much pressure on his behalf from various sources; and my cousin, Sir Frederick Borden, who sought an interview with me on behalf of Hughes, expressed the firm, and I believe the sincere, opinion that Hughes, under proper control, would be of great service to the country. I discussed with Hughes when I appointed him his extraordinary eccentricities. On one occasion when I impressed strongly upon him the perverse nature of his speech and conduct, he broke down, admitted that he often acted impetuously, and assured me that if he were appointed I could rely on his judgment and good sense. This promise was undoubtedly sincere but his temperament was too strong for him. He was under constant illusions that enemies were working against him. I told him on one occasion that I thoroughly agreed that he was beset by two unceasing enemies. Expecting a revelation he was intensely disappointed when I told him that they were his tongue and his pen. In my experience his moods might be divided into three categories; during about half of the time he was an able, reasonable and useful colleague, working with excellent judgement and indefatigable energy; for a certain other portion he was extremely excitable, impatient of control and almost impossible to work with; and during the remainder his conduct and speech were so eccentric as to justify the conclusion that his mind was unbalanced."

Rescinding the appointment of Hughes caused Borden as much soul searching as making it. Hughes had a gift of great value to any public figure: the appearance of standing four-square and unafraid between the common man and a shadowy but various host of tormentors called "they." "They" appeared in a dozen guises. One month they were the rapacious Yankees, trying to drive the wedge of reciprocity between Canada and the mother country; another month they were the haughty British, trying to deny Canada its rights. They were the incompetent English generals, throwing away the lives of Canadian boys to defend a useless and almost indefensible salient at Ypres. They were the English admirals who, but for Sam Hughes's personal warning against German submarines, would have let the first Canadian contingent cross the Atlantic all but unprotected. They were the brass hats at the War Office, bent on breaking up the Canadian divisions and dissuaded only by Sam Hughes's manliness and spunk. They were the proud and distant Governors General, trying to deny a fair hearing to a wronged Ontario Orangeman, but not quite getting away with it, not against Sam Hughes. They were the wicked munitions makers and bumbling corps commanders, giving Canadian infantrymen bad shells and trying to blame the result on bad rifles. They were the permanent officers swanking and posturing in front of the militia officers. They were the militia officers swanking and posturing in front of the sergeants and privates. They were the politicians conspiring and whispering behind plush curtains while far better men died in the mud of Flanders. They were the wretched creatures of the Pope of Rome, cowering among their beads and candles while the flower of the L.O.L. marched gladly forth to save mankind.

Hughes, largely at his own instigation, leaped in rank all the way from colonel to lieutenant general during his term in the Cabinet; yet he managed to give the impression that rank was distasteful to him. When he became Sir Sam, most people took his knighthood as a deserved tribute to a rough-and-ready man who probably didn't want it. In short, Hughes had been appointed to the Cabinet because he looked like a political asset at the time (his prestige in the Orange Lodge alone made him an invaluable makeweight against the Quebec nationalists, as the Liberal Toronto *Globe* sourly pointed out). And he continued to look like a political asset, for his blunders, numerous though they were, included few of the kind that arouse great popular indignation. Thus, Borden, once committed to him, had to ask himself again and again where the greatest danger lay: with Hughes raising modified hell as a member of the Cabinet or with Hughes raising unlimited hell as a former member. As Borden himself put the matter in his memoirs: "After his dismissal I sometimes heard expressions of surprise that I had not taken that action at an earlier date. . . . I knew that Hughes had a considerable following, the force of which was an undetermined factor, and, while I felt that his continued presence in the Government was a handicap rather than a support, I determined to let him continue until I was perfectly sure that his dismissal would not entail any serious danger to my Administration."

After his dismissal from the Cabinet, Hughes kept his seat in Parliament. In the summer of 1921, in his sixty-ninth year, he fell seriously ill in Ottawa and asked to be taken home to Lindsay. Someone with a good memory and a sense of chivalry recollected that, in his days as minister, one of the old man's favorite vanities had been riding back and forth on inspection visits aboard special trains. A special train was provided to bear him on his last journey. Before the train pulled out of the Ottawa station the conductor came to Hughes's private car and asked if the engineer should be instructed to travel slowly. "No!" the dying man commanded. "Tell 'em to go like blazes!"

XIV

The fateful hinge of Verdun—The counterhinge of the Somme—Enter the "landship," cistern, or reservoir, finally called the tank

THE fable that no news is good news ought, in theory, to apply with particular force to any large body of people under the imminent and continuous threat of death. For the front-line soldier of 1916 any prolongation of the status quo also meant a prolongation of life, and therefore should have had its compensations.

In fact, the status quo in the Ypres salient—leaving its dangers aside—had proved so totally miserable that for those who dwelt there the opposite of the fable had come true, and any news was good news. For the Canadians on the Western Front the late summer of 1916 was filled with red-letter days: the day they traded their Ross rifles for Lee-Enfields; the day they learned they were being pulled out of Flanders; the day they heard that, after sixteen months in defense, they were to move south to join the general offensive on the Somme.

At the beginning of 1916, the Western Front was still in the state of bloody paralysis that had set in with the fall of 1914. Like corporation directors preparing for a new business year, the German general staff and the still loosely co-ordinated French and British commands had spent much of the previous November and December weighing, modifying, and finally adopting their policies for the next twelve months. In so doing they repeated the pattern of 1914, when the French attacking eastward to the south and the Germans attacking westward to the north had become locked and immobile, like two men caught going opposite ways in a revolving door. This time the axis on which they sought to pivot was shorter, their heaving shoulders were closer together, and the direction toward which they struggled was reversed: the Allies thrusting eastward toward the north and the Germans westward toward the south.

There was now no hope on either side of an outflanking movement, for there were no flanks. But both commands saw, or thought they saw, pale gleams of light in the narrow prison of bog, forest, valley, and ridge that extended from the North Sea to the Alps. Nearly 300 divisions strained there in double shackles, each one of their millions of men both a captor and a captive. Groping in their separate ways for some means of breaking the deadlock, Von Falkenhayn, Chief of the German General Staff, and Joffre and Haig, the French and British commanders, were drawn inevitably toward the same solution. A massed attack on a narrow front might, if completely successful, achieve a breakthrough. Even if only moderately successful it might throw the enemy off balance, force him to pour his reserves into counterattacks, and thus wear him down by attrition.

By now the British had remedied their shortage of ammunition; the French and Germans had been relatively well supplied from the beginning. Thus, it was not difficult for either group of armies to persuade itself that, by attacking at a time and place of its own choosing, it stood to gain something—perhaps a good deal.

Von Falkenhayn chose to strike at Verdun. There he launched the longest and most brutal single battle of the war. By every criterion except the count of dead and wounded he was to end the loser, but strategically and psychologically his selection of Verdun was perhaps as good a one as he could have made.

Verdun was the fulcrum of the whole southern half of the Allied position. There, a hundred and forty miles straight ahead of Paris, the French clung to a salient on the right bank of the Meuse, a little crescent of ground that could not be given up without the risk of a disorderly rollback of fifty miles to the Marne.

Verdun offered prizes and disasters that could not be measured in miles or bodies. If Verdun fell Sedan would fall soon after, and France still remembered Sedan all too well and all too anxiously as the point of the Prussian breakthrough in 1870. And Verdun, like the Belgian cities of Liège and Namur—far downstream on the same river Meuse—was officially classified as a fortress. The swift envelopment of Liège and Namur in 1914 had been a profound shock not merely to the French armies but to the French nation. If their own Verdun should be lost now the effect on the country's morale might be decisive.

Studying these matters, Von Falkenhayn concluded the French would pour their last ounce of strength into Verdun before giving it up. Very well. Whether he took Verdun or not was not of the first importance. Merely by attacking, attacking, and attacking again he would, he promised the Kaiser, "bleed the forces of France to death."

Joffre, the French commander, knew nothing of his enemy's plan. He was bent on launching a spring or summer offensive of his own far to the north in Picardy. There, in the deep marshy valley of the Somme and on the slopes between the Somme and its tributary the Ancre, the British and French forces made their junction.

The British official war history has maintained that Joffre urged the Somme-Ancre hinge as a point of attack "solely because the British would be bound to take part in it."

On any other basis the ground offered an uninviting prospect, with peat bogs in the valley bottoms and great thickets of German wire, trench, and dugout, and sunken roadways looking down from the fortified uplands to the east. Haig would have preferred to try breaking out of the bulge at Ypres near the northern coast, and since there was no official unity of command, he was not obliged to defer to his French colleague. But he and his government yielded to the logic of numbers—the French still had far more men in the field than the British. It was agreed that on a total front of forty miles the French would strike on July 1, 1916, with forty divisions and the British with twenty-five.

The arrangement was made on February 14, nearly five months ahead of the target date. Exactly a week later Von Falkenhayn began his drive against Verdun. As he had reckoned they would, the French decided they must hold on, whatever the price. In so deciding they completed the blueprint for a battle that was to last ten months and cost a million casualties in about the ratio of five Frenchmen to four Germans. At the same time the whole design for the Somme offensive had to be changed. The French could contribute not forty divisions but sixteen. They could be responsible not for twenty-five miles of the front but for eight.

Yet whatever new sources of doubt all these sudden calculations added to the original plan for the Somme, some remnant of the plan had to be carried forward. To drop it would be to free the enemy for an unlimited stepping up of the assault at Verdun.

The British assault therefore began as scheduled, on July 1, 1916. As it proceeded through the summer and autumn, it crossed military frontiers as steep as those to be crossed two generations later by hydrogen bombs and artificial moons. Before the battle of the Somme was over in its far-off half century ago, it employed observation balloons hovering above lines of infantrymen with fixed bayonets; airplanes darting above plunging troops of cavalry horses; tanks rolling over trenches waist-deep in stagnant water.

At first the intimations of change were altogether missed by the field commanders. The British Fourth Army sent its assault infantry across No Man's Land girded and deployed as though for Waterloo: each man weighed down with his exact sixty-six pounds of gear and ammunition, each battalion walking straight ahead in waves, every soldier an arm's length from the soldier next to him and in step, every rifle at the high port.

No two men saw the horror and gallantry of the Somme from exactly the same point of vantage or in exactly the same perspective. A German soldier later described the first British assault in this way:

"The intense bombardment was realized by all to be the prelude to an infantry assault sooner or later. The men in the dugouts therefore waited ready, belts full of hand grenades around them, gripping their rifles and listening for the bombardment to lift from the front defense zone to the rear defenses. It was of vital importance to lose not a second in taking up positions in the open to meet the British infantry which would advance immediately behind the artillery barrage. Looking towards the British trenches through the long trench periscopes held up out of the dugout entrances, there could be seen a mass of steel helmets above the parapet showing that the storm troops were ready for the assault. At 7:30 A.M. the hurricane of shells ceased as suddenly as it had begun. Our men at once clambered up the steep shafts to daylight and ran singly or in groups to the nearest shell craters. The machine guns were pulled out of the dugouts and hurriedly placed in position, their crews dragging the heavy ammunition boxes up the steps and put to the guns. A rough firing line was thus rapidly established. As soon as the men were in position, a series of extended lines of infantry were seen moving forward from the British trenches. The first line appeared to continue without end to right and left. It was quickly followed by a second line, then a third and fourth.

"They came on at a steady easy pace as if expecting to find nothing alive in our front trenches. The front line, preceded by a thin line of skirmishers and bombers, was now halfway across No Man's Land. 'Get ready!' was passed along our front from crater to crater, and heads appeared over the crater edge as final positions were taken up for the best view, and machine guns mounted firmly in place.

"A few moments later, when the leading British line was within a hundred yards, the rattle of machine-gun and rifle fire broke out along the whole line of shell holes. Some fired kneeling so as to get a better target over the broken ground, while others, in the excitement of the moment, stood up regardless of their own safety to fire into the crowd of men in front of them. Red rockets sped up into the sky as a signal to the artillery, and immediately afterwards a mass of shell from the German batteries in the rear tore through the air and burst among the advancing lines. Whole sections seemed to fall, and the rear formations, moving in closer order, quickly scattered. The advance rapidly crumpled under this hail of shell and bullets. All along the line men could be seen throwing up their arms and collapsing, never to move again. Badly wounded rolled about in their agony, and others, less severely injured, crawled to the nearest shell hole for shelter. The British soldier, however, has no lack of courage, and once his hand is set to the plow he is not easily turned from his purpose. The extended lines, though badly shaken and with many gaps, now came on all the faster. Instead of a leisurely walk they covered the ground in short rushes at the double. Within a few minutes the leading troops had advanced to within a stone's throw of our front trench, and while some of us continued to fire at point-blank range, others threw hand grenades among them. The British bombers answered back, while the infantry rushed forward with fixed bayonets. The noise of battle became indescribable. The shouting of orders and the shrill cheers as the British charged forward could be heard above the violent and intense fusillade of machine guns and rifles and the bursting bombs and, above, the deep thunderings of the artillery and shell explosions. With all this were mingled the moans and groans of the wounded, the cries for help and the last screams of death. Again and again the extended lines of British infantry broke against the German defense like waves against a cliff, only to be beaten back.

"It was an amazing spectacle of unexampled gallantry, courage, and bulldog determination on both sides."

On that July 1, the British suffered more casualties than on any other day of the war. In so doing they accomplished little more than to persuade the German command—which had been more than half expecting the main attack in the neighborhood of Ypres—to commit its reserves to the Somme.

Within a day or so the Allies had traded the feeble hope of initiative for the heavy burden of commitment. Soon Haig and Joffre were quarreling over what to do next. The French had made some gains on the right, and Haig now felt his best chance of storming the long main ridge of the German position was to shift the weight of his attack from the center to the south.

But Joffre, with the fate of the French armies and of France itself still in a state of desperate balance at Verdun, insisted that the focal point of the Somme offensive remain in the center, toward the three miles of the ridge between Pozières and Thiepval. Joffre, in fact, gave Haig a direct order to attack toward Pozières and Thiepval. Haig refused, asserting in effect that the Somme was his battle and he would run it in his own way, whereupon the two commanders parted with declarations of good will and their difference still unsettled.

But the pattern of the battle was already firmly in place—an unending series of massive charges and minuscule gains, launched and contained at such ghastly cost to both sides that it was the Germans—the lesser sufferers—who first gave it the name of *Blutbad*.

Although the front was undeniably in motion, its tiniest agonized twitch or quiver could cost five, ten, or twenty thousand men. To create one narrow spur a mile deep the First Australian and New Zealand Corps alone paid with 23,000 casualties in a six-week period. In the midst of it one officer wrote: "We have just come out of a place so terrible a raving lunatic could never imagine the horror of the last thirteen days." Such bitter memories could not be dismissed as the personal nightmares of men close to the breaking point. Many years later the Australian official history had this comment to make: "Doubtless to the Commander-in-Chief, and possibly to the Cabinet, the use of terms implying leisurely progress brought some comfortable assurance of economy of life as well as of munitions; but to the front line the method merely appeared to be that of applying a battering-ram ten or fifteen times against the same part of the enemy's battlefront with the intention of penetrating for a mile, or possibly two, into the midst of his organized defenses. Even if the need for maintaining pressure be granted, the student will have difficulty in reconciling his intelligence to the actual tactics. To throw the several parts of any army corps, brigade after brigade . . . twenty times in succession against one of the strongest points in the enemy's defense may certainly be described as 'methodical,' but the claim that it was economic is entirely unjustified."

It was from the valiant but mangled Anzacs that the Canadian Corps took over an important sector of the Somme on September 4, 1916. Already, though the fact was but dimly understood by those who ushered it in, a new kind of warfare was in the making. It bore no relation at all to the swift and cleanly war of movement which the more optimistic of the Canadians had envisaged when they scraped the mud of Flanders from their boots and prepared to immerse them in the unknown and therefore more inviting mud of Picardy. But it did have, if not fluidity, at least a certain slow viscosity. And it did introduce the tank.

Nine years after its first appearance in combat and seven years after the Armistice, the credit for the tank's creation was still being contested before the British courts of law. By then two things had emerged: the chief inventor was a British military historian and fiction writer named Colonel Ernest Swinton; and if Swinton hadn't invented the tank someone else would have had to. Thanks to the machine gun, barbed wire, and the trench, the advantages of defense in military combat had again become as great as in the times when moated castles frowned down on unprotected archers.

Though the airplane was now in wide use, it had no power to break the deadlock on the ground below. Airplanes were useful for reconnaissance, but to the well-sheltered land masses their puny guns and primitive bombs were not even a major nuisance. Nor did the growing number of cannon do anything except add to the imbalance in favor of defense. Occasionally an army or corps commander, seeking a way to keep from herding his infantry unprotected across the last stretch of No Man's Land, sent tunnelers and mining parties burrowing beneath the enemy trenches to blow them up in the instant before a zero hour. But these chilling and fearful expeditions, though sometimes successful on a limited scale, had virtually been abandoned by the middle of 1916. A defending army was still an unbeatable army.

It was in response to these circumstances that Swinton evolved the tank. At first he received no encouragement from the War Office, but the incessantly inquiring Winston Churchill took him under protection, reasoning that Swinton's yet unborn vehicles were "landships" and therefore a proper concern of Churchill's Admiralty. Although Churchill was forced out of office by the disaster of Gallipoli, he helped Swinton obtain authority to go on with his experiments.

Exactly what kind of weapon was in the making no one knew for certain. But everyone agreed that it needed three properties: mobility to get across the mud and wire and through the craters; armor to stop machine-gun bullets; firepower to drive infantry from its trenches. By late summer sixty machines that, at least in theory, met these specifications were on the way to France, loaded on flatcars and mysteriously swathed in tarpaulins. The shapes beneath might have been tanks and that was why they were called tanks; cistern and reservoir were among the other names considered.

Haig's decision to send the tanks into battle as early as September 15, 1916, came to their inventor as a blow almost as bitter as his many earlier rebuffs from the War Office. One thing had always been acknowledged by all parties. Whether it was a useful weapon or not remained to be seen, but Swinton's apparatus was a secret weapon and must be so treated. It should not be employed until sufficient numbers were on hand to launch it in mass. In this conception Haig had concurred while the tanks were still coming off the drawing boards.

But suddenly Haig was bent on reactivating his stalled offensive at any cost. By gradual nibbling through July and August 1916, he had won a firm foothold on the high ground between the Somme and the Ancre. Now he was determined to clear the rest of the ridge before the winter set in and if possible roll down the reverse slope to the plain of Bapaume, an almost unheard-of bound of seven miles. Haig knew it was a gamble. So did Sir Henry Rawlinson, who commanded the army nominated to assault, the Fourth. "We shall have no reserves in hand except tired troops," Rawlinson cheerfully confided to his diary, "but success at this time would have a great effect throughout the world and might bring the Boche to terms. If we fail, we shall have all the winter in which to recuperate and there will be no counter-attack left in the enemy. It is worth the risk."

In his belief that the proper risks included unveiling the tank, Haig was almost alone. The War Minister, Lloyd George, protested against the C. in C.'s plan to support the September offensive with his handful of the weird new monsters and their half-trained crews. The British Minister of Munitions made a special visit to France to object in person. But Haig was adamant. The tanks would be used, and short of dismissing its first soldier, the War Cabinet could do nothing but acquiesce.

At first the Canadian Corps's role in the new attack was unspecified. The Canadians were attached to General Gough's Fifth Army, which was in reserve to the left of the assaulting Fourth Army. Their first instructions were to take a ruined sugar factory and a complex of German trenches in front of the town of Courcelette. From this position, under the far brow of the plateau between the Ancre and the Somme, the Germans threatened two Allied objectives—the main line of the Fourth Army's attack to the right and the high ground on the left at Thiepval.

In the first plan no mention had been made of the possibility that the Canadians might push through and take Courcelette itself. Later Gough amended this by instructing Byng, the Canadians' commander, "to occupy Courcelette at any time if it should be possible to do so without assistance." And Haig amended it still further with a message that "all preparations must be made" for capturing the town on the first afternoon of the attack.

The general attack had been under way for almost four hours and was going generally well when the order came to the Canadian Fifth and Seventh brigades, waiting far in the rear, to advance on Courcelette. To get into position they had to cross five miles of bare slopes and upland, most of it with no other landmarks than the bursts of enemy artillery fire. One battalion, the famous Princess Patricia's, arrived a few minutes behind its zero hour, overshot its start line, and actually found itself fixing bayonets for the assault in the middle of the enemy's outposts, with clusters of startled and fortunately demoralized Germans springing up from shell holes literally beneath their feet. Similarly the Royal 22d from Quebec and the Nova Scotia Rifles, who took the town itself, made their final dash from the open into territory so unknown that all they could do was draw an imaginary line between the outskirts of the town and the church steeple and make that their operations map.

Although the improvised attack at Courcelette was not so difficult or important as the dogged set-piece actions in Flanders, it represented the Canadians' most satisfying single engagement of the campaign to date. Gough, the army commander, acknowledged its special significance in a special message to the Fifth Brigade. In launching a major attack from the open "without any jumping-off place in the nature of trenches" the Canadians had done "something without parallel in the present campaign."

As for the tanks, they did not emerge as the heroes they might have been. Their supporters were disappointed; so, however, were their detractors. Their percentage of failure was much higher than their percentage of success, but they did have their successes. Of the sixty tanks in France, Haig got forty-two on the way to the Fourth Army front on the night before the attack, a strange night of moonlight and mist with five cavalry divisions wheeling into position in the cratered fields of the reserve areas and further ahead their outlandish successors-to-be crawling noisily toward their uncertain meeting place with history. Several tanks broke down. Others plunged through the roofs of abandoned dugouts and could not be hauled out. The number available for duty had shrunk to thirty-six by zero hour—thirty of these under the command of the Fourth Army and six attached to the Canadian Corps. And of this three dozen only one in three actually got far enough forward to help in the capture of a trench or a strong point. Four of the six tanks attached to the Canadians were knocked out by shells or mechanical failure, but the other two helped silence enemy machine guns outside Courcelette.

From this and other observations, Byng, the corps commander, concluded: "Without doubt the tanks are a moral support to infantry as long as they are in action, and a good deal of the shrapnel is diverted from the infantry on to them. . . . No action of the infantry should ever be made subservient to that of the tanks. They are a useful accessory to the infantry but nothing more."

Rawlinson, whose Fourth Army had been stopped far short of

its objectives, took an even more cautious view; until the tank proved itself more reliable no departure from "normal tactical methods" ought to be considered to bring it into battle. The Chief of the General Staff issued a general order that tanks were to be regarded as "entirely accessory" to the ordinary method of attack. They must not be allowed to interfere with the traditional interplay of artillery and infantry, either by depriving the infantry of its protective barrage or by bringing down an enemy barrage.

The Germans were even less impressed. At the level of the platoon and the company the new machines looked fearsome enough; one enemy private, flushed from his trench by one of the two effective tanks on the Canadian sector, complained in English that this was "not war but bloody butchery." But at the higher levels the German verdict was that the British had created nothing more formidable than something new to shoot at and absurdly easy to hit.

Haig's never very robust dream of striking a decisive blow before the end of the year still had its dying flickers. He himself was almost ready to break off the offensive, but Joffre and Foch, locked in the equally critical battle at Verdun, urged him to keep the pressure on.

The next two months brought gains of from a few yards to a mile or so on various sectors of the front and cleared the Germans finally from the highest ground. But the chief effect of this was to put the Allied winter positions on the reverse slope, where they were more vulnerable to artillery than they would have been a little further back. The Canadian Corps's main goals in this phase were a row of trenches just beyond Courcelette which they had wistfully named Kenora Trench, Regina Trench, and Desire Trench. They won the trench called Desire on November 18, the day on which Haig at last felt obliged to halt the whole Somme attack.

For some time the British commander's senior subordinates had been pressing the need of a long breathing spell on him. The fifty-five British and Dominion divisions in the West had suffered so heavily that they were more than 100,000 short of their full infantry strength. Haig was never a pessimist, but the best words he could find for the position on the Somme at the onset of the war's third winter were these: "The ground, sodden with rain and broken up everywhere by innumerable shell-holes, can only be described as a morass, almost bottomless in places: between the lines and for many thousands of yards behind them it is almost—and, in some localities, quite—impassable. The supply of food and ammunition is carried out with the greatest difficulty and immense labour, and the men are so much worn out by this and by the maintenance and construction of trenches that frequent reliefs—carried out under exhausting conditions—are unavoidable."

Yet weakened, weary, and despondent as the Allied armies were, the Central Powers were scarcely less so. They had been checked at Verdun and finally forced to abandon their attack there. After killing, wounding, and capturing 57,000 British soldiers on the first day of the Somme, they had found the terrible mathematics of the casualty lists slowly drawing even and then turning the other way. At the end of the year, the Germans' total casualties on the Somme stood at around 680,000, the Allies' at 630,000. Of these the Canadians, who had three divisions in major operations for most of eleven weeks and a fourth in minor operations for a few days, incurred 26,574. By the end of the year Canada had counted nearly 20,000 dead and 48,000 wounded or missing. In the hopeful days of August 1914 it had been estimated that barely a third that many would get overseas before the war was over.

John Masefield wrote this epitaph of the Somme: "Almost in every part of this old front our men had to go uphill to attack. The enemy had the lookout posts, with the fine views over France, and the sense of domination. Our men were down below, with no view of anything but of stronghold after stronghold, just up above, being made stronger daily." He predicted: "When the trenches are filled in and the plough has gone over them the ground will not keep the look of war. One summer with its flowers will cover most of the ruin that man can make, and then these places, from which the driving-back of the enemy began, will be hard indeed to trace, even with maps. Centre Way, Kiel Trench, Munster Alley and these other paths to glory will be deep under the corn, and gleaners will sing at Dead Mule Corner."

The British historian Liddell Hart found an explanation for the general failure of command: "In any profession where life careers are concerned it is human nature to follow the cue given from above. But a wider cause would seem to have been genuine self-delusion. In some cases this may have been induced by the confused idea of loyalty—'blind loyalty'—that the nineteenth-century military system had fostered; even here, the Fourth Army instructions, which omitted so many tactical points of vital importance, took pains to lay down with heavy emphasis that 'all criticism by subordinates of orders received from superior authority will in the end recoil on the heads of the critics.'"

One British general blamed the errors of command at all levels and in all armies on the scarcity of amateurs. Applauding the appointment to a high position of one such amateur, Haig's Chief of Intelligence, General Charteris, reflected: "He has one very strong asset—a very big job in civil life to go back to whenever he may wish. It is difficult for any regular professional soldier not to be influenced by consideration of his own future prospects."

XV

Quebec has its second thoughts about the war—
Ontario has its second thoughts about
Quebec—The fight over the schools
and the Mlles. Desloges

BARELY a week after the redoubtable Royal 22d Regiment had led the way into Courcelette at the cost of a third of its fighting strength, Sir Wilfrid Laurier rose to speak to a recruiting rally of 15,000 in the Montreal suburb of Maisonneuve. He was seventy-four years old now and it was less than a year since he had collapsed halfway through his address at a similar rally in Ontario.

But now he spoke out strongly and clearly. If the special anguish with which he had been living since 1914 might have been detected behind the words he chose, there was no sign of it in his voice.

"There are people who say we will not fight for England; will you then fight for France? I speak to you of French origin. If I were young like you and had the same health that I enjoy today, I would join those brave Canadians fighting today for the liberation of French territory. I would not have it said that the French Canadians do less for the liberation of France than the citizens of British origin. For my part I want to fight for England and also for France. To those who do not want to fight either for England or for France I say: *Will you fight for yourselves?*"

It was not among the old statesman's most eloquent speeches and certainly it was not among the most effective. At the most it could be said that his compatriots would still come to hear him and that they were still willing to hear him out. But it was too late for them to heed him, just as it was far, far too late—at least a hundred years too late, in his proud and lonely view—for him to say the things they would have heeded. They would have listened to a direct appeal to blood and race and the prejudice and animosities built into their past; this he would not utter.

The simple and tragic fact—as events were to prove, a fact of far greater tragedy to the country than to him—was that in this late summer of 1916 Sir Wilfrid Laurier was on the way to becoming a man without a country. For a short but crucial time he found himself a foreigner in the land of his ancestors. The most perfectly bilingual of Canadians, bilingual not merely in the dictionary sense but in heart and conduct and spirit, suddenly discovered that neither of Canada's great races really spoke his language at all. "I have lived too long!" he was soon to cry in protest while the gap that he and perhaps he alone could have closed grew deep and ugly.

Two years earlier, for a few incredible and quite misleading weeks, it had seemed possible that the gap was on the verge of being closed forever. During the late summer and early fall of 1914, French Canada and English Canada had given the appearance of being almost perfectly united. Except in the oratorical sense, no one in Canada knew the meaning of war, least of all a war whose scale and methods were without precedent. The war words, "pain" and "blood" and "sacrifice," had a ring of nobility and excitement but they did not yet carry the bitter echo of real experience or comprehension. When the government called for 25,000 men, the number had a robust sound, in which the whole country took pride. When 32,000 answered, the whole country was reassured, and it was doubly reassured when Sam Hughes said he had no thought, now or ever, of allowing any but volunteers to wear their country's uniform. Every Canadian automatically partook of the grandeur of so swift a reply to the call to arms; everyone who so wished could partake by proxy, enjoying the general surge of exaltation without the risk of personal inconvenience or suffering. As had been the habit of nearly all nations on the eve of nearly all wars since time began, Canada judged that those fated to die in her service would do so antiseptically, in small groups, and with their own approval and consent.

At first there seemed to be not a single person of influence in either French or English Canada who doubted the war's necessity and justness. The quarrels over the naval issue, with its charges and countercharges of disloyalty and of jingoism, were almost forgotten. A number of French-language newspapers began printing the Union Jack and Tricolor side by side on their mastheads.

One of them, *La Patrie*, carried the headline: *Vive la France et l'Angleterre et Dieu Sauve le Roi.*

Speaking in the debate on the Speech from the Throne at the special session of Parliament in August 1914, Laurier undoubtedly spoke for French Canada when he said: "It is our duty, more pressing upon us than all other duties, at once, on this first day of this extraordinary session of the Canadian parliament, to let Great Britain know, and to let the friends and foes of Great Britain know, that there is in Canada but one mind and one heart, and that all Canadians stand behind the mother country, conscious and proud that she is engaged in this war, not from any selfish motive, for any purpose of aggrandizement, but to maintain untarnished the honor of her name, to fulfill her obligations to her allies, to maintain her treaty obligations, and to save civilization from the unbridled lust of conquest and war.

"We are British subjects, and today we are face to face with the consequences which are involved in that proud fact. Long we have enjoyed the benefit of our British citizenship; today it is our duty to accept its responsibilities and its sacrifices. We have long said that when Great Britain is at war we are at war; today we realize that Great Britain is at war and that Canada is at war also."

Dissent from this declaration could be expected from Laurier's former follower and present enemy, the nationalist fire-eater Henri Bourassa. Bourassa was in France when war broke out, but he hurried home to write in *Le Devoir*, probably as much to his own astonishment as to everyone else's, that Canada had a "national duty to contribute, according to her resources and by fitting means of action, to the triumph and especially to the endurance of the combined efforts of France and England." And he went on: "I have not written and will not write one line, one word, to condemn the sending of Canadian troops to Europe." At the same time scarcely anyone noticed the rider he added: "But to render this contribution effective, Canada must begin by facing her real position resolutely, by taking an exact account of what can and what cannot be done, and ensure her own domestic security, before beginning or following up an effort which she will perhaps not be able to sustain to the end."

The attitude of the Roman Catholic hierarchy, to be modified considerably and even more considerably misrepresented in the heated years ahead, had at least some features that might have been designed in any good club on Pall Mall or St. James's Street. The Archbishop of Montreal, Monseigneur Bruchési, declared at once that both religion and patriotism required Catholics to give Britain their support. "If troops have to be sent to the other side, our brave young men will not hesitate to face the ordeal," he said. And a few weeks later, in mid-September, he spelled it out still more carefully: "England is engaged in a terrible war, which she sought to avoid at all costs. Loyal subjects, recognizing in her the protectress of our liberties, we owe her our most generous co-operation. Indifference at the present hour would be on our part a fault, and also the gravest error. Is it not evident that our fate is bound to the fate of her armies?"

Cardinal Bégin, the senior prelate in Canada, was attending the election of a new Pope in Rome. The daily *L'Action Sociale*, which everyone knew to speak for him even though it had not been acknowledged as an official organ, asserted: "We have the duty to grant to the mother country, in just and equitable proportions, the co-operation of which she has need from us." As to the measure of that co-operation, the paper insisted England was the final judge, "since from her derives the authority necessary to accomplish this great task, along with the burden of defending the Empire."

In a joint pastoral letter at the end of September 1914, the Canadian bishops said: "England counts on our help with perfect right and this help we are happy to say has been generously offered in men and in money." In the light of such pronouncements it was not surprising that *La Patrie* could conclude: "There are no longer French Canadians and English Canadians. Only one race now exists, united by the closest bonds in a common cause."

This ardent mood could scarcely have continued indefinitely. And things to dampen it soon appeared. Within a week or two Henri Bourassa had begun recoiling publicly from his first endorsement of the war. Just as swiftly he was assailed by shouts of contumely and rage from nine provinces, not the least violent of them from his own. And as was his habit and his genius, the more hotly his detractors railed, the more coldly and tellingly he railed back.

Thus Bourassa wrote gently in *Le Devoir* that the English were to be admired for adhering always to self-interest and Canada could not better demonstrate her loyalty to British traditions than by doing the same; that is, by taking care "to unite freely the interests of Canada to those of England when their interests are identical, to oppose Canada's interests to those of England when they are contrary, and to separate them when they are divergent."

And thus *La Patrie* urged that Bourassa be tried for high treason. Thus Bourassa icily invited his readers to compare "the liberty enjoyed and practiced in England even in time of war and under the ban of censors."

Thus Laurier tried to stir Quebec and shame Bourassa with the name of their people's greatest military hero: "If there are still a few drops of the blood of Dollard and his companions in the veins of Canadians who are present at this meeting, you will enlist in a body, for this cause is just as sacred as the one for which Dollard and his companions gave their lives."

Thus, at a public meeting in Ottawa, an army sergeant lurched to the speakers' platform with a Union Jack and ordered Bourassa to hold it aloft. Thus Bourassa put the flag quietly aside and said: "I am ready to wave the British flag in liberty, but I shall not do so under threats." Thus the meeting ended in a riot.

Bourassa was not the only influence in Quebec against the "English war." Some of the factors had very little to do with either the English or the war. In some cases it was a lack of tact, a small failure of good will and common sense rather than a large conflict of principle, that began to reverse the flow of sentiment. The most famous example did not materialize until somewhat later, but it reflected Sam Hughes's main approach to Quebec: his chief recruiting officer in that province was a Baptist clergyman.

Then too, Hughes's officers, with good military but bad political reasoning, refused to allow instruction in French. In the first surge of enlistments it soon became apparent that more men were coming forward than were needed and the recruiting officers sometimes gave a cool reception to men who spoke bad English. Under Hughes's crash program for raising the first contingents, the existing militia units—most of which were really not much more than social clubs—were used as gathering points for recruits, but their historic regimental names and with it their cohesiveness and identity disappeared. For the English-speaking units this was not serious. Provided it retained its officers and NCOs, a unit like the 48th Highlanders of Canada could change its name to the 15th Battalion and still remain a community. And former members who were posted to other battalions in the impersonal reshuffling were not, at least, among total strangers.

But recruits whose mother tongue was French found things more difficult. For them to be parted from their friends was a special hardship. It was not lessened by the fact that in the entire first overseas contingent only one of the company commanders of infantry was a French Canadian. The feeling that officers of their race were not appreciated or trusted received further impetus among French Canadians when Major General F.-L. Lessard, the senior Canadian officer, was sidetracked into an administrative job; many of his friends had expected he would be made commander of the first contingent. After much agitation the government at last authorized the formation of the Royal 22d as a distinctively French-Canadian battalion, but before this was done Laurier himself had had to make a special, private plea to Borden.

And so Ottawa's task of keeping the nation united was already made nearly impossible by two main factors—the growing reluctance of the Quebec nationalists to invest in the quarrels of a world they never made; the clumsiness and want of diplomacy of the English-speaking majority and of the government.

But it is a mistake to believe, as it is now commonly believed, that only French Canada had reservations about the degree to which Canada was obliged to participate in the First World War. The country's selective memory has left the impression with later generations that eight of the nine provinces came to the unanimous agreement that the war must be fought at any cost and that the ninth was unanimous in believing the whole enterprise to be foolish, extravagant, self-defeating, and perhaps even wicked. This assessment is grotesquely oversimplified. There were differences of opinion in Quebec and those differences had many shades. What is less well remembered is that there were similar differences in English Canada. Although there was a patriotic rush to join the colors in August of 1914, people born in Canada were not in the forefront. Even though they had been educated in the tradition of Drake and Kipling, of Elizabeth and Victoria, native-born Canadians supplied only 25 per cent of the strength of the first armed contingent sent abroad. Two recruits out of every three were immigrants from the British Isles. One whole battalion, the Princess Patricia's Canadian Light Infantry, was composed of men who had served in the Imperial forces before coming to Canada or in Canada's Boer War forces.

At this time conscription had not been seriously thought of—either in Canada or in England or in any other part of the Commonwealth. But English Canada had its own hard core of opposition to conscription, and when, much later, the issue became a real and urgent one, the English-language labor unions and the English-language farm organizations were to speak as firmly against it—even though not so intemperately—as the most rabid of the Quebec nationalists.

It was not until 1917 that official figures on the first military contingent were prepared and released. It was reported then that only twelve hundred French Canadians were included in the initial force of more than thirty thousand. Yet those who cared to maintain that this was a respectable figure—and there were many who did so maintain—could point out that Quebec was preponderantly a rural civilization and the figures of rural enlistment were low everywhere; that Quebec had large families and a high percentage of married men; moreover, and perhaps most tellingly, that if enlistment figures were to be taken as a yardstick of loyalty, then French Canadians suffered not nearly so much in comparison with English Canadians as English Canadians suffered in comparison with Canadians who had been born in the United Kingdom.

To some extent all these ratios of enlistment were the result of natural and historic impulses. The spread in them was greatly magnified by an irritant that had nothing to do with military matters.

The fathers of Confederation had wisely and unavoidably put the public schools under the jurisdiction of the provinces. But they had not been able to keep them out of federal politics. As the Dominion grew and acquired more provincial and local governments, the schools became a political, religious, economic, and racial issue of growing size. Manitoba, Saskatchewan, Alberta, and the Northwest Territories all had their variations of the main problem. Laurier felt his way through it as best he could. At first he supported the idea of completely denominational schools. Then he changed his mind. In the schools still under federal control he favored a compromise under which a Protestant or Catholic school board could order half an hour's religious teaching at the end of the day, but a child of the minority faith would not be obliged to stay and take part.

This middle-of-the-road stand put him under attack from both sides. Many clergymen of his own church were convinced he was offering the Catholics less than their due. The Orange Lodges, the Methodists, and other Protestants were equally certain he was offering the Catholics more than their due. At various times they described his position as insidious, iniquitous, oppressive, hideous, monstrous, and mad.

But Laurier had most of the country with him in his stubborn defense of tolerance. In 1913, however, a new factor entered the ancient dispute: the Ontario Department of Education's Regulation Seventeen.

Moving up the valleys of the Ottawa and St. Lawrence rivers, forming more distant pockets of settlement as far from home as the Niagara Peninsula, French Canadians had reached a population in Ontario of nearly a quarter of a million. They numbered almost one in ten by 1914. In scores of village and country schools their language was the only language taught or spoken.

The Ontario government decreed that both the teaching of English and teaching in English must be restored. Regulation Seventeen ordered that a child who arrived at school understanding only French might be taught in French until he had finished the first form. After that English must be his language of instruction. It was up to his parents and his teachers to see that, by then, his weaning to bilingualism was complete.

Some of the difficulties this raised were serious and practical. Many French-speaking parents of Ontario, like parents of all times and all places, had had sufficient trouble helping their children through the mysteries they could deal with in their own tongue. *Quatre-vingt-neuf plus quatre-vingt-neuf* was tough enough. But eighty-nine plus eighty-nine! What was this monster called eighty-nine that *les Anglais* had loosed on the habitant of the Ottawa Valley and his defenseless children?

Both the Conservatives and the Liberals were content to leave the issue in the realm of provincial affairs, where it belonged under the British North America Act. But Bourassa and the Quebec nationalists were not. Before the war's first Christmas, Bourassa's followers, bitterly plagiarizing from the appeals for aid to Belgium, were organizing mass meetings to support "the wounded of

Ontario." In one of his best-remembered bursts of polemic Bourassa wrote: "In the name of religion, liberty and faithfulness to the British flag French Canadians are enjoined to go and fight the Prussians of Europe. Shall we let the Prussians of Ontario impose their domination like masters in the very heart of the Canadian confederation, under the shelter of the British flag and British institutions?"

Bourassa did not always have the full support of the clergy or his province's other politicians. But now Cardinal Bégin, the senior prelate, made this declaration: "If the trial imposed on our brothers of Ontario must be prolonged, as please God it may not, it will be the noble duty of the French province of Quebec to support with its influence and all its strength those who fight until full justice be rendered them." Sir Lomer Gouin, the premier of Quebec, pleaded: "In the name of the justice and generosity of which England has given so many proofs and which cannot fail to animate every British citizen, as well as in the name of the struggles which our fathers waged to open to civilization the rich domains which are our common heritage, I ask that justice be done to the French minority of Ontario and even, if need be, that generosity be shown to them. In the name of the sublime expressions which it has given to human thought I ask for the French tongue the right to be heard on the lips of the schoolchildren of Ontario."

Philippe Landry, speaker of the Ottawa Senate, prepared to lead a fight in the courts against Regulation Seventeen and before it was ended he carried it to the Privy Council in England. He summed up the French position in twenty words: "We wish to have it settled whether Confederation has been for us a pact of honor or an infamous trap."

Landry quit his speakership of the Senate so he could feel free to go into the courts as a private lawyer.

The House of Commons knew perfectly well that it had no business in this provincial affair. But the urge to get into it anyway was irresistible. In May one of Laurier's most promising young bilingual supporters, Ernest Lapointe, introduced a motion asking Parliament to "respectfully suggest" to the Ontario provincial legislature "the wisdom of making it clear that the privilege of the children of French parentage of being taught in their mother tongue be not interfered with." When, amid loud protests, the motion was ruled in order, Laurier—even though he knew he was speaking against the wind—made a statement that summed up his country's dichotomy as well as any ever made:

"I know there is in the province of Ontario a sense of irritation at the position taken by some of my fellow countrymen of French blood in the province of Quebec, who have from the first deprecated the participation of Canada in the present war, and who have exerted their influence to attempt at least to prevent enlistment. Alas, it is true; too true. It is deplorable, and to me, as unintelligible as it is deplorable. It is true, alas, that there are in my province men of French origin who, when France is fighting the fight of heroism which stirs the blood of mankind, remain with their blood cold, who tell us: 'No, we will not lift a finger to assist Britain in defending the integrity of France, but we want our wrongs to be righted in Ontario.'

"Wrongs or no wrongs, there is a field of honor; there is a call of duty.

"I am not prepared to say that my fellow countrymen of French origin have no rights in Ontario; but I am prepared to say this. . . . Whether my countrymen have rights or no rights in Ontario, whether those rights are granted or denied, these considerations are no bar to the duty which the French Canadians owe to themselves and to the honor of their race to come forward in their fullest numbers and take part in the great struggle that is going on today in the land of their ancestors. . . .

"Under the present circumstances . . . only one language shall be taught in the schools of Ontario. I wonder if this new theory for bringing about unity of the Empire is to be applied in Wales . . . and in the Highlands of Scotland, or in Egypt, or in South Africa. Sir, if there is one thing which today stands to the glory of England —a feat unparalleled in the history of the world—it is that today on the battlefield in Flanders there are men who do not speak a word of English but who for England have come forward to fight and die. If the Britisher, when he went to India, to Malta, to South Africa, had implanted that new doctrine of 'one language and one language only' and had suppressed the language of the peoples who had just passed under his domination, do you believe, Sir, you would have seen that great and noble spectacle which has astonished and is still astonishing the world?

". . . I want every child in the province of Ontario to receive the benefit of an English education. Wherever he may go on this continent I want him to be able to speak the language of the great majority of the people on this continent. I want it, I say, not only because it is the law of the province but because of merely utilitarian considerations. No man on this continent is equipped for the battle of life unless he has an English education. . . . When I ask that every child of my own race should receive an English education, will you refuse us the privilege of education also in the language of our mothers and our fathers? That is all that I will ask today; I ask nothing more than that. . . . Is that an unnatural demand? Is that an obnoxious demand? Will the concession of it do harm to anybody? And will it be said that in the great province of Ontario there is a disposition to put a bar on knowledge and to stretch every child in the schools of Ontario upon a Procrustean bed and say that they shall all be measured alike, that no one shall have the privilege of a second education in a single language? I do not believe it. . . . I do not believe that any man will refuse us the benefit of a French education."

Laurier knew that for all its breadth of spirit, this speech was a speech, not a workable basis for action. When an editor told him he should have made it in a more appropriate place he replied unhappily: "What is the use of my going to Toronto or anywhere else in Ontario if I am to speak to deaf ears, ears voluntarily deaf? What is the use of trying to convince those whom I would address, if there is no possibility of changing their minds?" He could not, indeed, change the minds even of some members of his own party. He supported the Lapointe resolution, but when it went to a vote nearly a dozen western Liberals voted against it.

On the day when he had stood before the Commons to make his great plea for tolerance and understanding, Laurier, now halfway through his seventies, had seemed miraculously and shiningly young again. One newspaper report said: "His years dropped from him like a garment, and he seemed as vigorous and resolute as a man of thirty-five." But though the defeat of the resolution itself could not possibly have surprised a man of so much political experience, the break within his own party hit Laurier very hard. "I have lived too long!" he said when an emissary came to tell him that the Ontario Liberals too were on the verge of deserting him. He turned aside from the man who brought him the message and walked to the window of his office and looked out for a few moments in puzzlement and dismay on what was visible to him of his country. "I have lived too long," he repeated in bitter anguish. And then he added: "I have outlived Liberalism. The forces of prejudice in Ontario have been too much for my friends. It was a mistake for a French Roman Catholic to take the leadership." Laurier thereupon wrote out a note of resignation as leader of the party. The Ontario dissidents quickly came back into line and persuaded him to remain.

The fight was far from over. In the school question there were wheels within wheels. The sharpest dispute was not between Protestants and Catholics at all. In Ottawa and the Ottawa Valley a more bitter one erupted between French Catholics and Irish Catholics.

In shanty towns and logging camps and aboard their lumber barges, the Valley's French and Irish had discovered more than half a century before that they had very little in common but their view of God. And so some of the strongest opposition to the teaching of French in Ontario came from Irish Catholics.

Many of them feared their rights as a religious group might be harmed if they became identified with the—to them—more doubtful and less important rights of a racial and language group.

Bishop Fallon, of London, Ontario, was one of the main spokesmen of the anti-French faction in the Church. Bourassa classed him and his supporters with "Orange intriguers and English-Canadian Anglicizers." Equally dangerous enemies of French civilization in Canada, he insisted, were French Canadians weakened by the conquest and their centuries of colonial servitude. And "as to the prelates and priests who unite themselves to the worst enemies of the Church to snatch from the French Canadians the free enjoyment of their natural rights, they fail in their double duty of Catholic pastors and British subjects."

Much simpler, one-dimensional figures swirled around the periphery of the debate and added to its aggravations. An Ontario M.P. bawled at an Orange rally attended by Sam Hughes: "Never shall we let the French Canadians implant in Ontario the disgusting speech that they use." A Quebec senator bawled back at him: "Brutal maniac and ignoramus!"

But the struggle had more appealing participants. Especially the Desloges sisters of Ottawa.

Beatrice and Diane Desloges were the earnest teen-aged daughters of an earnest Ottawa French-Canadian family in which Papineau and Bourassa had long been heroes of only slightly lesser rank than Cartier, Laval, and Dollard.

The sisters were teachers at the Ecole Guigues in Ottawa. They were, of course, opposed to Regulation Seventeen, with what amounted to its delayed ban against their language.

In the first rounds of the fight a new Catholic Separate School Commission had been appointed in Ottawa. Two of its three members were of Irish descent. They had no inclination to defend the French language if at the same time they might jeopardize the Catholic religion. So when the Desloges sisters refused to help in the gradual liquidation of French as the language of instruction in their school, the commission fired them.

The sisters refused to be fired. They went back to their school and dug in as for a siege. The school commission took out an injunction ordering them out by law. The teachers led their pupils to a nearby Catholic chapel and school was held there while the young Mlles. Desloges found themselves compared again and again with those other teen-aged heroines, Jeanne d'Arc and Madeleine de Verchères.

The commission appointed two other teachers—both French-speaking also—to reopen the school from which Beatrice and Diane and their pupils had decamped. When the new ladies arrived to take over they had to run a gantlet of waving fists and hatpins. The police helped them reach their classrooms in safety, but it was only to find them empty.

The Desloges affair was followed by others much like it. French-speaking teachers in Ontario, and especially in Ottawa, went on strike by the score. Catholic separate schools closed all over the province and stayed closed for months rather than obey Regulation Seventeen.

At last, in October 1916, the Pope himself intervened. In a letter to Cardinal Bégin and the other senior prelates of Canada, Benedict XV ordered both his French-Canadian and Irish-Canadian followers to stop "this storm of rivalry and enmity." "Let the Catholics of the Dominion remember," he commanded, "that the one thing is to have Catholic schools and not to imperil their existence."

"Equitable teaching of French for French-Canadian children" was a matter of great importance, the Pope said, but it could not "be dealt with independently of the government." The Canadian bishops "in their earnest care for the salvation of souls" were not prevented from exercising "their utmost activity to make counsels of moderation prevail."

Thus those who wished to make a Holy War of Regulation Seventeen suffered one crushing defeat. Very soon another came. Senator Landry had carried the regulation through the Canadian courts to the highest court of all, the Privy Council in London. The Privy Council ruled it was within the law. These two decrees from the highest ecclesiastical and civil authorities brought a surrender of the strikers. The schools reopened. But the real cause of their closing was still far from settled. The ancient brew of religion and race was still fermenting. It had its dregs saved up. It had its new froth waiting.

Each day brought its changes in the main chemical process. Here is Sam Hughes leading with his prowlike chin once more as he tries to silence the hotheaded nationalist Armand Lavergne by offering to make him commander of a battalion if Lavergne will raise the battalion. Here is Lavergne storming back, and getting a far better press than Hughes in Quebec at least: "I consider it unwise and even criminal to put Canada in danger for a war over which we have not had and will not have any control. . . . It is not for us to defend England but for England to defend us. . . . My compatriots of French origin in Ontario, Canadians like you, sir, are now undergoing a regime worse than that imposed by the Prussians in Alsace-Lorraine, because they do not wish to abandon their mother tongue. Until they have been completely freed of this persecution, I cannot consider for an instant the idea of deserting their cause for a somewhat interesting adventure in a foreign country."

Here, inevitably, is Bourassa contesting for the mantle of Louis-Joseph Papineau with another of the great revolutionary's heirs. In one of the many inconsistencies that make up Canadian history, Talbot Papineau—like Henri Bourassa, a descendant of Louis-Joseph —had gone to the English war as a volunteer. Moreover, he had gone with the most English of all battalions, the Princess Patricia's, nearly all of whose men were born in England. So here is Talbot writing Cousin Henri from the front: "Can a nation's pride or patriotism be built upon the blood and suffering of others or upon the wealth garnered from the coffers of those who in anguish and blood-sweat are fighting the battles of freedom?" And here is Papineau publicly warning that if his cousin Henri has his way "whoever bears a French name in Canada will be an object of suspicion and possibly of hatred." Here is the impervious Bourassa storming back that Papineau was not a Roman Catholic, not a true French Canadian, since he had been educated in England, and that he had no right to speak for French Canadians; moreover, it made no sense for anyone to speak "of fighting for the preservation of French civilization in Europe while endeavoring to destroy it in America." His cousin, he was told politely, was playing into the hands of profiteers and jingoes.

Here is another master of abuse lashing at Bourassa from the bosom of the Church—Abbé J.-A. D'Amours proclaiming in the semi-official *Action Catholique:* "Your manners have misled a certain number of spirits, rather young, who have adopted your choleric and invective mania without having your facile talent for sophistry and popular oratory. It is not astonishing that you should be instinctively with the Germans. You have for a long time been a partisan of Kantian subjectivism and of the egotisms of the Nietzschean superman. . . . What would be today the condition of the poor French Canadians in Canada, in the British Empire and in the civilized world, if they had followed your directions, if in place of marching with the compatriots they had stood apart to attack craftily the present and past conduct of England, to enfeeble and depreciate the British effort against Germany and its barbarous and devasting tyranny?" Here is Bourassa confirming the streak of Anglophobia which was a part of his complex philosophy: "To his hereditary pride, which marks his cousinship with the northern German, have come to be added the obtuseness developed by insular isolation and alcoholism, and above all infatuation with his immense wealth and pride of domination over weak peoples. As a result, in spite of his remarkable faculties for government, and the general humanity of his proceedings—when cupidity and the desire of domination didn't push him to brutalities—the Anglo-Saxon does not know how to gain the confidence, much less the affection, of the peoples that he dominates."

And here is the mixed and unpredictable attitude of one of Bourassa's most brilliant followers, the other perpetually furious journalist, Olivar Asselin. Asselin assaults the ecclesiastical supporters of the war and partieularly the editor of *L'Action Catholique,* whom he calls "one of those little Jesuitical and Italian *abbés* such as there were four centuries ago and such as there are, alas, hardly any more

left, who wield with equal cleverness the canons of the Church
and the pen, and for whom no task is ever too hard, too wicked, or
too vile." And here is Asselin enlisting in the war he hates and explaining to his followers and friends: "I sometimes think that the
greatest need of our race is still to learn to despise life, when necessary; not to attach itself too much to well-being, to purely material
comfort; to be hard on itself and to be prodigal, on occasion, of
blood." And here are Asselin and the French-Canadian volunteers
who followed him to the colors being sent anticlimactically for garrison duty in Bermuda. Here is the colonel of another French-
Canadian unit on the verge of being dispersed for garrison duty urging the men in his command to desert.

XVI

The battle of Vimy Ridge

ON the northern plain of France, standing above slag heaps and beneath an overcast of smoke from the coal towns of Lille and Lens, two high columns of stone leap up from the summit of a long hill. Nearly any spring or summer day within the last forty years it has been possible to see a tourist or two, or perhaps ten or twenty or a hundred, walking carefully up the long, not very steep hill, up the steps to the shafts of stone, stopping to take a photograph or two, and then going back down the hill. Often there will be a graying and mildly complaining woman in tow. A boy or a girl might be there as well, grandchildren now most likely, children in the earlier years.

The place these people have come to is the ridge of Vimy. Though there are other places a good deal like Vimy Ridge on the industrial plains of northern Europe, there is none the same in the heart and history of Canada. Here in April 1917 the Canadian Corps fought and won a great battle. Here their country learned to its great pride and faint dismay that it had become an important factor in the destiny of nations.

The Vimy Ridge in 1917 stood at the heart of an escarpment, seven miles long, on which the Germans had anchored their whole position in northern Europe. Like Ypres and Verdun, Vimy was already a celebrated place name. The Germans had dug in there in 1914. The French had tried to dislodge them in 1915. Now, in April of 1917, the ridge had both a military and a spiritual meaning. It was part of a complex of forts, redoubts, dormitories, parlors, and passageways which in contrast to the muddy wallows of Ypres and the Somme seemed almost luxurious. On the high dry ground of the escarpment and the slopes leading up to it, the Germans had had two full years in which to build and improve their permanent trenches. Here the Hollywood version of a Prussian battalion commander with his monocle, his bird, and his bottle was not only possible but occasionally true.

Behind the front the Allied positions, centered on the old walled city of Arras, were a maze of caves and tunnels, many of them centuries old and left over from earlier wars. By careful attention and reworking, this honeycomb had achieved some of the utility of a good hard-rock mine. There were miles of wire for telephones and lights. There was a tramline and an underground hospital. Twenty-five thousand men could be housed safely in the hidden depths. When needed they could be moved through the tunnels and catacombs to the front line without the usual hazards of shelling on open roads, duckboards, or communications trenches.

But the attack from Arras had far more to recommend it than these local advantages. In a sense that could not be measured by the men waiting to rush up the hill of Vimy, the year in which they lived—and in which many of them died—was already in a state of crisis and convulsion unequaled by any other single year in man's whole stay on earth.

In the fifteen tumultuous months from September 1916 to November 1917 the Germans fired their high commander. The French fired their high commander. The British threw out their government. The beaten and bedraggled battalions of Russia turned their backs on their foes and began to fight their masters. The German high command, now resigned to the implacable fact that it could not win the war on the ground, forced the German government to accept a program of unrestricted war by submarine. The United States of America entered the war officially.

Some of these things had not happened by the early spring of 1917 and of those that had happened not all were known to the Allied soldiers who attacked east of Arras on April 9. At the tactical level the reason for attacking was plain enough. On the Western Front the line wavered as it curled past Arras. The Germans held a blunt salient toward the south of the city.

The Allied decision to attack there, like so many command decisions in the war of 1914–18, was mainly decreed by the lack of anything better to do. Decisions of equal moment were once assessed in this way by Haig's chief intelligence officer: "Allenby shares one peculiarity with Douglas Haig: he cannot explain verbally, with any lucidity at all, what his plans are. In a conference between the two of them it is rather amusing. DH hardly ever finishes a sentence, and Allenby's sentences, although finished, do not really convey exactly what he means. They understand one another perfectly, but as each of their particular staffs only understands their immediate superior a good deal of explanation of detail has to be gone into afterwards. . . . At these army conferences no one dares to interfere."

The night of April 8, 1917, was Easter Sunday. The strength of the Canadian Corps, including attached British troops, stood at 170,000. Fifteen thousand of its assault infantrymen moved into position through the tunnels from Arras.

Already little gaps had been cut in the barbed wire by special patrols, and larger holes had been made by an almost unlimited artillery bombardment of two weeks.

By four o'clock on the freezing morning of Easter Monday every battalion was in place, most of them no more than a hundred yards from the enemy. It rained on them through most of the night and then in the cold black of early morning the rain changed to sleet and snow. But by the start hour, every man in the assault force had been given a hot meal and a tot of rum to fortify him against the historic day ahead.

Up to that time no battle had been more carefully planned or mounted. Before they made their strange journey through the weird chalk tunnels from Arras, most of the assaulting infantry had gone through elaborate practice maneuvers. They had used white tapes to help them learn their routes of travel and their officers had pored for weeks over plasticine models of the ground ahead. And above them all the shape of the coming battle was being discerned and drawn by the pilots of the Royal Flying Corps, many of them Canadians too. As the R.F.C. pried behind the German lines, interceptors rose to meet them and one of the first and greatest of dogfights swirled above the waiting soldiers below.

In the last minutes of the cold night before the attack, the artillery finished its work. Besides the usual curtain of high explosives on the forward positions, a heavy barrage of gas shells was thrown into the German rear. The greatest and most decisive casualties of the gas were not men but horses. They died in hundreds, and when the infantry attack began, the German communications system was in chaos. The troops at the front ran short of ammunition. The artillery had no means of locomotion. The main Allied rush across the sleet-drenched hillside therefore was given a chance to succeed.

On some parts of the ridge the very depth and safety of the German trenches now betrayed their defenders. When the Allied artillery fire stopped it took as long for the German garrisons to clamber up to the surface as for the attacking troops to pour across the tiny strip of No Man's Land. In the first rush nearly 3500 Germans surrendered. In one of the many impregnable tunnels 150 German soldiers came up dazed and half dressed, with their hands aloft.

In any recital of military events there is a strong temptation to depend only on the memories of the victors. At Vimy Ridge an account by one of the defeated Germans says this: "No sooner had it been decided to abandon the battalion headquarters at the tunnel entrance than the first English appeared two hundred yards away and brought a machine gun into action at the Ruhleben House. Pursued by the fire of this troublesome gun, the battalion commander, his staff, and twenty men went back along the communications trench, knee-deep in mud, towards the second-line position; but most of the staff and all the men were killed or wounded before reaching it."

At a more practical level another German account of Vimy Ridge describes in this way the situation not long after dawn: "Nothing was yet known of the situation of the infantry on the ridge, since all telephone cables leading forward, including one buried six feet deep, had been broken, and patrols sent forward could bring no enlightenment."

The four Canadian divisions in the attack panted up the slope, some throwing grenades, some carrying awkward cylindrical Lewis guns on their hips, the great majority armed with bayonets and rifles and shooting through the rising fog and snow against an enemy they could not see. Not surprisingly, they achieved feats of great courage and folly. One officer, with only two men in support, leaped into one of the enemy trenches and captured two officers and seventy-five other ranks. By early morning of that famous Easter Monday the snow had stopped and those who had burst across the No Man's Land of Vimy and gained its height could look out on the great plain beyond. One of the Germans near by has reported the scene in this way: "The cessation of the snowstorm lifted the veil which had till now hidden the landscape, and we saw a remarkable sight. The air was suddenly clean and clear, filled with spring sunshine. The high ground . . . was covered with English troops standing about in large groups. The officers could easily be distinguished waving their short sticks in the air and hurrying from group to group to give instructions. For a few minutes the artillery fire almost ceased on both sides and complete silence fell upon the battlefield, as if all were lost in wonder. The battle itself seemed to hold its breath."

Though Vimy is rightly counted as one of the great Canadian military successes, it was not a decisive victory. Having been warned of the forthcoming attack by more than two weeks of heavy artillery bombardment, the Germans were already prepared to make an orderly withdrawal if they should lose their forward trenches. One German record says: "Innumerable crowds of working parties labored . . . at the repair and deepening of the defense system. Night and day in unbroken sequence trains from the Homeland laden with material and munitions reached the main depots. Mountains of shell were piled up in the ammunition dumps. The construction of the defenses and the organization of the troops were completed. The enemy could come."

Then too, the Allies were simply running out of sinew. The French had agreed to support the Arras offensive with another major offensive further to the south. But the poilus who had so staunchly given so much to save their country in 1914, 1915, and 1916 were now, through the sheer weight of misery and futility, in a state bordering on mutiny. Their officers, even up to the rank of army commander, were in the same condition. It was not surprising, therefore, that the French part of the attack of April 1917 was an unenthusiastic failure. Assaulting toward and through objectives with the tragic names of the Road of the Women and the Hill of No Name, the French were turned back everywhere. The British were beginning to lose their effectiveness too. Like the French, they had run out of time for training and were starting to run out of men. Many of their junior officers were beardless schoolboys. As for the other ranks, a colonel of no less a regiment than the immortal Black Watch had this to say of one large draft of reinforcements that reached him in the early stages of Arras: "These men, hastily put into kilts, had undergone no infantry training. . . .

Some could not fix bayonets and some could not load their rifles when they arrived."

The usually objective British official history, published after twenty years of careful retrospect, offers a reason why the Canadians did so well in the spring of 1917 while other equally gallant formations did relatively badly. "The capture of Fresnoy was the culminating point of brilliant successes by the Canadian Corps during the Arras battles, and the relieving feature of a day which many who witnessed it consider the blackest of the war. . . . One of the factors in this isolated success was undoubtedly the high standard of the Canadian infantry reinforcements. It has been pointed out that British divisions which began a long-drawn-out battle in a high state of efficiency suffered a very serious falling-off as the ranks of their battalions became filled with inadequately trained drafts. The Canadian drafts had not only as a rule undergone more training but were also rather older men and often of better physique. Thus a Canadian division appeared to deteriorate very little after taking part in several engagements at short intervals of time. The same applied to a great extent to the Australian and New Zealand troops, though the Australians, who maintained in the field more formations than the Canadians, from a smaller though more homogeneous population, were at a disadvantage by comparison with them."

The portents for the Allies, though reasonably good at Vimy, were far less hopeful elsewhere.

When the time came for the supporting French offensive, many of the French simply would not fight. As had happened at Ypres in 1915, thousands of colored colonial draftees were in the van of the battle, but had no idea what they were doing there. When the order reached them to leave their trenches and move into the killing hail of machine-gun fire, most of the Senegalese consulted their instincts and their logic and went the other way.

The morale of the French continental divisions was in a similar state. There had been many upheavals in the high command and before the April offensive the promising but colorless Robert-Georges Nivelle was given the desperate task of picking up after Joffre and Foch.

Nivelle's army was soon in a state of anarchy. Fifty divisions either mutinied outright or threatened mutiny. There were twenty thousand desertions by men who preferred a possible death by court-martial to a certain death by the German guns.

At last Henri Pétain replaced the broken Nivelle. Pétain shot
twenty soldiers after courts-martial. He exiled another hundred and
herded two hundred more into an artillery range and blew them
up. By these harsh measures, together with the memory of his
victory at Verdun, he restored the French Army as a military unit.

XVII

Conscription—Union government and the
fall of Laurier

IN the inner battle of Canada the triumph of Vimy Ridge settled very little. Sam Hughes, though spent in his power, was still very much present. So was Henri Bourassa, and the conflict in which they stood at opposite poles was very much alive. Borden kept trying to introduce a note of calm and Laurier struggled with all his great, defeated genius to help him.

But somewhat because of and somewhat in spite of all their efforts and desires, a new matter had come to engage the country's mind. This was conscription. Conscription had been for two centuries an especially ugly word in Canada. Conscription meant that an honest farm boy from Ontario went to fight for the British redcoats, whom he did not even like. Conscription meant, later on, that the Doukhobors and Mennonites, who had come to Canada as an active protest against conscription, were now, while exempted from military service, fair targets for the scorn and derision of their neighbors. Conscription meant, above everything else, that the young men of French Canada would be torn from their families to die in a struggle they neither approved nor understood.

Conscription was a witch word, all around the world, even among the nations most deeply committed to the war. The Australians and New Zealanders, when their best young men were dying as volunteers, voted against it. Great Britain did not introduce conscription until halfway through the war. The United States adopted conscription but rejected the war.

Borden had never made an absolute promise that he would not introduce compulsory service. In one statement, to be plagiarized nearly thirty years later by another Prime Minister, he had said:

"I hope conscription may not be necessary, but if it should prove the only effective method to preserve the existence of the state and of the institutions and liberties which we enjoy, I should consider it necessary and I should not hesitate to act." Laurier had promised explicitly that he would never support conscription. Bourassa goaded and tormented his fellow isolationists with continual reminders that whether they wanted it or not, whether their leaders intended it or not, conscription was sure to come. And in the trail of the Somme, of Vimy and Flanders, conscription did come, not as a mere subject for oratory, but as an immediate crisis.

For all its brilliant battle record the Canadian Corps was in difficulty. Its Fifth Division was not, in fact, a fighting unit, but a floating reinforcement depot. Even with the help of this subterfuge the other four divisions were having trouble in keeping up their strength. Canada's first—and then it had seemed handsome—commitment of manpower had now been multiplied not by two or three or five but by twenty. The capture of Vimy Ridge, which alone cost more than ten thousand casualties, only magnified a problem that had been building up for many months. Since the start of 1917 battle losses in the Canadian Corps had been outnumbering enlistments by as much as two to one.

Borden knew the rate of enlistment would have to be stepped up if the force was to be maintained. In 1916 he had introduced a system of national registration. His opponents correctly saw this as the forerunner of compulsory service.

In the spring of 1917 the Canadian Prime Minister was invited to a special conference of Imperial leaders in England. One of the chief reasons for the conference had been Borden's own angry complaint to his High Commissioner in London:

"During the past four months . . . the Canadian government (except for an occasional telegram from you to Sir Max Aitken) have had just what information could be gleaned from the daily press and no more. As to consultation, plans of campaign have been made and unmade, measures adopted and apparently abandoned and generally speaking steps of the most important and even vital character have been taken, postponed or rejected without the slightest consultation with the authorities of this Dominion."

At the conference Borden made his first acquaintance with the great South African leader Jan Christiaan Smuts, and won his support for a resolution in which he put Canada's position in this way: "The greatest intellects of the Empire in the past have miscalculated the conditions that would develop in the Dominions and have failed to foresee the relations of the Empire under the policy of developing full powers of self-government, which was supposed to have the tendency of weakening, if not severing, the ties which unite the Dominions to the Mother Country. The policy of complete control in domestic affairs, instead of weakening the ties which unite the Empire, has very greatly strengthened them. . . . The fact that one million men in the Dominions have taken up arms for the defense of the Empire's existence and the maintenance of its future influence is so significant a lesson that one would be unwise not to have it constantly in mind."

Borden scored his point heavily, and fourteen years later, in a historic enactment called the Statute of Westminster, it was to be made official.

Now, on his return to Canada, he felt himself under the stern duty of persuading his country to accept all the penalties of its growth in stature and independence. Conscription, Borden told the House of Commons on his return, could no longer be avoided.

"I myself stated to Parliament that nothing but voluntary enlistment was proposed by the government," he acknowledged. "But I returned to Canada impressed at once with the extreme gravity of the situation, and with a sense of responsibility for our further effort at the most critical period of the war. It is apparent to me that the voluntary system will not yield further substantial results. . . . It is my duty to announce to the House that early proposals will be made to provide, by compulsory military enlistment on a selective basis, such reinforcements as may be necessary to maintain the Canadian Army in the field."

Though he knew his decision would shake the country to its foundations, Borden had not guessed the shape of every tremor. One thing became instantly apparent. The simple triangle of Canadian politics dissolved and dispersed in all directions. Some of Borden's strongest supporters, particularly among the Quebec Nationalists, began deserting him at once. Henri Bourassa did not go so far as to advocate a rebellion, but he predicted one. "Conscription," he cried, "would soon transform the most peaceable, perhaps the most orderly, population of the two Americas into a revolutionary people."

Laurier, once more the man in the middle, could not take so resolutely uncomplicated a stand as either Borden or Bourassa. In the first days of the war he had given his full and ungrudging support to his natural Conservative enemies. He had consented to prolong the life of Parliament by a year. Although he had refused the offer of a coalition, he had no more wish than Borden to turn the war to partisan advantage.

Now he faced a less simple decision. He had supported Canada's entry into the war. He had urged his fellow Canadians to help fight it as free men acting freely. He had done his best to persuade them that the issues were worth fighting for. But he had also promised to do his best to see that no man would be sent overseas against his will.

Had he been able to guess all that was in front of him, Laurier might have seen that the two horses he was riding could never go in the same direction. Yet he could not ride one and turn the other loose.

He spoke privately to a friend of one side of his dilemma: "If I were to waver, to hesitate or to flinch, I would simply hand over the province of Quebec to the extremists. I would lose the respect of the people . . . and would deserve it. I would lose not only their respect but my self-respect also."

This was how Laurier tried to spell out his position toward Quebec. Toward Ontario he had a moment of bitterness and cynicism: "I am alarmed," he wrote in another private letter, ". . . Ontario is no longer Ontario; it is again the old province of Upper Canada, and again governed from London. . . . Upper Canada was governed from Downing Street with the instrumentality of the Family Compact sitting at York, now Toronto. Canada is now governed by a junta sitting at London, known as 'the round table,' with ramifications in Toronto, in Winnipeg, in Victoria, with Tories and Grits receiving their ideas from London, and insidiously forcing them on their respective parties."

Laurier made an equally outspoken judgment at a more down-to-earth level: "How many men will conscription bring in? Just a few slackers, exactly the same as in England. How many men has conscription brought to the ranks in England? An infinitesimal number, so small that the actual figures have never been given to the public. . . . It will be the same here. . . . Conscription will take in a few farmers and schoolboys."

Laurier knew perfectly well that conscription was inevitable. But when Borden urged him to help form a coalition and put it into effect he refused. He demanded an election. As for conscription itself, he did not oppose it outright. All he said was that a national referendum should be held before it went into force. It remained his contention that while constitutionally every able-bodied Canadian could be required to defend the country against military attack, neither the law nor his natural duty required anyone to fight outside Canada.

Borden went part of the way with this, but in his view the political and military necessities demanded that the government introduce conscription first and then ask the electors to ratify it. In one of their private conversations Borden, according to his recollection —which was never challenged by Laurier—put the proposition this way: "I suggest . . . that we form a coalition government, pass the [conscription] bill with the proviso that it shall not come into force until proclaimed by the governor-in-council after a general election. Parliament would then be dissolved and the coalition would make its appeal to the electorate. If it should receive their mandate conscription would be proclaimed and enforced. If, on the other hand, the coalition government should meet defeat, we shall have done our best and the responsibility will rest on others."

Borden at the same time offered Laurier the power of veto over the choice of men to run the Union government he was about to form. Laurier turned the offer down. Though he had many years ago given up any idea of living with Henri Bourassa, he still felt the need of living against him.

To an Ontario Liberal who knew of Borden's proposal for a coalition, Laurier wrote: "I wholly agree . . . that in a struggle such as the present one we must be prepared to give up the normal party divisions. . . . The only solution seems to me this: Have an appeal to the people, have it right away either in the form of a referendum or an election. Let the people decide, and if they decide in favor of conscription, as it seems to me they will . . . whatever influence I may have will be employed in pleading to the Quebec people that the question is settled by the verdict of the majority, and that all must loyally accept the issue and submit to the law: and this will be no light task, but a task to which I will devote myself with all my energy."

But the old leader of the Liberals, for all the careful study of his position and all the care with which he proclaimed it, was in a fast diminishing minority. His own party was breaking away from him. In the West it was in open rebellion, with Sir Clifford Sifton, the most influential of all western Liberals, the leading defector. In Ontario and the Maritimes, Laurier's strength fell away by the day and his despair mounted by the hour: "I have often thought of resigning," he wrote, "but whenever I sat down to think the matter out, my courage rose up against the difficulties which I saw impending were I to give up the fight, now especially that the fight has become a losing battle. Oh! but what a wrench at all my heart's strings!

"Yesterday it was Pardee, and today it will be Graham! Graham and Pardee as dear to me as my own brothers! Do not, however, think hard of them, for I do not. . . . The pain is not less acute on their side than on mine, and I know only too well the difficulties which face them. . . . How it will all end I venture not to predict. I still hope, perhaps against all hope, that when this nightmare is over, we may still maintain the party together."

Though he was greatly disappointed when his old adversary refused to join him, Borden understood the reasons quite plainly and put them plainly and generously in his memoirs many years later.

"If he [Laurier] had been ten or fifteen years younger, I am confident that he would have entered the proposed coalition. He held an unrivalled position in the affection and reverence of the French Canadians; and he was convinced that he would lose this pre-eminence if he should commit himself to a policy of compulsory military service. I am convinced that he underrated his influence and that Quebec would have followed where he led.

"But in addition to the personal motive," Borden went on, "there was I believe a higher influence. The prestige of Mr. Bourassa, not then perhaps at its highest point, was still sufficiently powerful to arouse in Sir Wilfrid's mind a grave apprehension as to the effect of violent propaganda led by his former follower. . . . In intimate conversation with Sir Wilfrid I concluded that he regarded Mr. Bourassa's teaching as inimical not only to the spirit of Canadian unity but to the best interests of the province of Quebec. Thus, an instinct of patriotism led Sir Wilfrid to believe that . . . his duty was to stand apart from the proposed coalition."

Having arrived at this fair estimate of his chief adversary's position, Borden was still resolved that he had to bring in conscription and that since an election over it was not inevitable, he had to find his support where he could. Accordingly, after nearly five months' negotiation and intriguing he swore ten of Laurier's rebellious, pro-conscription supporters into his new Union government as cabinet ministers and parliamentary secretaries. In turn he lost all but one of his Nationalist supporters from Quebec.

These shifts among the politicians had far less impact on the nation than the new upheaval of its basic feelings. Riots broke out throughout Quebec. As had been the case in the disputes over the schools, the Catholic Church spoke with no single voice. In the main its leaders urged the country's Catholics to obey the call to national registration because that was the law. But when it became evident that conscription was to follow, their opposition became clear-cut and violent.

Thus, Cardinal Bégin, the most influential of Canadian clerics, sternly forbade his churches to encourage a boycott of registration. But when the order for registration was followed by a proposal for conscription—a proposal which refused to exempt student priests —Bégin declared categorically: "This conscription law is a menace. . . . This military service . . . is not only a serious blow to the rights of the Church of Christ, independent in its domain . . . but it constitutes a fatal obstacle to the recruiting of ministers of God, shepherds of souls, as well as to that of the staff of clerical teachers, and through this fact it creates, in our society, an evil much worse than that which it is alleged to attempt to remedy."

Similarly the influential Archbishop Bruchési supported registration but denounced conscription: "We are nearing racial and religious war," he said.

At more junior levels, some—though not all—of the Catholic clergy were far less deferential to the civil power. One paper which, though it held no official standing, was widely read by the clergy urged that Quebec withdraw from Confederation: "Our faith, our language, our schools and the future of our children, the well-being of our families, the mission which Providence seems to have confided to our hands, to plant on the shores of the St. Lawrence a truly Christian civilization, appear to be passing away. The war came and the majority here again imposed upon us its arbitrary will. We are already crushed by an enormous debt, and today they wish to impose by force a law as unconstitutional as it is anti-

Canadian, which will send our sons and brothers to the European butchery, like so many cattle, to satisfy the appetite of a master."

Henri Bourassa's chief ally, Armand Lavergne, still, in spite of refusing Sam Hughes's invitation to recruit a battalion for overseas, held the odd tactical advantage of being a colonel in the militia. He proclaimed: "Canada is already practically bankrupt through this war, and now she is taking another step toward ruin and annexation." He would never accept conscription: "I will go to jail or be hanged or shot before . . ." The conscription of 1917 had its origin in 1899, he insisted, when Canada sent men to assist in crushing a small nation in the Transvaal, "which only wanted the right to live."

In another speech, Lavergne cried to a huge audience: "If the government passes this damned law, if you have a heart, if you are still descendants of those who were sent to the scaffold crying *'Vive la liberté! Vive l'indépendance!'*—you should take a pledge to disobey it."

No one sought to shoot, hang, or even silence Lavergne, although a highly public attempt—carried ultimately into the courts and there lost—was made to expel him from the Quebec Garrison Club.

Passions had risen so high that even the passionate Bourassa published a warning in *Le Devoir* against "sterile violence." But he was not in time, even if he really intended to be. Thousands of his followers went storming through the streets of Quebec and Montreal, smashing the windows of pro-conscription newspapers, and one little group of them actually made plans to blow up the home of the publisher of the Montreal *Star;* one of the plotters committed suicide when the police were closing in on him.

These were by no means the only factors that destroyed whatever hope of calm there might have been for the election of 1917. Borden was persuaded to make drastic and monstrously undemocratic changes in the rules of voting. Although Canada as yet had no female suffrage, a new bill gave the vote to the mothers, wives, and sisters of all men in the Army. Presumably they would vote for conscription, although the government gave more pious reasons for introducing the new measure. In another provision immigrants who had come from Germany, Austria, and other enemy countries and had been in Canada less than fifteen years were denied the right to vote.

Even without these special aids, Borden would have been in an almost unassailable position on election day. Bourassa at the last moment had decided to support Laurier, but he did no more than confirm the anti-conscriptionists in the decision they had already made to support the Liberal leader. At the same time many potential Laurier supporters—especially in Ontario and the West—took it that a vote for Laurier was a vote for Bourassa and decided this was a course they could not possibly follow.

When the results came in, conscription was overwhelmingly approved. But the division of the country—a division so sternly fought against since the time of Wolfe and Montcalm, sometimes forestalled and remedied, sometimes yielded to—had reached another climax. Borden's Union government, with its core of Conservatives and its disaffected Liberals, was elected with a great majority. Borden won 74 seats in Ontario to Laurier's 8. In the West, Borden won 55 seats and Laurier won 2. In Quebec, Laurier won by 62 to 3. It was closer in the Maritimes, but there Borden had an advantage of two to one. In summary, Canada had lost nearly as much ground in its struggle for unity as it had won in the previous one hundred and fifty-eight years since the Plains of Abraham.

XVIII

Passchendaele—The last German counterattack

AFTER its noisy preliminaries, conscription turned out to be an equally noisy failure. There were many categories of exemptions and when the act went into force the hearing of appeals took far more time than the swearing in and training of new soldiers. It was not only French Canadians who tried to evade the draft. Farmers' sons had been granted exemptions under certain conditions. They were demanded and granted in large numbers, and sometimes the men who were refused exemption stirred up demonstrations. In one of them, at Perth, Ontario, five hundred farmers jammed the streets. In another small Ontario town the local paper declared: "Every man taken from a Canadian farm destroys the power of Canada to feed the men at the Front. Every man taken from a Canadian farm makes more terrible the cry of starving women and children for whom our men are fighting. . . . Conscription . . . is a conspiracy of the rich and powerful against the lowly. Do you wish to enslave Canada's manhood to help the titled aristocrats?" A wealthy Winnipeg man created a *cause célèbre* by trying to buy his young and able son out of the draft by offering to subscribe to half a million dollars' worth of war bonds.

By the end of March 1918, the draft law had produced no more than twenty-two thousand reinforcements, far less than a tenth of the total Canadian force then serving overseas. Only two thousand of the men actually enrolled under the compulsory system were from Quebec, where the appeal boards were more sympathetic than in other parts of the country and the appeals were more numerous. The loud assaults against what little was left of the country's unity grew as the inevitable search for draft dodgers began.

In Quebec City a mob wrecked the local recruiting office and partly destroyed the offices of two local newspapers. The city was put under martial law and a military detachment from Ontario was rushed in to enforce it. The situation had become truly desperate, so much so that even the fiery Armand Lavergne was pleading for moderation.

But there was now no hope of ending the first small disturbance without a much greater one. Angry young anti-conscriptionists had been assaulting the soldiers from Ontario with ax handles and once or twice with their hunting rifles. Inevitably the troops were ordered to strike back with fixed bayonets and cavalry swords. At last the ugly climax arrived on the long night of April 1. Four civilians were killed and half a dozen soldiers were wounded. A kind of order was restored, but young Québecois fled by the hundred into the Laurentian Hills and some of them were heavily armed and in effect dared the police to come and get them.

The conflict between French Canada and the rest of Canada obscured and has almost blotted from the pages of history the fact that there were other conflicts over conscription too. Not long after the culmination of the Quebec riots five thousand farmers marched in a body on Ottawa demanding that the canceled exemptions to farmers' sons be restored. Although a large number of the delegation were from Quebec, more were from Ontario.

One of Borden's cabinet ministers, Frank B. Carvell, told the House of Commons, in a blunt answer to the growing wave of hostility toward Quebec: "There are thousands and tens of thousands, yes, hundreds of thousands, of people in the rest of Canada who have tried assiduously to evade military service." In addition to those who took refuge in the woods and mountains, hundreds of young men, not all from Quebec, fled to the United States. One party of Maritimers simply departed on a long voyage with the fishing fleet, and in the lumbering camps of Ontario and British Columbia there were other defaulters too.

By the time the war ended, conscription had added eighty thousand soldiers to the Army and nearly fifty thousand of these actually got overseas. About twenty thousand of these came from Quebec; about the same number from Quebec through one device or another simply refused to report to their draft boards.

These statistics were far less dismaying than others in the making at the scene of the war. In the last months of 1917 the Canadian

Corps was thrown again into the great killing ground of Flanders. This time its objective was the small and soon to be immortal village of Passchendaele, barely five miles beyond Ypres. Since the stalemate set in three years earlier, neither side, for all its millions of dead and wounded, had been able to win more than a few ruined little French and Belgian farmyards.

Haig's new plan, after his failure on the Somme and at Arras, was to move back and try again in the north. Here, he had persuaded himself, he could either break through and sweep up the coast of the North Sea or, failing that, wear the Germans into surrender. If the fighting was kept up "at the present intensity" for six more months, he predicted, Germany would run out of men.

Lloyd George tried to dissuade Haig from the Passchendaele attack, but did not have the courage to forbid it. Sir William Robertson, Chief of the Imperial General Staff and Haig's nominal superior, was skeptical of the plan too at first, but then was worn out and gave up the argument.

Throughout the long and deadly series of harangues and dissertations that followed in the British War Cabinet, the extraordinary relationship between the British Prime Minister and his commander at the front came into chilling focus. Lloyd George despised and distrusted Haig and considered him a wholesale murderer—but did not dare to dismiss him or risk his resignation. As for Haig, he did not despise Lloyd George but merely considered him a regrettable nuisance; the notion that he, an officer of cavalry and a lifetime professional soldier, should be compelled to discuss military strategy with a Welsh radical grated on Haig's every instinct, but in the main he kept his temper far better than did his civilian superior.

Yet it was touch and go whether Haig would have his way. At the end of a meeting of the War Cabinet's inner policy committee in mid-June, Lloyd George wrote a devastating critique of the new battle proposals. Whether he was really bent on exercising his authority as Prime Minister or on protecting his position in history is a nice question, in view of his ultimate capitulation. At any rate, the brilliant Welshman saw almost a dozen flaws and pitfalls in the enterprise in Flanders. While Haig and Robertson were suggesting a collapse of civilian morale in Germany they had forgotten that another costly failure might have disastrous effects on public opinion in Britain and the Empire. The Allies were equal to the Germans in guns and had only the barest advantage in manpower, and these calculations were based on the by no means sure assumption that the French had recovered from Verdun, their mutinies, and their turmoils of command.

For any reasonable chance of success in the kind of war being waged in Europe, the attack needed a decisive advantage in men and weapons. Lloyd George specifically asked how anyone could be sure that the new offensive would not end as Vimy Ridge had done with "brilliant preliminary successes, followed by weeks of desperate and sanguinary struggles, leading to nothing except perhaps the driving of the enemy back a few barren miles—beyond that nothing to show except a ghastly casualty list." His alternative plan was to stay on the defensive in the north, send artillery to Italy, and trust that the hitherto ineffective Italians might knock Austria out and thus destroy the Central Powers' whole position in the Balkans.

But Haig and his now persuaded boss, Robertson, marched back to Downing Street the next day and issued what amounted to an ultimatum. They had gone over their plan again and were sure it was sound; the inescapable implication was that the Cabinet could accept it or get new planners. Whether they liked it or not, neither soldier could afford the politicians' dream of fighting a war painlessly. They would never have got to be commanders if they had not realized that the object of war is to kill people—more of the enemy than your own, but if needed a great number of your own as well.

Robertson, confident of a superiority of numbers, said bluntly: "We should follow the principle of the gambler who has the heaviest purse and force our adversary's hand and make him go on spending until he is a pauper." Great mistakes of strategy, he was sure, had been made by "endeavoring to find a fresh way around."

Haig went on to a more detailed expansion over his battle map, his estimates of gains, and relative strengths and casualties on both sides. Lloyd George was unimpressed but still did not take a firm or final stand.

It was a month before the wavering Cabinet was half bullied and half coaxed into authorizing the commanders to go ahead with the new attack in Flanders. When he came to write his version of the discussions in his memoirs, Lloyd George's fury at having allowed himself to be overruled was entirely visited on Haig. Haig had lied to him about the simple facts, the Prime Minister said, blaming the whole "insane enterprise" on "inexhaustible vanity that will never admit a mistake . . . individuals who would rather that the million perish than that they . . . should own—even to themselves—that they were blunderers." Haig had achieved, his superior concluded when cause and effect could be weighed together, "a narrow and stubborn egotism unsurpassed among the records of disaster achieved by human complacency."

But Haig had his way at last and his massive attack exploded in midsummer with seventeen divisions ready to assault on a fifteen-mile front and seventeen more divisions in immediate reserve, a hundred thousand men in the first wave and almost a million more behind them as reinforcements and on the lines of communication.

The discussions and preparations had been so elaborate and prolonged that the Germans knew almost as much about them as the Allies. The Germans assigned their best defensive commanders to an arena almost perfect for defense. Because of the Flanders mud, which he knew would get worse with every day of the fall rains, Friedrich Sixt von Armin, the general assigned to stop the British, decided to change the hitherto almost unvaried system of trench defense. Instead of putting his Fourth German Army shoulder to shoulder in drenched and shallow furrows, Sixt von Armin built a mass of pillboxes—five lines of them in all—filled them with machine guns, and dispersed his infantry behind in relative safety and comfort but ready to move forward when and as the machine-gun posts were threatened.

The flat and marshy ground into which the British, Australians, and New Zealanders wallowed in the first weeks of the attack had no drainage system after the first bombardment wiped out the ditches and dikes. This country originally had belonged to the sea and—as was to occur in Holland in another war twenty-five years later—its defenses needed little disturbing before the whole landscape began seeking the sea again and became a quagmire.

Haig, the devoted cavalryman, had an idea that he could have his infantry and artillery make an initial break in the German front and then pour his mounted troops through. Failing that, he intended to thrust ahead with his new-fangled cavalry, the tanks.

But the cavalry proved even more helpless in the mud than the infantry. As for the tanks, one of their commanders on the ground was soon forced to the judgment that: "To anyone familiar with the terrain in Flanders it was almost inconceivable that this part of the line should have been selected. If a careful search had been made from the English Channel to Switzerland, no more unsuitable spot could have been discovered." The Tank Corps tried to warn General Gough's Fifth Army of the floods that would inevitably follow the bombardment and sent topographical diagrams to prove the point. It was answered with a staff officer's order: "Send us no more of these ridiculous maps."

Almost every one of the predictable disasters came true. The tanks were virtually useless and many of their crews had to bail out and be massacred in the mud. The German counterbarrage cut up the Allied communication wires. Infantry battalions got lost in the first dark dawn and fell under their own set artillery barrages. A disastrous rain began in the early morning. By nightfall three assault brigades of the Fifty-fifth Division had lost nearly three men out of four in killed, wounded, and missing, and Gough's Fifth Army had lost one in three. As the disastrous day went on Haig and Gough congratulated each other on a "great success" and Haig observed genially of the streams of wounded coming back to the field hospitals that they were "very cheery indeed."

It rained incessantly for four days and nights, and by the end of the first month the only provable result of the offensive was the loss of 75,000 Allied soldiers and 50,000 Germans. In the murderous sequence of attack and counterattack one little piece of wood changed hands nineteen times.

And this was only the start of what Lloyd George called "the bovine and brutal game of attrition." It went on and on, relieved by only a few particularly impossible stretches of rain. It went on through August, September, and October and into November. No one knows or will ever know how many casualties it cost, for, as Lloyd George admitted, there were not enough clerks to count them and the official and semi-official attempts to slant the figures in favor of various armies and commanders made the various estimates almost hopelessly contradictory. One of the most plausible reckonings was that of the British War Office—500,000 casualties to the Allies, 270,000 to the Germans.

An Australian officer recalled some of the more intimate details.

He saw them when the front had crept on from a position he was ordered to reconnoiter. "I got to one pillbox to find it just a mass of dead, and so I passed on carefully to the one ahead. Here I found about fifty men alive. . . . Never have I seen men so broken or demoralized. They were huddled up close behind the box in the last stages of exhaustion and fear. Fritz had been sniping them off all day, and had accounted for fifty-seven that day—the dead and dying lay in piles. The wounded were . . . unattended and weak, they groaned and moaned all over the place. . . . Some had been there four days already."

The Australians and New Zealanders, the immortal Anzac Corps, endured their share of the battle and then, worn out and half destroyed, were relieved by the Canadian Corps in late October.

If anything, the conditions of battle had worsened along with the weather. When he was ordered to take over the main burden of the offensive, the Canadian commander, Sir Arthur Currie, demanded a short postponement. Leaving aside the difficulties of the front-line soldier, the task of tugging ammunition, food, and reinforcements through the desolation of mud in the rear had become so serious that Currie insisted on time to get his guns in place. After a good deal of wrangling he won his point.

And thus it fell to the Canadians to capture Passchendaele and add it to Ypres and Vimy among the unforgettable place names of Canadian history.

One of the most graphic descriptions of the conditions the Canadians met has been provided by Kim Beattie, historian of the 48th Highlanders of Canada:

"The mud sea . . . was awful beyond words. Derelict guns, bodies, bloated horses and broken limbers were scattered wherever they looked. Had the plank road and duck-walks vanished into that quagmire they would still have been traced by the debris and the dead that flanked them.

"On the day that the First Division attacked, half of the battalion was detailed to the task of stretcher bearing. Carrying stretchers is an arduous job at any time, but at Passchendaele, where a man could only move a yard or so at a time without sinking to his thighs, and where the shells fell always about them and burst in the mud, it was work that defies description. Eight, ten and twelve men to a stretcher sometimes and all exhausted before one load was given into the hands of the CAMC.

"One sergeant, remembering a stretcher-bearing detail at Passchendaele, said this: 'It was the dirtiest job that ever I ordered men to do. They slaved like men, but I hoped it would never be so bad again. It was slippery, as were the stretchers and the wounded—what with the mud and blood. They sank to their waists. The poor wounded lads fell off at times and had to be fixed and put on again. It took hours for a trip.'"

It has been charged repeatedly that no one in a position of high command really understood what Passchendaele looked like, how deep the mud was, what certain death was decreed for the men ordered to attack into that hopeless plain. According to the British historian Liddell Hart, one highly placed officer from general headquarters made his first visit to the front after four months of battle. As he saw the awful swamp ahead he burst into tears: "Good God," he cried, "did we really send men to fight in that?"

The Canadians fought through this for nearly a month. With the sad poetry that so often rises in the hearts of men at the most abject stages of their most abject wars, the little ruins of bog and rubble ahead of them had been named Virtue Farm, Venture Farm, Vocation Farm, Venison Trench, Vanity Farm, Vine Cottage, and Vindictive Crossroads. At last the Canadian Corps won through them all and took the village of Passchendaele. It was a measure of the times that this was accounted one of the war's great victories. It yielded the Allied command about two square miles of mud.

The highly doubtful victory at Passchendaele was followed by a far more important one near the wood and town of Cambrai. This was further south, on drier ground, where with the Fort Garry Horse of Winnipeg in the van an attack of tanks, infantry, and cavalry dented the German front by as much as five miles.

But Cambrai, important though it was, proved only the prelude to the Germans' greatest and last attempt to win the war in one massive stroke. Russia by now had collapsed. Italy suffered the final disaster of Caporetto. The whole Eastern Front dissolved and the German command poured trainload after trainload of troops and guns to the west. In men the Germans increased their strength by a quarter, while the British strength, through battle wastage and the drying up of reinforcements, fell off by a quarter and the French were still struggling to recover their morale and will to fight.

Everyone on both sides knew that if the war went on much longer, the entry of the United States—which had now been made but had had no time to take effect—would probably turn the balance. So the German command took the inevitable gamble and staked everything on a massive assault in the west.

This final German offensive began on the first official day of the war's last spring, March 21, 1918. Six thousand guns had been assembled behind the attacking troops, a number unprecedented even in the massive Allied attacks on the Somme and in Flanders. By the end of the first day the Allied lines had been pushed back as much as forty miles. Forty miles in a day was, of course, an unbelievable advance in a war that had come to reckon forty yards in a month a gain worth mention in the communiqués.

The Germans had devised a new system of offense largely because, according to their sardonic records, "Haig's dispatches dealing with the attacks of 1917 were found most valuable, because they showed how not to do it." Their key man was an amazing sort of Colonel Blimp brought out of retirement and soon given the nickname of Durchbruchmüller, which in translation means "Breakthrough Müller." Müller's idea of breaking through was not to line his artillery up several miles behind the infantry and fire it for several hours before the attack, but to sneak it right up to the front and without even going through the ritual of ranging shots start shooting at what amounted to point-blank range. The surprise this brought to troops accustomed to stereotyped set-piece attacks was increased by another innovation. Instead of adhering to the traditional notion that an effective attack must be directed at all points of the defense, the Germans conceived and built "storm groups" of a few riflemen, a light machine gun or two, and a small mortar. Their task was to capture, surround, or just get behind the enemy positions in the assurance that stronger forces would be coming on behind them to exploit the confusion.

The Germans' dying *Putsch* came within only a small margin of winning the war or forcing an immediate armistice. Six days after the spring assault began, a poetic German soldier found himself, to his happy wonder, "in the English back areas . . . a land flowing with milk and honey. . . . Our men are hardly to be distinguished from English soldiers. . . . Everyone wears at least a leather jerkin, a waterproof, . . . English boots or some other beautiful thing. The horses are feeding on masses of oats and gorgeous food cake . . . and there is no doubt the army is looting with some zest."

The Germans were hypnotized by their greatest error, the error of believing that they had won the war. Rudolf Binding, the same man who made the observation quoted above, had this to say a day later:

"The advance of our infantry suddenly stopped near Albert. Nobody could understand why. Our armies had reported no enemy between Albert and Amiens. . . . Our way seemed entirely clear. I jumped into a car with orders to find out what was causing the stoppage in front. Our division was right in front of the advance and could not possibly be tired out. It was quite fresh. . . .

"As soon as I got near the town I began to see curious sights. Strange figures, which looked very little like soldiers and certainly showed no sign of advancing, were making their way back out of the town. There were men driving cows . . . others who carried a hen under one arm and a box of notepaper under the other. Men carrying a bottle of wine under their arm and another one open in their hand. . . . Men staggering. Men who could hardly walk. When I got into the town the streets were running with wine."

But despite these temporary indiscretions the German offensive stayed in motion. It bypassed Arras, overwhelmed Cambrai, and broke past the Somme and the Ancre almost to the old cathedral city of Amiens. By summer it was locked in a second Battle of the Marne with the fate of Paris itself in jeopardy, as it had been in 1914.

Even Haig, who almost never conceded the slightest possibility of failure, was forced by the third week of the assault to issue his famous order that the British must stand to "the last man."

The Canadians played only a minor part in the Allied defense, but it was enough to give their commander, Sir Arthur Currie, an occasion to send one of the most memorable of all messages from a general to his men: "Looking back with pride on the unbroken record of your glorious achievements, asking you to realize that today the fate of the British Empire hangs in the balance,

I place my trust in the Canadian Corps, knowing that where Canadians are engaged there can be no giving way. Under the orders of your devoted officers in the coming battle you will advance or fall where you stand, facing the enemy. To those who fall I say, you will not die but step into immortality. Your mothers will not lament your fate, but will be proud to have borne such sons. Your names will be revered forever by your grateful country and God will take you unto Himself."

This sort of rhetoric was going out of fashion in all armies—by 1918 a French or Australian officer, for instance, would quite possibly have been assassinated by his own troops for talking such sacrilegious claptrap. But the Canadians withstood Currie's words, fought very well in their limited defensive role, and then, in August, led the great Allied thrust that finally ended the war.

XIX

The Black Day and the Hundred Days—The battle in the air and Canada's part

THE exact date of the first assault was August 8, 1918—"the black day of the German Army," in the famous phrase of General Erich Ludendorff.

After Vimy, Passchendaele, and scores of lesser actions the Canadians had become associated with attack in the German mind. When they showed up in numbers on any part of the front the enemy commanders had come to expect an assault. Accordingly, a small part of the Canadian Corps was sent back to Flanders as a decoy and its main strength moved to its start line near Amiens only a few hours ahead of time. The Anzac Corps was deployed in a similar way. For once the deception worked. There were only six thinned-out divisions defending the German position before Amiens when the massive Allied drive began.

Nearly five hundred tanks supported the first thrusts and here they had solid ground to move on, not the marshy wallows of Flanders. In the first rush, which was helped by a providential mist, the Australians and Canadians stormed ahead eight miles on a front nearly fifteen miles wide. They were slowed down but then broke loose again, and as fall came on, the Americans launched a great offensive from the Argonne forest behind Verdun.

By October the Canadian Corps had suffered another 16,000 casualties, but in its last great drive, in which it had the temporary help of four British divisions, it overran, cut off, or otherwise completed the destruction of nearly fifty German divisions, a quarter of the whole remaining German force in the west. Cambrai, Douai, and at last Mons were added to the far-off, famous place names of Canadian history and the legendary Hundred Days of the Canadian Army were over.

When the time came to review the total Canadian war effort even the remarkable record on the ground could not surpass the record in the air.

Canada had no air force of its own in 1914–18. Sam Hughes, the unforgettable architect of the country's first military plans, had no knowledge of or confidence in flying machines. He allowed two small training planes, unassembled and packed in grease, to be bought and imported from the United States, but nobody knew or much cared what they were for and they languished in their crates. Canadians who wanted to fly either had to enlist direct in Britain's young Royal Flying Corps or seek transfers into it from the Canadian Army.

Ultimately nearly ten thousand Canadians got into the Royal Flying Corps and its successor, the Royal Air Force. They made up a quarter of the R.F.C.-R.A.F. fighting strength, and in the strange and primitive war being evolved in the sky—even more primitive than that being evolved below by the tanks—they were perhaps the most ingenious and adaptable of all the combat groups.

At first the slow little planes above the front were used only for the most rudimentary kind of reconnaissance. An Allied pilot who found himself in the same piece of sky as a German pilot could draw his revolver and duel it out as in a Western movie. Later the pilots were armed with hand carbines and then with machine guns, and finally the plane itself became a flying gun, with its cartridge belts built in.

Either through coincidence or some special aptitude, the Canadians in the Royal Flying Corps created a remarkable record in this kind of warfare. The most famous of them, Billy Bishop, destroyed seventy-two enemy planes, including five on his last day at the front. One of his friends, Roy Brown, encountered the legendary Manfred von Red Knight, Richthofen, and shot him down. Ray Collishaw was runner-up to Bishop with sixty German planes destroyed. Another of the astonishing young Canadian pilots, Billy Barker, won the Military Cross with two bars, the Distinguished Service Order and bar, and the Victoria Cross. Barker somehow survived a dogfight with sixty German planes during the final breakthrough of 1918. The official citation for his V.C.—carefully and skeptically checked, with the aid of photographs, as were all such citations—read thus:

"On the morning of October 27th, 1918, this officer observed an enemy two-seater over the Forêt de Mormal. He attacked this machine, and after a short burst it broke up in the air. At the same time a Fokker biplane attacked him, and he was wounded in the right thigh, but managed, despite this, to shoot down the enemy aeroplane in flames. He then found himself in the middle of a large formation of Fokkers, who attacked him from all directions, and was again severely wounded in the left thigh, but succeeded in driving down two of the enemy in a spin. He lost consciousness after this, and his machine fell out of control. On recovery he found himself being again attacked heavily by a large formation and, singling out one machine, he deliberately charged and drove it down in flames. During this fight his left elbow was shattered and he again fainted, and on regaining consciousness he found himself still being attacked, but, notwithstanding that he was now severely wounded in both legs and his left arm shattered, he dived on the nearest machine and shot it down in flames. Being greatly exhausted, he dived out of the fight to regain our lines, but was met by another formation which attacked and endeavored to cut him off, but after a hard fight he succeeded in breaking up this formation and reached our lines where he crashed on landing."

An eighteen-year-old boy from a village in Manitoba, Lieutenant Alan Arnett McLeod, won another Victoria Cross, with another fantastic citation:

"Set upon at 5,000 feet above the earth by 8 enemy machines, he so manoeuvred his aeroplane that his observer was able to shoot down three of his assailants. Then, although wounded in five places himself, when his petrol tank was set on fire he climbed out on one of the planes and by tipping the machine in descent kept the flames at one side while he continued to control it so that his observer could continue the battle with the machine gun. Then, when he had brought his burning machine to earth in No Man's Land, and before dropping from loss of blood, he saved the life of his equally gallant observer, helpless from six wounds, by dragging him out of the flaming wreckage, and this too under enemy fire."

The stories of Barker and McLeod and a few others almost as astonishing were not the inventions of fiction writers or romancing journalists. They emerged from the test of tough and doubting awards committees to whom the granting of a Victoria Cross was a matter of the most solemn decision. If the war that ended on November 11, 1918, proved nothing else it did again show the boundless variety of the human being—his infinite valor, endurance, and imagination along with his infinite folly.

When the whole reckoning was completed it was decided that Canada had sustained nearly a quarter of a million casualties, one in four of them fatal. When at last, to use Lloyd George's phrase, there was enough "clerk power" to assemble the figures for all nations on both sides, they came to 8,538,315 killed, 21,219,452 wounded, and 7,750,919 captured or missing. This awesome total of casualties did not include civilians.

XX

The hazards of peace—The Winnipeg
general strike

HAVING emerged from a difficult physical and moral test, Canada now faced an even more difficult intellectual test. The blacks and whites of Ypres and Vimy, of Parliament Hill and the anti-conscription rallies at Lafontaine Park, now began to melt into a less interesting gray. A time for quick speech and quick action had given way to a time for contemplation.

It was not a Buddha's serene contemplation of his eternal and accustomed navel. It was more like an adolescent's half-scared study of his first signs of a beard. Where did Canada go from here? Just as importantly, where did the individual Canadian go from here?

To each question the probable answers were dispiriting and anticlimactic. The soldiers coming home rolled their puttees extra tight, shined their shoes extra black, swung their arms extra high to bands playing extra loud—and wondered where to get a job. Good jobs were scarce and soon grew scarcer. Moreover, prices had gone up far more than wages. Voices of belittlement, gloom, and anger soon rose everywhere. The one that galled most of all was the voice that cried, unofficially but stridently, in the name of the United States: "We won the war!" Editorial writers and public speakers were proclaiming the message to the ends of the earth and in endless variations. They gave the American Expeditionary Force the foolish but maddening nickname "After England Failed." The Detroit *Free Press* summed up their viewpoint in a sentence: "A flood of American manhood set in the direction of the European battlefields and filled and swelled until it overwhelmed the enemy that had successfully resisted the combined military strength of half-a-dozen European nations."

The echoes of We-won-the-war were to linger on in Canada long after they had finished serving the United States as a drumbeat for the retreat from the League of Nations. They were to exacerbate Canadians' feeling toward their closest neighbors as the tariff had never done, and small wonder. For We-won-the-war represented the studied affront in its most unendurable form: a monstrous falsehood made further monstrous by the faint suspicion of truth.

But there were far more troublesome issues pressing for settlement as the troops came marching home. A new and more complicated war awaited them in their civil affairs.

It is to be doubted that before 1914 one Canadian in ten had heard the expression "class war." Not one in a thousand had used it. The name of Karl Marx meant scarcely more to the average Canadian of 1914 than the name of, say, Jean-Paul Sartre or the Dalai Lama means to the average Canadian of today. Socialism was a word, no more. Whatever debates and struggles had been waged on the outskirts of economic orthodoxy, the inner bastion had never been called on to defend itself. The methods and managers of capitalism had always been fair game for dissatisfied orators and voters, and in the days of Mackenzie, Papineau, and Riel they had, of course, even provoked a little musketry. But capitalism itself, though not precisely sacrosanct, was regarded as inevitable.

Now, suddenly, the very order of things—not the mere administration of society, but its root and nature—came under challenge. A really observant or discontented man might have seen the challenge looming even before the war; a very few particularly discontented ones had already enlisted in its service.

For the most part, these revolutionaries—Canada's first true revolutionaries, as distinct from its rebels—took their causes and their catechism secondhand. They borrowed their heroes—Keir Hardie, Ramsay MacDonald, Robert Owen, and Sidney Webb from Great Britain, Lenin and Trotsky from Russia, Eugene Debs, Emma Goldman, and Mother Jones from the U.S.A. They borrowed their martyrs, the Joe Hills and Tom Mooneys, and they borrowed their demons, the Rockefellers, Morgans, Schwabs, Du Ponts, and Armours. They borrowed their doctrine and their plan for action, not from the distant wellsprings of the *Communist*

Manifesto but from what appeared to be the freshly surging fountainhead of the I.W.W.

Today the Industrial Workers of the World of a half century ago resembles nothing so much as a yellowed newspaper cartoon made unintentionally comic by its extravagance and lack of subtlety. Its unwashed, unshaved, bomb-nursing image is a period piece to be smiled upon with the same indulgence as the companion image of the plug-hatted, diamond-studded, cigar-chewing Boss.

But in the second decade of the twentieth century the I.W.W. was a force to be taken in earnest. It had serious hopes—and indeed, it seemed briefly, reasonable expectations—of overthrowing not only the whole edifice of capital but the conventional goals of labor. At its organization meeting in Chicago in 1905, it assailed the traditional craft unions of employees almost as savagely as it assailed the employers. The preamble to the constitution read:

"The working class and the employing class have nothing in common. There can be no peace so long as hunger and want are found among millions of working people and the few, who make up the employing class, have all the good things of life.

"Between these two classes a struggle must go on until the workers of the world organize as a class, take production of the earth and the machinery of production and abolish the wage system.

"We find that the centering of the management of industries into fewer hands makes the trade unions unable to cope with the ever-growing power of the employing class. The trade unions foster a state of affairs which allows one set of workers to be pitted against another set of workers in the same industry, thereby helping to defeat one another in wage wars. Moreover, the trade unions aid the employing class to mislead the workers into belief that the working class have interests in common with their employers.

"These conditions can be changed and the interest of the working class upheld only by an organization formed in such a way that all its members in any one industry, or in all industries, if necessary, cease work whenever a strike or lockout is on in any department thereof, thus making an injury to one an injury to all.

"Instead of the conservative motto 'A fair day's wage for a fair day's work,' we must inscribe on our banners the revolutionary watchword 'Abolition of the wage system.'

"It is the historic mission of the working class to do away with Capitalism. The army of production must be organized, not only for the every-day struggle with the capitalists, but also to carry on production when Capitalism shall have been overthrown. By organizing industrially we are forming the structure of the new society within the shell of the old."

The I.W.W., personalized and much loved and hated as the Wobblies, soon became an important minority in U.S. labor and politics. The movement was at first slow to spread into Canada. Industrial sabotage and pacifist speechmaking were much more dangerous and, to the patriotic, much less palatable in a country at war than in a country officially neutral.

But by 1917 cynicism and discontent were rising to the surface in Canadian labor too. Labor, as a class, had been scarcely more enthusiastic about the war than French Canada; so long as the war continued to improve wages, erase unemployment, and increase the emolument of unions, the majority of labor leaders were willing to endorse, or at least allow to go by default, the general belief that the country was united in a righteous crusade. But the Russian revolution, the peace proposals of the Pope and Woodrow Wilson, the growing awareness of what a hideous senseless slaughter the world had really embarked upon, revived or gave rise to more equivocal attitudes. When conscription came in, and with it the realization that thousands of the country's patriotic munitions workers were about to be converted willingly or not into patriotic infantry privates and artillery gunners, many of the workers' spokesmen were as outraged as Henri Bourassa himself.

The president of the Trades and Labor Congress made a special pilgrimage to Quebec to declare that "organized labor would lay down its tools and refuse to work" before it would accept conscription; never would Canadian workmen allow themselves to be sent to the front to "protect profiteers" at home or "tricky politicians" abroad who, like Lloyd George, had "disgraced humanity."

Before long even the most inflamed pacifists of the Trades and Labor Congress were being outshouted by other voices crying out in the name of labor. The more militant I.W.W., having become the object of anti-sabotage and anti-sedition laws in the United

States, had sought cover under the new name One Big Union, and as One Big Union it found important allies in Australia and then in Canada. During the last year of the war the radical wing of labor was successfully challenging the Trades and Labor Congress in Winnipeg, Calgary, Vancouver, and northern Ontario. Strikes in the coal fields and lumber camps became almost commonplace and so, for the first time, did Marxist literature and oratory. The political arm of the I.W.W.-O.B.U., the Social Democratic party of Canada, set forth its aims thus:

"To educate the workers of Canada to a consciousness of their class position in society, their economic servitude to the owners of capital . . . to seize the reins of government and transform all capitalistic property into the collective property of the working class."

Before the war was over the revolutionary pamphleteers were assailing not only the sacred cause itself but its two most sacred symbols, the Christian Church and the Canadian soldier. The former was "palsied and staggering in its poverty of influence while Capitalism wallows in the filth of its own chaos"; the latter, to borrow the words of Jack London, was "a blind, heartless, soulless, murderous machine."

One of the many foreign-language papers that sprang up, with no stronger apparent editorial policy than to spread sedition, published a picture of a group of English aristocrats under the caption: "Exhibition of dangerous beasts." On the advice of the new national Director of Public Safety the government outlawed a dozen political, fraternal, and industrial organizations, including the I.W.W. and the Social Democratic party.

As the last year of war drifted untidily into the first year of peace, unrest was growing even among the British-to-the-core families that had proudly given sons to fight the Kaiser, had no knowledge of or curiosity about Marx, and would, in any case, have dismissed him as a foreigner. Across the country there were 169 strikes during 1918, almost two thirds as many as there had been in the four previous war years put together. Thousands of workingmen were dissatisfied with their wages and their hours. Hundreds of employers were appalled that in the name of some new device called collective bargaining they were suddenly forbidden to deal with their own men, man to man, but had to negotiate with strangers under strange new laws. Labor-management relations were still in such a primitive state that after it was discovered that it took $9.48 a week to keep a female laundry worker alive in Manitoba, the Canadian Manufacturers' Association objected to the government's proposal of a minimum wage of $9.50, the objection being based on the ground of increased costs of production and "the difficulty in dealing with the unemployable or shiftless class and the youth employees."

It was the relatively new conflict between craft unionism and industrial unionism that at last gathered all the chips together and left them teetering on a single belligerent shoulder. At a huge and noisy rally at Calgary in March 1919, the O.B.U. came officially into being in Canada with strong support from all four western provinces. Along with such ultimate goals as the overthrow of production for profit and the replacement of the parliamentary system of government with the Soviet system, it set forth as its immediate goals a working week of five six-hour days and an end to the "moss-covered and age-old" American Federation of Labor and its tradition of organizing by shop and by skill.

The Calgary convention broke up spoiling for a fight. It chose June 1 as the deadline for its then quite fanciful thirty-hour week, which was the same as choosing a deadline for a general strike.

In fact it was not necessary to wait that long. On May 1, 2000 workers in the metal trades of Winnipeg walked out, and it soon became apparent that the relatively moderate forty-four-hour week and eighty-five-cent-an-hour wage they asked for were to be little more than side issues. The bargaining had to be industry-wide, the nineteen separate unions of the Central Metal Trades Council insisted. All the chief employers were willing to bargain collectively, but only with their own employees. Building-trade workers had struck on the same day on a straight question of wages. Within a week fifty-two other unions voted to walk out in sympathy. On May 13 the Trades and Labor Council, the local body of the Congress, issued the long awaited decree: "A general strike has been called of all organizations affiliated with the Council."

Overnight Canada's third-largest city lay half paralyzed and stagnant. The streetcars stopped running. All but a handful of postmen walked off their beats. Cooks, waiters, bakers, and shoe clerks went on strike. So did teamsters, truck drivers, plumbers, carpenters, street cleaners, and garbage men; so did telephone operators, telegraph operators, elevator operators, butchers, milkmen, icemen, and breadmen. The firemen struck. Employees of the waterworks left only enough crews on duty to keep the pressure at thirty pounds—just sufficient to reach second stories. The police voted to strike, but remained on duty at the urging and "by permission" of the Strike Committee.

The Strike Committee set up a kind of presidium over the affairs of the city in the four-story headquarters of the Labor Temple. It poured out a stream of decrees and regulations. Not since the reign of Louis XIV had any civil power interfered so cavalierly in so many of the ordinary details of day-to-day life in Canada. Daily newspapers were closed down, creating a virtual monopoly of public information for the strikers' own *Western Labour News*. The telegraph companies were permitted to send news dispatches to other parts of Canada and the United States, but only after the copy had been cleared by a four-man board of censors. Motion-picture theaters and vaudeville and legitimate houses, at first shut down, were quickly reopened to help keep the streets clear of people who suddenly had nothing to do and nowhere to go.

Milk and bread deliveries were ordered resumed as hastily as they had been cut off. But cream was classed as an unproletarian luxury and remained under the ban. Several strike-bound cafés were ordered to reopen, but the waiters were instructed to serve only customers wearing union badges and the proprietors were warned that if their clients made any remarks derogatory to the strike the doors would be closed again. The provincial normal school was closed, but the school for the deaf-and-dumb was allowed to open.

Sympathy strikes broke out in a dozen other cities, including Toronto, Vancouver, Edmonton, and Calgary. But nowhere was the tie-up complete or general. It soon became apparent that the country as a whole was not headed for anarchy, and with this realization the momentarily stunned forces of law and order began asserting their existence in Winnipeg.

At the start this assertion was a gingerly one. The Dominion Cabinet's first reaction was that not of the highest agency of government but of a querulous employer. In the only statement immediately forthcoming from Ottawa, Postal Minister N. W. Rowell

assured Parliament that the postmen who had walked out had
done so "entirely without justification"; the postmen who had
remained on the job would find the government "standing absolutely behind them." Modest reinforcements were added to the
city's military and Mounted Police garrisons, but were kept out of
sight in their barracks.

It was ten days before the City Council could bring itself to pass
a resolution against sympathy strikes by civic employees, and even
then the vote was close. Mayor Charles Gray, in issuing an assurance that the people could count on having water, milk, basic
foodstuffs, and fire and police protection, had already acknowledged that "we are securing these rights by the sufferance of some
other authority than the constituted authority of the city government."

The first really organized counterattack against the strikers'
dictatorship came from a group of unreconstructed capitalists who
took the name Citizens Committee of 1000 and set up headquarters
in the Board of Trade building. The Committee of 1000—whose
membership ultimately grew to 10,000—offered volunteer firemen and policemen and emergency help in other public utilities.
Heartened by its support, the mayor overcame his feeling of help-
lessness and made another declaration: "The constituted authorities
are determined to stamp out the Bolshevik or Red element in
Winnipeg. The town is open; all business may go ahead as in the
past. No one section of the public has any right to dictate food
terms to any other section of the public. This principle will be
strictly adhered to by the constituted authorities."

The strike-bound newspapers mustered enough pressmen to start
putting out abbreviated editions again, and one of them, the *Free
Press*, set up a radio station on its roof and assured the outside
world that the city was still functioning and that there still had
been no violence.

T. C. Norris, the provincial premier, reminded the theater owners
and others operating under provincial license that they were *not*
doing business by permission of the Strike Committee and ordered
them to take down the permit cards saying that they were. Most
of the theaters obeyed.

Many unofficial spur-of-the-moment, non-union strikers—who
outnumbered the official, unionized strikers by about 18,000 to
12,000—began drifting back to their jobs. The cheerful clop-clop

of T. Eaton's delivery horses was heard again in the city streets. Scores of little stores followed the Big Store's example and retail trade returned to something resembling normal. At length two cabinet ministers showed up from Ottawa. The Minister of Labor ordered the postmen back to their jobs on pain of losing them permanently, and the Minister of the Interior bade the populace stand firm.

But the pendulum's return swing was far from steady. Whatever the immediate issues meant to them, thousands of returned men saw in their strike their first chance in years to cock a snoot at authority without fear of summary punishment. The mayor, the premier, the cabinet men from Ottawa, the Mounties, and the harassed employers represented all the world's sergeant majors, company commanders, and generals wrapped up in one ample and gloriously vulnerable target. And thus while the officers of the new and fast-growing veterans' associations passed resolutions condemning the strike, their members paraded through the streets cheering and upholding it. Three deputations, numbering 1000 to 2500 and finally 3000, marched on the provincial parliament buildings to boo the premier. Another procession marched to city hall to boo the mayor, and still another sailed up Wellington Crescent pointing at the houses of the rich and wrangling gaily and pointedly about who saw which house first.

On June 6 the mayor forbade all parades. On June 9 all but fifteen members of the city police force were fired, the Police Commission having demanded and failed to get from them a retraction of their first vote in support of the strike. The hitherto almost invisible Mounties began patrolling the streets and special constables from the Citizens Committee replaced the municipal force. On June 10 a mob set upon two of the new special officers at the corner of Portage and Main. The Mounties rode to their rescue with batons flying and the ensuing riot lasted five hours, although no one was seriously hurt.

A week later, and thirty-three days after the walkout had become general, the Ottawa government decided that what it had on its hands was nothing less than a seditious conspiracy. In a theatrical series of early-morning arrests, in which fifty Mounties and five hundred special policemen took part, a dozen of the most prominent strike leaders were bundled into automobiles and rushed to the nearby federal penitentiary at Stony Mountain. In the next few days three more of their alleged co-conspirators joined them there, having been picked up at places as far apart as Calgary and Montreal.

Of the men jailed in this roundup, five were ideally equipped for the role of Bolshevik plotters. They had guttural foreign names and swarthy foreign faces and all were known to have been, or believed to have been, born in Russia. But as the Crown set about the preparation of its case an awkward anticlimax appeared. There was hardly any evidence against the five "Russians" and the case against them had to be dropped. This left the Department of Justice to press its charges against ten impeccable Anglo-Saxons, two of whom, James S. Woodsworth and William Ivens, were ordained Christian ministers; two others, John Queen and A. A. Heaps, were aldermen of the city of Winnipeg; one, Fred Dixon, was a duly elected member of the Manitoba Lesislative Assembly; and the other five, R. B. Russell, R. J. Johns, George Armstrong, R. E. Bray, and William Pritchard, were labor-union officers of considerable seniority and prestige.

Before the trial began, the news of the arrests touched off a final convulsive outburst of violence around city hall and in Market Square just behind it. It took the Mounties and the militia six hours to break it up. By then one man was killed and another mortally wounded; thirty were in hospital and ninety-one in jail. By the middle of the next week the strike was over.

The central figure of the trial was Bob Russell, a thirty-year-old official of the Metal Workers, an unabashed and unrepentant Marxist and one of the strongest champions of the One Big Union, the child of the I.W.W. Russell stood trial first and alone. Through almost a month of day-and-night sittings, the prosecution, aided by an endless array of witnesess and letters to and from his friends, played back to him his own resounding clichés. "Yours for revolution." "Yours in revolt." "I see arising out of the unemployment now beginning to make itself manifest the most glorious opportunity to show the plug worker that the only solution to the question is to keep pointing to him the situation in Russia." "The blood that is spilled in Canada will depend on the working class. We must establish the same form of government as they have in Russia."

The jury brought down its verdict quickly. Russell was guilty of seditious conspiracy. The judge gave him two years. In the other trials that followed, five of the defendants, including one of the aldermen and one of the preachers, were sentenced to a year and another to six months. The other three were acquitted.

Viewed as a particular, self-contained event, the Winnipeg general strike of 1919 was not a major episode in Canadian affairs. In the larger mass of history it might easily be dismissed as a kind of geological fault, an anomaly born of the same passing disturbance as the contemporaneous Red Scare and Palmer raids across the border. In fact, the strike supplied the nation with a central focus for its restlessness and discontent. It had introduced, though in a raw and clumsy form, new political and economic ideas. Like a college boy savoring his first hangover, the country found its first gulp of the undiluted white mule of Marxism altogether too strong to stomach and swore off it for good. But the gentler apéritif of socialism was worthy of further experiment. And though the world that had been won with the winning of the war was in the main a disappointing world, it did not have to be accepted exactly as it stood. New alternatives had become visible: not just the same old alternatives of Grit or Tory, Tory or Grit, Union Man or Company Man or Boss, or Have or Have-Not. The system was susceptible of all sorts of variations, ready for every manner of tinkering. Canada was on the brink of its first real era of reform since Confederation. It was preparing to greet the Age of the Aging Turks.

XXI

The Age of the Aging Turks—The departure
of Robert Laird Borden

THE Aging Turks did not enter in a body. Nor did they emerge from the same points of the compass or proceed in step to the same unknown distances. They had no acknowledged leader; indeed, most of them were, or became, furious rivals. The one thing common to their philosophies was a sense of mission. Otherwise they were as motley as a band of Caribbean pirates. In their personal lives they were as respectable and careful as a gardenful of curates. A number of them actually were clergymen and most of the others were bachelors. Piety, rectitude, and celibacy never had so formidable a group of champions. The fire of youth was never more happily wedded to the God-fearing temperance of age. No large group of statesmen ever tried harder to follow, simultaneously, the stars of adventure and of safety.

Those who led most successfully were William Lyon Mackenzie King (bachelor) and James S. Woodsworth '(preacher). Those who pushed and urged on, urged back, and argued to the best effect were William Aberhart (preacher) and Richard Bedford Bennett (bachelor). Those who arrived later, but still in time to confirm the main directions, were Tommy Douglas (preacher), Maurice Duplessis (bachelor), and Ernest Manning (preacher). Of all Canada's main political figures between the 1920s and the 1950s, the only one who was not either a bachelor or a preacher was Arthur Meighen, and in the face he presented to the people he was the most austere and priestly of them all.

But these patterns still lay ahead in the years just after the First World War. Before their heirs began rearranging the reins of power, Laurier, Borden, and Bourassa had their separate farewells to make.

Laurier died in harness in his seventy-eighth year on February 17, 1919. Though he suffered two strokes in his last months, the black depression in which he had seen the collapse of his party's unity and the election of 1917 gave way near the end to his old serenity. In one of his last long letters he reminded a French-speaking colleague: "The soil, in our northern climes, is not as lavish as in the lands of the south, but it responds freely to labor and effort. In the humble settler's hut, his log cabin, one must not look for the abundant comfort of the old parishes, but there are always bread in the pantry, pork in the salting tub, warmth and gaiety at the fireside." In one of his last speeches, to a group of English-speaking Young Liberals, he said: "Many problems rise before you: problems of race division, problems of creed differences, problems of economic conflict, problems of national duty and national aspiration. Let me tell you that for the solution of these problems you have a safe guide, and unfailing light, if you remember that faith is better than doubt and love is better than hate." Laurier's last words, whispered as he pressed his wife's hand on his quiet deathbed, were: "*C'est fini.*"

Bourassa had another thirty-three years of life ahead of him, but his star had passed its zenith. He needed big issues to contest, big men to fight. He would never find another year to test his forensic genius like 1917, never find another giant like Wilfrid Laurier to bring crashing down to earth. Nearly two decades after their last great collision Bourassa was to mourn above its ashes: "I fought Laurier when he was at the height of his popularity. When he was the idol of Quebec I stood almost alone against him in defense of the principles for which I have fought all my life. But when he was betrayed by his Liberal friends, when he was downtrodden during the war, I came to him. The last letter Laurier wrote in his own hand, he wrote to me, and the answer I wrote came to him two days before his death. He knows now that although I fought him because of differences in principle, I loved him all my life; and he knew it then."

Bereft of his beloved victim, deprived of causes worthy of his anger, Bourassa now turned away from politics and took to lecturing and writing in praise of peace, the Church, and the French language. Noting his strange air of calm, the Toronto *Star* commented nervously: "He has been dead half-a-dozen times. But when he turns over in what some foolish beings think is his grave, more politicians take flight than if Gabriel had joined the other side." The warning was not needed; Mount Bourassa was never seen in full eruption again.

As for Robert Borden, his health and strength were failing. Few public servants ever had a better claim to honorable discharge than this faithful, solid, stolid man. No Prime Minister in the country's whole history had been cast in a more difficult role. True, Laurier had been drummed out of office, but at least for Laurier the drums rolled out loud and brave; at least they offered the solace of martyrdom. Borden, after his long apprenticeship of failure, had now known almost a decade of uninterrupted success, but his successes had never, somehow, looked heroic or even quite clean-cut. In their visible aspects there was always something to mar or dilute them just a little. His uncertain championing of tariff protection and a semi-colonial naval policy had won him an election in 1911. His reluctant adoption of conscription had won him another six years later. But these mixed triumphs made it easy for his enemies to charge and his friends to suspect that the welfare of the manufacturing interests, the respect of Westminister, and the sanctity of the Empire were things he held in too high esteem.

One of Borden's last major acts as Prime Minister had involved yet another massive handout to the persuasive proprietors of the Canadian Northern Railway, Sir William Mackenzie and Sir Donald Mann. The king and the duke had talked the Laurier and Borden administrations out of a literally incalculable fortune in cash, bond guarantees, and land on the promise to build and operate an essential national service. Now, from his huge castle overlooking Toronto Bay, Mackenzie pleaded bankruptcy. With the same stunned complaisance with which Canadian statesmen have nearly always responded to the cries of wealthy mendicants, Borden quickly put through a bill to pay off another $25,000,000 of the Canadian Northern's debts, and though the country already held it in trust, to buy the railway's stock for a further $10,000,000.

Equally openhanded settlements were in the making with the Grand Trunk and the Grand Trunk Pacific, two older companies that had also been financed, refinanced, subsidized, resubsidized, rescued, revived, and rewarded by the public purse a dozen times and now were for sale to the taxpayers, who already owned them in principle, in equity, and, almost certainly, in law.

To the last, Borden had tried to keep Mackenzie in business. At Mackenzie's importuning he made a personal visit to New York to meet a group of New York bankers (Otto Kahn himself was one of them) and see if he could persuade them to float a private bond issue for the C.N.R. The bankers indicated a willingness to discuss details. Borden's spirits rose momentarily, but only momentarily; the bankers' terms, it soon developed, might have been written by Sir William Mackenzie himself. They'd be quite happy to float the desired bond issue, and their sole condition was that the government of Canada must guarantee both the principal and the interest. Dazed and saddened, Borden returned to Ottawa and the bitter, thankless task of persuading Parliament to bail out the king and the duke just once more.

This enterprise, like most of Borden's public enterprises, was attended by contumely and dissent. Hardly anyone knew of, much less gave him the honor he deserved for, the dogged, quiet fight he had been waging behind the scenes to protect and fortify the still tender roots of Canadian nationhood. Hardly anyone knew of the hidden gusts of ire with which he had confronted even the Imperial Cabinet and the Governor General when they took his Tory principles (which to them still meant his automatic obedience to London) too much for granted.

Today Borden's brief duels with the Duke of Connaught and Bonar Law seem to verge on the seriocomic. But in their own time and setting they were of genuine importance. It was one thing for the choleric and half-mad Sam Hughes to quarrel with the royal Connaught. For the correct and careful Borden to speak up to the Governor General was something altogether different. This Borden had done with devastating effect when Connaught sought to order him to mount a recruiting drive in the still neutral United States. After several icy exchanges, during which he called the Governor General's attention to Canada's "complete power of self-government," Borden became personal:

"I hope that my colleagues and I shall not be found wanting in respect or indeed in admiration for the wide military experience of Your Royal Highness and the high position which you hold as a Field Marshal of His Majesty's Forces. It would appear to us that the matters under consideration do not call so much for the exercise of military skill or the application of military experience as the consideration of international law and the exercise of the commonplace quality of common sense."

The Governor General quietly caved in. So, in a more significant contretemps, did Bonar Law, who had tried, during the war, to brush aside Borden's demand that Westminster supply Canada with "more explicit information from time to time respecting conduct of the war." Law, the Canadian-born Colonial Secretary (later to become Britain's first Canadian-born Prime Minister), had replied that this wasn't "practicable," and with that arrogance toward colonials which so often betrays an ex-colonial, had notified Borden, moreover, that it was "very undesirable that the question should be raised."

Borden, who obviously was expected to apologize for his meddle-someness, steamed right back. "It can hardly be expected that we shall put four hundred thousand or five hundred thousand men in the field and willingly accept the position of having no more voice and receiving no more consideration than if we were toy automata. Any person cherishing such an expectation harbors an unfortunate and even dangerous delusion. Is this war being waged by the United Kingdom alone or is it being waged by the whole Empire? If I am correct in supposing that the second hypothesis must be accepted, then why do the statesmen of the British Isles arrogate to themselves solely the methods by which it shall be carried on . . . ?

"It is for them to suggest the method and not for us. If there is no available method and if we are expected to continue in the role of automata the whole situation must be reconsidered.

"Procrastination, indecision, inertia, doubt and hesitation and many other undesirable qualities have made themselves entirely too conspicuous in this war. During my recent visit to England a very prominent cabinet minister in speaking to the officers of another department said that he did not call them traitors but he asserted that they could not have acted differently if they had been traitors. . . . Another very able cabinet minister spoke of the shortage of guns, rifles, munitions, etc., but declared that the chief shortage was of brains."

This blunt communication was not addressed directly to Bonar Law, who by this time was Chancellor of the Exchequer and leader of the House of Commons, but to the Canadian High Commissioner, Sir George Perley.

Perley, however, passed it on either unexpurgated or in only slightly edited form, for Law almost immediately sent Borden a mass of documents so secret that they required—or perhaps for strategic reasons Law only pretended they required—the full panoply of the cloak and dagger. The papers crossed the Atlantic by hand. "They came," Borden recalled in his postwar memoirs, "in a strong canvas bag loaded heavily with lead. On the voyage this bag was kept on the bridge under direction to throw it overboard in case the ship should be subject to capture." Law urged Borden to show them to no one and burn them after reading.

A few months later, with the air of a man announcing a blinding discovery, a new Colonial Secretary informed Borden through the Governor General: "His Majesty's Government feel that fuller information should be given of the progress of events and of war policy than may have been possible hitherto and I think the most convenient way will be that I should send you a weekly letter for the personal and confidential information of yourself and your Prime Minister."

Almost simultaneously the British government announced the formation of an Imperial War Cabinet, which met at frequent intervals throughout the last two years of the war. Borden was in constant attendance, as, of course, were statesmen from the other dominions. There is no evidence to show that the Imperial War Cabinet took, or was asked to take, any crucial decisions in the actual conduct of the war. The decisions for all the British armed forces were still made by Lloyd George and Douglas Haig, frequently after one of their violent rows. But the Imperial War Cabinet at least offered Borden and the hitherto almost unheard-of and unheard-from leaders of the other dominions a forum in which they could speak their minds and be sure of an audience. A far more important assembly was the Imperial War Conference, summoned in 1917 to discuss political and economic relationships within the Empire and their possible readjustment after the war. Borden saw an opportunity here to get it firmly on the record that the dominions and India were entitled to a say in Imperial foreign policy. Accordingly, he sought out a noted fellow delegate, General Jan Christiaan Smuts of South Africa.

Smuts, though still in his forties, was already a world figure of the first magnitude. He had fought with distinction against the British in the Boer War and when honorable defeat became inevitable had thrown his full weight behind Louis Botha in pledging a genuine and workable peace.

Borden and Smuts had never met before, but each man already knew the other as an ally. Together they prepared a resolution which called for the preservation of "all existing powers of self-government . . . complete control of domestic affairs . . . full recognition of the Dominions as autonomous nations" and recognition, as well of "the right of the Dominions and India to an adequate voice in foreign policy and in foreign relations." To make sure the goal did not disappear in a thicket of generalizations, they demanded specifically that, once the war was over, arrangements be made for "continuous consultation in all matters of common Imperial concern, and for such necessary concerted action, founded on consultation, as the several Governments might determine."

Before they presented their resolution—the Canadian was the mover, the South African the seconder—Borden and Smuts enlisted the support not only of Australia, New Zealand, and Newfoundland but of Lloyd George and the British War Cabinet. Shortly after the formality of its passage was completed, Smuts told his new friend: "You and I have transformed the structure of the British Empire." Time was to prove the claim held a good deal of truth, although the ultimate transformation did not follow the Borden-Smuts blueprint in all its details. In both their countries a good deal of opposition was already developing to the idea of centralization of the Empire, a common foreign policy, and any threat of automatic involvement in the affairs of Whitehall and Downing Street.

Borden's last major acts as Prime Minister were also concerned, not with domestic affairs, but with the dominions' new position in the world.

Outside the Commonwealth, the changes in that magnificent and mysterious temple had gone almost unnoticed. At the peace conference and later at the charter meetings of the League of Nations and the International Labor Convention, Clemenceau of France, Wilson of the United States, and other influential foreigners found it almost impossible to understand why the dominions kept insisting on their separate delegations. London had always spoken for them all before; why not now? The fact that Lloyd George upheld the dominions in their demands only confirmed Clemenceau and Wil-

son in their suspicion that a master plan was afoot to give the
Empire voting control of the postwar world. But Borden could
see no equity in the arrangements first proposed for the peace conference: five delegates each from Britain, the United States, France,
Italy, and Japan; two each for the smaller Allied nations; none for
the dominions. In one of his infrequent attempts at humor he reminded Botha of South Africa of the need to "hold our own with
Patagonia."

Ultimately Canada, South Africa, India, and Australia were given
two delegates each and New Zealand one. In addition, India and
the four dominions were represented in the British delegation
through a series of revolving panels. And—Borden considered this
an even more significant triumph—the dominions signed the peace
treaty separately.

The battle had to be fought all over again, and on precisely the
same ground, as the scene shifted from Paris to Geneva. The right
of the dominions to seek election to the council of the League
and the governing body of the new labor organization was once
more challenged. The United States delegation led the opposition.

Borden turned plain ugly. Less than ten years before, he had
been half scared to death at the prospect of fighting an election
against Sir Wilfrid Laurier, and less than five years before, he had
allowed himself to be bullied like a schoolboy by the impecunious
millionaires Mackenzie and Mann and by the blustering Sam
Hughes. But now the quiet country lawyer from Grand Pré stood
in awe of no one.

In an angry letter to Lloyd George he accused the United States
—without going so far as a formal indictment—of trying to pack
the League with Pan-American satellites while trying to deny full
membership rights to the British dominions. "The Dominions," he
wrote angrily, "have maintained their place before the world during the past five years through sacrifices which no nation outside
of Europe has known. I am confident that the people of Canada
will not tamely submit to a dictation which declares that Liberia
or Cuba, Panama or Hedjaz, Haiti or Ecuador, must have a higher
place . . . than can be accorded to their own country." It was clear,
he said, that Canada's Parliament might order the country's withdrawal from both the Labor Convention and the League.

Lloyd George, who had been too preoccupied with other conference problems to give the dominions much active support, now

became alarmed. He promised to tackle President Wilson again. In a day or two Borden was invited to draft a set of proposed amendments to the Labor Convention and the covenant of the League and give them to the Big Three for their private consideration. In doing so he was unable to resist the opportunity to restate his country's basic position in somewhat more measured terms:

"Canada's effort in this struggle for democracy speaks for itself. She has not asked for representation on the Council or in the governing body unless it is accorded by the voice of the other members of the League and of the Convention. She has raised no objection to the nomination of Spain or Brazil, of whom one was at least neutral and the other took no active part in the war. But she cannot admit disqualification or accept a position inferior to that of the smaller States alluded to in the letter of April 29th.

"It is now proposed that Canada should become party to a Treaty by which she shall undertake to engage in active warlike operations against Germany in case that country at any time in the future should be guilty of aggression against France. I am not aware that any similar undertaking is proposed for Spain or Brazil or Greece or Belgium, or for any of the smaller states whose representatives are not debarred from election to the Council of the League or to the governing body of the Labour Convention. Canada is asked to make way for all these states except when effort and sacrifice are demanded; then, but not till then, she is accorded full and even prior representation. She is to be in the first line of the battle, but not even in the back seat of the Council. The submission of such a proposal to our Parliament would, in my opinion, be wholly futile. Indeed, I am convinced that it would be resented not only by Parliament but by the vast majority of the Canadian people."

Borden delivered his memo in person to Lloyd George. In spite of the considerable amount of steam he had got rid of, he was still fuming. As the two men sat chatting, Woodrow Wilson's name came up. Borden's blood pressure rose at once. Wilson, he growled, was sometimes as obstinate as a mule. Lloyd George laughed uneasily. "For heaven's sake," he implored, "don't look at me like that."

Almost by the hour the placid gentleman from Nova Scotia was accumulating new evidence that in the world of high diplomacy it didn't always pay to be too diplomatic. He had met Lloyd George just after breakfast. Just before lunch he was informed that the Big Three had agreed to support his amendments. During the morning's wait he had had ample time for second thoughts. As a lawyer he knew that lawyer's language—even when, as in this case, it was his own—often contains unsuspected loopholes.

No sooner had he received the news of the Big Three's acceptance of his proposals than he pressed in to spell his victory out in layman's language. Borden wrote the memorandum himself, and Lloyd George took it back into the private meeting room in the Quai d'Orsay where Clemenceau and Wilson were waiting to adjourn. It was signed.

"The question having been raised as to the meaning of Article IV of the League of Nations Covenant, we have been requested by Sir Robert Borden to state whether we concur in his view, that upon the true construction of the first and second paragraphs of that Article, representatives of the self-governing Dominions of the British Empire may be selected or named as members of the Council. We have no hesitation in expressing our entire concurrence in this view. If there were any doubt it would be entirely removed by the fact that the Articles of the Covenant are not subject to narrow or technical construction.

Dated at the Quai d'Orsay, Paris, the sixth day of May, 1919.

(*sgd.*) G. CLEMENCEAU
WOODROW WILSON
D. LLOYD GEORGE"

When Borden returned to Canada two weeks later he had a massive due bill awaiting him. He had been borrowing so long and so heavily from his reserves of health and strength that he was now literally exhausted. At the end of the year he announced his intention of resigning as Prime Minister and as leader of his party. The Cabinet persuaded him to postpone the decision until he had had a long rest, but after several months of travel he still found himself weak and tired. In mid-July 1920 he escorted his successor to the residence of the Governor General.

Along with the new decade, a new era in Canadian history had already begun. To what extent its legacy of growth, achievement, pride, and honorable strife was a legacy from Robert Laird Borden, not even those who said their farewells to him in person were agreed upon. Today hardly anyone says that he was a bad Prime Minister. Hardly anyone says that he was better than a merely good one. Sandwiched in history between the glittering Laurier and the suffocatingly durable Mackenzie King, he has seemed more and more normal to each succeeding generation, and therefore less and less exciting, and therefore less and less significant. Whether time will revise this judgment upward, no one can say. But if a public servant's net worth is the sum of his useful actions, minus his mistakes, multiplied by his difficulties, then Borden deserves his country's gratitude.

XXII

*The advent of Arthur Meighen—The expensive
luxury of lecturing Mackenzie King*

WHEN he left Rideau Hall on July 10, 1920, Arthur Meighen had just been sworn in as the youngest Prime Minister since Confederation. Besides his comparative youth—he was forty-six—he had great energy, a first-rate mind, a gift for oratory at least as impressive as Laurier's or Bourassa's, and a dozen years' experience in Parliament, the last seven as a cabinet minister.

He had everything he needed to succeed—except a chance to succeed. His prospects as Prime Minister were already hopeless before he became Prime Minister.

Among those who have studied Meighen's troubled career, the orthodox view is that on the day he succeeded Borden the world was his oyster; his failure to pry it open arose from defects of judgment and personality which became apparent only later on. It is, of course, incontestable that he made disastrous mistakes both as Prime Minister and as leader of the Opposition, and it is equally incontestable that the damage his mistakes caused him was usually aggravated by his cold, unyielding way with people. But long before Borden chose him as his heir, Meighen had more enemies than any politician can easily afford. Some he earned by his virtues, some he suffered for his faults. Some simply gravitated to him through circumstances he was too proud and independent to try to control.

Borden and Meighen first met on the platform of a railway station at Portage la Prairie, Manitoba, during the last year of the Boer War. Borden, still relatively new to his unwanted job as leader of the Opposition, was making his first trip through the West in the forlorn hope of shaking Laurier's grip on the farm vote. Though there was time for only a few words and a brief handshake, he was sufficiently impressed to make a few mental notes of the tall, apparently shy but obviously ambitious young lawyer from Ontario. When, six years and two general elections later, Meighen turned up on the Tory back benches in the House of Commons, he had already been put down as a man to watch. In 1913, two years after Borden's first government came to power, Meighen was made Solicitor General. For a politician of ordinary talent and ordinary temperament, this might have been the start of a long and steady rise; for the brilliant, icily egotistical Meighen, it was the beginning of the end.

As Borden found more and more of his time taken up by the central direction of the war and the growing demands of overseas diplomacy, he felt more and more the need of strong support from his Cabinet. There was no embarrassment of riches here. Sir Thomas White was showing qualities close to genius as Minister of Finance, but the job took all his time. Sir George Foster in Trade and Commerce was experienced, shrewd, and able, but he was growing too old for extra duties. Sam Hughes was causing enough trouble in his own department. Frederick Monk, who bore the title Minister of Public Works, was in reality a sort of ambassador from Quebec. Most of the other ministers were, at best, competent nonentities. The creation of the Unionist coalition in 1917 did little to improve the situation. The inevitable result was that the youthful, energetic, self-confident Meighen received and welcomed far more than his share of thorny and politically dangerous assignments.

It was Meighen who was given the job of investigating the mysterious J. Wesley Allison and other munitions profiteers. This undoubtedly raised his stock among the taxpayers, at least for a while, but some of his fellow Tories considered him unnecessarily zealous in searching out scandals for which the government itself had to bear the final blame. Sam Hughes once cursed him out loud in Borden's office.

It was Meighen who, as noted in an earlier chapter, was given the job of prolonging the ermined agony of Mackenzie and Mann when the king and the duke showed up on Parliament Hill in early 1914 demanding another forty-five million dollars. Meighen drafted the enabling legislation and fought it through against savage opposition, perhaps the most savage of all coming from another young Conservative lawyer and Prime Minister-to-be named Richard Bedford Bennett. Bennett, as a former counsel for the Canadian

Pacific, may have had special reasons for his special bitterness against the Canadian Northern and its promoters. Whether this was so or not, he did not hesitate to practice his gift for invective on the parliamentary colleague who was trying to defend and succor them.

It was Meighen who, apparently at his own suggestion and with no recorded twinge of conscience, invented and rammed into law the Wartime Elections Act of 1917. This shameless piece of gerry-mandering conferred a special franchise on the female relatives of soldiers and took the vote away from so-called "enemy aliens" who had been naturalized Canadians for less than fifteen years, and it had its desired effects. The first provision settled any doubt about the ultimate passage of conscription. The two provisions together broke the resistance of a handful of influential Liberals who had been holding out against Borden's repeated invitations to join him in a Union government. They also made it virtually certain that wherever Meighen was to go in the future he would have to go against the massed opposition of Quebec. And if any doubt had remained on this point, it was Meighen who, after the 1917 election, was given the job of escorting conscription officially and finally into the statutes.

As a Tory, a protectionist, and an Easterner, Meighen from the first had had to overcome the suspicion of the prairie farmers among whom he had chosen to live. After the Winnipeg strike labor held him in deep suspicion. He had by then been shifted to the Ministry of the Interior and with Senator Gideon Robertson, the Minister of Labor, was appointed one of Borden's two emissaries to the scene of the trouble. The strike leaders charged that neither cabinet minister ever sought or offered to give their side of the case a hearing. Meighen had not been in the city twenty-four hours before he was quoted as having said: "It is up to the citizens of Winnipeg to stand firm and resist the efforts made here to overturn proper authority. . . . There is absolutely no justification for the general strike." This was an honest and highly tenable point of view honestly put, but Meighen's willingness to put it before listening to a word of testimony from the strikers gave a certain edge to a Liberal M.P.'s charge that he was "the last man in the world to be selected as a mediator or conciliator . . . he stands in Canada as the apostle of arbitrary enactments and despotic legislation." A message of Meighen's to a Department of Justice representative—

not made public until some years later—would have added weight
to the charge if its contents had been made known then. On the
day the chief strike leaders were arrested the Minister of the Interior wired this advice: "Notwithstanding any doubt I have as to the
technical legality of the arrests and the detention at Stony Mountain,
I feel that rapid deportation is the best course now that the arrests
are made, and later we can consider ratification."

But Meighen's greatest handicap was not the unendearing things
his sense of national duty, party loyalty, and his perpetual rightness compelled him to do. A still greater handicap was the way he
did them—a reflection, as old George Foster put it, of his inability
to "curb a somewhat ebullient and acid and antagonizing criticism
and biting rejoinder."

This weakness could lead him into follies of the most pointless
kind. He treated the House of Commons to a particularly gratui-
tous example two weeks after William Lyon Mackenzie King had
made his first speech as Laurier's successor and leader of the Opposition. Some twenty-five years earlier, the two men had been
classmates at the University of Toronto, occasional rivals in the
student debates at Hart House, and good enough friends that
Meighen addressed King by his nickname Rex. Now that they
found themselves in opposite camps politically, each of them moving up fast, Meighen felt some compulsion to establish their rivalry
as a personal matter and so proclaim it to all the world.

King's maiden speech as Liberal leader had not been a great
success, a circumstance which only accented the heavy-handedness
with which Meighen "complimented" him on it. "The courtesies
of debate" demanded that a speech by the leader of the Opposition
receive the attention of a reply—"even though," Meighen added,
"that address be little more than a repetition, perhaps for the
tenth time, of the same remarks uttered by himself as well as by
many of his followers."

The usually sophisticated Meighen went on with his speech. He
was suddenly helpless under the spell of his own campus oratory.
"The congratulations," he continued, "of honorable gentlemen on
this side of the House are due however to the leader of the Opposition by reason of the very manifest evidence of the determination
on the part of his followers to show fidelity to his leadership—
evidence that came frequently to our ears in the way of applause
and which was all the more pronounced and impressive when we

recall the long succession of demagogic platitudes that evoked that applause. He read a lecture which he has read, I think, every time he has stood upon his feet since he entered the House about duties to the people of members of the Government and members of the House, duties that I venture in all humility to suggest every member of this House was thoroughly aware of, thoroughly conscious of, long before the House received this rather nauseating reminder from the honorable gentleman."

On Demosthenes plunged, having sport at the expense of the village idiot: "If I have one suggestion to offer to the fair rose of expectancy of His Majesty's loyal Opposition, it is that when we have a concrete subject before the House for debate he would be good enough to offer some remarks which really bear upon the merits of the issue and leave out of consideration, if he possibly can, these old, hackneyed phrases, 'democracy,' 'autocracy of executives' and all the rest of it which have no more relevancy to this discussion than were he to discuss the merits of the government of Japan."

When it became King's duty, a few months later, to congratulate his tormentor on the latter's accession to the office of Prime Minister, he turned a cheek as round and innocent as a newborn babe's. "Perhaps," he beamed across the floor of the Commons, "the Prime Minister will permit me to say in public what I have already said to him privately: that on personal grounds it was to me a source both of pride and of pleasure to learn that His Excellency had chosen as his first adviser one who in university days was a fellow undergraduate and whose friendship, through a quarter of a century, has survived the vicissitudes of time, not excepting the differences of party warfare and the acrimonies of political debate. I can promise him that in seeking to fulfill the demands of public obligation I shall strive with him to preserve the highest traditions of our public life, and to be governed in all things by its amenities and never by its animosities."

No doubt the acerb Meighen squirmed under this ooze as King had never squirmed under Meighen's lash. *More damned platitudes! More damned cant! What a wretched little man poor little Rex has become!* Meighen might have found the occasion more challenging if he had known that King's real thoughts had been set down in a letter to a friend just before Meighen became Prime Minister: "My impression is that Sir Thomas White will be chosen. If he is not, it will probably be Meighen. White is in every way a better stamp of man for Prime Minister. Meighen . . . lacks frankness in debate; he is a Tory of the Tories. Sir Thomas White is a man of character and ability. For the country's sake, I should prefer to see Sir Thomas White chosen. Politically, it would be an advantage to our party were Meighen selected."

And Meighen might have found the future less disastrous if he had been able to read a more recent, ominously non-platitudinous entry in King's diary: "I could not help exclaiming 'Good for him' when I read of Meighen having won out, and achieved his ambition, immediately I added, walking up and down with feelings of satisfaction, 'It is too good to be true.' Meighen is a Tory through and through, the very antithesis of myself in thought and feeling on political matters. I can fight him naturally, the issues will become clear and distinct. The hypocrisy of a false union in the Gov't will be more than ever disclosed. It is the beginning of a speedy end to the Unionist administration."

King was not the only man who saw trouble ahead for Meighen. Although the Tory backbenchers, in the main, stood in awe of him, it was a different story in the Cabinet, where both Meighen and the political realities were better known. Borden circulated a ballot among his parliamentary followers. The party's spear-bearers gave Meighen a clear majority. But three members of the Cabinet —C. J. Doherty in Justice, J. A. Calder in Immigration and Colonization, and C. C. Ballentyne in Marine and Fisheries and Naval Service—announced they were still unwilling to serve under him. Calder put it bluntly in a brief note to the retiring Prime Minister: "I am convinced Meighen is absolutely out of the question in so far as Quebec is concerned. In addition I know that several ministers will immediately retire should he be the choice. In case however it is decided to revert to the old order of things and reconstruct the Conservative Party in the hope of success at the second general election it might be advisable to select Meighen as leader at this time. Personally however I doubt very much the wisdom of this course as I do not think Meighen possesses the necessary qualities to ensure his success as a leader at any time in the future."

Through one last tour de force of persistence, Borden wore the holdouts down and won them to a grudging acceptance of his grudgingly chosen heir. The Age of the Aging Turks was now begun and Arthur Meighen stood briefly in its forefront, partly of it, partly in its way, and doomed to become its first serious casualty.

XXIII

*William Lyon Mackenzie King—The two women
in his life—The labor conciliator and
the disciple of Laurier*

MY desire, my inclination, is all for politics: Mackenzie King,
diary, January 1919.

Although he was six months and one day younger than the
"youthful" Meighen, when they met as rival leaders of the country's
two great political parties King was, in everything except the
professional and physical senses, an old man. Emotionally and
spiritually he was already a tragic prisoner of the past, lonely cura-
tor of a treasure house of family memories beclouded by misfor-
tune, and victim of a mother complex of almost frightening per-
vasiveness. And in the years not far ahead he was to become the
acolyte of a private cult of mysticism in which the dead and the
living conversed in everyday language about everyday matters;
in which stone and marble ruins gathered from the corners of the
earth and spread over the lovely Gatineau Hills had a meaning for
him and him alone; in which, during the last quarter century of
his life, the only animate things for which he could find love and
affection were a series of Irish terriers named Pat.

Throughout his public career, the complexity of King's inner
nature and inner thoughts remained largely hidden, even to his
closest associates. He had his own kind of reserve, but most people
who came in contact with it put it down, unlike Meighen's reserve,
to shyness rather than to the lack of human warmth. The country
King ruled so long saw him mainly as orthodox, almost boringly
respectable, not a stand-patter but far from the radical he imagined
himself to be—one of the few people whom the labels small-*l*
liberal and small-*c* conservative seemed to suit equally well and
without serious contradiction.

Certainly there had been nothing in his first forty-five years to suggest that King's round, Tweedledum-like figure concealed strange depths and chasms. This was before the age of amateur psychiatry, and to the naked eye King seemed as cheerful, commonplace, and well adjusted as an elderly waitress at Childs.

For any visible sign of excitement in the early biographical details, it was necessary to go back to a time long before King was born. These were the half-heroic, half-lunatic years in the late 1830s when King's grandfather, the first mayor of Toronto, led an armed revolt against the overfed despots who ruled Upper Canada, met with an ignominious rout, and was forced to flee into exile. William Lyon Mackenzie's daughter Isabel was born in New York seven years before her father was allowed to come home under an amnesty. Although in later years the Little Rebel began to have a few second thoughts about his early life, his daughter's passionate devotion to his memory never wavered. She gave her first son her father's full name and in countless tales and little sermons imparted to him her own fierce pride in bearing her father's blood.

Somewhere in King's boyhood the two blazing shadows changed places. The part that belonged to his grandfather never grew less, but the part that belonged to his mother grew constantly greater. From his early youth almost until his death, it was not merely the strongest force in his personal life, it was almost the only force. At times his life was vastly enriched by it, at times almost engulfed.

Isabel King was an easy woman to love, full of cheerful spirits in spite of her iron character and iron will, a gay and affectionate companion to her husband and their two daughters and two sons. Willie left their home in Berlin, Ontario, before his seventeenth birthday to begin his higher education at the University of Toronto. Throughout his five years there and during his later postgraduate studies at the University of Chicago and at Harvard he corresponded steadily and tenderly not only with his mother but with his father, his brother, and his two sisters.

It was through this correspondence that the world not long ago learned of King's first and last full-fledged encounter with romantic love. For good and obvious reasons the custodians of King's papers have permitted the lady in the case to be referred to only as Miss —.

In 1897, while he was in Chicago, King fell ill of typhoid fever.

During his three weeks in hospital he and one of his nurses formed an attachment which not only survived his transfer to Harvard but grew in ardor. Within a year King was on the verge of proposing. So great was the spell of family loyalty that he prepared his conscience by invoking the ghostly blessing of his grandfather Mackenzie. "His mantle has fallen upon me," he promised his diary staunchly, "and it shall be taken up and worn. I never felt it could be done before. I see it now. With Miss —— by my side I can stand out against all the world and stand out I will. His voice, his words, shall be heard in Canada again and the cause he so nobly fought shall be carried on."

But if the Little Rebel was not in a position to demur, Willie's living relatives were under no such handicap. They were shocked and horrified at the idea of his marrying before he was well embarked on a career. They were shocked and horrified at the idea of his marrying a nurse, a profession then considered socially somewhere between parlormaid and governess. Although Willie was a grown man of almost twenty-four, they were plainly shocked at the idea of his marrying at all.

His sister Jennie wrote him plaintively. "What we all did hope and believe was that you would make a name for yourself that would help us all. You will never know the sacrifices that have been made for you."

His father wrote him sternly. "I can conceive of scarcely anything that would be more prejudicial to yourself and those whom you love. . . . You have a position and prospects now that, if wisely used, will make your future, but otherwise not. If you do what you think of doing, you will simply blast your prospects and all the hopes we have so fondly cherished. . . . I had confidently counted on your giving me very valuable assistance [in providing for the family]; no one can do as much for sisters as a brother, and especially one who has your opportunities. Say and think and feel what you like, your striking out on your own account in the way you have spoken of means an end to all such hopes and expectations. I think your first duty is to those at home; it is a duty that should outweigh every other consideration."

His mother wrote him tearfully. "The struggles have been long and hard at home and I think you will not think me selfish when I say I had counted on you to help lift the cloud. Things are looking brighter than they were but no matter *which way* we turn it must take time to lift the burden off our shoulders. I have built castles without number for you. Are all these dreams but to end in dreams? I am getting old now Willie and disappointment wearies and the heart grows sick. Sometimes when I hear you talk so much what you would do for those that suffer I think charity begins at home and as you do so shall it be done unto you. I am not grasping for myself but I do feel for your sisters and I know you who have such a big heart will not forsake me."

Sadly for all of them, there was more than mere possessiveness behind these pleas. Although Willie had financed his own post-graduate studies almost wholly through scholarships and occasional bits of journalism, his father was in debt. After a promising start, John King's career as a lawyer had gone sour and he was reduced to scheming for jobs in the public service.

For once the younger King, later to earn renown as one of the world's greatest compromisers, could find no way to compromise. He tried, all through a long and tortured summer. Tried through letters to his father, to his sisters, to his mother, a torrent of letters to the baffled and unhappy Miss ——; hopeful letters, despairing letters, self-justifying letters, self-accusing letters. At times he feared he was close to a nervous breakdown. At last, in September 1898, a year and a half after their first meeting, the ill-starred lovers agreed to part. Miss —— married within two years. King, of course, remained a bachelor throughout his life.

Partly perhaps because of a need to sublimate his disappointment, partly perhaps because of a need to feel she had been right and therefore that he had been right in heeding her advice, King now became almost wholly dependent on his mother for emotional warmth and surcease.

From that point on his diary is full of filial sighs (and if the prose calls to mind the plush and genteel dust of Victoria's time, why not? Victoria was still Queen). "Mother is such a little girl. She is so bright, cheerful, good, happy and lovely. She has so much grit and courage in her. I have met no woman so true & lovely a woman as my mother." And then, ten months after the break with Miss ——: "If I can only win such a wife as I have such a mother, how infinitely happy!"

And, after a visit from his mother in Ottawa: "I feel very sorry to see her go and have felt a sad loneliness every time I have thought of her which has been very often. She is, I think, the purest and sweetest soul that God ever made. She is all tenderness & love, all devotion, knows nothing of selfishness and thinks only of others. Her heart has explained to me the mystery of God's creation and she lives in the light of His love. It is like coming near to an angel to be with her, and where she has been there is a holy calm and purity seems to remain when she has gone. The more I think & see of her the more I love her and the greater do I believe her to be. She is as young too in heart & feeling as a girl of 15, in beauty she is wonderfully fair. Everyone looks with admiration on her."

His letters were equally devoted: "I have no less than five photographs of you in my room, three on the mantel over the grate, one hanging in a frame and one in the Cedar of Lebanon frame. One I often take down & put on my table as I have it now, and when I read Margaret Ogilvie I had it in my hand most of the time. But these pictures are less often before me than the image of you I have constantly in my mind. Trenholm said to me one night, 'There is no mistaking who your sweetheart is!' "

King still had a few warily platonic flirtations to side-step before his bachelorhood was confirmed and more or less accepted. Ten years after his first meeting with Miss —— Sir Wilfrid Laurier himself tried to interest him in a young widow. "The right person would be a great help to you in public life," Sir Wilfrid observed, and then went on to describe the widow as being good, clever, kind, capable, and rich. King agreed to meet her at Laurier's home but fled as soon as he decently could and reassured his diary: "Unless she can surpass in my judgment any woman I have yet seen as the one with whose nature my nature could best blend, I will not allow wealth, position or aught else to tempt me. . . . I will never be controlled save by my heart."

His heart belonged to Mother until his earthly end. Even now, a decade after his death and four decades after hers, his favorite oil painting of her still hangs in the study of King's Ottawa residence, overlooking her son's favorite leather chesterfield. The same light he kept burning before it for forty years still burns night and day.

Isabel King did not live to see her son in the office of Prime Minister—nor, in fact, did she ever demand that he rise to any explicit position in any explicit field. All she asked was that he make the most of himself and his opportunities.

And this part of her dream she did see well on the way to ful-

fillment. Between scholarships at Chicago and Harvard he took a
summer job on the Toronto *Mail and Empire* and persuaded the
editor to turn him loose among the scandalous sweatshops of the
garment industry. He found girls as young as nine being paid as little
as a dollar a week, and took clippings of his four carefully doc-
umented stories to William Mulock, who as Postmaster General was
also in charge of federal labor affairs. Mulock gave him a hundred
dollars in pay and a hundred dollars in expenses to find out whether
his own postal department was buying mailbags and postmen's uniforms from sweatshops. King's answer, received in due course, was
such a convincing "Yes!" that the Post Office drew up a new
contract form requiring its suppliers to improve wages, hours, and
sanitary conditions. Shortly afterward other government departments followed suit on Sir Wilfrid Laurier's personal instructions.

Three years later, as King was completing his formal education
on a tour of Europe, Mulock offered him the job of editor and
manager of a new government publication to be called the *Labour
Gazette*. King had his heart set on a teaching appointment at
Harvard, but the only opening there was uncertain and part-time,
and after a good deal of soul searching he accepted the Ottawa
offer. Soon he was Deputy Minister of Labor and a star performer
in the new science called Conciliation. His instinct and his intelligence both told him that real social justice still lay well beyond
the horizon and that in any given dispute between the employer
and the workingman, the preponderance of right was almost certain to be on the side of the workingman. But his realism also told
him that it would be folly to attempt to achieve too much too soon.

It was from this basic position—sympathy for the worker, patience with the boss—that he approached forty-one separate labor
disputes and achieved settlements in thirty-nine of them. He wrote
two important laws requiring a cooling-off period and a conciliation hearing before there could be a strike or lockout in a mine, a
railway, or any other public utility. His reputation as a negotiator
spread so quickly that President Teddy Roosevelt borrowed him
from Laurier to go to England and warn the British government,
secretly, to warn the Japanese government, secretly, to stop sending emigrants to the United States. (This remarkable channel of
communication was recommended, in Roosevelt's judgment, by two
considerations: first, Britain and Japan were allies; second, King had
already managed to persuade the Japanese government to accept

"voluntarily" a Canadian policy of discrimination against immigrants from the Far East.)

By 1906, to the disgust and indignation of many other senior
civil servants, the young Deputy Minister of Labor was made a
Commander of the Order of St. Michael and St. George. He already
had a firm understanding with Laurier that he would soon be leaving the civil service to go into politics and that, if all went well,
Labor would be set up as a separate department and he would be its
first minister. All this shortly took place according to plan.

In 1908 he was nominated Liberal candidate for his home constituency of Waterloo North and won the seat comfortably as
Laurier went back into office with another handsome majority.
For the last two years of the Laurier administration he served un-
eventfully and unspectacularly as Labor Minister—and then, after
the election of 1911, found himself rejected, unemployed, and half
stunned amid the wreckage of Laurier's reciprocity treaty and
naval bill.

For several months after the 1911 election defeat the rejected
young ex-minister scarcely knew where to turn. The sudden reversal of his fortunes was difficult enough to absorb in itself. To
add to his anguish, Laurier seemed to be growing cooler toward
him. This ought not to have surprised him, for during the election
campaign King's support of the two main Laurier policies had been
oblique and halfhearted. The simple fact was that two out of three
voters in his riding were of German descent and a high proportion
were engaged in manufacturing. The idea of trying to sell them
on arming against Germany and also surrendering their tariff protection struck the hardheaded, ambitious young Labor Minister as
so dangerous that, while he could not disassociate himself from the
party platform, he could and did contain his enthusiasm for it.
Laurier never rebuked him directly, nor were the two men ever close
to a break. Nevertheless, King waited in vain for his chief to persuade some dispensable backbencher to resign his seat in the House
of Commons in the defeated cabinet member's favor.

As he did so often in moments of confusion and doubt, King
turned to his Maker. God, he was certain six weeks after the
debacle and so wrote in his diary, still had him singled out as a
future Prime Minister. But then he fell into a long period of depression. The divine mandate momentarily forgotten, he talked of

abandoning politics forever, reflecting gloomily: "I thought how odd in a way it was that with the kind of ability I have & service I might be rendering I should in a sense be walking the streets."

But walk the streets he continued to do, in the figurative sense, for another two and a half years. He refused to consider going into business. He turned down an invitation to work for a newspaper at what, for those times, would have been a highly respectable salary, and kept himself and his family going on the income from his savings, a £300 annual gift from a friend in London, and a $2500-a-year job writing speeches and propaganda for the party.

He remained marooned thus until mid-1914. And then, miraculously, a golden sail hove into sight. Above it flew the ensign of the richest man in the world, John D. Rockefeller.

XXIV

King and the Rockefellers—Mother Jones and the Colorado mines—A plan that worked

THE Rockefellers were just coming to grips with a discovery that had been causing distress to reformed privateers for several thousand years: It is not always possible to wipe out the past simply by hauling down the skull and crossbones. John D., Sr., his early raids on the American economy far behind him, was in retirement, jovially doling out his personal dimes to golf caddies and small boys and his newly formed foundation's millions to worthy charities. John D., Jr., was busy trying, among other things, to improve the family's record and reputation as an employer. But to the consternation of both, the name of Rockefeller had entered the language not merely as a name but as a word. To millions it had become and stubbornly remained a symbol of all that was reactionary and cruel in American Big Business.

This truth had come home to them with sickening impact in the coal mines of Colorado. All the major mines had gone on strike there in September 1913. Superficially the main issue was recognition of the United Mine Workers of America, but there were other issues far more grave and fundamental. Most of the grimy, strong-backed men digging coal in the mountain wilderness of southern Colorado were immigrants from Italy, the Balkans, and Mexico who knew little of collective bargaining and cared little about its principles. But they knew too well that the abundant, generous America of their dreams had failed them, herded them somehow into company houses in company towns, put them into perpetual debt to company stores at company-dictated wages of a thousand dollars a year, provided them with no local government but the company, no means of seeking redress from their real or fancied grievances except by appealing from one foreman or manager to another. In a post-mortem report on the strike, an official investigator for the United States Commission on Industrial Relations summed up their condition in these words: "This domination has been carried to such an extreme that two entire counties of Southern Colorado have been deprived of popular government, while large groups of their citizens have been stripped of their liberties, robbed of portions of their earnings, subjected to ruthless persecution and abuse, and reduced to a state of economic and political serfdom."

The other side of the coin was just as ugly. Under the auspices of the Western Federation of Miners, now supplanted by the U.M.W., union organizers in the high-rock country of Colorado, Idaho, Nevada, and Montana had built their own record of brutality and cynicism. One Federation thug alone, a former Ontario farm boy who lived under the name of Harry Orchard, gunned down or blew up at least twenty men, including a former state governor. Orchard had been caught by now and jailed for life and his chief employer was left unpunished only through the skill of the greatest of criminal lawyers, Clarence Darrow, but the tradition of union lawlessness still gaped like a raw wound. No charge that capital could make against labor or labor against capital was so lurid that it could not easily be proved by a selection of already proved facts. Between the two extremes there was little room for reason or for mercy.

The union organizers in Colorado prepared for the inevitable walkout by leasing land outside the company towns and putting up a forest of tents. At the designated hour nine thousand miners marched across the flinty canyon floors and mountain ledges beside their wives and children.

From then on events in Colorado followed the course of a nightmarish cliché, the plot of a bad proletarian play. The company guards came in. More organizers came in. The strikebreakers came in. Rocks flew, names were called. The state militia came in.

Miraculously, the bloodshed did not begin until seven months after the walkout. Then a head-on clash outside Ludlow, Colorado. Six miners shot to death. Two women and eleven children trapped and suffocated in dugout cellars when the militia—thinking that men with guns must be below—poured paraffin on and set fire to the tents above.

As all the world knew by nightfall, the biggest of the mine employers was the Colorado Fuel & Iron Company and the biggest shareholders in Colorado Fuel & Iron were John D. Rockefeller, Sr., and his son. The name their lavish philanthropies had begun to raise from the mud was abruptly dragged down again. Pickets marched before their head office on Broadway. Newspapers and magazines, many of them no more radical than the Rockefellers themselves, asked pointed questions. President Wilson allowed it to be known that he was among those interested in hearing the answers.

John D., Jr., was summarily hauled before a special subcommittee of Congress. His lame, ill-informed testimony clearly demonstrated neither he nor his father had any real conception of their guilt. They had been perfectly content to follow the traditional dictum of the absentee proprietor: "Put a good man in charge. If he does a bad job, fire him. If he does a good job, leave him alone." Under this venerable rule it was easy and almost mandatory to accept the monthly reports from their Denver office at their precise face value. Who was in a better position than the officials on the spot to say whether the men really wanted a union or whether the talk all started with paid Red agitators? Who was really dissatisfied with hours and wages—the solid, loyal core of the work force or a few chronic malcontents and pithead lawyers? Who objected to buying at the company store and living in a company house—the decent, respectable wives and mothers or a few noisy slatterns who couldn't keep accounts or keep house anywhere?

After the Ludlow massacre the Rockefellers began to wonder uneasily whether the palatable answers they had been getting from Denver were really the right ones. In the hope of finding out they instructed their foundation, which they had recently endowed with its first hundred million dollars, to make an independent study of labor and industrial relations, with particular attention to what was going on in Colorado

King had known James D. Greene, secretary of the foundation, at Harvard, and Greene suggested that the by now internationally known labor expert from Canada be asked to come to New York for a consulation. The outcome was that John D., Jr., hired him to conduct the study in person at a salary of $12,000 a year.

This solved King's financial problems but did not leave him wholly at peace. He had recently been nominated as official Liberal candidate for York North, his grandfather Mackenzie's riding, and he knew that if he became an expatriate he would have no chance of election. He disposed of the matter by maintaining his apartment in Ottawa and entering a minute in the diary: "To North York I still cling. I must carry that riding for grandfather's sake, then the future must determine its own destiny which will be as God intends and as I may measure up to the great opportunities that are mine."

He had some misgivings too about the logic of an arrangement which found him, a champion of labor, going to work for a concern reputed to be labor's archenemy. But with his ready genius for self-justification he defended and acquitted himself on four separate grounds, all carefully recorded in the diary: (1) He would never even have thought of associating himself with any Rockefeller enterprise if it had not been for the "strongly endorsed opinion" of his old teacher, President Eliot of Harvard. (2) Besides, working for the Rockefeller Foundation was not the same as working for a Rockefeller corporation. (3) He could do far more for labor by educating the Rockefellers and appealing to their good instincts than by fighting them. (4) Within four months of their first meeting he had discovered: "I know of no man living whose character I admire more [than John D., Jr.'s]. . . . Of all the men who have yet come into my life I have more to be grateful for for the friendship which has sprung up out of our association together than for any other like association yet formed." Although the United States did not enter the war until 1917 King was able to recall, retroactively, in 1920, a fifth reason for his decision of 1914: By furthering better relations between capital and labor and thus increasing production in vital war industries he had materially aided the Allied cause.

His doubts at rest, the verbal calisthenics out of the way, King proceeded to do a valuable job for his employers, for their strike-bound employees, and for the long-haul cause of industrial peace. He began by coaching John D., Jr., through a hearing before the United States Commission on Industrial Relations; the commission was hostile, but thawed out slightly after Rockefeller announced his intention of visiting the mines to see for himself what reforms were needed and how best to put them into effect.

King then arranged a theoretically impossible meeting in New York between John D., Jr., and a mine leaders' deputation headed by old Mother Jones, the Madame Defarge of the union revolution. They got along fine. The octogenarian hellcat ended up shaking the billionaire boss by the hand and sternly reminding her fellow emissaries that he was their friend and was doing his best, even if he didn't know much. Rockefeller did not immediately announce his opinion of Mother Jones, but later described her, according to his biographer, as the "marvelous, vigorous, courageous organizer of the United Mine Workers of America."

In the actual settlement of the strike, which was over before he paid his first visit to Colorado, King played no direct part. But in persuading Rockefeller, and then persuading Rockefeller to admit in public that he could not fob off his own responsibilities on remote, high-paid hirelings, he did much to create the atmosphere in which a settlement became possible. He followed this with a much more conspicuous and concrete accomplishment—the invention and successful promotion of the Rockefeller Plan of Industrial Representation.

On the management-labor scene of today, where "paternalism" is a dirty word, King's Rockefeller Plan would be widely condemned and, indeed, declared unlawful; it was the blueprint, thinly disguised, for a company union. Nevertheless, in Colorado and in 1915, the Plan offered a large step ahead. Its basis was to be a cadre of workers' representatives to confer with management on recreation, health, housing, and other sources of grievance. No miner was to be fired because of union activity, and meetings—even union meetings—were to be permitted on company property. The employees would be allowed to hire their own doctors and ministers. There was no provision for collective bargaining.

King wisely retired to the background and gave the Rockefellers the task and the kudos of selling his Plan to their local officials as well as to their workers. As a first step he persuaded John D., Jr., to accompany him on a trip to the mines, where federal troops had restored an uneasy and sullen peace.

Before they went back East even J. F. Welborn, the Rockefellers' Colorado viceroy—to whom even a company union reeked of sloth and socialism—was showing signs of enthusiasm for the Plan. The miners, won over partly by the good manners and palpably good intentions of John D., Jr., endorsed it in a secret ballot. Variations of it, many of them worked out by King himself, were soon in effect in hundreds of other business and industrial concerns. The Wagner Act of 1935, with its ban on company unions, meant that all of King's labor and management agreements had to be canceled or rewritten, but for twenty years they were to serve the times and the conditions of which they were born, and serve them well.

XXV

Industry and Humanity—King becomes
his party's leader

AMID these triumphs in places far afield, King the out-of-office politician had sadly neglected his new constituency of York North. During 1916 and the first half of 1917, in spite of the urgent invitations and pleas of the local party workers, he visited the constituency only twice.

He had no heart for going down with the Laurier ship a second time, as he knew he must do once the lines were drawn, the fateful conscription issue brought in the open, the genteel ballot-box stuffing of the Tories' Wartime Elections Act arranged, Liberals deserting right and left to Borden's Union standard.

Less than two months before election day King was on the verge of running out altogether, leaving Laurier and the local organization to find another candidate where they might. Laurier looked him sternly in the eye and said: "You must run." He was defeated by a thousand votes, far from a disgrace considering the crushing majorities conscription and the Unionists were piling up everywhere but in Quebec.

He had little time to regret the result, for a far greater sorrow awaited him the next day. Against his own will and at her insistence, he had left his mother desperately ill in Ottawa to attend to the last stages of the campaign. A message intercepted him on his way home: she was dead.

More than one baffled student of Mackenzie King has concluded that there were occasions in his career when his right hand simply could not have known what his left hand was doing. The overwhelming weight of evidence suggests something quite different.

The two hands were, indeed, often engaged in seemingly incompatible tasks, but the total man knew precisely what each of them was up to and he invariably approved and applauded them both. For him consistency was no jewel but a Woolworth bauble unworthy of a second glance from any man of serious purpose.

Thus, during 1918, King divided his time in two main ways. With his right hand he served as an industrial consultant to some of the world's largest corporations—Standard Oil of New Jersey, Bethlehem Steel, and General Electric were among them—at average fees of a thousand dollars a week plus expenses. With his left hand he completed a book which, in effect, challenged the whole edifice of capitalism. The book was called *Industry and Humanity* and it summarized the convictions he had acquired in twenty years of close contact with management and labor in roles as varied as cub reporter poking around the sweatshops of Toronto, as professional mediator and federal cabinet minister, as adviser to the shockingly rich and champion of the shockingly poor.

The main theses of *Industry and Humanity* were neither new nor particularly daring. The Community was under no obligation to sit uncomplainingly by while labor and capital engaged in incessant dogfights for which the Community ultimately would pay. The Community had a right to appoint its own representatives to sit with capital, labor, and management on the directorates of business. "Working men and women have come to realize that, in the ever-changing conditions of Industry, they exist as atoms in a human tide so vast, and subject to such ceaseless ebb and flow, that the effort to secure collective stability becomes the first requisite of existence itself. . . ." They "find themselves . . . possessed of little save their skill and energy—human beings who work with equipment which belongs to others, in establishments owned by others, upon materials the property of others and who leave to others the disposition of the wealth they have helped to produce. . . ." Capitalism "gives little heed to the individual lives that suffer or are sacrificed by its rapid transitions; it is slow to concede to Labor, in Labor's struggle against world forces, facilities of combination like unto its own. . . ." "In the conflict between the temporary interests of selfish individuals and the permanent welfare of nations, the latter alone is entitled to consideration. Wherever, in social or industrial relations, the claims of Industry and Humanity are opposed, those of Industry must make way."

The novelty lay not in the proposition itself but in the apparent paradoxes between it and the source: a special confidant of Big Business urging interference with Big Business; a disciple of old-fashioned, capital-*L* Liberalism demanding that the State move in on free enterprise and the free individual.

King's only objective biographer, Bruce Hutchison, believes that few, if any, Liberals could have read King's book; if they had he could never have become leader of their party. Another biographer, the less critical MacGregor Dawson, offers evidence to suggest that his capitalist friends read it but, after brushing through its thickets of piety and platitude, simply couldn't understand it. John D. Rockefeller, Jr., admitted tactfully that he found it "too philosophical and somewhat long," but he had no other hard feelings.

In any case, Rockefeller shortly recommended King to an almost equally wealthy industrialist and philanthropist, Andrew Carnegie. At this stage the Carnegie Trusts were a few million dollars better endowed than the Rockefeller Foundation, and King was offered a salary of $25,000 a year to surpervise the distribution of their funds. As an added incentive he could count on a lump payment of $100,000 if he wished to write a biography of old Mr. Carnegie, who was then in his last year of life.

But King's future was already committed elsewhere. He now intended to return to Canada, succeed the failing Sir Wilfrid Laurier as leader of the Liberal party, and then become Prime Minister. But first he spent the first three weeks of the new year in feigned torment, building up the self-image of a man about to make a mighty sacrifice. Thus, reflecting on the Carnegie proposition, his diary exclaimed: "Were I to go the world over, it is impossible to conceive anywhere on either side of the Ocean, where an opening more attractive could be presented."

But hold! There is something more to be considered: "The primrose path does not make for greatness in any true sense."

On the other hand, could he be truly "independent" on the modest salary of a party leader? Still, duty transcends all: "There seems to be a call to me . . . a call through the necessities of the party, the need for leadership . . . I should rather serve my own country than any other land, tho' service for humanity would command me anywhere."

Less than a month after King finished these soliloquies, on February 17, 1919, Sir Wilfrid Laurier died. Had King turned his careful actuary's mind to a precise summary of his chances to succeed his departed chieftain, it would then have read something like this:

Credit: Borden's Union government was beginning to crumble. The Liberals who had strayed to its side at the time of conscription would be welcomed back—indeed, coaxed back if needed—to their old and proper political home. But none of them could be considered a serious candidate to succeed the leader they had deserted, however honorable their reasons for deserting might have been.

Debit: King's own wartime record. He was not so naïve as to expect that his enemies, present and future, inside the party and out, would forget that he—a single man of forty—had accepted a job in the United States only a few days after his country went to war and that he kept it, or others like it, until shortly after the Armistice.

Credit: No innuendo could be drawn from his wartime activities that could not be refuted by a straightforward recital of the facts. The hint of draft dodging was preposterous. Until 1918 there was no draft to dodge. If there had been, King would not have been beyond its reach in the United States. When the draft did come, his age group was never called. As for his failure to fly to Sam Hughes's standard in the first rush of volunteers, he could claim that while ostensibly working for various U.S. industrial giants he had actually been performing vague heroics for Canada and democracy on the production line. Much more convincingly he could—and in his own good time did—point to the pathetic degree to which his family were dependent on him and to the suddenness with which they had been swallowed up by tragedy. His older sister died in 1915. His father died in 1916. His mother died in 1917. His brother became a helpless invalid. King knew the inevitable attempts to smear him as a coward would force him to speak openly of memories almost too fresh and painful to endure. But if this was one of the costs of a career in politics, he was ready to pay it and be done with the matter.

Debit: King's political inexperience.

Credit: His chief rival's excess of experience. This rival was W. S. Fielding, former premier of Nova Scotia, Laurier's Finance Minister and best-known colleague for fifteen years. But Fielding was over seventy, hardly an age to begin rebuilding a party still not recovered form the Unionist schism.

Debit: Lady Laurier was known to be supporting Fielding. King, to his disappointment, had not been invited to be a pallbearer at the funeral.

Credit: Whether with unbridled enthusiasm or not, King had stuck with Laurier and the party through two disastrous elections and eight desert years. Fielding had never gone over to the Unionists, but he had voted for conscription in the House of Commons. He would be no asset in Quebec, the only province in which the party could be reasonably sure of strength. King would be an asset there.

King played his hand as warily as a Mississippi gambler nursing a good hole card but still needing to fill. He arranged to leave unsettled the offer to go to work for Carnegie, and when Rockefeller asked him to make a short trip to England, he quickly agreed. This way he could watch the beginnings of the fight for power in the Liberal party and still avoid getting into it until he was ready. In the confused and sensitive state in which the party found itself, a wrong word, an unfortunate inflection, an ill-judged handshake, a premature bargain, might spell ruin. The election of Laurier's successor was not to take place until August. With an ocean separating him from the early skirmishes, King could hope to reap the advantages of being both available and a little hard to get.

When he returned to Canada in July he was given a prominent place on the Liberal resolutions committee, whose task it was to bring the party platform up to date. It was not a startling platform. In Empire affairs it called for autonomy for the dominions, with a special warning against Borden's goal of regular Imperial consultations; the Liberals feared the trap of overcentralization. In trade the platform stood for lower tariffs, particularly on tools for primary production, an increase in the Empire preference, an attempt to bring reciprocity with the United States back to life. In industry it stood for a slightly watered-down version of the gospel according to William Lyon Mackenzie King.

King spoke to the labor resolution, and under the rules of the Convention this had to serve as his one and only appeal for the party leadership. As he began, eight of Canada's nine provincial premiers were in his audience. Only Ontario was without a Liberal administration and it was only two months away from kicking the Conservatives out in favor of a Farmers' government. Canada was still Liberal at heart, whatever convulsions the war had wrought at

Ottawa. The man who could win this convention, King was well aware, could win the country. He could win it here and now.

The proposals King put to the Convention were all palatable and fairly traditional. He and the party strategists were in favor of unemployment insurance, sickness insurance, old-age pensions, widows' pensions, and maternity benefits. They were in favor of a place for labor and the community in the management of business. They were against government by order in council, the high cost of living, profiteering, and Chinese immigrants.

He finished his speech with a glowing eulogy of Sir Wilfrid Laurier. King was never an inspired speaker, but on this, perhaps the most crucial single occasion of his entire political life, he came close to eloquence. At the end his hearers were on their feet amid "tremendous cheering."

When the balloting began it was still, nevertheless, touch and go between King and Fielding. King led on each of the three votes, but only after each of the other two candidates had withdrawn did he scrape through with the needed clear majority, 476 to Fielding's 438.

There was no one left to share the moment with, no father, no mother, no sister Isabel. His second sister, Jennie, was married and his brother, Max, was two thousand miles away, dying in a sanatorium. He turned again to the whitely hearkening pages of the diary: "Just before the result of the last ballot was announced, I sat quietly waiting on the platform. . . . The majority was better than I had anticipated. I was too heavy of heart and soul to appreciate the tumult of applause, my thoughts were of dear mother & father & little Bell all of whom I felt to be very close to me, of grandfather & Sir Wilfrid also. I thought: it is right, it is the call of duty. I have sought nothing, it has come. It has come from God. The dear loved ones know and are about, they are alive and with me in this great everlasting Now and Here."

XXVI

*The pull of gravity and the U.S.A.—"WLW, the
Nation's Station, Cincinnati!"—The Black and
Tans and the surge of nationalism—The tour
of the Prince of Wales*

AMID the moral, economic, and intellectual upheaval of the 1920s,
Canada had a private upheaval of its own. Painfully and uncertainly,
with much beating of its newly hairy chest, the country began to
be less a British country and more an American country.

The shift did not become visible all at once and what became
visible was full of paradox. Britain was seldom more admired. The
United States was seldom more resented. For millions of Canadians
the war had restored the Empire of their schooldays to its invincible, infallible best. The Englishman they knew in person, or
thought they knew, was no longer a patronizing egotist, but a
heroic, lovable combination of Kipling's Tommy Atkins and Bruce
Bairnsfather's Old Bill. The war had made the Yankee, in spite
of Teddy Roosevelt's earlier advice, a man who spoke loudly,
carried a small stick, and swung it rather late.

Yet gravity was not a force to be obeyed or disobeyed as a simple
matter of preference. The great massif of the U.S.A., still half molten
among a thousand volcanic fires, exercised a pull that Canadians
might deplore and fear but could not resist. Between 1900 and
1921 there were nearly a million and a half immigrants from the
United States into Canada—more than from the whole of the Commonwealth. Two and a half million Americans had either been
born in Canada themselves or born to parents born in Canada. Americans were busily setting up as branch managers or independent
owners in Canadian business and high finance; already, according
to the *Financial Post*, one dollar out of every two in Canadian industry was an American dollar. Another survey judged that by 1922
there were six thousand doctors and clergymen of Canadian origin

in the United States and twelve thousand teachers. Through stinginess or necessity, many of the most influential Canadian newspapers depended for much of their important world news on American correspondents, some of whom, not unnaturally, were anti-British and even, it sometimes appeared, anti-Canadian.

Those essentially American institutions, radio, the popular magazines, and the motion pictures, were all moving toward their zenith. It was an unlucky Canadian boy indeed who had not experienced the ecstasy of hearing a crystal set cry forth the siren songs of a whole generation: *KDKA, Pittsburgh! KOA, Denver! WLW, the Nation's Station, Cincinnati!* Who could possibly get through the 1920s without becoming a familiar of Rudolph Valentino, Mary Pickford, Douglas Fairbanks, Charlie Chaplin, Pola Negri, and the Talmadge girls? Who could escape or conceivably desire to escape the acquaintance of Octavus Roy Cohen's Florian Slappey, Mary Roberts Rinehart's Tish, Arthur Train's Mr. Tutt, or a dozen of their peers from the pages of the *Saturday Evening Post?*

More than forty Canadian Rotary Clubs sent delegates to Rotary's thirteenth annual convention at Los Angeles. Kiwanis International held its convention in the same year at Toronto and five thousand delegates and twenty-five thousand spectators cheered with indiscriminate fervor while a Tattoo and Pageant at the Exhibition Grounds brought forth a lunatic mixture of Wolfe's British Redcoats, the Minutemen of Concord, the U. S. Blues, the U. S. Grays, the Canadians of Passchendaele, and the Yanks of the Meuse-Argonne.

To say that Canada, at this period, had a conscious desire to ape the United States would be rather like saying that the tides ape the moon when they are only yielding to its pull. It was possible for Canadians to remain immensely irritated by the we-won-the-war talk from the other side of the border and by other social, political, and business frictions while still turning, usually a little behind, into the mainstream of North American history.

Thus, in the immediate aftermath of the war, the United States had a deflationary depression and Canada had a deflationary depression too. Coal strikes broke out in the United States; coal strikes broke out in Canada. The United States embarked on prohibition; so—usually a little before, sometimes a little later—did almost all the provinces of Canada. The United States spawned the prohibition gangster; Canada spawned the prohibition rumrunner to keep him supplied. The American female developed invisible busts and hips, the boyish bob, bells on her garters, and a taste for cigarettes and gin; the Canadian female sought to do the same. Oddly, in one of the few reversals of the customary order, it was the Canadian woman who was first to get the vote.

The Ku Klux Klan sprang to arms in Dixie; it followed suit, after a manner of speaking, in Saskatchewan. (Discomfited to find an almost total lack of Negroes to keep in their place, the saviors of the white race burned a few crosses in warning to the province's Chinese laundrymen and café owners and then disbanded.)

None of this was to say that Canada lacked the desire or means to create an identity of its own. Louis Hémon's famous novel of life on the agricultural frontier of Quebec, *Maria Chapdelaine*, had already reached the phenomenal sale of a quarter of a million copies. Stephen Leacock went back for a visit to England, not as a young man who had gone out to the colonies many years before, but as a fully assimilated Canadian reflecting on a common crisis: "I am sorry to have to tell you that now we have prohibition it is becoming increasingly difficult to get a drink. In fact sometimes, especially in the very early morning, it is most inconvenient and almost impossible." Robert W. Service had a new book out, as did Mazo de la Roche. The beloved natural-history writer Ernest Thompson Seton, Lucy Maud Montgomery, creator of Anne of Green Gables, and the much respected sky pilot from Glengarry, Ralph Connor, still had large followings inside the country as well as out. A handful of rebellious and militantly Canadian artists known as the Group of Seven were painting bold native landscapes and stirring up as much attention as and far more argument than Cornelius Krieghoff and Paul Kane had created in earlier times. Walter Allward, the sculptor, was at work on the Vimy Ridge Memorial. Emma Lajeunesse, known to the world as Madame Albani, was the best-remembered Canadian in the field of music, and there were other individual performers and choral and instrumental groups of at least modest reputation. An ex-army tentshow troupe called the Dumbells stormed the country's heart and imagination as no native entertainers had ever done before. Sir Frederick Banting discovered insulin—a miracle as great as the miracle that his countrymen instantly recognized him as one of their greatest men.

In spite of the growth of North Americanism, Britain remained a main factor—probably the main factor—in the amendment of

Canada's spiritual and political loyalties. The country's feeling for the mother country was as rich in surface contradictions as its feeling for the United States. The whole Empire was undergoing an attack of mixed feelings and Canada was not immune. The Borden-Smuts plan for a kind of Imperial foreign affairs committee, approved unanimously at the War Conference of 1917, had lost much of its steam against a rising head wind of second thoughts and caveats. Having signed the Covenant of the League or having been committed to it by Lloyd George's government, the dominions and the colonies now were faced with the chilling fact that one of the League's two essential members, the United States, had withdrawn from it. Woodrow Wilson lay dying and repudiated, and so, it was not too early to suspect, was the whole Geneva dream. In the meantime any nation whose name still stood on the documents could be ordered forthwith to war whether it believed in the causes or not.

Already thus involved in yet unborn struggles through Geneva, most of the dominions had become loth to risk further involvement through Whitehall and Downing Street. The Imperial Conference agreed upon in 1917 was not convened until the middle of 1921. It produced not the resounding declarations of solidarity that Borden and Smuts had at first hoped for, but a series of polite equivocations. Its most far-reaching effect, ironically, was Britain's decision not to renew its Pacific treaty with Japan. This was taken under the urging of Arthur Meighen, who was acting under the urging of the new U.S. government of Warren Harding.

The Empire's discovery that it could not achieve complete independence for its parts while at the same time achieving complete unity of the whole was accompanied by another, partly parallel discovery: the nationalist movements that had been making life difficult for the Foreign and Colonial offices even before the reign of George III were astir almost everywhere.

Ireland was the only pressing trouble spot, but there the trouble was as dark and hideous as anything since the Indian Mutiny and the Black Hole of Calcutta. The Irish had been revolting sporadically against English rule at least as early as the time of Henry II—usually with good reason. The Dublin Easter uprising of 1916 set the country in flames again and the flames were still alight five years later. The clandestine Irish Republican Army by now claimed a strength of 100,000. The British, no longer able to find Irishmen willing to fight the I.R.A., had recruited a special police force in

England. This much feared and hated little army—the Black and Tans—found itself half besieging and half besieged by a desperate and baleful enemy it seldom even saw. It was a war of darkened cellars, silent streets, dark shapes in trenchcoats hurrying through the fog, the sudden terrifying sound of marchers in the night. No man on either side could ever be sure his next wary step around a quiet street corner would not be his last. The Irish wanted to declare it officially a war, but could not hope to win except by guerrilla tactics. The English denied it was a war; they claimed it was simply a struggle between the law and the lawless. Both sides turned more and more to terror—to bombings, incendiarism, betrayals, reprisals, ambuscades, and murder. The dead, wounded, and injured ran into the thousands. The revolutionists destroyed, among other things, at least eight hundred barracks and nearly a hundred courthouses. The Black and Tans set fire to whole villages.

The influence of Ireland on the rest of the world had always been strong, in good times or in bad. Potato famines, political flights, and the lure of adventure had sent nearly five million emigrants forth from Ireland since the 1840s, and by 1920 they and their descendants living abroad were believed to number around twenty-five million. Half of these were in the United States. There were substantial numbers in England, Canada, and the other English-speaking parts of the Empire. Undoubtedly the "Irish question"—in which virtually everyone's sympathies lay with Ireland through instinct or some degree of common experience—helped accelerate the postwar rush of nationalism all around the world.

Australia was moving toward the left politically and was already pacifist enough to have rejected conscription during the war. Many of the new men of Labor there were talking republicanism in the open and even trying to get it put into their state and federal platforms. New Zealand remained stoutly monarchist, but it was a far different question in South Africa. There General Hertzog opened an election campaign with a plea for secession and the restoration of the old Boer republic. Jan Christiaan Smuts, the champion of Empire, beat him back, but Smuts's majority in a House of 134 members was nevertheless no more than 22.

Egypt, officially a British protectorate, was in the throes of a struggle whose central issue, despite all high-sounding language, was whether the British were ready to be kicked out or not. They were not; they needed the Suez Canal and wanted the Sudan. Accordingly, when a popular fellah agitator demanded the protectors be expelled, they deported him as an enemy of the Sultan. England was having other difficulties with its mandate in Palestine, where half a million Moslems and sixty-five thousand Christians were beginning a long struggle to block the Balfour plan for a Jewish national home. In India, Mahatma Gandhi was preaching civil disobedience and winning converts by the tens of millions.

Probably not one Canadian in five was knowingly affected by these distant issues and events. And those who were spurred to action or to cries for action were, in the main, only expressing attitudes settled long before. The most highly vocal Canadian nationalists of the postwar years were the same men who had played the same roles before and during the war. Henri Bourassa reappeared to lead a rally on behalf of the Self-Determination League for Ireland. At another meeting his faithful lieutenant, Armand Lavergne, denounced England as "the greatest murderer of small nations." Lindsay Crawford, a Toronto editor and propagandist, declaimed: "To ask the Irish in Canada to honor a flag stained with the blood of their people and to declare loyalty to a Throne that rests on the might of armed assassins, is to ask them to profane the temples of their fathers and to betray their Motherland in her hour of greatest agony."

Inevitably the Irish debate in Canada degenerated into another half-religious, half-political, and essentially private quarrel between the Orangemen of Ulster and the Catholics of the southern counties. The Orangemen were no more temperate than the Catholics. One Orange meeting, summoned in Toronto to hear from a Belfast lodge brother, applauded wildly at these words: "The only force that stands firmly arrayed against Fenianism, Bolshevism [and] terrorism in Ireland today is, as regards Ulster, the institution of Orangeism. With rebel Ireland [under Home Rule] as a base for German submarines during the war the end might well have been otherwise. It was Ulster that saved the Empire in this emergency by refusing to have Home Rule."

Another cheering Toronto meeting heard another visitor from Belfast refer to a projected conciliation meeting in London and then cry: "I would to God that we had the lads who laid down their lives and sleep with your Canadians on the Somme, and there would be no peace conference today."

Whatever stirrings of the new nationalism he might have noticed, the average Canadian felt far less violently about them than that. He might express some degree of impatience to see Canada with a flag of its own, to have "O Canada" installed as the national anthem, and to see the abolition of the right to appeal decisions of Canadian courts to the Privy Council in London. He might have a lingering resentment and jealousy of the overbearing Yankees. But for the time being there were no issues over which he had much interest in shedding his own or anybody else's blood. He could get along with the Yankees if he had to—and he was beginning to realize that he probably had to. And even though its house rules and bylaws needed modernizing every now and then, the Empire was still a first-rate club. What better evidence could anyone ask than the dashing impression the young Prince of Wales was creating on its behalf throughout the world?

One of the gaily irresistible heir apparent's first main duties after the Armistice had been to visit Canada and the United States. This triumphal tour was followed by another one, equally successful, to Australia and New Zealand. And the last months of 1921 and the first months of 1922 found him in India, amid scenes of pageantry and splendor that surely had not been surpassed since Antony's visit to Egypt. While an admiring world followed his every move, the Prince swept through a procession of sights and sounds, places and people whose very names were a chant of riches, of magic and of majesty . . . tiger hunting in Nepal, the races at Poona, a durbar at Baroda, polo and pigsticking at Jodhpur; devil dances by Tibetan monks and softer ones by the dancing girls of Manipur; cannon of gold and silver, gold and silver thrones on the backs of jeweled elephants, floors of gold, walls of teak and marble; maharajahs, kings, princes, lords, and nawabs; the towers and tribal huts of Indore, Bhopal and Gwalior, Peshawar, Karachi and Hyderabad, Bihar and Orissa, the Khyber Pass and Lucknow and Delhi and Oudh.

Even *The Times*'s correspondent felt this was no occasion for restraint: "[It] has been one grand pageant of color, movement, light and music; of flags, decorated streets, palaces and temples; of swarming populations, of troops in brilliant uniforms, from the half-wild horsemen and armor-clad warriors from the Middle Ages to the superbly trained and magnificent regiments of today; of elephants, camels, oxen and horses, all in gorgeous trappings; of crocodiles in tanks and motor-cars; of British Army bands and the weird throbbings of native drums and the clanging temple bells; of hot sun by day on yellow land, dark foliage and white houses with kites wheeling overhead, and clear crystal nights, with jackals howling in the starlight."

Reading of these Imperial wonders, as most Canadians were doing every day in late 1921 and early 1922, it was difficult not to feel a surge of excitement at being a shareholder in them by virtue of ties and privileges denied to ordinary mortals. It was almost as good as reading G. A. Henty again or being back with the old Fourth Reader and Russell's Balaclava and Byron's Waterloo.

XXVII

*The farmers try their strength—The rise of
the Progressives and the beginning
of their fall*

THE Winnipeg strike had spoken to the country in the simple idiom of the political cartoonist and the pamphleteer. It was a clash of absolutes: in one view, anarchy and Red revolt against order and decency; in another, plutocratic greed and oppression against the rights of man. In truth, of course, its roots were deeper and more tangled than either combatant could see. Its fruits could not be measured in broken heads, man-hours of employment lost, or man-days spent in jail.

It was not only labor that emerged from 1918 intent on a better deal and aware of the advantages of seeking it through common action. The farmers, still by far the country's largest and most important occupational group, were off in hot pursuit of their own special interests too.

For many of them the war had brought their first real taste of abundance. The prices they got for everything they raised or grew went up and up and up. So did the amounts they sold. The country's total wheat acreage almost doubled between 1913 and 1919. The price per bushel tripled. Unable to borrow money abroad to pay for the war, full of the conviction that high taxation defeats its own ends, the government had relied on food exports for its largest source of cash. The value of meat shipped abroad increased fifteen times and of livestock three and a half times. Cheese and butter production doubled.

Moreover, there were things to buy with the extra cash, for although normal trade dried up, the domestic manufacture of clothing, furniture, tobacco, and most other consumer goods increased. How well off this made the farmer either in absolute or comparative terms, there was no way of establishing, for farm statistics were even more plastic then than now. A government supporter produced a record for 1918 in the House of Commons to show that, while they numbered more than half the population, Canada's farm families paid less than a twenty-fifth of the nation's total income tax. Approximately half the country took this as proof that, even after the agricultural boom, the farmer was living in poverty; the other half took it as proof that he was cheating.

Arithmetic, in any case, was not the issue. The farmer had glimpsed and partaken of a better world and felt it should be still better. He had seen government emerge as a more pervasive force in the life of the individual than it had been since the days of the Family Compact. The government took his sons off to war. Or, if it chose, it allowed them to stay home. During 1917 and 1918 it marketed his wheat at a guaranteed price. Both the old parties were talking mightily about social security; whether the farmer would get his share of it, now or ever, might depend on the next election. And the next election would not offer the usual simple though unexciting choice between the low-tariff Grits and the high-tariff Tories. The Tories could be depended on as usual to offer protection to manufacturing and industry at the expense of agriculture. But the Grits could not be counted on to press for outright reciprocity; Mackenzie King was already pussyfooting on the tariff issue with the slogan: "Not free but freer trade." Then too, King was a known labor man. With labor emerging as a class capable of militant action, could agriculture afford the luxury of remaining a disorganized conglomeration of individuals?

So ran some of the farmer's thoughts during the last years of the war and the first year of the peace. How far they would have carried him along the road to political insurrection if the price of wheat had held is not worth much speculation. In fact the farmers' political uprising was already well launched while No. 1 Northern was still well over two dollars a bushel.

Various agricultural groups, most of them the outgrowth of marketing co-operatives, were preparing to bid for government office in the western provinces. But it was in Ontario, traditionally Tory, traditionally protectionist, traditionally—though inaccurately—thought of as preponderantly urban, that the first farmers' government reached office.

On the morning of October 20, 1919, the Conservative Sir William

Hearst bore every appearance of being the provincial premier most nearly certain to succeed himself. He had gone to the polls in Ontario with 76 seats to his combined opposition's 32. He had won 12 of the last 21 by-elections. The opposition Liberals had no chance to improve their standing until their federal parent's embarrassing record on conscription could be lived down. The third party in the contest, the United Farmers of Ontario, had a paltry 3 seats in a legislature of 108.

By nightfall Hearst was crushed and his party was in eclipse. The premier lost his own seat and saw only 25 of 100 fellow Tories elected. The Liberals held their own with 29 seats. The Farmers' 45 was the largest group of all. On the same day five federal by-elections were held, and Farm candidates won three of them.

This twin bombshell brought consternation and dismay to scores of old-line politicians. But in the ranks of the national Liberal organization there were many notable exceptions. Chief among them was Mackenzie King, who had won his party's leadership barely ten weeks before. Before the day was over he wrote exultantly in his diary: "It means as sure as I am writing that I shall be called on to form a government at the next general election if no serious mistakes are made in the interval."

The prophecy, accurate as it proved to be, was not a remarkable one. The remarkable thing was that *before* the upset in Ontario, King had perceived the swift rush of the agrarian movement and had carefully begun work on a master plan to deal with it: first, to avoid a direct collision; second, to woo it into an alliance; third, to swallow it. During his first two months as Liberal leader he had spent far more time worrying about the as yet unformed national Farm party than about the Conservative government it was his main goal to overthrow.

One of the first decisions he had to make as Liberal leader was to choose a constituency in which to seek his own parliamentary seat. The forthcoming federal by-elections offered him his pick of two—one near at hand in Ontario and one far away in Prince Edward Island. At first he favored the Ontario riding, but when a Farm candidate appeared to oppose him, King refused to run and took the long way home by way of the Atlantic Ocean and an acclamation. Nor did he find this retreat in the least embarrassing. On the contrary, he made it part of an experiment in reading the weather. For his own part, he explained: "I should feel that I was placing both myself and the Party in a false position, were I to consider accepting any nomination which would have the effect at this time of placing me in an attitude of apparent antagonism to the Farmers of our own Province."

Like any true scientist, he knew his experiment would be useless without a control. Accordingly, when a bold Liberal insisted on running against a Farm nominee in the Saskatchewan by-election, King converted him into a sort of human placebo pill. He extended his own strong personal support to the candidate and saw the man lose his deposit.

King needed no more evidence that his master plan was sound. To attempt anything so crude and direct as dividing and conquering the Farmers at this stage might prove suicidal. Now that they had discovered their own strength, it was doubly dangerous to provoke them. A high official of the triumphant Ontario group was already daring anybody—anybody at all—to stick just one toe across the line. "Liberalism has been more progressive than Conservatism, but only in a degree. Both systems were bad and of late years were running mates identified only by name. . . . We have passed through an orgy of corruption that is a disgrace to true Canadians and was only made possible by the utter failure of machine party politics to defend the rights of the people. . . . Something better must be found. . . . We do not purpose to look back like Lot's wife in the days of old. We will not worship idols though they be Dewart or Hearst, King or Borden."

To risk further inflaming men already thus inflamed was not in King's nature. Not divide and conquer: caress and envelop. King pondered for a week and then committed to his diary the outlines of strategy and philosophy that were to be his beacon for the next two years. There was little in it to recall the brave spectacle of his grandfather Mackenzie riding into battle against the redcoats. There was no echo of the noble calls to arms of Sir Wilfrid Laurier. But as a practical manual for politicians, it was, as King well knew, worth more than a brigade of white horses and the sound of a thousand trumpets.

"The win of the Farmers," he noted dispassionately, "creates a serious outlook for the Liberal Party whilst it spells complete ruin to the old Tory Party. The farmers' movement is a people's movement & as such the truest kind of Liberalism. The same is true of

Labor, which has also shown its strength combined with Liberals, in B.C. against the present Government. One thing is certain, the Union Government is doomed completely. Whether the Liberal Party will survive the Farmer-Labor combination depends on our conciliatory attitude. . . . Liberalism to hold its own must make clear that it stands for the essential reforms the Farmers and Labor are advocating. I have always done that & indeed as I see the situation, I am the only man who by natural sympathies & past record can bring these three groups into alliance & to a single front, should it come to the formation of a Ministry in Federal affairs later on. I welcome these new forces, as shewing our men in the ranks of Liberalism that we are right in a progressive platform, also as shewing 'the interests' that a wise conservative leadership of radical forces is better than reactionary Toryism. Time will have its effect on these 'sectional' movements. Two parties in the end will be necessary & I shall win the Leadership of the Liberal and other radical forces, thru' being true to Liberal principles."

Within three months King's silver-lined cloud had taken a definite shape. In January 1920 a hundred delegates from four provinces attended a special conference of the Canadian Council of Agriculture in Winnipeg and departed as the founders of a new political party. They borrowed the name Progressive from the U.S. mavericks of Robert La Follette and shortly chose as their leader a respected ex-Liberal and ex-Unionist named Thomas Alexander Crerar.

By midsummer Arthur Meighen was installed as Borden's successor as the Conservative Prime Minister and a brand new political triangle was in place. It was less robust and exciting than the Borden-Laurier-Bourassa triangle had been, but it had its own kind of flavor too.

All three members had their eyes firmly, and to the exclusion of all else, on the next election, which Meighen could call at any time and was obliged to call no later than 1922. All three began to campaign immediately.

King, having already decided that his most dangerous foes were the Progressives, proceeded to claim them publicly as blood kin. The Conservatives, from whom he feared nothing, he spoke of as an evil menace to society.

Meighen fought both his opponents as best he could. Crerar, who was already threatened with a party split between the doctrinaire liberals and the us-first farmers, bore down on the one issue on which all his Progressive followers could agree—free trade. This brought him and Meighen careering at each other like two bull moose in full rut, while King stepped delicately out of their way.

Meighen was as scathing and superior with Crerar as he had ever been with King. His brilliant scorn dripped over on the populace at large, which he lectured from coast to coast like an angry schoolmaster.

"The public mind," he reminded the public sternly, "is confused with a veritable babel of uninformed tongues. A great many people seem to have lost all sense of values, of proportion and of numbers. Extravagance in thought is as great as the undoubted extravagance in living. Thousands of people are mentally chasing rainbows, striving for the unattainable, anxious to better their lot, but seemingly unwilling to do it in the old-fashioned way by hard, honest, intelligent effort."

He warned of "free wreckers" and hinted at Reds in the ranks of the farmers. Why couldn't the rural voters have enough sense to understand that they really understood nothing? "Free trade," he explained with weary patience, "has depopulated rural England; it has filled the emigrant ships with fugitives from her shores; it has scattered the manhood of Great Britain through the fields and workshops of the United States; it has starved and repressed the nascent industries of Ireland; it has reversed the supremacy that Britain held through centuries in the industrial life of the world, and caused her to concede the place to other great competing nations who adopted a different policy."

Crerar in return proclaimed that Meighen and his Tory protection were tools of big business and the ubiquitous "interests." The tariff existed to keep prices up and further enrich the rich. Moreover, under its broad umbrella, millions of dollars of watered stock had been unloaded on a public already victimized. To what extent were campaign handouts from the wealthy protected manufacturers responsible for protection?

King campaigned as vigorously as either of the other two, but he had more opportunity to choose and occasionally vary his ground. He coolly claimed for his party a large share of the credit for the Farmers' victory over the Tories in Ontario. Wherever Crerar went in 1920 and the early months of 1921, he found that King had been there ahead, strewing his path with not altogether welcome olive branches.

"As Liberals," King said, "we mistake altogether the significance of these agrarian movements if we do not see in them evidence of Liberal thought and feeling on the part of those who are advocating and supporting their policies. . . . In so far as these movements are in the nature of protest against arbitrary behavior on the part of the administration, and are evidence of the determination of those engaged in agriculture to secure a wider measure of economic freedom, there can be only one attitude toward them on the part of all true Liberals, and that an attitude of wholehearted approval and co-operation in an endeavor to obtain reforms already too long delayed."

In the West, King stressed lower tariffs, without, however, going all the way on free trade. In the East he soft-pedaled the tariff but proclaimed that some degree of protection was vital for the good of the country. He goaded Meighen at every opportunity for his "autocracy and absolutism." "There is an invisible government by the big interests of this country," he declared. "Meighen and the others around him are the playthings in the scheme of these great forces."

King's plan for taming the Progressives did not, however, yield all the results he had hoped for. Crerar reacted to the first steps of the mating dance with a disappointing lack of ardor. Later, after the election had been called, King tried to persuade him to withdraw Progressives from certain ridings in return for the withdrawal of Liberals in others. But Crerar was unwilling or unable to persuade his enthusiastic party workers to enter into any such arrangement. During the last months of the campaign King, partly through pique and partly through growing confidence, began urging the farmers to abandon the party of "class aims and class ambitions." ("These wretched Progressives" he called them in a letter to his brother.)

There were other matters to be ventilated and argued on the hustings. The brief but severe depression of 1920–22, during which wheat dropped to $1.00 from a high of $2.50, was an extra nail in Meighen's coffin. The aftermath of conscription alone probably would have made his re-election impossible, and he was even in wrong with the arch-Imperialists for having sided with the United States against Great Britain in aborting the treaty with Japan.

When the votes were counted in December 1921, the political map of Canada had been transformed into a Balkan nightmare. A country that had seen itself a decade before as serenely on the way to national unity had become a jigsaw of isolated tribes, merchant guilds, and husbandmen. The outgoing Conservative government failed to win a single seat in five of the nine provinces. The Liberals won all 65 seats in Quebec, all 16 in Nova Scotia, and 5 of 11 in New Brunswick. The Progressives won 37 out of 52 in the prairie provinces. Only from Ontario and British Columbia, both carried by the Conservatives, was there to be any real variety of representation in Ottawa. In the aggregate the Liberals had 117 seats, just one short of an absolute majority. The Progressives were next with 64. The Conservatives' tattered 50 did not include Meighen himself; nine other members of his Cabinet went down with him.

Three days before New Year's, King was sworn into office to begin his career as Prime Minister. It was a disorganized and ambiguous country he had been given the task of ruling, but his greatest talent was for dealing with the disorganized and the ambiguous. Meighen and the Tories were in rout and apparent ruin. King's one threat was Crerar and the Progressives, and they were, as King had told himself and the electorate, a splinter group whose only future lay in decent suicide. King conferred with Crerar and offered him and his party a few seats in the Cabinet. But Crerar held out for stronger control over government policy than King was willing to give. He was entitled to make his party the official opposition, but he let this privilege go by default to Meighen and the Tories. He was undoubtedly influenced by the fact that the Progressives could not agree among themselves whether to remain a class group promoting the interests of the farmer or to seek a place as a genuine national party independent of class.

King had even less trouble than he had expected in swallowing the Progressives up. By the end of the decade hardly a trace of them was left.

XXVIII

The Chanak affair—Canada rejects the motto "Ready, aye, ready!"

THE first two years of peace, according to a reliable statistician of the time, saw the start or continuation of at least twenty-five separate wars. One of them was still smoldering in the fall of 1922 and, although no Canadian fired a shot in it, it was for Canada one of the most significant events of the decade.

Theoretically the total defeat of Germany in 1918 also meant the total defeat of Turkey. Theoretically this was confirmed when the Allies dictated a treaty to the Sultan which put them in control of the Dardanelles, the Sea of Marmara, and the Bosporus. Standing thus astride both banks of the great and vital moat between Europe and Asia Minor—commanding the Black Sea and the Mediterranean, within a short cruiser run of Suez—Britain, France, and Italy had all they wanted in that part of the world.

Not so Turkey's neighbor and recent enemy, Greece. The Greek government claimed and was given Gallipoli and Smyrna by a great-power commission on which Sir Robert Borden was pressed into service as the British representative.

To see that the Greek occupation was carried out as painlessly as possible and to supervise the disarmament of its own troops, the Turkish government at Constantinople sent a brilliant young officer named Mustapha Kemal across the straits to the interior of Asia Minor. Once safely out of range of the Allied warships and the thin screen of Allied soldiers along the Dardanelles and the Bosporus, Kemal ordered 80,000 Turkish soldiers to remain in uniform, formed a "government" of his own, and announced his intention of fighting on until the Greeks were driven out and Constantinople itself was free.

A year of stalemate followed, punctuated by the massacre of Turks by Greeks and Greeks by Turks. France signed a separate peace with Kemal, and Italy began losing interest in the whole affair. A few French and Italian troops remained with a larger contingent of British in the land garrison at Chanak, on the Dardanelles. Between them and the rebellious Kemal there was only the Greek occupation army in Smyrna.

On August 26, 1922, after an emissary to London had been rebuffed, Kemal threw his army into an all-out attack against the hapless Greeks. In two weeks the Greeks were crushed and the ancient capital of Smyrna burned.

As the Turkish army paused among the flames the hopelessly outnumbered Allied garrison at Chanak was trapped. The only immediate defense for the Dardanelles was a fifteen-month-old proclamation setting up a strip of neutral zones beside the Straits, and since it had never been recognized by Kemal, there was no certainty that he would recognize neutrality now.

Up to this point the Canadian government had had no communication on the new crisis whatever. Then, on September 15, London sent urgent secret cables to the four British dominions asking them to participate in the defense of Constantinople and the Straits.

This sudden four-alarm call to arms was not nearly so startling as the manner in which it was announced. Even before the official appeal reached Ottawa that redoubtable man of action, Winston Churchill, had released a press statement in his capacity as Colonial Secretary. The statement had Prime Minister Lloyd George's blessing, and the Associated Press dispatch that reached Canada read as follows: "London: Great Britain has invited Canada and the other British Dominions to be represented by contingents in the British force taking part in an effective defence of the neutral zone in the Near East, it was authoritatively reported today. The semi-official announcement of the invitation to the Dominions said that they had been invited to participate in the defence of those interests for which they had already made enormous sacrifices."

This was far more than a diplomatic news leak; it was a tidal wave. Leaving aside the shattering prospect of another war, it resurrected old, vexed, and basic questions that were supposed to be already settled. Was London still making foreign policy unilaterally and arbitrarily for the Empire? Were the dominions still expected to fight blindly in defense of decisions made in Westminster with or without their consent or knowledge?

The answer had been a staunch and unanimous "No!" in the comradely, chastening days of the Imperial War Cabinet, the Imperial War Conference, and Versailles. Now it appeared, in London's view, to have reverted to the *status quo ante* "Yes!" Moreover, in case of hesitation by the political leaders of the dominions, London apparently felt it proper to appeal over their heads to their people.

Mackenzie King read the story in the newspapers several hours before Winston Churchill's official appeal for help arrived in his office. By then New Zealand had already received its cable from Churchill and had replied with an offer to send troops at once; this was in the papers too.

To King the whole enterprise reeked of Imperial arrogance and bluster and he lost no time in committing his thoughts to the diary: "I confess it annoyed me. It is drafted designedly to play the imperial game, to test out centralization vs. autonomy as regards European wars. . . . I have thought out my plans. . . . No contingent will go without parliament being summoned in first instance. . . . I shall not commit myself one way or the other, but keep the responsibility for prlt. I do not believe prlt. would sanction the sending of a contingent. The French Canadians will be opposed. I believe most if not all our members in Ont. and the maritime provinces will be opposed. I am not so sure of B.C. I feel confident the Progressives will be opposed almost to a man. It is the time now to bring them into the Government . . . to strengthen us in our attitude of refusing to send a contingent without sanction of prlt. . . . New Zealand has offered a contingent—naturally she looks to the Br. Navy for everything. Australia will probably follow her example. I doubt if S. Africa will. I feel sure she won't. I am sure the people of Canada are against participation in this European war."

At the same time King cabled Lloyd George protesting the premature press release. But public opinion was already afire. For the next ten days the country resounded with exhortations to war and prayers for peace.

Clergymen cried for preparations to mobilize. Militia depots were crowded with volunteers. The Red Cross and the Salvation Army offered to reorganize their wartime services. The Liberal Toronto *Globe* declared, taut-lipped: "If the Turk attacks Constantinople he attacks Canada." The Conservative Montreal *Star* spoke for the ours-not-to-reason-why faction: "If the British Government, with its special sources of information, decided that a firm stand must be taken on the Dardanelles, it would be an act of mad and egotistic folly for a journal or Government 3,000 miles away to set up a different view." Some papers and public speakers thought no decision could be taken until the Canadian government had more information. Others, such as the Toronto *Star*, laid the whole affair to "propagandists," and *Le Droit* of Ottawa saw Canada's duty as to refuse Britain's request.

During the first full day of the crisis the Canadian Cabinet met almost continuously. King's attitude hardened almost by the hour and the Cabinet followed his lead unquestioningly. No Canadian troops would be offered until Parliament's consent had been asked, and Parliament's consent would not be asked until the Cabinet itself was ready to make a recommendation.

Lloyd George cabled again: "The attitude of Canada at this moment is of great importance. We do not ask for any immediate decision to send troops. Were large reinforcements to prove necessary we should immediately summon Parliament here and should notify you of our decision to do so at once. It is presumably not necessary for you to summon Parliament till then and we hope that it may not be necessary at all. A definite statement, however, that Canada will stand by the Empire in the event of terms of Armistice being broken will do much to ensure maintenance of peace."

King replied coldly: "We have not found it necessary to reassert the loyalty of Canada to the British Empire. . . . Should it become necessary to summon Parliament, Canada, by decision of its Parliament, will so act as to carry out the full duty of the Canadian people." He still refused to budge after a further appeal from Winston Churchill to join in "a quiet but decisive demonstration that the British Empire is not to be threatened or bluffed."

It seems evident from the painstaking, persevering way in which Lloyd George and Churchill sought to elicit a declaration of unquestioning support from the Canadian Prime Minister that they mistook his stubbornness for mere density. Arthur Meighen knew King too well, and from too far back, to make the same mistake. He recognized that for all the fencing over diplomatic niceties something much deeper was involved: by some wild freak of history, his tiresome little college friend Rex King had been placed in a position to influence the whole future course of the Empire, and little Rex, in his tiresome, mealymouthed way—as Meighen saw it—might do that indispensable institution untold harm unless someone headed him off.

Since Parliament was not in session, Meighen was obliged to make his views heard from the public platform. At Belleville, Ontario, five days after the dispatch of the first appeal for aid from London, he announced sternly: "This being a grave question of foreign policy, it is the duty of every good citizen to give the Government every opportunity to live up to the sterling aspirations of the British Empire. I am giving them that opportunity."

When this Jovian ultimatum was unanswered after three days, Meighen made another speech in Toronto. This time his ordinance rang out as resoundingly as a six-gun salute: "When Britain's message came, then Canada should have said: 'Ready, aye, ready; we stand by you.'"

The Chanak crisis died down as quickly as it had erupted. Kemal's troops moved into the neutral zone and found themselves separated from the British garrison only by a slender barricade of barbed wire. A process of spontaneous decombustion set in as the commanders on the ground and their political superiors in Angora, London, and Paris realized they were no more than a few feet and a single pistol shot from another war. Another peace conference was speedily arranged on conditions acceptable to all the key parties except the Sultan of Turkey and the King of Greece, each of whom fled into exile.

This "oriental imbroglio," as it was disdainfully described by Henri Bourassa, proved to be a bench mark in the evolution of Canada's foreign policy. It depicted a far sharper line between the basic positions of King and Meighen than that which actually existed, but it did show unmistakably that the line was there. Meighen's simple and long to be remembered "Ready, aye, ready!" represented an attitude toward the Empire far less watchful and independent than Borden had intended when he and Smuts devised their scheme for common action in international affairs. King's frigid correctness toward Great Britain implied an indifference more pronounced than he actually felt.

Nevertheless, the affair in Turkey did offer a point from which it can be seen that the events preceding it and the events that followed it were all part of the same landscape, hewed in the same contours. The Conservatives were what might be described as federal Imperialists. The arrangement between the mother country and the dominions that would have suited them best would have been not unlike that undertaken between the provinces and Canada by the British North America Act. Each member would have full control of its own domestic affairs. They would all act together in foreign affairs with Britain acknowledged to be—Borden used the phrase approvingly, with no hint of Orwellian irony—first among equals.

King was an isolationist before Chanak and he remained an isolationist up to and most of the way through 1939. He and his party saw precisely eye to eye with the Conservatives on the need to avoid commitments on matters in which they were not consulted. But they differed on the means. King feared that by asking to be consulted automatically, he would become automatically involved. He wanted to be consulted only when his country was involved already.

Perhaps there was no anti-British bias in this attitude. King might have been equally suspicious of too much Imperial solidarity if the Empire to which his country belonged had been a Roman Empire, a Mandarin Empire, or a North American Empire. He was as wary of foreign entanglements, in his own way, as Henry Cabot Lodge or Henri Bourassa. Had it been otherwise he could never have obtained power or kept it, for as a Liberal, an anti-conscriptionist, and the successor to Laurier, his own most indispensable entanglement was a highly domestic one, with Quebec and its 65 parliamentary seats.

He was even more cautious toward the League of Nations than toward the Empire. He never paid more than lip service to the League, and when the time came he helped in its destruction. That was to be much later, but in the early 1920s alone he compiled a considerable record of skepticism toward collective security. While he was still Leader of the Opposition he recoiled from a suggestion that Canada accept a mandate over Armenia, whose people were being exterminated by the Russians on one side and the Turks on the other. (The United States, given a similar opportunity, turned its back on Armenia too.)

King had nothing to say for the League in his campaign for office in 1921 and he had nothing of importance to say for it afterward. He was asked to be a delegate at the League's Assembly. He declined. He was asked to take the presidency of the League's parallel arm, the International Labor Conference. He declined. His chosen deputy, Senator Raoul Dandurand, rose at Geneva to announce his Prime Minister's stand on world security: "We live in a fireproof house far from inflammable materials."

King, as Borden and Meighen had done before him, tried to water down Article X of the League of Nations Covenant, the clause that could send any signatory to war "in case of threat or danger of aggression." He repudiated the Treaty of Sèvres, a non-League settlement which preceded the trouble in Turkey. He made certain that Canada did not become a party to the new treaty at Lausanne or to the more important Locarno pacts involving France and Germany. The one treaty in which he took pride and personal interest concerned, by a lamentable accident, not mighty principles or the sweeping destiny of nations—but halibut. This occurred in March 1923, when King arranged for a member of his Cabinet to sign an agreement on fisheries with the United States; up to then the British ambassador had acted as Canada's signing power.

It was in the same year that King himself went to London to put an end to the Borden-Smuts dream of a central Empire. Odd and illogical things had happened since the man from Grand Pré and the man from Pretoria sold the Welshman, Lloyd George, on a new unity beneath the Union Jack. Less than a decade before, it had been unthinkable that Canada, South Africa, and Wales should all be heard and heeded with something like equal respect in the councils of His Majesty. Now it was not only granted that they should be heard and heeded; it was desired. And so, having won the right to be listened to, Canada decided not to speak. King turned away from Westminster with as much determination as he had turned away at the time of Chanak.

His basic position was best summarized in a memo from one of his chief advisers at the conference, O. D. Skelton. Skelton was referring to one of the many attempts to set up some kind of main authority or consulting body.

"This proposal [Skelton wrote from London] is simply another variant of the endless schemes for establishing a central government here. Parliament or Council or Secretariat, it matters not, so long as the machinery of control can somehow be established in London. . . . It may be that the 'permanent organization' will be pictured as a mere statistical and fact-finding body, but on such wide questions, questions of policy, it could not be merely this even to start and would soon develop into something much more active and executive. It would commit us to a central review of every important economic activity of our government, and would for example give good ground for intervention if we proposed a reciprocity arrangement with the U.S. It is superfluous because each government has access to all the material facts and can collect and judge them; if then common action is desired, that can be effected between the governments concerned."

King almost certainly would have arrived at this position with or without advice. The way he acted on it is described in a diary entry of November 5, 1923:

"At three o'clock there was a secret session of what purported to be the Prime Ministers. . . . Lord Curzon explained that the conference was for the purpose of considering the statement . . . on foreign policy. . . . It was really an effort to commit the conference to a common foreign policy and I had a most difficult and unpleasant hour or two strongly opposing many of the paragraphs that were inserted. I protested against our assuming the rights of a cabinet in the determination of foreign policy and maintained that at most we could give advice on matters on which we were fully informed and concerning which we were prepared to accept responsibility.

"I pointed out that we had, in a communication to the Foreign Office, refused to recognize the telegraph despatches which were sent to us as giving us any real opportunity of discussion or shaping foreign policy and that we had refused to regard their acceptance as more than for purposes of information. . . .

"I protested . . . against the Government's foreign policy . . . I protested strongly against trying to shape the affairs of Europe . . . I pointed out that it might be necessary for the Government to consider . . . an invitation to subsequent conferences if their purpose was to have the Dominions committed to matters over which their Parliaments had no control. . . . I succeeded by absolutely refusing to sanction certain of the Clauses . . . I was very outspoken and perhaps too much so."

King, the most careful and maidenly of men, had reached an unprecedented peak of anger. He outraged everybody. Lord Curzon said that he was "obstinate and stupid." Jan Christiaan Smuts looked him in the eye and, twinkling only slightly, announced: "Mackenzie King, you are a very terrible person."

King took these remarks as compliments. It will never be possible to make anything like an objective appraisal of this astonishing man and his career until his official, semi-official, and private papers are opened to objective inspection. But according to his official biographer, the diplomatic pressures to which King was subjected in London were aggravated by far more attractive social pressures. "He is," noted an Opposition member of Parliament in the Canadian House of Commons, "a young Prime Minister and Shakespeare says something about the temptations of 'silken dalliance.' There is a silken dalliance in the drawing rooms of London."

King, almost certainly still a virgin and a terrified one at that, was half hypnotized by the scent and rustle of the drawing rooms. One of his private secretaries predicted in high alarm that "extraordinary pressure" would be brought on him but from "unsuspected directions too." "Beware," the secretary warned a colleague, "lest your knight be unhorsed."

King himself, after sifting hundreds of social invitations and accepting a large number of them, made this summary for his future guidance:

"Were I attending another Conference I should refrain wholly from accepting any luncheon engagements and would make it a point to retire early in the evening. The irregularity of meals, lack of exercise and numerous engagements have made extremely difficult the thought and care which should have been given to the Conference itself."

XXIX

The emergence of the Left—James Woodsworth and Tim Buck

WHILE the deceptively strong-looking Progressive party began its march to oblivion, a deceptively weak-looking group of two Laborites began a longer journey in the approximate direction of the stars.

It would be an exaggeration to say that no one noted the election in 1921 of William Irvine and James Shaver Woodsworth to the House of Commons. Irvine was well known and highly respected in western Canada as a leftist clergyman from Calgary. Woodsworth was even better known as one of the agitators who had been briefly jailed at the time of the Winnipeg strike. To his regret he was never brought to trial. The indictment against him consisted of six counts. Five were based on angry and biased but scarcely seditious reports and editorials he had written for a labor paper. The sixth consisted simply of two quotations he had used from the prophet Isaiah.

"Woe unto them that decree unrighteous decrees, and that write grievousness which they have prescribed; to turn aside the needy from judgment, and to take away the right of the poor of my people, that widows may be their prey and that they may rob the fatherless."

"And they shall build houses, and inhabit them; and they shall plant vineyards, and eat the fruit of them. They shall not build, and another inhabit; they shall not plant, and another eat; for as the days of a tree are the days of my people, and mine elect shall long enjoy the work of their hands."

It was perhaps not so strange as it seemed that the confused, nervous, and none too bright federal prosecutors of 1919 should have locked Woodsworth up for quoting from the prophets. He was just the sort of man who, full of surface gentleness and frailty combined with a maddening perseverance and strength of will, drives stronger men to helpless resentment and to acts of folly and fatuity. He was, in his way and in the most admirable sense, a rather Chaplinesque figure.

Like the little stray whom Chaplin made immortal, Woodsworth had a faith in ultimate goodness and was content to put up with all the rebuffs of a more cynical world to help achieve it. Each had a great inner dignity, but no special regard for the usual trappings of dignity. Woodsworth, with his little well-trimmed beard, bore little physical resemblance to Chaplin, with his little well-trimmed mustache, although they were both small in stature. Nor did Woodsworth ever become a tramp, although he endured poverty with a high heart and cheerfully descended from his pulpit as a Methodist minister to become a longshoreman when he felt doubts about the church.

And in the long run he triumphed, triumphed over life and its hardships and left the world a better place, with his friends better off for his being there and his adversaries glaring impotently after him down the length of long dusty roads or pursuing him hotly around corners with waving nightsticks.

Although she never drew this particular comparison, Woodsworth's wife, a staunch friend and supporter through forty cheerful years, must have been thinking of something of the kind when she told a reporter after his death: "If James had more sense of humor he'd never have amounted to anything. He could never see how funny he looked, one little man struggling against the whole world."

Woodsworth and Irvine took their seats together in the new Parliament of 1922. "I wish to state," Irvine told the Speaker of the Commons, "that the honorable Member for Winnipeg Centre is the leader of the labor group—and I am the group."

Irvine went on more seriously: "But even if we are small I should like to say, without any presumption whatsoever, that a small living seed, however small it may be, is greater than a dead trunk."

During the next twenty years—even in the face of his wildly unpopular political attitudes—Woodsworth was to see the small living seed grow into one of the strongest political and social forces in his country's life. Only nationalism, as reflected by King, Bourassa, and Borden, and occasionally by Woodsworth himself, played as strong a part in the country's evolution as did Woodsworth's doctrine of welfare-state socialism.

Woodsworth never won more than a handful of parliamentary supporters either in the early days as a Laborite or later as founder and leader of the larger party called the Co-operative Commonwealth Federation; nor did he ever achieve a large popular vote. Nevertheless, the older parties recognized him and the half-articulate yearning for reform among the population at large as a force too strong to ignore or minimize.

Under the patient goading of Woodsworth the Liberals moved further and faster toward the left than they had intended and the Conservatives did not dare fall far behind. Except in Saskatchewan, where an offshoot of his national party achieved power and introduced a few government factories, a bus line, and a fur-marketing service and stimulated the move to co-operatives, Woodsworth and the C.C.F. achieved virtually nothing in the area of doctrinaire business socialism. They attached much less importance to this, in any event, than to an increase in social welfare. Here Woodsworth's supporters can and do claim—and only the narrowest kind of hairsplitting can refute them—that he was the most influential advocate of old-age pensions, family allowances, unemployment insurance, and national health insurance. He forced the creation of a divorce court for Canada's largest province in the face of the stern opposition of religious groups and the older political parties. He led a fight, successful after fifteen years, for the repeal of Section 98 of the Criminal Code, an enactment designed after the Winnipeg strike to strengthen the law against undesirable aliens and Red agitators, but which, in fact, could be used and occasionally was used to interfere with civil liberty.

About the same time that Woodsworth and his Laborites were embarking on the national political seas, another small but hopeful party was making its beginning. It was inevitable that Canada, like almost all countries, should aquire its own Communist movement in the wake of the Russian revolution. It was equally inevitable that the acquisition should be carried out in an atmosphere of intrigue, mystery, and—in the eyes of the more nervous—awful menace.

In the confusion of Russia's military collapse, accompanied and followed by the bloody struggle for power between the Czarists, the Bolsheviks, and the Mensheviks, Canada had been one of a dozen nations to send "help" in the shape of armed forces. A brigade of Canadian artillery disembarked at Archangel two months before the Armistice; four thousand troops landed at Vladivostok; and there were other small contingents around Murmansk and in southern Russia. The various Allied Expeditionary Forces in Russia or near its borders included British, Americans, French, Italians, Czechoslovaks, Serbs, Rumanians, Poles, Japanese, Australians, New Zealanders, and South Africans, and at one time they numbered more than half a million. Canada's Conservative government at first sought to suggest that their purpose was not to intervene in Russia's internal affairs, but to "check German expansion and influence." But it soon had to be admitted that most of the military visitors, including those from Canada, were actually fighting the Red Army. One of the Canadian groups was forced to wage a two-hundred-mile rearguard action before being rescued by the British fleet at Archangel. The other units were soon withdrawn voluntarily.

The knowledge that Canada had already been in a form of armed combat against the new Bolshevik government did little to allay the fears of Bolshevism that were already spreading through the world. Then, of course, there was the only partial accident that these distant events coincided to the month with the beginning of the Winnipeg strike. While not more than one or two of the strike leaders could accurately be described as Communists, many of the leaders and their supporters were already borrowing the language of Marx, Engels, and Lenin and, not surprisingly, were widely believed to mean what they said.

The war of nerves was almost universal and nowhere did it create more anxiety than in the United States. There were strikes almost everywhere, including a paralyzing general walkout in Seattle. A bomb exploded on the doorstep of Attorney General A. Mitchell Palmer, who then rounded up six thousand radicals, labor leaders, and pamphleteers in a series of nation-wide raids on New Year's Day 1920.

Palmer assessed the danger and justified his reaction to it in the most lurid and chilling terms: "Like a prairie-fire the blaze of revolution was sweeping over every American institution of law and order. It was eating its way into the homes of the American workman, its sharp tongues of revolutionary heat were licking the altars of the churches, leaping into the belfry of the school bell, crawling into the sacred corners of American homes, seeking to

replace marriage vows with libertine laws, burning up the foundations of society."

Postmaster General A. S. Burleson felt no less strongly: "The
doctrines of the Bolsheviki, Communists, anarchists and kindred
organizations are being spread broadcast throughout the United
States by agents of revolutionary socialism, co-operating for the
purpose of precipitating a revolution through violence and by unlawful and unconstitutional means."

The editor of the responsible and reliable *Canadian Annual Review*
quoted—in a context which suggested he believed it to be accurate
—an American estimate that in Canada alone there were already
68,000 members enrolled in underground soviets bent on seizing
control of the country by force.

The objects of the domestic Bolsheviks were, of course, exactly
as stated by these and other adversaries. The error was in placing
their strength and potential far too high, an error which not only
led to unnecessarily repressive measures but unquestionably helped
the tiny handful of real anarchists by making it easier for them to
attract the support and services of adventurers and opportunists
and even of a number of those "crackpot idealists" who later were
to become so prominent a species in the demonology of anti-com-
munism.

In Canada, according to evidence obtained through later seizures
of the party records, testimony of undercover police agents, and
other means, it is doubtful whether the 68,000 true-red, off-with-
their-heads Communists mentioned in the *Canadian Annual Review*
actually numbered as many as a hundred.

Indeed, in the years of maximum jitters, 1919 and 1920, there
was no Communist organization in Canada. The O.B.U. was often
mistaken for one and so were a number of other militant labor groups
which often imitated the party jargon.

The charter meeting of the Canadian Communist party was not
held until May 1921. The whole proceedings were carried out
with the stealthy panoply and muffled trumpet blasts of a true
conspiracy; not a single one of the cinematic clichés was overlooked.

The meeting was convened, secretly, in a barn near Guelph,
Ontario. The guiding spirits were three organizers sent from
Moscow by the Communist International. The senior member of the
delegation was a Latvian who was introduced to the Canadian postu-

lants only as Charles Scott. Scott had brought three thousand dollars from Moscow to finance the launchings. He explained that it would be necessary for the Canadian party, before being admitted to the Communist International, to abide by its Theses and Statutes. These were accepted. One sample excerpt read: "The Communist International makes its aims to put up an armed struggle for the overthrow of the international bourgeoisie and to create an international Soviet Republic as a transition stage to the complete abolition of the state."

In another passage the means to the end were itemized: "Violent defeat of the bourgeoisie, the confiscation of its property, the annihilation of the entire bourgeois governmental apparatus, parliamentary, judicial, military, bureaucratic, administrative, municipal."

The party's charter members were instructed in and quickly adopted the stock underground paraphernalia of codes, ciphers, and cover names. They divided and overlapped in two organizations—one a surface, or "A," party, called the Workers' Party of Canada; the other an underground, or "Z," party, called the Communist party. The object of this charade was to enable the pioneer comrades to seek new recruits through the relatively innocuous "A" party while still stoking up the revolutionary fires in the hidden crucible of the "Z" party.

No one plunged into these exciting ventures with more zest than a young novitiate who entered the "Z" party as an invented J. Page and enlisted in the "A" party in his true identity as Tim Buck. An immigrant machinist from England who had first heard the gospel of the Left straight from the lips of Keir Hardie, Buck was almost immediately made the party's industrial director, a position in which his chief duty was to foment labor unrest.

But his timing was unlucky. Prosperity was already on the way. Hardly anyone was interested in striking. By 1923, the Red scare was so far in the past that when a Canadian delegation went to the Fourth World Congress of the Comintern in Moscow, it was instructed that it was now safe for the party to come into the open. This assessment proved all too true. When the comrades emerged into the daylight, it was only to be greeted by a wave of staggering indifference. Having liquidated his subterranean alter ego, J. Page, Tim Buck manfully attempted to do two men's work as prophet of disaster. But to most ears his trumpet of doom sounded thin and vaguely comic among the singing cash registers and chattering ticker tapes. His own old union paid him the thin compliment of canceling his membership, but most people had neither the time nor the inclination to take him seriously.

A somehow touching glimpse of the problems of a revolutionary in a contented society emerged in an interview the present writer once had with a police officer in connection with a magazine article on Buck. Both the Toronto city police and the Royal Canadian Mounted Police were shadowing him as dutiful watchdogs of the state. One plain-clothes man who was detailed to the job during that period believes there were days when it wouldn't have taken much to persuade Buck that he was riding the wrong horse. "Once I picked Tim up at his house right after breakfast and tailed him all day," the officer recalled. "He just seemed to be wandering around, talking to a guy here, talking to a guy there, disappearing into his office for a couple of hours and then coming out and talking to another guy. He didn't even seem to be able to work up an argument. I tailed him right up to eleven-thirty at night and then he got on a streetcar and I got on after him.

"It had been a trying, useless day for both of us," Buck's old shadow went on, "and I sat down in the streetcar beside him. He didn't know I was tailing him, but I'd known him before I joined the force. 'Tim,' I said, 'that revolution of yours doesn't seem to be going so hot.' 'No,' he said. 'No, it doesn't.' And then he said: 'You know, it should have spread on into Germany. If it had the whole world would have caught fire.' He sure sounded discouraged that night."

But the dead hand of prosperity gave Buck's personal career an unexpected lift. He had only two superiors in the Canadian party, Jack MacDonald, the secretary, and Maurice Spector, a fellow delegate to the Comintern, and both men began to wonder whether the Comintern's line was the most effective one for Canada after all. Each began toying with a separate heresy. The word for Spector's heresy was Trotskyism—the belief that no revolution means anything unless it's going on everywhere, all the time, and at breakneck speed. The name for MacDonald's heresy was right opportunism—a belief in the value of gradual, peaceful leftist gains.

At that particular moment, the official line lay in between. Spector was expelled from the party with a minimum of ceremony. MacDonald, as the national leader, presented a more delicate case.

The Executive Committee appealed by cable to the Anglo-American section of the Comintern in Moscow. Moscow's reply read: PLACE BEFORE MACDONALD DEMAND THAT HE AS MEMBER OF PARTY AND CC [CENTRAL COMMITTEE] MUST OPENLY ADMIT AND IMMEDIATELY ABANDON RIGHT OPPORTUNISTIC POSITION COMMA UNCONDITIONALLY AGREES TO CARRY ON RESOLUTE STRUGGLE AGAINST ALL RIGHT ELEMENTS IN PARTY UNCONDITIONALLY ACCEPTS CI PARTY LINE AND DISCIPLINE INFORMING HIM FAILURE TO ACCEPT THESE CONDITIONS OF THE TENTH ECCI [EXECUTIVE COMMITTEE COMMUNIST INTERNATIONAL] PLENUM MEANS EXPULSION FROM THE PARTY.

The cable was addressed to Buck, who thus was proclaimed heir designate. He succeeded ten days later, when MacDonald, having been given that length of time to recant, refused to do so.

More fallow fields lay not far ahead for Buck and the party. But in the meantime he remained a failure in success, just as Woodsworth, leader of the nation's other leftist party, was beginning to achieve success in failure.

XXX

*Prohibition in the United States and rumrunning
in Canada—"Lean up against the counter
and make a gurgling sigh."*

MOST Canadians born later than, say, 1910 are under the impression that their country came almost wholly unscathed through the social, moral, and political ordeal of prohibition. Nothing could be further from the truth. Canada did escape the great consolidated headache of a Volstead Act, but the headache it took piecemeal was nevertheless a memorable one.

Except to collect sales and excise taxes and duties Ottawa stayed largely clear of the liquor traffic during the war and postwar years. The provinces were left to write their own regulations—and in many cases to rewrite them and then rewrite them again. Prohibition, semi-prohibition, and the open bar raced back and forth through the statute books of the nine provinces like the lights on a busy switchboard, but there was never any time after 1921 when at least two or three of the provinces weren't at least damp. And even in those that were bone-dry there were almost invariably warehouses stacked to the eaves with beverages which, although forbidden to local consumers, it was perfectly legal to export. Ontario and Quebec both denied booze to their own citizens but allowed some of the world's largest distilleries and breweries to go on making it as fast as they could.

Thus, to anyone interested in assuaging the sudden thirst of a hundred million Americans, Canada was the promised land, a smuggler's paradise—an Andorra with a border four thousand miles long, and an undefended border at that. At each end lay enough open water to float a thousand Majorcas.

The last weepy pre-Volstead drunk had not finished his last pre-Volstead highball before the first relief shipments were on the way.

Some went in schooners out of Lunenburg for dark coves in Maine, some from Victoria and Vancouver to lie off Puget Sound. Some went by skiff and fast launch from Windsor to Detroit, some by truck or bicycle or even on foot down lonely prairie trails from towns like Estevan, Saskatchewan, toward towns like Portal, North Dakota. Most Canadians soon became aware of these enterprises, which grew in scope and variety. Their reactions ranged from indifference to amusement; hardly anyone was outraged except the dries, and they were too busy trying to save their fellow citizens to worry unduly about any possible peril to the U.S.A.—which, after all, had just removed itself from peril anyway.

Moreover, the rumrunning and border slipping broke no Canadian law, as various governments, including the one at Ottawa, repeatedly and correctly reminded the public. It took half a dozen years or more before Canada fully comprehended the impossibility of providing both an operating base and the raw materials for a multi-billion-dollar criminal industry while itself remaining untouched by the crimes involved. Then the knowledge came home with savage impact, almost enough to wreck the country's most durable political dynasty.

For the time being, however, prohibition was much too good a thing to leave to the Yankees. It was a far fresher topic of discussion than those old stand-bys, the tariff and the Empire. It even had a slight edge on the weather; a person could actually do something about it. Before the war it had been an issue that might or might not turn up in an election. Now it could not fail to turn up in some form, in any and all elections—and with women now eligible to vote it offered endless new opportunities for cajolery on both sides and a new element of uncertainty.

By the early 1920s the patterns of liquor law had begun to sort themselves out, but they were still a remarkable hodgepodge. Quebec and British Columbia were unabashedly wet. Their annual profits from liquor exceeded, respectively, five million dollars and three million. There were rumors that a fleet of some twenty light aircraft were ferrying whisky across the Quebec border into New England. Seven bandits killed a Montreal bank-car driver in a quarter-million-dollar holdup, and during the trial that led to the hanging of four of them it became apparent that shooting up banks was really only their spare-time work; smuggling was their real business.

Manitoba and Alberta were dry, but both were on the verge of changing.

Saskatchewan had just gone wet after a harrowing experience. When prohibition was introduced it had been decreed that the province's sixty liquor export houses would still be able to ship spirits out of the country, but after February 1, 1921, they would not be allowed to replenish their stocks through further imports. Before the cutoff date they all built up enormous stockpiles and went happily on consigning the stuff in bond to destinations outside the province. The government had no objection to this export traffic, but unfortunately large quantities of warehouse whisky kept showing up on the breath of the province's own captive teetotalers. It was then decreed that all the liquor warehouses would have to move to Regina, Moose Jaw, or Saskatoon, where it would be easier for the law to help guard them against seepage. Even this did not work, and in 1923 the province closed down the export houses completely. During this period the prairies had a number of bank robberies, hitherto a rarity there.

Both New Brunswick and Prince Edward Island were dry. New Brunswick had export warehouses and experienced complications not unlike Saskatchewan's. In one two-day sweep in tiny Prince Edward Island prohibition agents seized 1100 gallons of rum and fourteen cases of whisky.

Nova Scotia was wet for a time, a circumstance that made rumrunning all the more attractive to its fishing captains, who had an additional source of cargo at the nearby French island of St. Pierre. This led to a special set of problems, which were described thus in the Charlottetown *Guardian*:

"It [the traffic] is not only immense, but is the cause of evil consequences to the Lunenburg fishing fleet.

"In 1921 there were 113 fishing vessels out from Gloucester. There were only 72 in 1924, and there will not be more than 30 in 1925. Not only will the catch of fish be very much restricted, but the fishermen themselves will have to go elsewhere for employment, because where a vessel engaged in fishing would carry twenty-five hands, vessels rumrunning need only carry six or seven. The profits in 1924 were so large, however, that the vessel owners, as a rule, succumbed to the temptation of the business.

"For the use of the vessels they receive from $100 to $120 per month, and the captains average about $500 per month. In addition bonuses are paid for the successful landing of the cargo. The captain and crew are paid only to carry the liquor to Rum Row. They remain beyond the twelve-mile limit, as secure against the law as ordinary freighters.

"Property in the vicinity of the quays at St. Pierre has advanced very much in price; $100,000 was refused recently for one warehouse property which was purchased a few years ago for $2,000."

Ontario's law was the weirdest contraption of all. The province was considered to be prohibitionist and, indeed, it was difficult to obtain a drink of scotch, rye, irish, gin, rum, or any beer worthy of the name. However, the powerful grape growers' lobby had persuaded the government to stop short of outlawing wine. This could be bought freely in strengths up to 28 per cent, a potency generally considered to be more conducive to straightforward guzzling than to gracious living. The government had issued permits allowing their 30,000 holders to make their own wine at home.

After much agitation beer up to 4.4 proof was allowed later on. Anyone who could get a prescription could buy enough hard spirits for medicinal use. (Stephen Leacock reported: "It is necessary to go to a drugstore . . . and lean up against the counter and make a gurgling sigh like apoplexy. One often sees these apoplexy cases lined up four deep.")

South of the 49th Parallel and its adjoining waters the harassed U.S. revenue agents were doing what they could to secure their borders against alcohol from abroad. What they could do, unfortunately, was sometimes what they had no right to do. They organized a "Dry Navy" of half a dozen high-speed patrol boats for use on the Atlantic coast and five motor cutters for the Great Lakes. Occasionally the Dry Navy searched or seized Canadian and British ships outside U.S. waters and sought to seal up liquor on passenger ships in U.S. ports. Britain was particularly touchy about any suggestion of interference with its maritime rights, and when in the midst of these minor irritations the U.S. government without notice or discussion announced it was extending the three-mile limit to twelve miles, the irritation became acute.

Under this unilateral authority the British trawler *Gamma*, sailing out of Halifax with 2000 cases of whisky, was fired on and captured off (but more than three miles off) Montauk Point by a

U.S. patrol boat. Shortly afterward a U.S. federal judge sustained the seizure of the Canadian schooner *Grace and Ruby* six miles offshore, ruling: "The seas are free to all countries . but the mere fact that the *Grace and Ruby* was beyond the three-mile limit does not make the seizure unlawful."

Sir Auckland Geddes, the British ambassador, protested direct to President Harding on these and other violations of the three-mile limit. The U. S. Cabinet thereupon agreed that the limit should be respected except in the case of vessels "which actually established communication with the United States by means of their own crews or small boats." This recognized what everybody knew already: the wronged *Grace and Ruby*, like many other mother ships of the rum fleet, had been seeking to hide behind the three-mile limit while trans-shipping its liquor to smaller craft for the final run to shore.

But although a settlement based not merely on law but on respect for the law now seemed in sight, relations worsened when the U. S. Attorney General, later backed by Judge Learned Hand, decreed that "any foreign vessel entering an American port with liquor on board as cargo, or in stores, comes under the Prohibition Enforcement Law and is to be dealt with accordingly." In short, the luxury liners of Cunard and other foreign shipping firms sailing into New York would have to close the bar three miles out, throw any unused liquor overboard, and serve nothing stronger than tea on the return voyage. United States opinion was as much opposed to this enactment as was British opinion. "The one thing we can be sure of," the New York *Tribune* warned, "is that our ports and shipping will suffer. Foreign lines can be shifted to Canadian ports. Unless the Supreme Court reverses Judge Hand, Congress should promptly take steps to tie the Volstead Act safely at home, where it can be enforced without ruining vital American business and without initiating futile squabbles with other nations."

Public opinion in Canada was not unaffected by business considerations either. Much of the export booze was the product of Canadian industry and the rest passed through Canadian wholesalers. In the first full year of the Volstead Act the import of whisky into Canada increased from an annual $5,500,000 worth to $23,000,000. "Rum-running," the *Financial Post* pointed out realistically, "has provided a tidy bit towards Canada's favorable balance of trade." The Toronto *Saturday Night* said haughtily: "A good many people in the United States, including certain Washington officials, are evidently of the opinion that it is Canada's duty to assist that country in enforcing the Volstead Act. One enthusiast writes that if it takes a hundred thousand men to police our borders in order that no smuggling of liquor may take place, it is the duty of Canada to perform that service." The Americans, *Saturday Night* went on, had brought the hazards of the Volstead Act on themselves through their own folly.

In March 1923 the U. S. Secretary of State officially asked Canada to decline clearance papers to vessels with cargoes of liquor destined to ports in the United States unless a U.S. permit authorizing its entry was presented first. After three months Mackenzie King's government replied coolly that "the government of Canada had carefully investigated the matter and had ascertained that the provisions of the law were being properly observed." There existed "no provisions in the custom laws or regulations which would warrant refusal of clearance to a foreign port simply because of the fact that the entry of such liquor, without special permits, was prohibited at the foreign port in question." The government of Canada therefore "regretted their inability to adopt the suggestion put forth by the United States government in regard to this matter."

But it gradually became apparent that, leaving international incidents and local crime aside, there were aspects to the rumrunning problem that Canada had not fully appreciated. Smuggling is a two-way street, both economically and morally. A ship, a small vessel, or a truck that can safely transport a cargo of contraband in one direction may be able to—and will certainly be tempted to—transport a different kind of contraband in the other direction on the return journey. A nation that yawns when its citizens break another nation's laws invites a loss of respect for its own laws.

Canada, rather disconcertingly, discovered that smuggling was not as great a help to the balance of trade as it had been first supposed. The return traffic was threatening a number of Canadian industries, large and small, with extinction or near extinction. *Saturday Night*, which had taken so lofty an attitude toward American complaints two years earlier, summed up the other side of the equation in high alarm:

"Smuggling into Canada has of late years assumed such immense proportions and has increased with such startling rapidity that it has become a national menace. Hon. Jacques Bureau, Minister of Customs, is quoted as saying that at least fifty million dollars of foreign goods are smuggled into Canada every year. This is, of course, only an estimate, and no one can really have an adequate idea of the extent of a business which thrives on secrecy, never advertises, and prefers to blush and smuggle unseen. But its extent may be measured by the results; by the Canadian factories which have reduced or suspended operations because they cannot meet this unfair competition; by the workmen whose families are very close to the bread line, because Canadian merchants have preferred the cheap goods, coming by the underground route, to those made by Canadian factories which have honestly paid the duties on their raw materials; and by the prosperity of the smuggling communities which have entrenched themselves here and there along the international boundary line between Canada and the United States."

Although the larger ships of the rum fleet were not suitable for handling return cargoes, land conditions for two-way smuggling were ideal, particularly on the lonely frontiers between Maine and New Brunswick, between the southern townships of Quebec and Maine and Vermont, and between Manitoba, Saskatchewan, and Alberta and Minnesota, North Dakota, and Montana.

Once barely passable for anything but a horse and buggy, the side roads on both sides of the border were improving. They were an immense aid to crime as well as to honest business. A brisk two-way trade in stolen cars, based on the experience and organization of the border bootleggers, soon developed. Stolen goods of other kinds moved past the darkened lonely customs sheds with little trouble.

Representatives of the textile and allied industries were beginning to complain vociferously against the enormous increase in smuggling. Many firms were being driven to the verge of bankruptcy. Canadian tobacco manufacturers, who, like textile and garment makers, had always depended on the protective tariff to stay in business, were equally concerned. King re-examined his attitude on the whole smuggling question and in mid-1924 a new treaty was signed by both countries: Canada granted U.S. revenuers the right to search suspected rumrunners up to twelve miles from shore.

There was to be closer exchange of information on suspected cargoes on both sides and more care in granting clearance papers when there was any suspicion of intent to smuggle. Stolen property would be returned to the country of origin. But in fact and in practice it was far too loose an arrangement to cause the bootleggers and runners of contraband more than minor inconvenience.

XXXI

Another close victory for the government—
The customs scandal comes into the open—
The barge Tremblay, *Chicago Benny,*
Joseph Bisaillon, *and* Moses Aziz

NEITHER King nor anyone in his Cabinet yet realized or was ready to admit that smuggling was a really serious question. The Prime Minister was prepared, when confronted with samplings of the unpleasant truth, to make sounds of polite concern, preferably in a low voice. He still had his hands full maintaining his precarious mastery of Parliament, although his hopes were high for the next election. But any suggestion of an underground crime wave, any whisper of scandal or laxity in the government service, would be particularly embarrassing now. Besides, it wasn't warranted—or at least King had himself persuaded so.

When a delegation of prominent businessmen came to urge on him the need of tightened laws and tighter enforcement of the existing laws, he received them with grave attention. He was interested to learn that they had formed themselves into a Commercial Protective Association and were prepared to offer the authorities all possible co-operation.

The meeting did not bestir King as much as his hearers had hoped, but it did, in due course, produce two concrete results. The penalties for smuggling were stiffened and the government offered the Protective Association the services of one of its most efficient private eyes. This was Walter Duncan, an investigator for the Department of Finance. Duncan was authorized to hire a small staff and he himself was given the power to examine witnesses under oath, to break into premises and safes, and to seize books and records.

Duncan chose as his first target one of the most incredible sitting ducks in the annals of public malfeasance. Whatever could be said of him, Joseph Edgar Alfred Bisaillon, chief preventive officer for the Department of Customs at Montreal, was never a man to hide his light under a bushel. He was already modestly famous as a protagonist in two of the most bizarre and mystifying episodes in the history of the customs service.

The first was known as the Lortie–St. George case. In 1919 a wagon drawn by a single horse drove up to the Canada Steamship docks in Montreal. The driver dismounted and unloaded two trunks. He gave the baggageman two first-class tickets to Cornwall, Ontario, sixty miles upstream, and asked to have the trunks checked. As the baggageman dragged the trunks across the counter, he heard something rattling inside and called a customs officer. The officer found a key to fit and discovered that the trunks contained $35,000 worth of narcotics. He locked the trunks again and awaited developments. Shortly two women arrived to make sure the trunks had been properly dispatched and to pick up the baggage checks. The customs officer stepped forward and asked them if they had the keys to the trunks. No, they said calmly, they hadn't; the trunks belonged to an acquaintance of theirs, a Dr. Lortie, in France, who had asked them to have them forwarded to Cornwall as a favor.

By this time a second customs officer had been called into the consultation—Joseph Bisaillon. Shortly afterward the women were allowed to go. No one searched them or made any attempt to check their story or their identities. When notified of the presence of the drugs, however, the R.C.M.P. took a less casual view and after a considerable search found the women and brought them to trial. At the trial, although the evidence was still strong enough to bring down the conviction of both accused, neither Bisaillon nor his fellow customs officer could identify either one. The judge warned Bisaillon and the other officer of the penalties for perjury, but they stuck to the story that they had never seen the women before.

That night the drugs, which had been released to the safekeeping of the Montreal chief of police, were stolen. One of the persons automatically questioned was a Chicago Benny Rose, a gangster who had come north to exact what share of the tribute he could along the new caravan trail staked out by prohibition. Chicago Benny admitted readily enough that he had been planning to steal the drugs, in partnership with Louis Morel, a former acquaintance of Bisaillon's in the Customs Department who had resigned from the civil service for a life of crime. But Chicago Benny insisted someone double-crossed him and Morel by hoisting the drugs twenty-four hours too soon; he intimated that his number-one suspect was Bisaillon.

Now, five years later and several degrees in rank higher in the Customs Department, Bisaillon had just emerged in an equally intriguing role from the equally intriguing barge *Tremblay* case.

In November 1924—just about the time Walter Duncan was beginning his investigations on behalf of the Commercial Protective Association—the Quebec City office of the provincial Liquor Commission was advised to watch for a certain barge sailing up the St. Lawrence.

The barge appeared, labored on past the city without stopping to clear customs, and disappeared into the night. The Liquor Commission sent a patrol along the banks in search of the waddling ghost ship and caught up to it the following midnight, moored in a quiet cove near the village of St. Sulpice.

Eight trucks had already begun unloading 16,000 gallons of alcohol on which no duty had been paid and whose likeliest point of origin seemed the French island of St. Pierre.

The detachment from the Liquor Commission seized the barge and arrested the captain and crew and two American passengers who said they owned the cargo.

The boarding party prepared to go on to Montreal for further instructions. Before they could cast adrift, however, a stranger rode in from the night in a Model-T Ford. His name was Duval, and he said he was a customs officer acting for Chief Preventive Officer Bisaillon, who also had been warned to watch out for the barge *Tremblay*.

Bisaillon was one of the first men aboard when the vessel docked at Montreal. He notified the new masters of the ship, the men from the Quebec Liquor Commission, that as officials of a provincial government they were inferior in authority to him, an officer of the Dominion government. He ordered them ashore and they meekly complied, first telling him that the captain and the crew and the two Americans were under arrest. Bisaillon immediately permitted the two Americans to escape and then impounded the cargo for the Crown.

This led him into court again, along with the barge captain and certain members of the crew. The charge was conspiracy, its burden that Bisaillon had made arrangements to steer the vessel's 16,000 gallons of alcohol to a safe harbor, duty-free. The intervention of the Quebec Liquor Commission had been a stroke of bad luck, partly balanced by the fortunate escape of the owners of the cargo.

The case was dismissed for want of evidence—not, however, before Bisaillon was compelled to admit to some remarkable book-keeping habits. Since the only matter at issue now was the affair of the barge *Tremblay*, nothing immediate came of the disclosure that at least $69,000 of government money had found its way into Bisaillon's personal bank account—all of it, he insisted, being re-turned to the Receiver General in an orderly and businesslike way.

Inspector Duncan—working quietly for the Commercial Protec-tive Association—had no difficulty in gathering further information on Bisaillon. He ran a customs brokerage business of his own in his spare time. He was a well-known landowner in the famous smuggler's cove of Rock Island, one of those picturesque Canadian–New England villages where some of the houses were actually partly in Canada and partly in the United States. Bisaillon owned one whole house on each side of the border and it was common gossip that he made good and rather obvious use of them.

Duncan, the detective, was reporting to and working closely with R. P. Sparks, chairman of the Commercial Protective Asso-ciation, which now claimed among its concerned supporters such august organizations as the Montreal and Toronto Boards of Trade and the Canadian Manufacturers' Association. Both men had ex-pected the automatic dismissal of Bisaillon by the Customs Depart-ment or at least his suspension pending a full inquiry into his activities. Montreal was the smuggling capital of Canada, and per-haps of North America, and for a man of Bisaillon's background to continue as the district's chief anti-smuggling warden seemed as imprudent as putting a known rapist in charge of a school for wayward girls.

Nevertheless, neither the genial Minister of Customs, Jacques Bureau, nor his deputy, R. R. Farrow, gave the slightest indication that they had even been reading the papers during the barge *Tremblay* hearings. Two months later Bisaillon was still their chief preventive officer in Montreal. Sparks visited Bureau's office to inquire discreetly whether any action was contemplated, but he learned nothing. Duncan, the detective, added a new entry to his own file on Bisaillon; at an early period of his career the chief preventive officer had, in the presence of two other customs officers, offered a fourth customs officer a standing bribe of $100 a week.

Early in February 1925, eight months after the original interview with Mackenzie King, Sparks wrote the Prime Minister in his capacity as chairman of the business group asking that a parliamentary committee be appointed to investigate the customs service.

On February 21, after an inconclusive interview with Jacques Bureau, the Customs Minister, Sparks petitioned the Prime Minister again: "The acquittal of Bisaillon . . . creates a new situation. I think you should be in possession of certain information which we have in reference to this matter, as he is the key to the whole smuggling situation. . . . Might I again repeat what I think I have said to you before that, from the standpoint of loss of revenue, I think the smuggling business is second only to the loss occasioned by the Canadian National Railways."

Sparks wrote again, four days later: "After four months' investigation by a staff of trained investigators, we are convinced that at least half of the smuggling now going on could be prevented within a month by an energetic policy on behalf of the department, and further that, with necessary amendments to the Act, 90 per cent of the smuggling could ultimately be prevented. Might I further express the opinion that smuggling is increasing at an alarming rate, rather than decreasing, as the minister states."

He returned to what he and his detectives considered to be the one problem that could be isolated and corrected in an instant: "I took up with the Minister of Customs the question of the continuation of Mr. Bisaillon as chief preventive officer at Montreal. I pointed out that the business community had lost confidence in Mr. Bisaillon. I had with me at the time a number of reports on this man, one of which I read to the minister."

Not a word of reply had been received from the Prime Minister or his office. King was shielding Bureau as stubbornly as Bureau was shielding Bisaillon. The Protective Association wrote again on March 20. Finally, in the middle of April, a two-sentence reply came from one of King's secretaries to say that the letter of the 20th instant had been received and "same will receive due consideration."

Late that summer King made two fairly routine decisions. They were only distantly connected. He called a general election for October, and he arranged for his Customs Minister, Jacques Bureau, to be appointed to the Senate in September.

Except for one meeting at Three Rivers, Quebec, where Bureau
was angrily shouted down, smuggling barely created a ripple in the
campaign. Neither King nor Meighen found much to talk about
except the tariff, although to his later embarrassment King outlined
a plan for reform of the Senate. The only surprise about the result
—and surprise was probably too strong a word for an enterprise
carried out in such an atmosphere of boredom—was that the government's position, instead of becoming slightly stronger, became
slightly weaker. The Liberals lost 16 seats and ended up with 101.
The Conservatives shot up from 49 to 116. The tottering Progressives still had 25, so that with luck, prudence, and proper respect
for the remnant of the farmers' party, King had a chance to get
through another term by holding the support of two minorities.

Lord Byng, the Governor General, offered King the chance to
try, and King accepted. He still hoped the next session or two
would enable him somehow to bolster up his party's fading stock
with the voters and—just as crucially—his own stock within the
party. The latter, after his second successive failure to win a clear
majority in Parliament, was now at so low an ebb that there was
open talk of replacing him—perhaps with Charles A. Dunning,
premier of Saskatchewan and the rising star of Liberalism that King
himself had been a mere five years before.

If he could get through a few months and survive a few divisions,
King might then ask the Governor General for a dissolution and
go back to the voters again with his head, though bowed, still
not fatally bloodied. For the moment, having lost his own seat, he
had to seek another through a by-election. A reasonably safe riding was arranged in Prince Albert, but in the meantime the House
began sitting in January, with Ernest Lapointe, the Justice Minister, at the head of the Liberals and King listening in the lobbies.

Less than a month after the Speech from the Throne, Lapointe
asked for an adjournment until the middle of March. On the surface
the object of this was innocent enough: to postpone serious business
until the Prime Minister had won his by-election and could be
officially present and heard.

Ordinarily Lapointe's motion might have been accepted with
little or no debate But beneath the placid surface of the House
on that dull February day in 1926, there seethed a witch's brew of
skepticism and distrust such as no Canadian Parliament had seen
since the best fencing days of Macdonald and Laurier.

Much had happened since Jacques Bureau and King had so pointedly refused to answer the Commercial Protective Association's repeated requests for a cleanup in the Customs Department. The most significant thing was that R. P. Sparks, the association's chairman, had run out of patience. As evidence from the private detectives piled up, Sparks went to the veteran Conservative M.P. Harry H. Stevens and put the whole dossier in front of him. Stevens consulted his party leader, Arthur Meighen.

The Tories now had a fistful of cards. The next question was how to play them.

The Liberals knew the Tories knew something. But how much? Stevens had put a motion on the order paper calling for an investigation of the Customs Department and then had withdrawn it.

The Tories knew the Liberals knew they knew something. But how well?

Who would make the first move? King, sitting behind the curtains to the lobbies, hoped no one would, at least until he could win a seat and take his place on the floor of the House. Meighen and Stevens had to proceed with caution too. At any sign of undue haste while the investigations were still going on, their opponents would certainly accuse them of jeopardizing the public interest in order to play politics.

What, they had to discover, could Lapointe's real motive be in asking for a six-week recess only three weeks after the session began? The obvious one seemed too obvious, and besides it was not convincing. The new government had already won one vote on an amendment and was in no immediate need of King's physical attendance.

Could it be that King, having scraped through one election by suppressing the customs scandal, hoped to scrape through another by breaking it wide open? Could it be that the Liberals intended to use the six-week parliamentary recess to make a splashy announcement of the mess themselves? Claim credit for uncovering it themselves? Claim credit for announcing it themselves without reck of the cost to themselves? Get the worst of it over while the Commons was still dispersed and powerless to throw them out in the first wave of indignation? Then, having stolen the thunder from a Tory exposé that could not be avoided anyway . . .

If King got his adjournment now he might win everything. But if the customs thing were brought out—now—he could not get his adjournment. The Progressives, who held the power to decide, would not dare vote to go back home and leave this horror untended on the nation's doorstep. Stevens and Meighen, weighing the odds and what they knew of the workings of Mackenzie King's mind, decided it was time to act. The House had now been circling warily around Lapointe's motion to adjourn for a whole afternoon and evening.

At a few minutes before midnight Harry Stevens, a former grocer from British Columbia, took the floor and began to display the contents of his sample trunk. He offered the barge *Tremblay* and the Lortie–St. George case. He offered Joseph Bisaillon: "The worst of crooks, he is the intimate of ministers, the petted favorite of this government. The recipient of a moderate salary, he rolls in wealth and opulence, a typical debauched and debauching public official."

He offered petty larceny and grand larceny. He offered the scalp of the old minister, Jacques Bureau: "Already nine filing cabinets filled with records containing damaging evidence have been removed from the custody and the care of that institution known as the government, taken away to the home of an ex-minister, and there destroyed."

He offered the scalp of the new minister, George Boivin: "No warehouse receipt was surrendered; no order was given; simply a jingle of the phone, a familiar voice, and $200,000 worth of alcohol was turned loose. I repeat, Mr. Speaker, that the exchequer of Canada was defrauded in that deal alone of over $200,000, either by gross incompetence or connivance."

He offered honest indignation: "I charge the government with knowledge for a year, or almost a year—members of the government including the Prime Minister, the Minister of Justice, the Minister of Marine, the ex-Minister of Customs—this government with knowledge, with positive knowledge, with abundance of proof, that the grossest violations of the customs laws were being perpetrated in this country."

On and on Stevens went, until four o'clock in the morning, outlining what he frequently repeated was only the barest skeleton of the skeleton in the closet. To get even a respectable part of the whole story, he insisted, it would be necessary to convene a parliamentary committee.

At first only the new minister, George Boivin, was ready to talk back. He had known what was coming when he saw Stevens' notice of motion on the order paper; most of the government backbenchers were literally stunned to silence.

By the next afternoon the Liberals had had time to plan a holding action which might somehow tide them over until King's return. As Stevens and Meighen had suspected it might, the government tried to board the band wagon of the exposé itself, admit the charges concerning people like Bisaillon, deny the charges against the Cabinet itself, and create the impression that all was well now that keen, alert young George Boivin had replaced bumbling, well-meaning old Jacques Bureau.

After three days the amendment to adjourn was defeated, the House went back to its regular business, and a nine-man committee was struck off to go into the affairs of the Customs Department in more searching detail.

The committee reported back in June 1926. It came bearing approximately everything Stevens had said it would, and a little more. There was a wealth of verse to support each chapter of his first spate of charges and now there were a few new chapters too.

Perhaps the most startling one went back to the rumrunners. Many Canadians still regarded them as a rather romantic breed of men, somewhere between Long John Silver and Robin Hood— gay adventurers braving the guns of the U. S. Coast Guard to maintain freedom of the seas and a friendly neighbor's right to a harmless drink. But now, it developed, not nearly all the liquor being smuggled out of Canada was being smuggled into the United States. Millions of dollars' worth was being smuggled back into Canada at a heavy cost to the Canadian taxpayer.

It worked like this. Canadian distillers or wholesalers paid excise tax only on the whisky they sold in Canada. When they sent a shipment to a foreign destination it went out under bond. They posted a forfeit of twice the value of the cargo to ensure that it reached its foreign destination; this bond was returned on presentation of a receipt from the foreign port of entry.

Most of the receipts were, as everyone knew, forged. A cargo of whisky bonded for and addressed to Mexico or Nassau would be unloaded for Boston off the North Atlantic coast. In due course a receipt would come back from Mexico or Nassau; the distiller made his profit, the shipper made his profit, the customs inspector —not always, but sometimes—made his profit, and the deserving,

parched American got his drink. If anyone suffered in the transaction, no Canadian did.

But as the parliamentary committee's investigations soon showed,
this delightfully cynical way of doing business was also robbing
the Canadian treasury blind. In addition to their "legitimate" boot-
legging to the United States, distillers and other shippers were
bonding Canadian whisky to Mexico, Puerto Rico, Venezuela, Peru,
and other foreign lands and then unloading it, tax-free and duty-
free, in Canada. Receipts were easy to come by and they were
seldom closely scrutinized. The amount of difficulty depended only
on how comatose or corruptible the customs officials happened to
be.

Under this system of intramural smuggling one ship, according
to its records, made three return journeys to the Bahamas in a
week. Another vessel made a round trip to Peru in two days. In
the three years ending in 1925 almost six million gallons of liquor
left Halifax and Saint John under bond. A committee member
claimed that "not one gallon of it left the shores of the Maritimes,
and because it did not, at the rate of $9 a gallon excise, the Treasury
lost $52,481,340."

One imaginative bootlegger found an ingenious way of beating
the heavy Canadian duty on genuine imported scotch. The scotch
did, in fact, come from Scotland. In fiction it was bound not for
Canada but for Japan. Its route was through the Welland Canal to
Port Arthur, then by train to the Vancouver docks. But somewhere
between Lachine on the St. Lawrence and Port Arthur on Lake
Superior the whisky disappeared. The Customs Department accepted the word of a known bootlegger that it had in fact been
offloaded at Buffalo and therefore was not liable to Canadian duty.
The committee estimated the loss to the Canadian Treasury in this
one episode at between $420,000 and $700,000.

It was disillusioning enough for Parliament and the nation to
learn that not all rumrunners were patriots in disguise, plucking
tail feathers from the American Eagle for the common good. An
infinitely more sobering and shameful truth became apparent as
George Boivin, the new minister, was drawn personally into the
inquiry.

Far from approaching his new job like a Galahad, Boivin had
approached it like a man who has inherited a concession. One of
the problems awaiting him was how to dispose of the 16,000

gallons of alcohol that had run aground with Joseph Bisaillon's plans for the barge *Tremblay*. He found this easy enough to solve.

Among the new aristocracy of legal bootleggers, W. J. Hushion was one whom Boivin was pleased to call a friend. Hushion, a former member of Parliament, was now chiefly engaged as a senior officer and owner of Dominion Distilleries—a leading exporter to the United States and, according to the firm's books, other foreign countries as far distant as Japan. There was no more logical man to whom to sell the contraband from the barge *Tremblay*. Boivin let Hushion have the entire shipment at 36 cents a gallon, tax-free. The price was fair and no tax was collectible, for it had been established and certified that the alcohol was not officially drinkable. It was denatured alcohol—that is, rubbing alcohol—and under the law Hushion would be allowed to resell it only to hospitals and a few other rigidly specified types of consumer.

So far so good. But having sold Hushion the contents of the barge *Tremblay* as rubbing alcohol, tax-free, the Minister of Customs now permitted Hushion to export it to the United States as drinking liquor. (How he was to get it through the Volstead pickets was, of course, none of the Canadian Customs Department's affair.)

In short, Boivin gave his friend the best of both worlds. What the government sold him as poison it allowed him to resell as non-poison, with the price and tax advantages on his side in both cases. If it was not poison, the government was defrauded of about $200,000. If it was poison, only the people who drank it were defrauded. (To complete the story, it is possible that the ultimate consumers survived, for according to further evidence it was not plain denatured alcohol anyway, but "special" denatured and susceptible of "defusing" in the hands of a good chemist.)

The story that held Parliament's attention longest, however, and probably played the greatest single part in bringing down the government, was not one involving huge sums of money, rich conspirators, chases by moonlight, or any of the other paraphernalia of high intrigue. It revolved around an insignificant little country bootlegger named Moses Aziz.

Moses Aziz lived in Caraquet, New Brunswick, a small town near the Bay of Chaleur. In the summer of 1925, a raid on his premises disclosed him to be in possession of several hundred dollars' worth of contraband liquor. It was his third offense and he was sentenced to a year in jail.

One of the first messages George Boivin found awaiting him when he relieved Jacques Bureau as Minister of Customs in September was a letter from J. G. Robichaud, the Liberal candidate in Gloucester, asking that Aziz's sentence be stayed. Boivin, a lawyer, wasn't sure why Aziz—having been convicted—wasn't in jail already. Nor was he sure how he, the Minister of Customs, could overrule a decision of the courts. But, as he explained innocently to the parliamentary committee, he wasn't certain of legal practice in New Brunswick. He gave his fellow Liberal what comfort he could by promising to talk to him about the case on the latter's forthcoming trip to Ottawa.

Late in September a much more urgent message came from Robichaud to Boivin. "Will you please consult with the Honorable Mr. Lapointe [the Minister of Justice] about the proceedings instituted against Mr. A. M. Aziz, Caraquet. I attach the greatest importance to this affair, since in the actual circumstances I need the help of all my friends. Mr. Aziz is of the highest help to us during this campaign and we cannot do without his services."

Any qualms Boivin may have felt about the legal niceties vanished. If the party needed help, who was he to quibble about the law? Lapointe was not available for advice, but Boivin wired the local customs officer in New Brunswick: "Am directed to request you to stay execution of warrant of commitment against Moses Aziz pending further investigation. Arrange with magistrate accordingly."

Robichaud, the local candidate, retained the seat for the Liberals in the fall election, presumably with the help of Aziz. The latter continued in his state of freedom, his one-year jail sentence unserved, unreviewed by any court, unaffected by anything except the private arrangement of two Liberal members of Parliament. Five months later Moses Aziz was still free. Boivin now had two explanations for his own conduct in the affair. One was for the House of Commons, where he could say what he wished to say and pay as much or as little attention to anyone else as he chose. The other explanation was for the parliamentary committee, where he was subject to the hazards of cross-examination.

Before the tough-minded committee he admitted again and again, abjectly and without reservation, that he had had no right to interfere with Moses Aziz's sentence once the courts had pronounced it. The reason he gave for having seemed to believe otherwise was that he had been new to his job and rushed for time and hadn't stopped to remember that the minister's pre-trial right to lay, withhold, or withdraw charges against violators of the Customs Act conferred no similar post-trial rights.

In the House itself, where the audience was less critical, Boivin was correspondingly less frank. The hungry Tories, certain they had a major quarry at bay, demanded he come to the confessional again before the nation's highest tribunal. He refused, and refused again and again—at first petulantly and rather pathetically, then sullenly, then indignantly. Amid blizzards of red herrings and tornadoes of invective from both sides of the House, Boivin stood his untenable ground. He had pleaded guilty once, before the private inquisition. It was too much to ask that he plead guilty again, before the public jury. He declined flatly to admit to any wrongdoing. He was not to have another chance to do so, for within six weeks he was dead—his friends said of the strain of trying to repair a world he never made, his enemies said of worry over his own tragic failings, the doctors said of appendicitis.

XXXII

The Constitutional Crisis—The Liberals
evade a desperate defeat and Meighen makes
way for R. B. Bennett

BY the time the parliamentary committee brought in its report
Mackenzie King had won his by-election and was back in the
House as the besieged government's commander.

He made no attempt to deny what had gone on within the corrupt little principality of the Customs Department. His main concern was to see that in whatever opaque and distant cloudland the
blame came to rest, it would be nowhere near the eyrie of the
Cabinet. If, he tried to reason, Jacques Bureau was responsible,
it would still be unfair to pin the whole responsibility for his
action on the government. If the government was deceived by
Bureau, so was the Opposition. "I will take for the moment the
three years 1922, 1923, and 1924, the first three of this government in office. I ask honorable members if there is a single one of
their number in this House who had not the highest respect for the
integrity, the ability, and the honesty of Hon. Jacques Bureau."

King sought to claim for the government most of the credit for
the activities of Walter Duncan, the detective. As for the *homme
fatal*, Joseph Bisaillon, it was true he had not been dismissed until
ten months after the first complaint and dossier were laid on the
Prime Minister's desk. He had been kept on so long, King maintained, only to avoid frightening off his accomplices before they
could be trapped.

To suit the predicament of his new Customs Minister, Boivin,
King had even loftier words: "I ask honorable members, when they
are recording their votes, to remember that every man who goes
into public life sooner or later is certain to be subjected to the kind
of thing to which my honorable friend is being subjected today.

I say to honorable members, judge by the judgment wherewith you expect to be judged, 'for with what judgment ye judge, ye shall be judged; and with what measure ye mete, it shall be measured to you again.'"

Most of this, as everyone in the House knew, was window-dressing for Hansard and posterity. The fate of the government was unlikely to be decided either by the verses of Holy Writ or by the Satanic plots of the smuggling trade. The real contest would be less a contest of principle than of footwork and horse trading.

Although the committee's report contained many unpleasant truths and suggested several embarrassing remedies, King would have been glad enough to accept it. It recommended the dismissal of six senior customs officials and the compulsory retirement of three others, including the Deputy Minister. It called for an honest attempt to help the United States curtail the activities of the rum-runners. To cut down intramural smuggling in Canada it suggested that all liquor leaving Canadian distilleries be subject to sales and excise tax, whether it was marked for export or not. On the thorny question of who was to blame for past sins and errors, the report read simply: "The evidence . . . leads to the general conclusion that for a long time the Department of Customs and Excise has been slowly degenerating in efficiency, and that the process was greatly accelerated in the last few years. Apparently the Hon. Jacques Bureau, then Minister of Customs, failed to appreciate and properly discharge the responsibilities of his office, and as a result there was a lack of efficient, continuous and vigorous control of subordinates by the headquarters staff at Ottawa."

But this meat was far from strong enough for Harry Stevens and the hungry Tories. To the motion in support of the report Stevens proposed an amendment censuring the Prime Minister and the government for failing to take prompt remedial action and specifically censuring George Boivin for interfering with the courts in the case of Moses Aziz.

Here, politically at least, was the only question that mattered Would Parliament be content with reprimanding the elderly and safely rid-of Jacques Bureau or would it go so far as to reprimand the whole government? In the latter instance the government would automatically fall and King's personal career would almost certainly be destroyed.

The immovable 116 Tories were six too few to defeat the government by themselves. The 101 rock-firm Grits needed to find at least twenty-two friends before they could embalm the customs scandal beside Senator Bureau. Twenty-four of the uncommitted votes were held by Progressives and two by Independents. The other two belonged to J. S. Woodsworth and his Labor "group," the original group of William Irvine having been replaced by A. A. Heaps.

As the fourth long day of debate wore on and the time drew near for the divisions, King was already ahead in both the footwork and the horse trading. At an appropriate moment he injected a shrewd, King-size irrelevancy for the special benefit of the Progressives: What they were being asked to decide, really, was whether Arthur Meighen should rule the country or not, whether the country should have high tariff or low tariff. This feat of gamesmanship was sure to make the spokesmen of the western farmers think twice before throwing the Liberals out.

More importantly, King had made an advantageous deal with J. S. Woodsworth. The Prime Minister had promised Woodsworth at last to bring in old-age pensions and to liberalize the Immigration Act, the Naturalization Act, and the Criminal Code, all objectives close to Woodsworth's heart. He had, moreover, offered Woodsworth the Ministry of Labor. The gentle maverick from Winnipeg turned this latter proposal down. Although both men denied any bargain had been struck, it was now implicit in their whole relationship that in any real contest between the Liberals and the Conservatives, Woodsworth and anyone he could carry with him would vote Liberal.

As the House prepared to divide on the fateful Stevens amendment, with its full indictment of the government, Woodsworth tried to come to King's rescue. That he found the task distasteful he could not conceal. In a memorable passage of his two-hour speech he said: "I had occasion the other day in looking into the law books . to notice the penalties enacted for several different forms of crime; they happened to be on one page of the statutes. This legislation, I may say, was all passed at the same time in 1919, and there was one to this effect: that any person who is suffering from venereal disease in communicable form who knowingly or by culpable negligence communicates such disease is subject to a fine not exceeding $500 or to imprisonment for a term not exceeding six months. Another law on the same page provides that for stealing an automobile the punishment is two years and not less than one year without the option of a fine. Then we come to the legislation with regard to sedition and we find that there the penalty at present for what is practically criticizing the authorities is twenty years. For ruining a life, six months with the option of a fine; for stealing an automobile, two years; for criticizing a government, twenty years, a pretty fair indication, let me say, of the relative values according to the standards which now exist. I have given these penalties. What is the penalty for debauching a government department? A senatorship."

Nevertheless, Woodsworth, feeling "the question is inseparable . . . from the question of who shall administer our affairs," sought to smother the Stevens impeachment under the ether mask of a further investigation.

But the maneuver failed; while Woodsworth led most of the uncommitted members into the Liberal camp, half a dozen of them voted against him, and his plea to reprieve the government failed by two votes.

By now it was midnight. The failure of Woodsworth's motion did not officially constitute a defeat for the government, but it made defeat certain. Still, there were five more hours of hoarse and bitter talking to be done before the sitting broke up in a bleary dawn. There were also three more divisions to be taken—two on votes to adjourn, one on a Speaker's ruling. Two of the three went against the government. But the government was still in office and technically in control at daybreak, for the Stevens motion still had not been put to a vote.

King's time had run out, but not his resourcefulness. His ancient enemy, Arthur Meighen, might have his scalp—there was no longer any hope of preventing that—but there was still a chance to deny him the satisfaction of waving it aloft. King saw a way, even in this extremity, to avoid the final humiliation of becoming the first Prime Minister in Canadian history to be overthrown by a vote in the House of Commons. During the weekend he went to see the Governor General three times, the last time on Monday shortly after noon, slightly less than two hours before he was to meet the House and, it was universally presumed, offer himself for the *coup de grâce*.

The proposal he had to offer Lord Byng struck the Governor

General as outrageous. But King not only offered it, he insisted on it. He desired a dissolution of Parliament and a new election. His government had been in control of the Fifteenth Parliament since its first sitting nearly six months before. It had suffered no defeat on a major motion or a major amendment. Now, as the leader of the government and His Excellency's sworn adviser, King advised that His Excellency dissolve the House of Commons.

For nearly four decades some of the world's best reporters and political analysts have been trying to decide exactly what words passed between King and Byng during those historic discussions, and exactly what lay behind each man's words. There were no witnesses and no agreed statements. Each man went to his grave with a version of the events and an explanation for his part in them that were at considerable variance with the other's.

In any case King asked for a dissolution. If it were granted he could still fight the new election as Prime Minister, at least technically unrebuked and unrepudiated by Parliament. Aside from the help this might afford his party's faltering morale, it would be worth something at the polls. If Byng refused him there were other potential gains to hope for—nebulous and uncertain gains to be sure, and largely dependent on how Arthur Meighen should react to an as yet purely hypothetical situation. But when there is no other course open, the prudent man at least gives luck a chance.

Byng did refuse this dissolution, as was his perfect right. King thereupon made his way along the meandering Ottawa Driveway to Parliament Hill, entered a House crammed with expectant witnesses to his defeat, glanced at the packed galleries, bowed to the Speaker, announced that his government had resigned, and moved that the House adjourn.

Meighen, momentarily and unprecedentedly at a loss, began fumbling for words. King interrupted him coldly: "I might say that this motion is not debatable." Meighen proposed, nevertheless, that since they were already near the end of the session there should be a conference between him and the Prime Minister. "There is no Prime Minister," King said stonily. Moreover, there was no government.

The Governor General had rejected the advice of the previous government that the House be dissolved. There could be no new one until someone assumed, as His Excellency's new adviser, the responsibility for that decision.

It was an open dare, and Meighen could not resist taking it up. When the Governor General sent for him later in the day and asked if he could form a government and keep it in office, Meighen said he thought he could and was sworn in as Prime Minister.

From its first day, this brief and raucous Fifteenth Parliament had been far less an instrument of government than a contest in cleverness between Mackenzie King and Arthur Meighen. It had devoted a considerable part of the first six months to the gambits, ploys, and counterploys, the motions, amendments, and subamendments, the deals and counterdeals of the principals and their seconds, and so far nothing of the least consequence had been settled except that both King and Meighen were growing in adroitness and parliamentary skill. Now the weary backbenchers sensed that another round in their private war of extermination was at hand, and they looked forward to it with scant enthusiasm.

The Progressives were particularly fed up. Having sustained King through six months of rough weather, often at the cost of much soul searching, they had just heard him, in effect, order them home under the most exasperating of circumstances. It was only eight months since they had fought one election; now those who wished to remain in Parliament would have to go to the trouble and expense of fighting another, and moreover they would not be able to tell their constituents that they had accomplished a single thing except to survive a few noisy speeches.

The position this feeling led them to was a fantastic one, but no more fantastic than the Fifteenth Parliament itself. The Progressives decided to give their support to Meighen—Meighen, the high-tariff man, the spokesman of big business, the enemy of the farmer, the selfsame ogre their party had been created to destroy.

Nevertheless, if Meighen would promise to attempt no immediate changes in the tariff, finish up the session's business quickly, and get them back home by early summer they would make no undue effort to defeat him. It was not an unconditional bargain, but it was far better than Meighen had hoped for.

Meighen's new government got through its first day easily; the day was devoted to the happy formality of concluding the customs trial and pronouncing the old government guilty as charged by Harry Stevens.

King bore the ordeal stoically. His turn, he was certain, was coming. He fully expected the second day's events to bring his old Varsity colleague, Arthur Meighen, crashing down to his final ruin. To speed this end he abruptly introduced a motion which, theoretically, the Progressives could not oppose: "That the fiscal policy of the government, as enunciated by the present Prime Minister when leader of His Majesty's Opposition, will prove detrimental to the country's continued prosperity and prejudicial to national unity." No Progressive could possibly vote against it. Nevertheless, no fewer than ten Progressives did, enough to give the Conservatives a seven-vote margin.

To all intents Meighen was safely over the highest hurdle he would have to face. He had beaten poor little Rex after all, in spite of all his guile and slipperiness. He should now be able, at the very least, to muddle safely through the session.

But King still had two arrows in his quiver. The Tories hardly felt the first tiny prick of the first one at all.

His temporary sympathizer, J. S. Woodsworth, gave King the cue he was waiting for. Woodsworth, speaking of King's anti-tariff resolution, deplored "the decision given the other day by His Excellency the Governor General." Immediately half a dozen members sprang up to argue whether it was proper for an M.P. to discuss or criticize the representative of the Crown.

This was made to order for Mackenzie King. No one was half so anxious to discuss and criticize the Governor General as he; no one realized half so well how dangerous that enterprise could be. Here was a heaven-sent opportunity to rush to His Excellency's defense and simultaneously knock His Excellency black and blue.

King sought the Speaker's eye. No member, he observed, when he had been recognized, had the right to criticize the Crown in a disrespectful way. Then, shifting expertly from the general to the particular, he turned to the issue that was to guide him back to power. The name it later received was the Constitutional Crisis and King introduced it in three steps.

First, the staunch, scornful words for anyone who would dare speak disrespectfully of the Governor General: "The honorable member was speaking of His Excellency's right to take the course he had taken in not accepting the advice of the then Prime Minister and sending for another member of this House to give him advice. That itself may be a perfectly constitutional position in certain contingencies. I want to make it clear from His Excellency's point of view, because I desire to see justice done to His Excellency in this matter."

Second, just the barest hint that the Governor General might have made a mistake: "His Excellency is being criticized . . . I am here to defend, for the time being, if you wish, the position taken by His Excellency. When I advised His Excellency that I thought dissolution was essential my advice was not taken. . . ."

Third, the inescapable conclusion that if anyone was to blame it was Arthur Meighen, who must accept the blame for any error or misdeed of the Governor General along with the blame for any of his own: "It is not His Excellency that is being discussed in this matter, it is the present Prime Minister who has accepted the responsibility of carrying on the business of this House without a dissolution. . . . We must wait to see whether the present Prime Minister can fulfill the undertaking which he then gave and what His Excellency may do in the circumstances."

That was the first of King's remaining arrows. He retrieved it for later use from the hide of the almost oblivious victim. Then he loosed the second one, and this one stung a little more.

Under a law since modified, any member of Parliament appointed to the Cabinet had to resign and seek re-election before he could take his place in the House. Thus Meighen had become Prime Minister but had temporarily lost his right to sit in Parliament. He would not have a parliamentary seat until a by-election could be arranged and won.

To carry on in his absence Meighen appointed seven acting ministers. By appointing these floor commanders as acting ministers only—a rank in which they drew no cabinet pay—he made it lawful, or thought he made it lawful, for them to continue sitting in the Commons before seeking re-election.

Here was the second of King's remaining arrows. He let it go with an almost deafening twang during one of the few peaceful interludes Parliament had known in weeks.

The House at last had gone into Committee of Supply. After the non-stop carnival behind them, the scene was one of blissful tedium as the members drowsed over the cool, non-contentious voice of the clerk.

To provide for the purchase of 650 copies of the Canadian Parliamentary Guide, $1950

The former Customs Minister, George Boivin, inquired amiably whether there had been any increase in the price of the *Guide.* Sir George Perley, the Acting Secretary of State, said there hadn't been and the item was carried.

Salaries, including Governor General's secretary additional to salary authorized by R.S.c.4, $3600; John Guy at $1500 and George Johnson at $1380 . . . $35,370. Contingencies . . . $66,000.

Mackenzie King asked pleasantly for the salary of the Governor General's secretary. It was $2400 and the supplement brought it to $6000. Item carried. Amid these familiar, reassuring rites, the members were at last getting down to the homely day-to-day business of keeping house for the nation. It would not have been surprising to see some of the older members loosen their galluses and quietly begin reading their home-town papers. But then, as suddenly as some messenger from the gods come to shout a warning to the lotus-eaters, King was before them again, his composure gone, his face flushed, his voice rising to a pitch of calculated anger.

"We are now," he cried into the shattered tranquillity of the warm June evening, "voting large sums of public money to different honorable gentlemen opposite who are supposed to be administering several departments of the government. Before we proceed any further I would like to discover from those honorable gentlemen to what extent they have complied with constitutional practice in the matter of assuming office. I would like," King added, "to ask my honorable friend who is leading the House whether he has taken any oath of office of any kind since he undertook to lead the House, or even before doing so."

Ten weeks later Meighen was still unable to recall the ensuing performance without shuddering. On the eve of an election, about to expire of wounds he was not yet aware of having sustained, he sought to put the spectacle in terms an audience of rural Ontario voters could understand. "Mr. King and his followers," he ruminated in despair and incredulity, "seemed determined that the House of Commons should be used only as a prize ring. They fixed up and moved a fantastic fabric of phraseology, the end effect of which was to declare that the government as constituted was not legally a government at all."

In the wild and clamorous argument King was greatly aided by the fact that his enemy could not address the House of Commons in person. With King speaking for the Liberals and Meighen prompting the Tories, the debate nevertheless produced some of the best and most learned parliamentary oratory since Confederation, along with some of the most unbridled nonsense and utter billingsgate. King's contention that the government had no right to office was based on one main point: all but one of Meighen's housekeeping ministers had been sworn in as members of an earlier Tory Cabinet. But their previous oath did not bind them now.

In the fine print of the Constitution it could be maintained that Meighen's shadow cabinet had no right to run the country at all.

Talk about smuggling! The Tories had smuggled themselves into possession of the government.

King's former Finance Minister, J. A. Robb, put it in a motion. The Commons debated the proposition for most of two days and nights, ending up at 2:15 A.M. on the day after the fifty-ninth anniversary of Confederation. The long and stormy argument produced the kind of infighting at which King was at his superb and incredible best. He knew exactly when to bully, precisely when to coax, when to raise his voice, when to lower it.

Although the hapless and of course silent Governor General's action in accepting Meighen and his Cabinet was the only matter officially under debate, King kept referring to Byng's refusal of a dissolution. He did this with repeated declarations of esteem and even affection for Byng. He went out of his way time after time to say that Byng had been quite within his rights in refusing the dissolution. But if Meighen, Byng's new adviser, proved unable to form and sustain a stable government, it would mean that Meighen, not Byng, had failed in his duty to the Crown.

There were precedents on both sides. The question of dissolution was only obliquely before the House, as a side issue to the Liberal motion that Meighen's shadow cabinet had not been properly sworn.

But King's repeated references to dissolution so scattered the energy and talent of the hard-pressed Tories that instead of defending their Cabinet's right to office they spent hours talking about old precedents in Tasmania and what Queen Victoria said to Palmerston in 1857.

Meighen might have been able to handle this situation, but all he could do was sit and suffer in the lobbies while King did combat with his caretakers. The chief of these and acting Prime Minister was Sir Henry Drayton, a rather nice gentleman nearing his sixtieth birthday and no fit opponent for the pudgy tiger on the other side of the floor.

In their contest there was only one prize. All 116 Conservatives would, of course, vote Conservative. All 101 Liberals would vote Liberal. There were four strays—Woodsworth and his party of one, plus two independents. The decision would rest with the 24 Progressives. Their short affair with the Tories had been unnatural and loveless from the start and when King commanded them to come home most of them did. The Liberals won the division, 96 to 95. Byng, now certain that neither party could control the country, granted the Conservatives the dissolution he had refused the Liberals. He was again quite within his rights, but King was now equipped with a lethal weapon for the forthcoming election. In Canada's bursting rush of nationalism words like "autonomy," "sovereignty," and "independence" had become almost sacred. King, after his impressive performances as a friendly enemy of the British Raj at London in 1923, and again during the Constitutional debate, had become the acknowledged heir of all these magic symbols. In less than a week he had been reprieved from the need of fighting an election on the sordid customs scandal and had become a kind of Canadian George Washington.

Meighen, on the other hand, was saddled not only with his unenviable position in the Constitutional Crisis but with two other political errors of the first magnitude. The first was his "Ready, aye, ready!" speech at the time of Chanak, the speech that implied Canada should be willing to come to the military support of Britain without question or delay in any time of trouble. The second was a lame retreat from Chanak.

In 1925, after Chanak but before the Constitutional Crisis, Meighen tried to repair his position with the anti-Imperialists and particularly with Quebec. He had never had anything to expect but disaster in the ancient province, where his record, under Borden, as sponsor of conscription was remembered with abiding bitterness. In the 1925 election, when he carried the country, he and his party returned only 4 members of Quebec's 65.

But two months later Meighen entered a by-election campaign there. It was in the riding of Bagot, deep in enemy country up the Saguenay on the Baie de Ha! Ha!

Meighen prepared himself by making what was, in effect, a complete repudiation of his Chanak speech. Canada should not be "ready, aye, ready" for any future wars of Britain. In an address he made for the first time at Hamilton, he urged that before Canada sent any more men to fight abroad there should be a plebiscite.

Then he went off to the lovely Baie de Ha! Ha! There he made dozens of speeches. Most of these were at *assemblées contradic-toires*, at which both or all candidates meet, usually several times an evening, and the chairman holds a watch and allows each speaker three minutes. Meighen made an astonishingly strong showing, easily strong enough to erase the canard that he was afraid to show his face in Quebec. Nevertheless, his candidate was soundly defeated.

He had, however, committed one of the great errors of Canadian politics. King, who made a practice of pacifying and courting everyone, could never have made it. But Meighen was now in wrong with the anti-Imperialists for the Chanak speech and as much in wrong with the Imperialists for the Hamilton speech. Inconsistency in the shrewd and palpably deft King was something the voters could forgive. But they could not forgive the same thing in Meighen, tall and upright, the very figure of rectitude.

In the election Meighen fought brilliantly. He could always out-talk King and he outtalked him again on the hustings. In theory he tore his little college friend apart: The Constitutional maneuver, he announced, was "a work of guile; it was a plant; it was a piece of verbal chicanery; it was a wily, sinister artifice to take advantage of men untrained in legal reasoning; it was, in plain language, a fraud." King had tried to hang on to the premiership "like a lobster with lockjaw."

But with the spot of 60 of Quebec's 65 seats, King won easily, 116 to 91, plus more than 30 Farmers and Progressives who could be counted on for support in a pinch.

Meighen was now finished as a major political figure. His party held a convention in Winnipeg, and although Meighen made it clear he was not seeking a renomination, it was equally clear that he would have had little chance of getting it. Howard Ferguson, premier of Ontario and probably next to Meighen himself the most influential member of the party, strode to the platform in the Amphitheatre Rink and, amid an almost deafening hubbub, denounced his leader roundly for the Hamilton speech. "Inappropriate and inadvisable . . . the grossest kind of violation of unity in Canada . . . if the convention chooses to endorse Mr. Meighen I would dissociate myself entirely from the activities . . ."

Meighen was nominated but refused to allow his name to stand.

Richard Bedford Bennett, a long-standing rival of his, was chosen leader of the party on the second ballot. Thus Meighen, for all major purposes, passed into his country's history as one of the great parliamentarians of all time, gifted with rare lucidity and logic, a magnificent speaking voice and the presence to match it, but not much good at fighting windmills.

XXXIII

The splendid euphoria of the rumrunning
days—The Diamond Jubilee and the
Briand-Kellogg Pact

NOW, in the last years of the twenties, Canada began to share the Great American Boom. The country had vastly changed its character. People were moving mainly into the cities, but they were also moving into the North. The great metal finds of the early part of the century had forced the railroads to go and take them out. Their fingers, stretching into the Canadian Shield, had greatly changed the traditionally lateral shape of the country. Men by the thousands were moving into the bush to harvest, first of all, its pulpwood, then its nickel, copper, silver, lead, zinc, and gold. Nearly three hundred million dollars in metal came out of the Shield in 1928, a very sizable amount in the currency and the Canada of those times. Pulp and paper were producing nearly twice as much. Iron had not been found close enough to transportation to start bringing it out, and oil in quantity had not been found at all.

Mechanization had started on the farms, and so had industrialization in the cities. The country had begun to make use of its immense resources of hydroelectric power. The pole of gravity had begun to move, to the general advantage, away from the farms and the small towns to the cities and the North.

It was a poor man indeed who couldn't buy his family at least a secondhand Model-A Ford, a Chevrolet, a Chandler, or a Buick. In the cities it was a poorer man who couldn't take his family to the local theater to see Lillian Gish or Norma Talmadge. In the rural parts the town hall above the barbershop was usually filled with Swiss Bell Ringers or other musicians called the Bluebird Five.

It was a happy time. The per capita income was almost five hundred dollars—in British Columbia it was almost six hundred.

That meant a man with two children had an annual pay of nearly two thousand dollars, a very handsome amount in those times and places.

The Canadian Pacific Railway was enlarging those familiar landmarks the Empress Hotel in Victoria, the Palliser in Calgary, and the Saskatchewan in Regina, and had just finished the largest hotel in the British Empire, the Royal York in Toronto. The Canadian National was enlarging the Chateau Laurier in Ottawa and beginning the Vancouver in Vancouver and the Nova Scotian in Halifax. The Canadian Pacific bought the largest steam locomotive in the British Empire. The Canadian National built the biggest oil locomotive in the world.

Thousands of British immigrants were seeking a place in Canada and a share in its new prosperity, but many objected that the standards of health and character demanded were far too rigid. Ramsay MacDonald, who had been visiting the country with a group of British M.P.s, complained: "The opportunities for migration are innumerable, but you can't start migrating with a shovel and just transport people in bunches or heaps from one country to another."

Much of the trouble about immigration stemmed from the harvest trains that ran into the West, jammed with broke and bewildered men quite literally on the auction block. Many of them were unemployed from England, where the boom never did quite catch up with the labor market. A visiting British M.P. put the matter bluntly in a speech at the Canadian National Exhibition. The lack of system in their reception had compelled them to introduce themselves to Canada "fighting like wolves after odd jobs after they arrive and barely subsisting through long, hard winters, thrown upon the charity of whatever municipality they have drifted to." He urged they be settled in groups of 5000 or more, somewhat like the Selkirk Settlers or the Barr Colony. King denied there was any discrimination against the British settlers.

The fact was that 8500 men came to Canada under assisted loans, and 7000 of them went back home. As the agriculture-minded *Manitoba Free Press* said, the experiment could not be shown as "anything but a failure."

Canada was recovering gradually from its bias against individual Englishmen, but there was still an unsympathetic disposition, especially in the West, to regard even the most forlorn little Cockney wanderer as the ne'er-do-well son of an earl living on a remittance from the family he had disgraced. Let one of them express even the mildest disapproval of the glue-and-cardboard raisin pie in a Chinese restaurant or come out against the flyspecks in the sugar and he would be widely denounced as one of those arrogant Limeys bent on running the Colonies.

Canada was still engaged in an old dispute with its other leading relative over the now almost ten-year-old matter of the rumrunners. This flared up again when two U.S. patrol vessels chased a Canadian ship named the *I'm Alone* for two days and 215 miles, finally caught it in their gunsights, and sank it with cannon fire.

Canada was still allowing liquor to be run across the border, even after the customs mess. In its first wave of outrage Parliament had passed a resolution demanding that no more shipments of booze be allowed to be sent out of the country addressed to the United States. King never put it into effect. Indeed, boats carrying Canadian liquor were loading constantly in Windsor in full view of the U.S. customs station across the short mile of the Detroit River and proceeding undisturbed to land their cargo on the far side.

The weird arrangement in existence was that when Canadian liquor was on the way to the United States, the Canadian authorities, having granted the necessary papers, would then telephone the American authorities at the port of destination to warn them the contraband was on the way.

Frequently the American officials, who had become just as cynical as—and, it must be suspected, even more corrupt than—the Canadian officials, merely sat and looked on. A Canadian officer in Bridgeburg, Ontario, reported to the Department of National Revenue, the successor to the Department of Customs and Excise, that his opposite number across the fifteen-minute run to Buffalo had asked him to stop making phone calls about impending shipments of rum and write him once a week.

According to one M.P., there were five thousand cases in which Canadian customs agents had cleared rumrunners with the boat wrongly named and the captain wrongly named. An unbelievable number of the boats were called *Daisy* and their skippers Bill Smith.

The Canadian Minister of National Revenue, W. D. Euler, had inherited this Gilbert-and-Sullivan situation from George Boivin and Jacques Bureau, and he viewed it with calm and unconcern. In the House he spoke of an adventure of his own. "I was offered safe

conduct by a liquor exporter and went out on a launch on the
Detroit River. I could see the United States customs office on the
other shore and I could see it was not very difficult to detect any
boats that left the Canadian shore to go to the American side. While
in Windsor I got into conversation with a man engaged in the
business of exporting liquor. I asked him, 'Do you cross in the
daytime?' He answered, 'Yes, quite often.' I said, 'How is it they
do not get you?' He replied with a smile, 'It just happens that they
are not there when we go across.'"

At one time there were actually ninety docks in Windsor mainly
serving the liquor trade. Thirty of them were closed up after the
Ontario Liquor Control Board charged that at least some of them
were "switching back" liquor into Ontario.

In a prosecution against one of the Windsor warehouses, a government attorney estimated that the liquor traffic across the Detroit
River was about a million dollars' worth a month. The United
States Prohibition Bureau issued a statement saying that four
fifths of the illegal alcohol coming into the United States came
through Detroit, and in defense of its inability to stop it maintained
that, in order to do so, it would need the whole United States Army
and Navy.

The United States tried to extradite a bagful of Canadian distillers, wholesalers, even bankers and railway officials. The intention
was to charge them with conspiracy to defeat the Volstead Act, but
the case was quietly dropped when it became apparent that no
Canadian court was likely to take the extradition request seriously.

The government stuck to its basic position that liquor in most
parts of Canada was a legally manufactured product, that the government had no right under the existing law to forbid its export
and didn't intend to change the law, since to do so would set an
impossible precedent.

One notable sympathizer in this was the explosive little congressman from New York, Fiorello La Guardia. In his view the U.S.
proposal that Canada change its own laws to fit the requirements
of the Volstead Act was completely indefensible; indeed, he splut-
tered in the House of Representatives, there had never been "a
more outrageous, cheap proposition in the history of the world."
A slightly less passionate defender of Canada's position was
Mackenzie King's part-time ally, J. S. Woodsworth, who wondered
innocently in the Canadian House of Commons whether Canada's

staunch attitude might not be unconsciously influenced by the huge campaign donations both the Liberal and Conservative parties were getting from the distillers.

In the meantime, although the British consul in New Orleans indignantly demanded, and obtained, the release from U.S. custody of the survivors of the *I'm Alone* and other protests were made in their behalf in Washington, most of the rumrunners working the high seas regarded the affair as nothing more serious than a bad break in a game in which the odds were all on their side. In *Maclean's* Thomas Wayling extracted this interesting sidelight from an old sea captain working off the Gaspé coast.

"I was not interested in his rum, but how he got it ashore," Wayling wrote. " 'It was easy,' he said. This was in the days when the de luxe cruiser *Margaret* was the flagship of the preventive service. 'That *Margaret*,' he said, 'she don' know nodding. We go out, twenty, thirty launch to the rumrunners. We load up, then all together we go lak hell for shore. The *Margaret* she chase us. We go twenty way, the *Margaret* she go only one way.'

" 'But she's sure to catch somebody.'

" 'Oh, sure,' he said casually, 'but it don't do her no good. Whoever she catch up wid throws the liquor overboard, and the *Margaret* she can do nodding.'

" 'But he loses the liquor.'

" 'No, he don't lose nodding. The liquor she's in sacks and all tied togedder wid rope. A long rope is tie on wid a buoy. He go out and pull it up.'

" 'Well, why doesn't the *Margaret* find the buoy and pull up the liquor?'

" 'When de *Margaret* she's dere, de buoy she's not. When we trow de buoy overboard we tie on de sack of salt. That sinks the buoy. Two, three days the sea she wash away the salt, the buoy she come up.' "

The fantastic adventures of the Volstead Act were by no means confined to Windsor and the Atlantic and Gulf coasts. On the long and empty prairie border between Saskatchewan and Alberta on the north and North Dakota and Montana on the south, anyone who was content to smuggle a few bottles merely had to walk through a clump of wolf willow or Saskatoon berries and hand them over. But a person with more ambition could easily whisk them through by the carload. This created its own regional gangland. A frequent visitor to the town in southern Saskatchewan where this writer grew up was a fairly important bootlegger from Lignite, North Dakota, who had acquired a set of possessions that looked as exotic, at least in that dusty little town in Saskatchewan, as the whole contents of *The Arabian Nights*. First of all his car, an authentic Duesenberg, top down, open to view, as long, low, and glossy as Cleopatra's barge. It was all nickel and red, with a set of exhausts shining like a pipe organ.

This would have been a staggering enough sight, but the man from North Dakota filled his Duesenberg with blondes. There were usually four or five of them clustered around him like a bouquet of wax gardenias.

At the end of the procession he led into town came two black Buicks full of colored baseball players. This was the time of tournament baseball in the West, a time when almost every town of any size had its one- or two-day tournament for a thousand dollars or more, and when colored men were still not allowed in organized baseball and therefore the best of them played in the unorganized tournaments. Two of the greatest men who ever pitched a baseball, John Donaldson and Satchel Paige, had no other place to earn a livelihood but on the prairies.

The gangster from North Dakota had neither Paige nor Donaldson, but he had a good ball team, easily good enough to play against Hap Felsch and Swede Risberg, the white stars of the Chicago White Sox who had been disqualified from organized baseball for their part in the fixed World Series of 1919.

When the cavalcade from North Dakota swept into one of the small towns of southern Saskatchewan, it was far more exciting than the arrival of the circus. Nobody in that vicinity had ever seen a Duesenberg before, nobody had ever seen a gangster before, nobody had seen a manufactured blonde before, nobody had seen a colored man before. Suddenly the streets were alive with them all, honking, shouting, giggling, staring back in a not unfriendly way at the goggle-eyed farm boys.

Volstead prosperity, however picturesque, was only a tiny part of the general prosperity through 1926, 1927, and 1928 and—people insisted on believing in spite of signs to the contrary—into 1929. Even those battered playthings of the gods the dirt farmers were collecting their share of it. Wheat prices were good and except for local accidents of nature the crops were good. Canada was producing a tenth of the whole world supply of it; of every five bushels sold on the export market two came from Canada.

Trouble lay not far ahead as Europe, still behind North America in the postwar recovery, began producing more of its own grain and setting up higher duties against imports. After debating tariffs for a good century, as though they were a sort of private preserve, Canada was soon to get a shattering dose of them from Herbert Hoover and the Smoot-Hawley Bill. Moreover, thousands of Canadians who had been working in the United States while still living in Canada faced the threat of much tougher border-crossing regulations; 200,000 French Canadians who had moved to New Hampshire in the last decade came briefly under the shadow of deportation until the U. S. Immigration Service ruled they were not subject to the new quotas on foreigners.

But these things still lay ahead in the years just before 1929. During the decade the total volume of exports went up by three quarters, the real national income by half, real wages by a fifth, and population by 15 per cent.

Mackenzie King went to another Imperial Conference in 1926 and helped confirm, in a less acrimonious atmosphere than that of 1923, the principle of full autonomy within the Empire in war and in peace. This, along with the now pervasive mood of optimism, provided the last needed note of prelude to Canada's Diamond Jubilee in 1927.

Perhaps Canada will never know another occasion when all the circumstances—an unclouded world horizon, a good and reassuring place within the Empire, an honest and rising pride in itself—will make for such a happy celebration. Children were still innocent enough to enjoy parades and prize-giving days. Adults were still willing to put on their hard collars and best millinery and go forth to listen to interminable speeches by the most obscure politicians and clergymen. About the whole proceedings of the Diamond Jubilee, which reached their climax on July 1, 1927, there was an air of unaffected, unsophisticated joy. The country was alive with strawberry festivals, ice-cream festivals, fowl suppers, three-legged races, egg-and-spoon races, baseball games between the fat men and the thin men, historical pageants featuring weirdly made-up and costumed Iroquois and fur traders, hymns, sermons, oratorical contests, millions of Union Jacks, tens of thousands of lithographed portraits of King George and Queen Mary.

The Prince of Wales came out for another visit, along with his brother Prince George and Prime Minister Stanley Baldwin. Among other things, he dedicated the new Memorial Chamber of the Peace Tower, built in memory of Canada's 60,000 war dead and containing a Book of Remembrance inscribed with all their names. Mr. Baldwin told the Montreal Canadian Club: "Nothing can stop you; you may some day be the greatest nation in the world." To make sure the visitors understood there was no serious flaw in the fabric of mutual esteem, Premier Taschereau assured the Prince in a speech at Quebec: "Some day you will reign over the greatest Empire in the world. Canada will be, and will wish to remain, part of that Empire."

King George V sent his message of congratulation, as did the Prime Ministers of the other dominions. The local Council of Women in Toronto made the pleasant discovery that twenty-seven daughters of Confederation were still living and gave a banquet in their honor. The new carillon in the Peace Tower played "God Save the King," "O Canada," and "The Maple Leaf" over a special radio network and was heard all over Canada and almost all over the world.

Charles Lindbergh flew *The Spirit of St. Louis* to Ottawa. Bliss Carman wrote a special poem. There were special books and special postage stamps, and every schoolchild who didn't play hooky from his school's commemorative exercises received a special bronze medal.

In these sunny times there was, of course, no beclouding thought of war. In 1928 King had a brief fling with world government. His wary approach to collective security within the Empire and within the League of Nations had now relaxed a good deal. He made a trip to Paris to sign the Briand-Kellogg Pact for the renunciation of war and went on to Geneva to accept election as a vice-president of the League's Assembly. He returned to assure Parliament that under the terms of Briand and Kellogg "even those nations who are parties to the Covenant of the League have gone a step further in agreeing formally to renounce war at any and all times." In reply to skeptical questioning by the Opposition, he demanded indignantly to know why they should wish to show distrust to other nations. "Because," R. B. Bennett answered him, "we have had experience."

Neither of the parties to this exchange knew that King, the new apostle of collective safety, was a few years hence to play a leading part in sinking the League. And although Canada and the world were fast nearing the end of their salad days, no one knew that either.

XXXIV

The market crash and the Depression—King's
historic Five-Cent Piece

OCTOBER 29, 1929, is commonly accepted as the date of the end
of the boom. This probably is an undeserved compliment to, or
criticism of, the world's stock markets.

Unemployment was approaching noticeable, if not critical, proportions as early as September. The world was reaching for such an
overdose of economic nationalism that it could scarcely have failed
to bring on years of chaos. Herbert Hoover, the real father of the
Smoot-Hawley Bill, had failed in his first try to ram his towering
tariff wall through the U. S. Congress, but he had declared himself long ago on the principle behind it and he was not to fail
on his second attempt.

Nor was Hoover by any means the only enemy of a return to
the law of supply and demand and a reasonably natural flow of
goods among the nations. The whole world, after exchanging a
few pleasantries at the peace conference, had been drifting steadily
back to an unabashed policy of dog-eat-dog. As a Canadian Royal
Commission put it later: "All the weapons in the arsenal of economic autarchy were brought into play. Weak positions were protected, high-cost producers were kept in production and obsolete
equipment was preserved by rising tariffs, import quotas, cartels,
government subsidies, 'rationalization,' restriction schemes, stabi-
lization of prices, etc."

Canada, of course, had been tempted by these measures and
succumbed at one time or other, and at least in some degree to all
of them.

Ironically, just a few months before the market crash the country
had embarked on one of its own most disastrous adventures in

world trade. After the big crop of 1928 the Wheat Pools had an unsold carry-over of about a hundred million bushels. The next year's crop was much smaller, and through most of 1929 the Pools kept Canadian wheat off the world market, confident that good prices would get better. Precisely the opposite happened. There were huge crops in the Argentine, the United States, and Australia, and the red-faced Canadian salesmen who had watched their produce begin dropping from a peak of $1.60 in July were forced to the unhappy conclusion that they were not only on a falling market but on a glutted market. Moreover, they had lost some of their European customers forever, for the Argentine, which had been content to sell its crop at the going price, had for the first time in history outsold Canada. And as a final hazard to Canada's unsold surplus of 1929, Germany in 1930 raised its import duty on wheat to a shattering $1.62 a bushel. In Italy the tariff jumped to $1.07 and in France to 85 cents.

With perhaps two hundred million dollars' worth of their wheat still in the elevators as they passed through a cold Christmas, Canadian farmers had to appeal to the governments of the prairie provinces for an advance to help them to the end of winter. In the meantime business of every kind throughout the West had been delivered an extra blow at a time when it could least be afforded. The railways and shipping companies, with their fall tonnages cut by almost two thirds, suffered too.

The world's real wealth, its actual goods, was in imbalance and this was a far larger factor in the Depression than the miscalculations of those who held only slips of paper from the stock exchanges—and these often only 10 or 20 per cent paid for on margin.

Nevertheless, the rise and fall of the stock market was something everyone could understand and take part in personally, or at least follow as a spectator. If the participant came out of it unhurt or not too badly hurt, he might even have enjoyed it, for its sense of immediacy and quick crescendo and crash gave it an air of mighty drama. While it lasted, it was the sinking of the *Titanic*, Balto's race to Nome, the Halifax Explosion, and Doc Dafoe's fight to save the Dionne quintuplets all rolled up in one.

The giddily new-rich office boys lighting cigars with dollar bills did really exist. The little old ladies staring at the brokers' boards like uncomprehending, merry robins were not a work of fiction. The hockey players driving up to the Montreal Forum behind their personal chauffeurs were not mere inventions. Nor were a hundred other heroes the crazed market paid homage to On the Way Up.

No more were the tottering assortment of dupes, fools, and outright villains it mocked and reviled On the Way Down. They too were briefly real, even if their setting was as fanciful as an opium dream.

No one will ever know how much was made On the Way Up or how much lost On the Way Down. It cannot be said, except as a guess, that the two figures even matched. For all were using phony money under lunatic rules. Interest rates in New York went as high as 20 per cent. In Canada it was by no means an unusual thing for a person who had no real money of his own to borrow money at 10 or 12 per cent to buy a stock yielding 1 per cent or even much less. One issue was selling across Canada at twenty-eight hundred times its annual earnings; most investors feel that when the price rises to much more than thirty or forty times earnings, it is time to take a careful look.

The greatest holocaust occurred, of course, on Wall Street. But considering their more limited financial capacity, Canadians got taken about as handsomely as anyone. From the highs of 1929 to the lows of 1931, the combined shares of thirty-five Canadian blue-chips dropped nearly five billion dollars in listed price. Lesser issues probably went down as much again. International Nickel alone slumped nearly a billion in the total price of its shares; Imperial Oil more than eight hundred million; Canadian Pacific Railway more than half a billion. In terms of individual shares, Brazilian Traction dropped from 82 to 12; B-A Oil from 36 to 8; Cockshutt from 53 to 4; Winnipeg Electric from 109 to 10—and so on and on.

As though their venture in blue-sky buying and panic selling hadn't been enough for the suckers to reflect upon, they learned shortly after the first shock of awakening that they had been playing with a third kind of fire—unbridled piracy. As early as the first part of November, the *Financial Post* launched a series of exposés that in time led to the revelation that practically every one of Canada's largest mining brokerage firms had been plundering its customers without let or conscience. By the time the startled authorities had finished looking into the reeking mess for themselves, sixteen senior partners and officers of eight of the country's best-known brokerage houses were sentenced to terms in jail up to five years and fined up to $425,000.

By mid-1930 the U.S.A. had four million unemployed. Canadian statistics were haphazard, but those available pointed to around four hundred thousand. And it was to get much worse through most of the next three years before a slow upturn began and finally reached a moderate breakthrough in 1937.

Among those who had jobs, thousands were living on less than subsistence pay. The worst case uncovered by any official agency was of a girl factory worker in Montreal getting a dollar and a half for a seventy-five-hour week. The needle trades were paying home-workshop employees an average of fifty cents a day. Able-bodied men, some of them heads of families, were getting as little as six dollars a week. In Saskatchewan during a two-year period, the average earnings of more than a hundred doctors in the dust bowl was twenty-seven dollars a month.

The Depression was well into its third and in some places its fourth year before anything like systematic relief became general. In relatively rich Toronto a family of seven was entitled to food vouchers worth just under seven dollars a week. In Saskatchewan a family of five could expect ten dollars a month plus a ninety-eight-pound sack of flour. They were forbidden to squander any of the money on fruit or any vegetables except potatoes and dried beans. Most relief rations, as the rebellious Manitoba judge Lewis St. George Stubbs once snapped, were not enough to live on and not enough to die on.

In fact there was almost no starvation in the Depression as a coroner would define starvation. A much greater tragedy was demoralization: the demoralization of able and willing men standing on street corners selling apples for a nickel; of sad, terrified girls standing on other street corners selling themselves for two dollars, one dollar, fifty cents, anything; of an unending procession of "hobos" knocking on the back doors of friendly restaurants for the scraps left on luckier people's plates, hitting the rods again, knocking at the back doors of the next town, hitting the rods; of children going to school without shoes and proper books; the demoralization even of those not themselves faced with hardship but unable to face its specter; the demoralization of a nation fast losing its anchors and assurances.

Even the usually unshakable Mackenzie King was shaken, though less, apparently, by the catastrophe itself than by his inability to argue or maneuver his way around it. He handled the

Depression exactly as though it were another parliamentary opponent. His strategy seemed to be to wait it out, watch for it to make a mistake, then pounce on it and destroy it.

Actually it was King who made all the mistakes—one of them probably the most costly one, politically, of his whole career. In spite of himself he became rattled and cantankerous under constant petitions and attacks. It was many months before he would admit there was an unemployment problem at all. Then the furthest he would go was to announce that if by any chance there was a problem it wasn't serious enough to warrant intervention by the Dominion.

In his speeches outside the House during the six months after the market crash, he talked about everything but unemployment. He was on the move fairly constantly, for he had already decided to call an election in the summer of 1930 and wished to begin seeing to his fences. During a long trip through the West, he referred constantly to the Conservatives' position on protection and spoke vaguely of their loyalty to the Interests. At Prince Albert he was against racial and religious prejudice. At Edmonton he became an advocate of a railway or road from the Peace River country to the Pacific. In Winnipeg he talked of external affairs. He carefully chose non-political occasions and non-political platforms to make addresses of welcome to Ramsay MacDonald and to the Japanese envoy. He unveiled a tablet at a Toronto church and took to the radio to open a Montreal bridge. He returned to Toronto to make a speech on Liberalism.

But he was forced ultimately to emerge from behind the cloud banks of public oratory and face the last session of Parliament. In one of his few serious statements on unemployment outside the House he had already begun to fall into one of those awkward traps Arthur Meighen had been so good at seeking out.

A delegation of western public officials came to see him just after the session opened to ask that Ottawa help the municipalities and provinces in financing relief. King listened to them with growing impatience, which he contained for two hours. But at last he burst forth with the accusation that they were "stirring up and aggravating" the whole situation. Unemployment, he insisted, was "not abnormal."

Early in April he was still stoutly defending his refusal to help the provinces on the ground that to do so would be to invade their rights under the British North America Act. He was on perfectly sound ground; moreover, he put a few strands of barbed wire around it by observing that without exception the provincial premiers had delivered New Year's messages alluding to "prosperity" in their provinces.

J. S. Woodsworth broke in to snip the barbed wire in one sentence. "Do governments ever declare that there is anything but prosperity during their regime?"

Suddenly King was ranting as crudely as some Latin-American dictator. The Liberals had been in power in Ottawa since 1921. They'd reduced the public debt and reduced taxes. But now the Tories and Progressives were saying to the wise and prudent Liberals: raise taxes. And give the proceeds "to whom, if you please?"

He answered his own question in a litany of outrage: "To a Tory government in the province of British Columbia; to a Progressive government in the province of Alberta; to a Tory government in the province of Saskatchewan; to a Progressive government in the province of Manitoba; to a Tory government in the province of Ontario; to a Tory government in the province of New Brunswick; to a Tory government in the province of Nova Scotia." And to cap the indictment he fairly shouted: "No request has come from or been made on behalf of either Quebec or Prince Edward Island, where there are Liberal governments."

An intruding heckler tried to get in his way, but King brushed him aside and plunged recklessly on: "May I conclude? . . . So far as giving money from this federal treasury to provincial governments is concerned, in relation to this question of unemployment as it exists today, I might be prepared to go a certain length possibly in meeting one or two of the western provinces that have Progressive premiers . . . but I would not give one cent to any Tory government."

After a detonation of cries of "Shame!" he bludgeoned his way back into possession of the floor through sheer persistence and lung power: "May I repeat what I have said? With respect to giving moneys out of the federal treasury to any Tory government in this country for these alleged unemployment purposes, with these governments situated as they are today, with policies diametrically opposed to those of this government, I would not give them a five-cent piece."

Thus King's famous Five-Cent Piece speech might as well have been remembered as the One-Cent Piece speech. Except as the tiniest of footnotes, the difference could have meant nothing to history.

XXXV

King loses his confidence—Bennett
inherits the Depression

KING was soon in the middle of the election, listening to those awful, irretrievable words played back to him from all quarters and from every manner of mankind. Like some landlocked Philip Nolan sentenced to make perpetual amends for a single utterance, he roamed the hustings as the tormented captive of his past.

Let him commence the most rational address on the St. Lawrence Waterway and announce the proposed cost of it, and some local wag was certain to bring down the house by bellowing "Five-Cent Piece!"

Let him reach full flight during the most eloquent defense of the C.N.R., and an outraged clubwoman would screech "Five-Cent Piece!"—and there he was, flailing and floundering back to earth like a mortally wounded pigeon. The dreaded words pursued him everywhere. He heard them in Charlottetown, P.E.I., and in Victoria, B.C. He heard them in Chilliwack and Saskatoon, in Edmonton and Sherbrooke, in Brandon, Barrie, and North Bay.

And most horribly of all, even before the campaign began, he heard them repeatedly from Richard Bedford Bennett, the man he had to beat to save his ministry.

On the surface R. B. Bennett was already half a century out of date when he attained the leadership of the Conservative party. If some demented Marxist had been seeking an effigy to stick pins into, he might well have made it in Bennett's exact likeness. He was a multimillionaire; he earned his first million or so as a corporation lawyer and the rest had been inherited.

He wore a plug hat, tail coat, and striped trousers and, in the words of a reporter, "shoes that glisten—almost gloat." These adorned a towering and commanding frame on which years of good eating and no exercise had deposited a definite paunch.

His face was round, but there was no mirth in it; it gave only a sense of immense concentration, intelligence, and strength.

"When he laughs," remarked that staunchest of Tory editors Grattan O'Leary, "it is as though he were making a good-natured concession to the weaknesses of others."

Bennett talked a great deal, in a firm, resounding voice and at almost incredible rates of speed. A whole mythology had grown up around this memorable voice and the way in which he used it. In his earlier days in the West it had won him the nickname Richard "Bonfire" Bennett. He had been clocked at 220 words a minute, and after he came to Ottawa the Hansard reporters were said to lay out extra pencils and hope for the best every time he caught the Speaker's eye.

One observer referred with respect to "his blustering three-fisted way of smashing out words." After one of his radio speeches another said: "One cannot help but think he looked on the microphone as a public meeting or a mob."

The only thing lacking in the classic image of a domineering capitalist was the big cigar. He neither smoked nor drank and, like King, he was a bachelor—though not nearly so timid a one.

He was born at Hopewell Hill, in the same corner of New Brunswick as Max Aitken and Bonar Law. Aitken became his fastest friend and they remained friends after the former had become Lord Beaverbrook and the latter Viscount Bennett of Mickleham, Calgary, and Hopewell. In later years Bennett tried to encourage the innocent fiction that he had known a youth of poverty, but in fact his father was a well-to-do shipbuilder. By the time he took a friend's advice to go West he had suffered somewhat fewer than the usual hardships of a law student. He had worked hard and had become highly competent at his profession and it was not long before he was getting corporation work from both the C.P.R. and the Hudson's Bay Company. With the help of his real estate investments he was soon a rich man. He became much richer—in fact the richest politician in Canadian history—after a friend of his New Brunswick days, Mrs. E. B. Eddy, left him the match factory that still bears her husband's name.

Sir Robert Borden met Bennett for the first time during the same western tour on which he first saw Arthur Meighen. Bennett was then a thirty-two-year-old member of the legislature of the North-west Territories. He struck Borden as "overflowing with energy and enthusiasm." He arrived in the House of Commons as a Conservative M.P. in 1911 and soon began fulfilling his leader's prediction that his "future course in life would be conspicuous." Indeed it was, and never more so than when he was assailing Borden's own railway policies on the floor of the House and taking Meighen apart for daring to defend them. Borden accepted this with relative calm. He had far too few good young men. Also he was philosopher enough to appreciate that as an old C.P.R. hand Bennett could not be expected to applaud the government for bestowing millions of public money on the C.P.R.'s impecunious and bankrupt competitors, Mackenzie and Mann. Meighen, with every reason, took the matter more personally; no one, before or since, ever gave him so thorough a public trouncing. The two men never became friends.

Except for a few rare occasions when a situation turned up that happened to match his florid, headlong style of oratory, Bennett's parliamentary career had been an oddly unspectacular one. He had played an important part as a committee cross-examiner during the unearthing of the customs scandal, but was much less effective when the question was aired and debated in the House itself. During the climactic day of the Constitutional Crisis he was not in the House at all; private business had called him back to Calgary.

Until he succeeded to the party leadership most of the public probably remembered him best from the distant days of 1917 when, as director of the National Service Board, he attempted to set up a national registration scheme. The plan, being both unpopular and voluntary, was doomed to fail from the start. When it was liquidated, Bennett handed over the million and a half cards he had collected to Meighen, who was beginning the even more thankless task of enforcing the infinitely more unpopular conscription program. Neither man knew it then, but the slight difference between their two roles made it possible for Bennett to get at least some support from Quebec in the years ahead. Meighen, of course, could get none.

As the two party leaders crisscrossed the country in the election spring of 1930, the staunchest Tory would have admitted that Bennett's strongest asset was King. Aside from the memory of the Five-Cent Piece and the unadmitted burden of unemployment,

King hobbled himself with so many semi-private quarrels that he fell further and further in his real opponent's rear.

Bennett had no need to campaign against anyone but King, but King felt some suicidal need to campaign against those detested Tory provincial premiers. At Regina he charged J. T. M. Anderson with delaying public works in order to project unemployment into politics. "It will be my pleasant duty," Anderson replied, "from now on to do all in my power to bring about the defeat of the King government."

King feuded constantly with Howard Ferguson, of Ontario, over the Five-Cent Piece, the St. Lawrence River power question, and half a dozen other issues he should have been fighting out, if at all, against Bennett. He accused J. B. M. Baxter, of New Brunswick, of giving employment on the roads even to women and children. Baxter as much as admitted it and King was now campaigning against Santa Claus. He never did come wholly to grips with either of the two real issues, the Depression and the tariff. He never did come wholly to grips with Bennett.

King had always been a loner, and now, with everything falling apart, including his own political instinct, he was pathetically alone. Even in Quebec, where he had always been able to count on all the electioneering help he needed and an almost automatic dividend of sixty seats, he could stir no spark of enthusiasm. It was not until a week before polling day that Premier L. A. Taschereau made his first speech in his federal chieftain's behalf. Then he could find no more ringing appeal to his compatriots than: "Mackenzie King is a friend of our race. He respects our traditions, reverences all that we hold sacred, and merits your support. I have nothing to say against Mr. Bennett, but I must say I don't like his friends."

Bennett won a clear majority in this 1930 election with 138 seats. Of these, twenty-five were from Quebec, where Meighen had been able to win only four in 1926. The Liberals had 88 seats across the Dominion.

Almost overnight, almost before there was time to trade places in the House of Commons, the two men traded complexions. King had stumbled through the election in a fog of helpless unreality. Now he was a tiger again, thirsting for blood. Bennett had been an avenging angel demanding the head of a government that had neglected the national crisis of unemployment. Now he was the voice of calm and sobriety asking: what crisis?

During the campaign the new Prime Minister had promised, if elected, to call an immediate special session of Parliament to deal with the problems of the jobless. This he did six weeks after his election.

For King the opening of the Seventeenth Parliament offered his first real taste of the delights of Opposition in nearly a decade. It obviously gave him far more pleasure than had anything in his last few months of office. He remarked, in reply to the Speech from the Throne, that only a few months ago the new Prime Minister had been blaming the Depression and unemployment—which King now admitted to be not only real but serious—on "the policies of the Ottawa government." But now, overnight, Bennett had decided and so announced that the true villain was "exceptional economic conditions." Bennett had insisted that by substituting his good government for King's bad government he could bail the country out. He had made "wholesale and unqualified promises and pledges of all classes and description." Where, King demanded, did he propose to begin fulfilling them?

Bennett started retreating at once. To begin with, the press had misquoted him on some of his pre-election pledges. At any rate, Rome wasn't built in a day. "This government purposes to go forward with the program which it has outlined. It does not purpose to undertake it completely in one session or in two sessions, because no promises of that character were made."

For the time being, what he had to offer and all he had to offer toward easing unemployment was twenty million dollars for public works. There might be more later, but that was all for now.

In any case, make-work projects were mere palliatives, not remedies. The real solution lay with the tariff, not a conventional, middling tariff such as other Conservatives had stood for since John A.'s time, but one of much sterner stuff, a sort of Canadian Smoot-Hawley. Close out foreign goods and keep Canadian jobs and Canadian money in Canada. "We propose," Bennett said, "that so far as may be reasonably possible the requirements of the ten million people living on the northern half of this continent shall be provided by Canadian producers." King replied with heavy-handed references to Bennett's election promise to "blast his way into the markets of the world."

The country followed these pronouncements and maneuvers with amusement, hope, anxiety, and a certain amount of indifference. Life was still going on in a million and a half Canadian homes, and beside its not altogether grim realities the jousting of the two portly bachelors at Ottawa had a little of the air of a charade.

XXXVI

*The great bonanza of Beauharnois—A few
hundred thousand dollars for a few
enterprising senators*

THERE were really two distinct phases to the Depression—the first, when everybody wondered when it would end; the second, when everybody wondered if it would end. One man's dividing line was not precisely the same as another's, nor was one region's the same as another's, nor one industry's the same as another's. If all the bearings could have been averaged out, the height of land would probably have been fixed at somewhere between the middle of 1931 and the middle of 1932.

Counting the ragged edges at the beginning and the end, the Depression lasted almost as long in Canada as the two world wars put together. In its presence a million and a half Canadians were born, three quarters of a million were married, and another three quarters of a million died. Life went on, and, until it crossed the escarpment between hope and despair, it went on in a fairly comfortable and familiar way.

In 1931 Canada won eighty-six firsts at the International Live Stock and Grain Exposition in Chicago. The failure of the celebrated Herman Trelle to retain his title as world wheat king was widely regretted, but he and his countrymen still carried off sixty-eight prizes out of seventy-two for hard-spring. The provincial treasurer of Alberta expressed confidence that the road was beginning to rise toward prosperity. Captain Angus Walters' splendid schooner, *Bluenose*, won its seventh straight fisherman's international sailing race, defeating the *Gertrude L. Thebaud*. Bennett went to London and signed the Statute of Westminster, putting the final seal on the conception of autonomy that Borden had begun spelling out at the Peace Conference and King had enlarged on at the Imperial Conferences of 1923 and 1926.

Special masses were said throughout the country for Jean de Brébeuf and seven other Jesuit martyrs just canonized at St. Peter's. The Orange Grand Lodge of British America celebrated its 100th anniversary and the 240th anniversary of the Battle of the Boyne by passing resolutions against a national flag and the use of French on postage stamps. The president of the Toronto Board of Trade said that recovery had started and urged an immediate reduction of the income tax. The government of Prince Edward Island expressed gratitude for sound economic conditions. The president of the Imperial Order Daughters of the Empire referred to five main issues in her address to the annual meeting: unemployment relief, child welfare, Empire trade, communism, and undesirable literature. The Catholic Women's League passed a resolution against birth control and divorce. The premier of Nova Scotia assailed those who were spreading "glum talk." The National Council of Women passed a resolution demanding stricter laws against white slavery. Except where the dust was beginning to blow up on the prairies, the face of the country still had a clean, scrubbed look and its heart was full of steady purpose and naïve good cheer.

The miracle is not that there was so much old-fashioned innocence still abroad after a year and a half of Depression. The miracle was that so much of it survived Beauharnois.

When Parliament dissolved for the 1930 election, the first fumes of a new public scandal lingered behind in the silent green chamber of the House of Commons. A private concern, the Beauharnois Power Corporation Limited, had for some years held extremely important power rights on a stretch of the St. Lawrence River near Montreal. To make it possible to use them, Ottawa's approval of a diversion canal had been required and granted. The promoters thereupon began putting more water into their stock than into their canal.

A week before the last session under the Liberal government, Robert Gardiner, of the United Farmers of Alberta, charged in the Commons that through a false prospectus the company was well on the way to defrauding the public of some thirty million dollars. Moreover, during the preparations necessary for so ambitious an enterprise, the president of the company, R. O. Sweezey, had written an indiscreet letter to J. Alderic Raymond, hotelier and businessman, of Montreal. Alderic Raymond was the brother of Senator Donat Raymond, the Liberal party treasurer for Quebec.

Sweezey, the promoter, instructed the senator's brother: "Enlist with our syndicate two or three individuals who, in addition to paying some cash as their fair share, can assist us in getting our rights extended or enlarged so as to develop the entire available flow of the St. Lawrence at this point. As the whole situation is within the Province of Quebec, our influence has to be exerted only in political circles."

The next chapter had to wait a full year. During his last few days in Opposition, Bennett, on the basis of the Raymond letter and the impending stock flotation, had been demanding a full investigation of the Beauharnois company. When he returned to the House of Commons as Prime Minister, he had more urgent things on his mind, among them the knowledge that his own party had taken thirty thousand dollars from the Sweezey interests before he himself ordered it to take no more. He was, at any rate, no longer in a hurry to ventilate the subject. King was in even less hurry, for reasons that soon became clear.

Except for the persistence of the little United Farmers of Alberta group, the matter might have remained dormant indefinitely. But in May 1931 the Alberta farmers concluded they had been stalled off long enough. They looked the massed and silent phalanx of city slickers square in the eye and demanded a recorded vote to decide whether Beauharnois should be debated immediately or not.

King and Bennett eyed each other across the floor of the House, each wondering whether he dared lead his followers into the "nay" lobby, each afraid to do so lest the other might then reap an advantage by voting virtuously "aye."

Bennett at last made the first move and suddenly the whole House, Tory and Grit alike, was milling toward the banner of the farmers like a yeoman army mustering against the barons. "The scene," J. S. Woodsworth reflected later with un-Woodsworthian malice, "was one of the most ludicrous I have ever seen in this House." When the astonished tellers had finished counting, they announced one of the most one-sided verdicts in recent parliamentary history—147 in favor of ventilating the Beauharnois affair, 21 against.

Within a month Beauharnois was before a parliamentary committee. It took only a few sittings to establish the outlines of the most barefaced public steal in more than fifty years. The company had paid at least $700,000 into the Liberal party's campaign funds. Three of the party's leading members—all respected senators, one the party's national treasurer, one its Quebec treasurer—had also accepted or extorted huge profits for themselves. While this was going on the Liberal government was handing over to the company almost priceless rights on the St. Lawrence along with a heaven-sent opportunity to fleece the investing public.

On the Beauharnois side of these transactions the chief malefactor was Robert Oliver Sweezey, a forty-seven-year-old Montreal engineer, broker, and businessman. As early as 1912, when he was working for Lord Beaverbrook, Sweezey had studied the St. Lawrence's untapped power resources and concluded, as had others before him, that the fifteen turbulent miles between Lake St. Francis and Lake St. Louis constituted one of Canada's most valuable unused natural resources. Beaverbrook lost interest in the St. Lawrence as he became drawn more and more toward England, but in the early 1920s Sweezey decided to form a syndicate to build a power plant on his favorite stretch of the river.

Quebec controlled the power rights and Ottawa the navigation rights. Without Ottawa's clearance the canal needed for a power plant could not be built.

On the government side of the seedy drama now unfolding the protagonists were Donat Raymond and his fellow senators Andrew Haydon and Wilfrid Laurier McDougald. Raymond joined the syndicate early and made half a million dollars on his own account besides collecting $200,000 for the party.

The parliamentary committee soon learned that Haydon, the national treasurer and organizer, had collected half a million dollars of Sweezey and Beauharnois money for the Liberal party. In addition he virtually forced Sweezey to pay his law firm $50,000 for helping to arrange the needed permissions from Ottawa, and in addition to that he had his firm placed on a retainer of $15,000 a year.

Senator McDougald collected no money for the Liberal party, but he collected a very large amount for himself. No one was in a better position to do so, for he was a big man in both politics and high finance. He had begun life as a country doctor in northern Ontario, made some fast money in mining, and given up the healing arts forever. He took up business in Montreal, continued to prosper, and began to make the right friends. He soon became as familiar a figure in the lobby of the Chateau Laurier as in the St. James's Club in Montreal. In either place he was recognized by his field marks: a virile shock of black wavy hair surmounting a haberdasher's totem of patent-leather button shoes, dove-gray spats, silk gloves, and morning clothes, often with a small orchid in the lapel.

Before McDougald was forty-five Mackenzie King appointed him to the Senate. Other honors had preceded this, and others followed. In the year of decision on the Beauharnois application he held four distinct public offices in which he could influence the decision. He was chairman of the Montreal Harbor Commission. He was a member of the National Advisory Council on the St. Lawrence Waterway. Besides being an ordinary member of the Senate, he was a member of the Senate's special committee on the St. Lawrence. He was also—although this, understandably, was a secret known only to a very few—one of Beauharnois's largest shareholders.

He acquired his first million dollars' worth of stock as an outright gouge and split it down the middle with Robert A. C. Henry, an influential civil servant who helped him extract it. In this mere prelude the powerful senator and the powerful bureaucrat set up a dummy company of their own and made a dummy application for the same water rights they knew Sweezey and other promoters would be seeking later on.

Then they informed Sweezey that if he wanted fast action on his own application he had better buy out their own worthless corporation. Sweezey did, for two thousand shares in his own syndicate—worth about five hundred dollars each.

Once the deal was made events moved swiftly. Henry, through a lucky coincidence, was promoted to the position of Deputy Minister of Railways and Canals. This made him the top administrative officer of the government department which could, and almost immediately did, push through the order in council granting Beauharnois its franchise.

Up to this crucial point, the point of the government's decision to give the company what it wanted, McDougald and Henry had kept their Beauharnois interests hidden behind a series of false fronts. But once the Beauharnois franchise was granted and no one could accuse them, as brand-new stockholders, of influencing an

action already taken, they felt free to come above ground. With
the help of options and stock splits they soon had Robert Sweezey
where the camel had the Arab—halfway out of the tent. McDougald
became chairman of the board. Henry resigned from the Department of Railways and Canals to become vice-president and general
manager. Sweezey hung on as president.

When he took the witness stand to explain his vast scale of
bribery, Sweezey, the buyer of men and governments, made a not
altogether convincing effort to depict himself as an innocent who
had fallen among thieves. When his memory flagged at one point,
he fingered his pince-nez and pleaded fastidiously: "It was a very
distasteful thing to me and I personally preferred not to know or
remember anything about it." He paid nearly half a million dollars
in "legal fees," a large percentage of which actually went, according to the gossip of the press gallery, for everything from
cases of the best scotch to bevies of the best ladies from Hull.
He cheerfully settled individual expense accounts up to $50,000
without asking for itemized statements.

Sweezey once pressed $125,000 on a casual acquaintance on the
strength of a knowing nudge in the ribs. John Aird, Jr., son of the
eminent banker, heard of the delay Sweezey was having in his plans
for Beauharnois, went to see him, and mentioned discreetly that
he thought a donation to the Ontario Conservative party might be
appreciated. Theoretically, Sweezey had nothing to ask of the
Ontario government, but he was well aware that if it chose it could
seriously delay his plans in Quebec. "Gratefulness," Aird reminded
him gently, "is always regarded as an important factor in dealing
with democratic governments."

The promoter, certain that he was speaking to an official emissary,
promptly forked over $125,000. Aird as promptly put it in his
personal bank account and left it there. When it came his turn to
testify before the parliamentary interrogators he said he'd never
had any connection with the Ontario Conservative party and
never pretended to have. The money was a fee for some advice
that Aird, a non-practicing engineer and a failure in half a dozen
fields, said he had given Sweezey on how to procure a contract
with the Ontario Hydro-Electric Commission.

Aird was unable to remember the nature of the "advice" and
Sweezey stuck stubbornly to his story that he had been led to

believe his company was buying the good will of the Ontario Tories.

R. B. Bennett was so shaken by this public exchange that he put in a transatlantic telephone call to Howard Ferguson, the former premier of Ontario, recently appointed Canadian High Commissioner in London. Back through three thousand miles of Atlantic static came Ferguson's rasping guarantee: "They can dig right through to China; they will get nothing on me." (They never did either; nor did this first committee or a follow-up investigation in Ontario ever get anything from young John Aird except his blandly reiterated claim that Sweezey, in effect, gave him $125,000 for nothing.)

Most of the witnesses at the Beauharnois investigation were cooperative and reasonably frank. Once a member of the committee asked Bob Henry, the former civil servant and now general manager of Beauharnois, a blunt question: Was it true that he and Senator McDougald had filed their original St. Lawrence application in order to force anyone who might thereafter undertake to develop that part of the river "to take care of McDougald and Henry?"

"I guess you can put it that way," Henry said pleasantly.

Senator Raymond appeared before the committee and admitted both the huge party donation and the huge personal profit he had acquired from Beauharnois. Senator Haydon was too ill to testify in person, but consented to be examined at his home. He confirmed the Beauharnois donations to the Liberal party and his private dealings with the company. Neither senator would acknowledge the slightest feeling of wrongdoing; they both appeared convinced that they had acted in a perfectly normal and ethical manner.

McDougald was by all odds the least outgiving of the principals. When the committee summoned him to appear he refused, falling back on his immunity as a senator from the commands of the Commons.

For a day or two the press was full of rumors that the committee would send the sergeant at arms to fetch him and, if he still refused to come, lock him up in the tower of the House of Commons. This delightfully medieval prospect was not nearly so impossible as it sounded. As recently as 1913 an earlier utilities promoter had gone to the tower in Ottawa for refusing to answer a subpoena from the House. The papers recalled that he slept on a davenport with a uniformed policeman on an adjoining one and had lamb chops and hash-brown potatoes for breakfast. The vision of McDougald, the multimillionaire fashion plate, in similar surroundings added to the sense of public excitement that had already kept the inquiry on the front pages through most of July.

When McDougald still refused to communicate with the committee except through his lawyer, Bennett threatened either to call a Royal Commission or to rush through a constitutional amendment abolishing Senate immunity.

At last, on the second-last day of the hearings, the senator presented himself for examination. Except that he was dressed much more conservatively than usual in a plain blue business suit, there was no visible change in his usual demeanor.

As he entered the historic Railway Committee room, the scene not so long before of the explosive customs investigation, it was jammed to its paneled rafters. At least five hundred people crowded the corridors outside. From afar the bell summoning ordinary M.P.s to the regular sittings of the House clanged and scolded for a full five minutes. It was mostly in vain. Nobody was missing this if he could help it.

To some McDougald was disappointingly unruffled. He took approximately the same basic position as his fellow senators had done. There was nothing to deny, nothing to defend, nothing to apologize for. He had made money from Beauharnois, certainly—but only as an honest businessman. He had never used the slightest influence in any of his public offices to advance his private interests or the interests of the power firm of which he was now the chairman.

An outraged M.P. read back to him a declaration he had made in the Senate in 1928, when he was acquiring shares in the company through one of his blinds: "I want to say here," the senator had declaimed, "and to say it with emphasis, that I do not own a dollar's worth of stock in this enterprise, and have no interest in or association with that company in any way, shape, or form." McDougald, confronted with evidence to the contrary, now ran to cover behind a thicket of his front men and the fine print in his original statement.

As the senator alternately swaggered and slithered through his cross-examination, the story of Beauharnois appeared to be nearing a merciful end. The thing had at last come down to the dregs.

There could be no more shame to taste, no more good, respected names to soil.

But there was one more name: William Lyon Mackenzie King. The exhibit that contained it had been uncovered first by the committee's shocked auditors. The members saw it privately and for a week could not quite bring themselves to make it public. But now, with McDougald on the stand, they put it on the table. There, as suddenly, unbelievably, and theatrically as an apparition from Shakespeare, lay a slip of paper to show that, only a year before, the company that had been busy suborning a Canadian government had paid a rather large hotel and travel bill for the head of that government.

Just before plunging into the election campaign of the previous spring King had gone to Bermuda for a short holiday in company with Andrew Haydon, the party treasurer. Before they left, King urged McDougald to join them; the Prime Minister and the senator had been enjoying Easter together off and on for years. When they checked out of their hotel, McDougald picked up the bill for all three. Later a voucher went from McDougald's office to the treasurer's office at Beauharnois. It was paid and, according to the stamp on the voucher, the proceeds were credited to McDougald's private account.

The voucher read: "Expenses of trip to Bermuda, Hon. W. L. Mackenzie King and self: Hotel, Bermuda $288.53. Fares, Montreal to Bermuda and return, $395.04. Hotel, New York $168.75. Total, $852.32."

McDougald, who had been warned the voucher might come up and therefore had time to prepare an explanation, produced a story of bookkeeping so muddled and accounting so confused that he himself was still amending it when the subject arose again seven months later in the Senate. It boiled down to two main points: He had, indeed, paid part of King's hotel bill in Bermuda, as a friend but not as an officer of his company. He had not intended to recover the money from Beauharnois; the voucher that said he had recovered it went forward through an error of his secretary.

The next day King, gray and trembling, rose in the House of Commons on a point of privilege to say substantially the same things. When he had gone to pay his own bill in Bermuda he found that McDougald had paid it already, but he considered the matter a personal one and was sure McDougald would do the same.

Therefore he forgot it. He had not traveled with McDougald either to Bermuda or back to Canada. McDougald had not paid his hotel bill in New York. He was "horrified" when he learned the Bermuda bill had gone back to Beauharnois.

It may or may not have occurred to King that if it was improper for the Prime Minister to accept expensive entertainment from a large company doing business with his government, it might also be improper to accept the same kind of entertainment from the chief officer of the same company.

He appeared to believe quite earnestly that the only point at stake was which of McDougald's pockets the money came from. No one in Parliament argued the question with him, then or later. R. B. Bennett himself nodded sympathetically throughout King's painful statement on the matter and at the end there was moderate applause from both sides of the floor.

The committe lost little time in bringing down its report, which "strongly condemned" Senators McDougald and Haydon; chided but did not condemn Senator Raymond; suggested that John Aird and anyone else who had extracted campaign funds "improperly" return them to the company at once; charged Sweezey with the misuse of company funds but nothing more serious; suggested Henry be fired; and urged refinancing of the whole development "in such a manner as will best serve the people of Canada."

Under the stock-watering schemes carried through thus far, the inquiry disclosed that the promoters already had all their own money back, plus a cash profit of more than two million dollars, plus common shares once worth seventeen million dollars but now down to four million. The next step they had been planning would have left them still owning 1,600,000 of a total of 1,800,000 shares, with an additional forty-six million dollars of public money invested in the company, all their own money back, and full voting control for the next ten years even if they sold all their stock.

As Bennett, the efficient lawyer of big business, strode into this scene of corporate blight and rapine, some semblance of order began to emerge. McDougald resigned his Senate seat, but Raymond and Haydon clung stubbornly to theirs. Sweezey and Henry were allowed to quit the company. But for many years Beauharnois was to be a white elephant not unlike the old Canadian Northern Railway—too useful to allow to die and almost too expensive to feed.

With the Tory government fated to run the gantlet of four more years of depression, the Liberals' responsibility for Beauharnois was almost completely forgotten before the voters had a chance to pass their own verdict on it. The result was no verdict at all; it might never have happened.

King's instinct seemed to tell him this was how it would be. For after the brief humiliation of the Bermuda disclosures, he recovered his composure and within ten days was attempting to plant the suggestion that whatever had gone wrong with the country's political morals, it was mostly the fault of the Conservatives.

For his part, he did not condone party donations of the size just made known, although he was pleased that the committee had discovered no evidence they had influenced the conduct of his recent government. It was really, to come right down to it, none of his affair anyway. He made it a rule never to know where the party's funds were coming from. If he did know, it might unconsciously prejudice his judgment.

Now as for the present Prime Minister—at this point the effortless, hydromatic shift of gears, a device he practiced on Bennett as maddeningly as he ever practiced it on Meighen—now as for the present Prime Minister, King was sure he must take the same attitude. Why, of course Bennett couldn't allow himself to know who was supporting the Conservative party and with what sums. He elaborated in his friendliest tone: "If it be true that my right honorable friend had knowledge of all who were contributors to his party fund, what will the country be thinking today of the changes which have been made in the tariff in connection with cottons, in connection with woolens, in connection with rayon and silk? What about iron and steel, boots and shoes, gasoline, magazines, sugar refining; what about income taxes, what about agricultural manufacturers, what about motorcar manufacturers, and what about electrical-goods manufacturers?"

Bennett burst in, enraged but almost helpless: "This is disgraceful!"

King went on piling his honorable friend elbow-deep in red herrings. What was needed was a special inquiry into the whole question of campaign funds. If Liberals had been abusing the traditional right of political parties to seek financial help of their sympathizers, let them be exposed. If Liberals had allowed their political decisions to be affected by party donations, seek them out.

If Conservatives had been guilty of similar transgressions, let them answer for it too.

It was regrettably true that the Conservatives, with their greater appeal to big business, probably had ten dollars to spend on elections to the Liberals' one. Let an impartial commission be charged to get at all the facts. "In addition," King went on, offering the country still one more thing to think about besides Beauharnois, "there should be a measure to make it the law of the land that voting shall be compulsory."

The crowning affront to Bennett, who somehow was now being called to account for the sins of his enemy, was a little sermon in which King managed both to repudiate and to embrace his erring friends and to make his own part in the affair appear not only exemplary but rather noble.

"We all have our friendships," he declaimed. "Are we to understand that every man is responsible for every act of his friends? . . . I ask this honorable House: Is there any relationship closer than that of father and son? Will honorable members opposite or will any member of this Parliament or anyone in this country say that because a son commits indiscretions and does things which will not bear the light of day his father is responsible for those acts, that as a result of them his father has been corrupted? He may break his father's heart, but he will not break his father's character. He may even help to reveal something of the beauty and the strength of a father's character, and what is true of that very intimate relationship of life is also true of the less intimate but hardly less sacred relationship of human friendship." In the same address he spoke favorably of Canadian unity, the Diamond Jubilee of Confederation, Dominion-provincial harmony, and the Briand-Kellogg peace pact.

Bennett, the champion non-stop orator of his time, circled the reef of syllogisms for two days, but only really pierced it once. "I have always held," he growled during one of King's acrobatic feats of self-justification, "that the receiver of stolen goods was a criminal."

Without turning a hair King replied with a lecture on the necessity of sticking to the point.

XXXVII

R. B. Bennett comes to office—The unlucky
coincidence with Herbert Hoover

LONG before harvesttime in 1931 the heartland of Canada was reeling under a disaster that both embraced and eclipsed the national disaster. Anybody in need merely of a roof could find roofs to spare on the wheat plains, from which the first small exodus of the defeated had already begun. With that one exception, the West shared virtually every trouble and deprivation known to any part of Canada. It also had a whole special and semi-private set of its own.

In the southwestern part of Manitoba, the whole of southern Saskatchewan, and most of southern Alberta they began discarding the Olympian, impersonal word "depression" and using the more intimate and concrete word "drought." At first "drought" meant only what the dictionary intended it to mean—an appalling and almost total lack of moisture. But as the years went on it came to stand for almost everything that was hard and hostile in the day-to-day business of living. It still meant, above everything, drought itself, but it also stood for dust, hail, rust, and sometimes frost. It stood for fifty-cent wheat and hardly any of that. It stood for grasshoppers and Russian thistle. It stood for relief—relief food, relief clothes, relief bedding, relief seed, relief fodder, relief coal, relief binder twine. It stood for taxes unpaid, mortgage payments unpaid, bank loans unavailable, homeless men sleeping in the hayloft, hungry men turned away from the door, darkened boarded-up windows on the next farm down the road, plowshares striking against hardpan, the last crushing signal that the topsoil was gone and with it the land itself.

Against the assault of the drought and its choking winds, fields

that once yielded thirty bushels to the acre blew away or were
held precariously together by a wiry mesh of Russian thistle, the
only thing that would grow. The elevation of this hated weed to
the rank of a kind of household god was in itself a measure of the
times. In the worst parts of the dust bowl they not only welcomed
it for what it could do to save the land until the rains came back;
they chopped it up with straw and fed it to their scrawny cattle
to keep them alive through the winter.

The whole Depression, with its weighty abstractions—world
marketing, Empire preferences, high tariffs, and the like—was by
no means beyond the farmer's understanding. But the drought was
a constant physical presence, something he could not avoid seeing
and feeling and touching and smelling every day of his life,
something that jostled and harassed him from dawn to dawn and
sometimes bore down the strongest men as terribly and finally
as it bore down the weak.

If some vengeful Old Testament prophet had been setting the
conditions of life on the prairies from 1930 through 1937 he might
have arranged it just the way it turned out to be.

The individual accidents and inventions of nature and of man
might each have belonged to some harsher, larger plan, each reinforcing and aggravating the others. First the break in prices. Then
the tax war, which made farm goods harder to sell and manufactured goods more costly to buy. Then the endless obstacle race
to get a crop in the ground, see it through the spring and summer,
and bring it to the elevators in the fall. By 1933 per capita income
in Saskatchewan had dropped to $135—barely a quarter the 1929
level. The relative price structure had been so dislocated that for
every bushel of wheat it cost to buy a pair of shoes or a suit
of clothes in 1929, it cost slightly more than two bushels in 1931
or 1932. In a hard year in a hard-hit district, a man might easily
seed, cultivate, cut, stook, and thresh four or five acres to buy his
wife a cotton dress.

The question of whether to thresh at all was often a crucial
one. "Thresh?" Dan Christmas used to cry incredulously on the
dried-up flats of the Souris River. "Thresh? Me thresh? Hell, man,
even a jack rabbit wouldn't dare start across my farm without
packing a lunch."

In one year, with virtually its whole population already on food,
clothing, and fuel relief, the municipality of Kisbey arranged to

supply relief binder twine. It got rid of fifty-five cents' worth. That was all the entire municipality had use for. Sometimes even seeding was a desperate risk. "It's been so dry," a man in southern Manitoba said, "we're afraid to touch the land. If we stir it up it will drift with the least wind. It has us scared."

In 1934 D. B. MacRae of the Regina *Leader-Post* and R. M. Scott of the Winnipeg *Free Press* made a leisurely tour of southwestern Manitoba and southeastern Saskatchewan. Their unemotional, re-strained reports of what they saw and heard offer one of the best single accounts of what life was like behind the statistics. In only one of a hundred or more districts they visited did they find as few as 50 per cent of the families on relief. In scores the percentage ran upward of 80, 90, and 95. Near Bengough, Saskatchewan, they discovered an area where every farmer was drawing relief but one. They asked a neighbor to explain the exception and got the sardonic reply: "I guess he's had no luck yet."

"The word 'relief,'" MacRae and Scott observed, "used to scare self-sustaining people. Now it scares only governments wonder-ing when it is going to stop."

By now, in 1934, virtually all the western municipal govern-ments were bankrupt in fact or in name, and so were the provincial governments. Federal grants and loans, grudging and woefully small, kept them going somehow. The painful job of passing on the food, seed, and clothing vouchers to the man at the end of the line often fell to his neighbors. "So the municipal secretaries are taking applications for relief. These will be scrutinized by the reeves and councillors, many of whom are on relief themselves. Men come in and give statements of their crop returns, the number of horses and cattle, their gardens and what they will need. It is pitiful to hear a man affirming that he had 125 acres of wheat acreage and harvested 60 bushels of wheat."

MacRae and Scott dissected the books of a man near Cadillac, acknowledged to be one of the best farmers in the district, one of the miraculous few who had managed to stay off relief altogether. This is what was involved: He gathered and threshed 400 bushels of wheat from 150 acres. His 30 acres of oats were a complete failure, meaning he'd have to buy oats for the winter's feed and the spring's seed—if he could. His threshing cost him $12 an hour for six hours—$72. His binder twine cost $18 and binder repairs another $9. Out of his 400 bushels he would need 150 for seed in the spring, leaving 250 to sell—for $150 at sixty cents a bushel.

"Subtract his threshing, twine and repair bill alone and his net is $50. The taxes on his 320 acres are $109. How to stretch that $50 to cover taxes, groceries for himself, wife and three children, not to mention clothing and replace bed clothes, etc., in the home is a job for a magician. He will have enough potatoes and some milk and butter for winter and guesses he will 'pull through somehow.'"

Through the eternal dust, peering toward baked beds of alkali, people saw mirages as near and inviting as the phantom oases of the Sahara. Lakes shimmered and beckoned crazily in the savage heat of the afternoon. The bleared orange sun went down night after night into purple thunderheads; they might as well have been mirages too. Yet the oases in the deserts of dust and in the darkening sky were better to cling to than nothing at all. "This land gave forty bushels to the acre. It was a great country when she was going right. She'll do it again. . . ." "It's as good land as there is outdoors. . . ." "You see those fine houses and barns dotting the countryside? You see the horses and cattle, the motorcars? Well, they didn't come out of the air. They came out of the soil and the labor of the people. A country that was no good couldn't do things like that."

Although they were the Depression's worst sufferers in material terms, the two million people trapped in or by the Palliser Triangle did at least have their mirages. Nor were they placed in the hideous position—as were millions of better-off people in the cities and towns—of being able to improve their own condition only at a direct and often brutal cost to someone else.

For being an age of poverty it became, inevitably, an age of squeeze. The squeeze operated everywhere, and with particular virulence in business, the retail trades, and manufacturing. In its worst aspects it threw aside the ordinary processes of hard, honest competitive bargaining and replaced it with a system that fed on want and desperation. It was a mean and predatory system and by definition only the very few could profit from it.

In its most pervasive form, the squeeze began with the mass sellers of consumer goods—the department stores and the chain stores. In 1934 Harry Stevens, the erstwhile scourge of the Customs Department, persuaded Bennett to turn him and a committee loose on the buying-and-selling policies of these merchandising colossi. There was little difficulty in collecting chapter and verse on them. They were squeezing one another in a ceaseless war of cut prices and loss leaders. In their private struggle for advantage, and sometimes for bare survival, they passed the squeeze on to their suppliers, who, in turn, could either go out of business or pass it on in turn to their employees.

The department store and the chain store no longer found out what it cost to make a certain set of furniture or a certain suit of clothes, then bought it at a reasonable markup from the manufacturer and passed it on with their own markup to the customer. Now the store decided first of all the price at which it would sell. Then it decreed the price at which it would buy. The manufacturer could take it or leave it. He, in turn, no longer paid his help what they needed to live on, or even what the law said they must get. He paid what he could afford to pay, or what he felt like paying, take it or leave it.

And there was no job so miserable or ill paid that someone couldn't be found who would be glad to take it. The most vulnerable point in the whole conscienceless edifice was the worker's bench, where thousands of women and children were drawing far less than the minimum wage and working far longer than the maximum hours. Enforcing the wage-and-hours laws was almost as difficult as enforcing the Volstead Act in the United States. Policing whole industries, many of them, like the needle trades, full of tiny hole-in-the-wall factories, was impossible. And even when a sweatshop proprietor was caught red-handed, his employees were reluctant to testify against him for fear of losing their jobs.

A skilled tailor in Winnipeg, a man who had spent more than twenty-five years learning his trade, was one of the relatively few who were persuaded to speak up. He had been working ten hours a day to make a camel-pile overcoat a day. For this he was paid at first a dollar a day, later reduced to eighty cents. The investigator was sympathetic but incredulous. Surely, with his qualifications, he could have demanded something more—at least a dollar and a half a day.

"No." The words were obviously born of experience. "If I don't work for a dollar a day they'll get a man on relief to do it for fifty cents."

In a Quebec factory a family of six collected total wages of twenty dollars a week. A girl in Toronto—where the minimum wage was twelve and a half dollars a week—worked full time for eighteen successive weekly pay envelopes of between four and eight dollars. The envelopes, supplied by a bank, carried this message: "Your pay envelope and one of our savings account pass books make a strong team that can help you to financial independence." The man or woman with a job was only slightly less helpless before the squeeze than the man or woman without one, and the jobless were now around seven hundred thousand. A million and a half people of a total population of ten million were dependent on relief.

It was an unhappy coincidence for R. B. Bennett, and probably for his country, that his only term in office overlapped the only term of Herbert Hoover. By the time Bennett settled into office Hoover was well on his way to becoming the great North American whipping boy, the symbol to millions of all that went wrong before the crash and all that got worse afterward.

And Bennett looked like Hoover, acted like Hoover, and talked like Hoover. Perhaps he did so entirely through his natural inclination, without either consciously or unconsciously heeding Hoover's example. There is no doubt that on most basic matters the two men would have thought alike even if they had inhabited different planets.

They were, of course, very much of the same planet. They were both born in the 1870s, one in a small town in New Brunswick, one in a small town in Iowa; both hard-working, clean-living, God-fearing, and ambitious; both well on the way to wealth before the age of thirty; both tall and a little more than robust; both full of confidence and, in public, empty of humor; both men of unchallengeable courage and old-fashioned honor; both at least as far to the right as their own conservative parties; both convinced that government was a necessary and costly evil which, so long as someone had to run it, might as well be run on solid business lines; both more certain than any politician dared say out loud that any man who couldn't make an abundant living in the northern part of North America was either lazy or willfully stupid.

Behind these streaming, high-held colors Hoover rode up to, through, and beyond the market crash with the benignly absent-minded air of a cavalry colonel inspecting the guard.

By March 1930, with Wall Street still plunging toward deeper chaos and the bread lines and soup kitchens gathering new patrons by the tens of thousands, he announced that "all the evidences indicate that the worst effects . . . will have been passed during the next sixty days." When the effects did not pass he reacted somewhat as the bewildered Mackenzie King had done in Canada. "Gentlemen," Hoover told a delegation that came to see him in June asking for more public works, "you have come sixty days too late. The Depression is over." Talk of hunger made him impatient. "Nobody is actually starving," he said in one typical statement. "The hobos, for example, are better fed than they have ever been. One hobo in New York got ten meals in one day."

R. B. Bennett, commencing his tenure as a fellow head of government, was less blind to his surroundings than Hoover, but this was a difference of degree only, like the other differences between them. Both men were suspicious of large-scale relief payments of any kind, and both looked on make-work public construction as a second-last resort, only slightly less unspeakable than the dole.

They both were morally certain that a great deal of the Depression lay in people's minds. "What this country needs," Hoover told a visitor early in 1931, "is a great big laugh. There seems to be a condition of hysteria. If someone could get off a joke every ten days, I think our troubles would be over." A few months later Bennett was saying essentially the same thing to a convention of traveling salesmen. "As you travel through the country, try to sound a note of confidence in all your contacts."

As unemployment in the United States climbed from four million to eight million, and then to twelve million, Hoover continued to scold about exaggeration and defeatism. On his first trip back to his home city as Prime Minister, Bennett lectured the Board of Trade on the "morose and solemn way some men walk down the streets of Calgary."

The President refused to talk to the leaders of an army of jobless veterans, whom he obviously considered too shiftless to work. To an audience of Albertans beginning to feel the pinch of low prices and crop failure, the Prime Minister said sternly: "I cannot make up my mind why this country between the lakes and the mountains should experience the Depression, why people who have lived here for years should now find themselves without an accumulation of goods, sometimes without the bare necessities of life."

To Hoover "the sole function of government" was "to bring about a condition favorable to the beneficial development of private enterprise." Bennett put it more moderately: "Governments cannot

do everything. They can tax you and you can pay the taxes, grudgingly or otherwise. But you must look beyond that."

Even if the comparisons had not been constantly staring them in
the face and dinning in their ears, Canadians doubtless would have
borrowed all the Hoover jokes for Bennett. The Americans had
Hoover Wagons, which were engineless or permanently out-of-gas
automobiles drawn by mules or horses. The Canadian name was
Bennett Buggies. The Americans called shanty towns and hobo
jungles Hoovervilles. Hoover Blankets were newspapers worn as
bedding or an extra layer of clothes. Bennett Coffee was boiled
wheat or barley. A Bennett Barnyard was an abandoned farm.

Except for a brief visit to Washington by Bennett the two men
had little direct contact. The very similarity of their ideas, having
put them on opposite sides of a tariff wall, left them with little
occasion for doing business together. It was mutual instinct, not
any arrangement or agreement, that kept them in step. Nowhere
were they in step so firmly and unfalteringly as in the province
where they both felt most at home—the province of the dollar.

To say that they were both sound-money men would be an
extreme understatement. They were sacred-money men. This does
not necessarily mean that they held their own personal money in
especial awe or reverence. They just happened to believe, passionately and without the slightest reservation, that a hard dollar
and all that went with it was essential to the ultimate health of their
nations and the survival of the system under which they had chosen
to live.

If Hoover seemed indifferent to the fact that the average relief
rate in New York City stood at $2.39 a family a week, it was not
because he thought such things didn't matter. What he thought was
they didn't matter nearly so much as protecting the country's currency. If Bennett seemed content that ranchers were selling cattle
at fifty cents a hundredweight and seamstresses working for a nickel
an hour, it was not that he really considered these scales of payment
adequate or proper. He happened to believe, quite literally, that if
Canada allowed depression spending to shake its credit the country
would be irreparably ruined.

When Britain went off the gold standard, Hoover was plunged in
grief. Gold, he lamented, had been "enshrined in human instincts
for over ten thousand years." Years later he still shuddered at the
thought that the United States had almost been forced to follow

Britain's example. "Never was our nation in greater peril," he said solemnly.

"How," Bennett asked a hushed banquet gathering of the Toronto Board of Trade, "can you go out and deliberately inflate the dollar of the country, knowing as you do that it will make it worth between fifty and sixty cents or possibly less? What is the effect abroad? . . . Confidence is gone. And with the departure of confidence, credit goes. And with credit," he warned in the voice of one who has looked on Armageddon, "goes the country!" When John Maynard Keynes urged the world to stop hoarding and spend its way out of the Depression, the "fools and madmen" he denounced for rejecting his advice were the Hoovers and the Bennetts. Their opinion of him was precisely the same as his of them.

When Hoover left the White House, Bennett still had half his term to run and his astounding conversion to the New Deal was two years in the future. If anything, the advent of the free-spending Roosevelt at first spurred the Prime Minister to greater efforts in his defense of the spartan life and the inviolate dollar. He made more speeches outside the House than had been Mackenzie King's custom, and much better ones. He was most at home before boards of trade, but he carried the gospel without fear or discrimination to unbelievers and believers alike.

Canada, he never tired of reminding his audience, owed nine billion dollars on which the annual interest was more than four hundred million. Let there be even the hint of a default, let there be the least suggestion of paying the money back in cheap, inflated money, let there be the slightest tremor of uncertainty among the bondholders, and the country was as good as finished. As a debtor nation, Canada would commit a "great folly" if it tried to copy the shorter hours and higher wages of Roosevelt's N.R.A. Deep into 1934 his main message was still that "we must pause and consider before embarking upon enterprises calling for the expenditure of large sums of public money."

He was so obsessed with the need for fiscal salvation that he took it for granted that the most gaunt and hard-pressed dirt farmer, the most pinched and frightened salesclerk, must share his feeling. To him it was simply a matter of common sense and patriotism. What right-thinking Canadian would put his own transitory comfort and welfare ahead of the nation itself?

For all who understood the real nature of the crisis he had words of solace and encouragement. "There has never been a time in recent years in Canada," he assured the people proudly in 1933, "when there was so much money available in banks and financial institutions. Why? Because the very conditions that obtain in this country insist that the banks shall be in a position where they can meet the demands of their depositors. No, there is no shortage of currency."

In October of that year a hopeful procession of Alberta farmers streamed across the prairie to hear him speak at Lethbridge. He promised them that Ottawa would continue to help with public works and other relief undertakings but "would not at this time engage in any large scale of expenditures." He reminded them that the root cause of the world's predicament was its "mad frenzy of hopes to make money without working." To see his countrymen bravely exorcising the evil had made him proud to be a Canadian as he had never been before: "Do you suppose I, who met and struggled with adversity in this new country during my early years, have no appreciation of your hardships, your anxieties, your fears?"

He assured an assembly of students in Toronto that "one of the greatest assets any man or woman can have on entering on life's struggle is poverty."

Even his ceremonial greetings to the people were full of exhortations to have faith in a sound financial policy. His New Year's message of 1933 focused on the point that "financing we have to do for unemployment measures during the Depression will be a charge on the productive resources of tomorrow."

From London in 1934 he cabled back this extraordinary sentiment for Thanksgiving Day: "Canadians should be especially thankful for the manifold blessings that Providence has bestowed upon them. Notwithstanding trials and tribulations, they have abundant reason for thanksgiving. Not the least of the ways by which they can show their thankfulness is by using their savings to preserve the financial integrity of their Dominion by renewing at a lesser rate of interest the loans that they made to their country in other days, not only continuing a safe investment but also rendering a real service to Canada."

XXXVIII

The Left makes its bid—Disappointments for the C.C.F. and the Communists, for Woodsworth and Tim Buck

THE Depression was not regretted by everyone. After wandering for a decade in a wasteland of contented capitalists and full dinner pails, Tim Buck and the senior comrades of the Canadian Communist party saw their beacon shining clear and steady and miraculously close at hand. It was almost exactly as Marx and Lenin had promised it would be. Capitalism's final stage of decay had set in at last. The party would now proceed to the task ordained for it half a century before it was born. It would take all possible steps to hasten the collapse, then pick up the pieces and reshape them into one of the proletarian states of a proletarian world.

The invitingly desolate winter of 1930 was not half over before Buck was in Moscow awaiting detailed instructions in person. He was allowed to explain his plans for Canada in a speech to the Plenum of the Sixth World Congress of the Communist International. Having recently witnessed and assisted in the Kremlin's swift erasure of his only two rivals for the leadership of the Canadian party, he felt his way ahead cautiously.

Spontaneous strikes in Canada, he explained apologetically, seldom grew so large or went so far as spontaneous strikes in the United States. "The political value of these strikes, therefore," he went on, "tends to be less unless we ourselves can prepare them in certain industries. The result is that we have adopted a policy of developing demands in many industries and on this basis sharpening relations and developing strike movements." The Comintern decided this was satisfactory so far as it went, but instructed him, in writing, to add three more planks to the party's program: more activity among the foreign-born, among the French Canadians, and among the "poor" farmers.

Not even in the days of the Winnipeg strike had the opportunities for agitprop (spelled out for a growing list of new members as agitation and propaganda) been so promising. While King and Bennett tossed the Depression back and forth with the wheezy agility of two Y.M.C.A. elders playing with a medicine ball, Woodsworth sat hesitantly on the sidelines. His Co-operative Commonwealth Federation was still years away, which meant there was a yawning gap in the national political structure; except in a few ridings there was no place to cast a vote for the Left or any vote of loud and unmistakable protest. A discontented elector could protest against the Grits by voting for the Tories or against the Tories by voting for the Grits, but to protest against them both usually involved supporting a regional or occupational group like the Independent Labor party or the United Farmers of Alberta.

Buck redoubled his efforts to move his thin but eager cadre of cardholders into the vacuum. The first thing he did was to attend to the orders of Moscow. He set up or seized control of a dozen front groups for the ethnic minorities, revived a French-language party journal, and formed an agrarian wing called the Farmers Unity League. Through another of the party's old pros, Tom Ewen, he established a new labor front, the Workers Unity League. According to the best estimates, the total apparatus might have claimed various degrees of allegiance from twelve thousand party members, forty or fifty thousand bona fide fellow travelers, and perhaps another hundred and fifty thousand "sympathizers" who weren't fully aware what they were sympathizing with.

Working already fallow ground in the troubled coal fields of Nova Scotia and southern Saskatchewan, Ewen's labor section helped organize at least two major strikes during 1931, in the second of which three men were killed. It was established later that all four leaders of the Saskatchewan outbreak were members both of the Workers Unity League and of the party itself.

How much further Buck and his inner cabinet might have gone if they had been permitted to go unchecked must always remain a matter of conjecture. In the early evening of August 11, 1931, eighteen officers of the Royal Canadian Mounted Police and the Toronto and Ontario police forces were ushered into the office of Major General V. A. S. Williams, commissioner of the Ontario police, to receive a special assignment. The commissioner closed the door and announced: "Gentlemen, we are going to strike a death-blow at the Communist party."

Three quarters of an hour later simultaneous raids were made at Buck's six-room brick house in Toronto, at the national offices of the Communist party, and at the nearby headquarters of the Workers Unity League. Buck, on his way between home and office at the zero hour, was arrested half an hour afterward. By the next afternoon eight of his most active subordinates had been picked up too, all—as in the case of Buck himself—without histrionics on either side. The Attorney General of Ontario charged the nine men under Section 98 of the Criminal Code with being members and officers of an unlawful association and of being parties to a seditious conspiracy.

Their sensational and dramatic trial resulted in the discharge of one of the accused, whom the Crown admitted it was not prepared to prove a member of the party after all. Almost from the beginning it was apparent that under the law as it stood the other eight had no defense. The raids on Buck's home and on the party's office had produced a small hillock of evidence of the party's record, its aims, and its plans for carrying them out. This was swollen by a series of revelations by Sergeant John Leopold, an R.C.M.P. officer who had gone underground while the party itself was still underground, joined its Regina branch under the name of Esselwein, and remained a trusted member until 1928.

The jury took only two hours to decide that the party was unlawful. Since Section 98 made membership in an unlawful organization a crime and since none of the accused denied his party membership, the verdict of guilty was automatic. Buck, Tom Ewen, and five others were sentenced to five years and the eighth defendant to two.

Despite this apparently crushing setback, the party now had a new whirlwind to reap. While the persuasive and indefatigable little Buck campaigned for new recruits in the workshops and chow lines of Kingston penitentiary, the comrades who remained at liberty set out to make him a martyr. They had several things running for them. The chief of them was Bennett's open canonization of sound money even at the apparent cost of human pity. The second was the law under which Buck and his friends had gone to jail. Thousands of people whose respect for British justice was as deep and abiding as the Communists' contempt for it had never been able to reconcile themselves to Section 98, in which they saw the principle of guilt by association and an attempt to outlaw ideas. The party quickly hatched another "non-partisan" front to get "The Eight" out of jail and repeal Section 98.

In October 1932, in the tenth month of Buck's sentence, the cell blocks at Kingston were swept by riots. Today, even after a public trial (at which Buck was sentenced to serve another nine months), an endless series of debates in Parliament, and a special inquiry that did not bring down its findings until 1938, Buck's precise part in organizing the riots is still a subject of debate. But one fact did emerge, as sudden and chilling as a cry in the night: while Buck stood shouting in his cell, two of the prison guards, one using a shotgun and one a pistol, fired five shots into the cell from the floor of the cell block forty-five feet away. His was the only cell fired on in the whole prison. The only explanation Bennett's Justice Minister, Hugh Guthrie, was able to offer was: "I suppose it was to frighten or cow him. . . . The situation was serious and Buck was one who had been encouraging the disorders."

In the troubled conscience of the nation the case of Rex versus Buck abruptly became the case of Buck versus Rex. To the charge of political persecution Buck's strident friends added the charge of attempted assassination. By the spring of 1933 the Communist-inspired Canadian Labor Defense League claimed it had 200,000 names to a petition for his release. Bennett expressed suspicion of the signatures, but in November 1934 the Communist leader was paroled after serving slightly more than half his five years and nine months.

His welcome back to the world outside was as carefully staged as a May Day march-past at Lenin's tomb. On the night of his first public appearance, Maple Leaf Gardens in Toronto was packed with seventeen thousand people. Thirty-four athletes from the Young Workers Sporting Association bore the returning martyr to the flood-lit speakers' platform. The chairman of the reception, another party veteran, announced apologetically that it would be necessary to play "God Save the King." The feeble peals of the electric organ were drowned out by boos and hisses.

Buck stepped forward into the spotlight, his face gray with three years' prison pallor, his weight thirty pounds below its customary 150. He stood there in the light, tiny and alone, and then raised his arm in the clenched-fist Communist salute. An unregenerate capitalist who had attended the rally in a spirit of curiosity recalled later: "Tim looked like an unconquerable pygmy defying the sun and the moon and all the stars. When he started speaking there wasn't a dry eye in the house, including mine."

Buck played it for all it was worth, and it was worth a good deal. He made a well-staged tour of the country. At many stops the comrades greeted him with flowers and bands. In Blairmore, Alberta, they declared a public holiday and renamed the main street Tim Buck Boulevard. In Victoria, the very Shangri-la of the bourgeoisie, he filled the auditorium of the Chamber of Commerce.

For all these outward signs of progress, the Communist party got more credit than it deserved for the turbulence and strife of the hungry thirties. The fact that the 1931 trial made it an outlaw organization was no serious handicap, for its numerous fronts were still lawful. They initiated relatively few disturbances themselves, but the eager persistence with which they infiltrated and sometimes abducted other people's strikes, riots, parades, and protest marches made them appear much larger than life.

The party's most effective arm was the Workers Unity League, which in 1935 launched an abortive march on Ottawa from the western relief camps. The camps had been set up for the benefit— and, as many of them complained bitterly, the containment—of that sad order of companionship described on the official relief rolls as Single Homeless Persons. For years they roamed like pathetic locusts across the lean prairie, through stagnating dockyards and timber limits, in and out of overpopulated mining camps and overcrowded employment offices. Resourceful as they became at finding odd jobs or at plain scrounging, most of them sooner or later had to apply for local relief. Many municipalities, particularly the villages and small towns, simply lacked the wherewithal, and in some cases the inclination, to help these needy strangers. At the request of the municipalities, supported by the provinces, Bennett agreed to pay for their support. Special settlements were built for them and they were given food and clothing for clearing land or cutting wood at between ten and twenty cents a day.

The plan was better conceived than executed. Ottawa placed a ceiling expenditure of forty cents per day per person on food, clothing, shelter, and fuel and put the camps in charge of the Army. Thus an extra psychological hazard was added to the hazard of austere and unnatural living conditions. In some camps the army administrators treated the inmates as a species of subprivate, regimented them sternly, and showed them woefully little of the one thing they perhaps needed most of all—respect.

By 1935 the bored and disgusted inmates—some of whom had been living in the camps for four years—were walking out by the hundred. In late spring nearly a thousand broke camp in British Columbia and began heading East by freight. By the time they reached Calgary their ranks had swollen to 1300, they were firmly organized under an avowed Communist and Workers Unity League member named Arthur Evans, and they had declared their intention of going all the way to Ottawa to force the government to take the Army out of the camps and pay the residents fifty cents an hour.

Bennett ordered the Mounted Police to stop them at Regina. For a week, their numbers now increased to 2000, they bivouacked in a local sports stadium and ate off the proceeds of a tag day and the casual charity of a city that was half sympathetic and half terrified.

Bennett agreed to meet Evans and seven of his lieutenants and, while the rank and file stayed behind in Regina, brought them to Ottawa at government expense. It was not a successful meeting. Bennett had learned to his great distaste that the chief of the eight leaders, Evans, was a Communist and that his seven aides admitted to having been born outside Canada. When Evans began haranguing the Prime Minister in soapbox jargon, Bennett reminded him quietly that they both came from Alberta, where Evans had once been jailed for stealing union funds.

"You're a liar!" Evans shrilled back.

On the way back to Regina after two unfruitful hours of discussion, Evans stopped off at Sudbury to promise that the strikers would now continue to Ottawa as scheduled and to threaten that if the police interfered the streets of Regina would run red with blood.

These two utterances, together with Evans' open boast of being a Communist, probably did more to speed the defeat of the On-to-Ottawa march than all the Mounties put together. By playing the role of the pasteboard Red agitator more faithfully than Bennett played the role of the cartoon capitalist, Evans had sacrificed most of his moral support from the public at large. By the time Evans arrived back in Regina, the R.C.M.P. officer in charge there had ordered the local population to stop giving the marchers money or handouts and had forbidden further public meetings. The marchers would be sent home in special trains and fed on the way by the government. A transit camp was ready not far outside the city for those willing to go there and wait for transport. But no one would be allowed to go further east and those who were determined to stay in Regina faced the prospect of being starved out.

The climax came swiftly. Evans, obviously intent on inciting a riot, called a mass meeting in Market Square for the evening of July 1. The Mounties marched in deliberately unarmed, along with a detachment of city police, who were armed. The ensuing melee lasted almost four hours in the square itself and took another two to peter out in the side streets. There were a hundred injured. One man was killed: a city detective dragged behind the city jail and beaten to death with sticks and fists. Of 130 marchers arrested, 24 came to trial and 9 drew sentences of between six and fourteen months.

The rest went home quietly. They had convinced Bennett that the relief camps were a failure, for he began disbanding them almost at once. They had given a clumsy novice anarchist a chance to pick up some experience—probably without much day-to-day guidance from his leader, for Buck, under constant surveillance and as a ticket-of-leave man from Kingston, was forbidden to make inflammatory speeches. The one thing the tragic pilgrimage had not accomplished was the thing its now disheartened originals had set out to accomplish. When they dispersed to begin all over again in the railway yards and hobo jungles there were as many Single Homeless Persons as ever, and if their average lot in life had been changed it was slightly for the worse.

In his own efforts to provide a rallying point for the country's inarticulate and leaderless third force, J. S. Woodsworth faced a set of problems different from Buck's. But his problems were no less numerous.

Some were of his own making. He was neither an organizer nor an opportunist. While Buck was hurrying back from Moscow with his marching orders, Woodsworth was still arguing doggedly about the divorce laws and unemployment insurance. Until mid-1932 he had no time and made almost no attempt to gather up the odds and ends of the democratic Left and persuade them to offer a united front against the older parties. Not until July 1933 did the Co-operative Commonwealth Federation hold its first national convention and draft its manifesto, and even then there was great confusion about who was going to follow it and in what direction.

There were splits and threats of splits between labor members and farmer members; between the national organization and the provincial organizations; between affiliated groups and the new party; between affiliated groups and other affiliated groups; between the right-wing leftists and the left-wing leftists.

At first the C.C.F. seemed hopeful that it could somehow absorb everybody who wasn't an out-and-out Tory, an out-and-out Grit, or an out-and-out Communist, but this dream expired in the din of platform building. Even the members of the new party's formidable intellectual wing had trouble agreeing whether the numerous industries and utilities they proposed to socialize should be confiscated outright or acquired through compensation to the owners. Woodsworth insisted on his own way on this point—he was in favor of compensation—and under the guidance of a group of brilliant young university teachers the manifesto passed the 1933 convention with only one dissenting vote.

Although the preamble was careful to speak up for democratic methods and against change by violence, the text sounded to millions like outright Bolshevism. No matter how Woodsworth and his brains trust scented them, the words that counted all reeked of Marxist brimstone. Socialization of the banks and insurance companies; socialization of transportation, communications, electric power; socialized mining, socialized pulp and paper, socialized milk, socialized bread, socialized coal, socialized gasoline. And all of it presided over by an organization its sponsors described innocently as "a National Planning Commission consisting of a small body of economists, engineers and statisticians assisted by an appropriate technical staff [whose task] will be to plan for the production, distribution and exchange of all goods and services necessary to the efficient functioning of the economy." To hands-off Tories and laissez-faire Grits, who still made up more than half the population, the vision of bureaucracy run wild was as distasteful as the manifesto's blunt summary: "No C.C.F. government will rest content until it has eradicated capitalism."

Nevertheless, it was a mixed kind of hostility that greeted the new party. Through exposure to his patient, innocent kind of honesty, many of Woodsworth's political enemies had also become personal well-wishers. One of them, J. R. MacNicol, was prepared to forgive him on the ground that he knew not what he did. "When I look into his gentle eyes, when I observe his kindly smile, his sympathetic countenance, I know that although in my opinion he preaches communism . . . he is not a communist." The colorful Quebec orator Jean-François Pouliot put it in two opposite ways at once: "The only difference between Woodsworth and Gandhi is the goat and the spinning wheel. [Woodsworth and the C.C.F.] will be the czars of Canada."

Others viewed the C.C.F. with more serious alarm. Robert J. Manion, the Conservative Minister of Railways, could see no difference at all between it and the Communists. Both movements stood for "a system based on tyranny and oppression and the outlawing of personal freedom." The Archbishop of Montreal had all his priests read a pastoral letter denouncing the C.C.F. by name as resting on "a materialistic conception of the social order which precisely constitutes the anti-Christian character of socialism."

The inevitable overture from the Communists—the traditional kiss of death for non-Communist leftist parties in Europe—arrived before the 1935 general election. Buck and his national organizer, Sam Carr, wrote: "The united front is the only guarantee that a great number of working-class representatives will be sent into the next House of Commons. . . . We are of the opinion that an agreement can be arrived at between the Communist election committee and the C.C.F., making possible an elimination of any possibility of splits in the working-class vote and mutual support on the basis of a minimum program of the immediate needs of the toilers of Canada."

Woodsworth's reply closed the correspondence: "A real united front involves an agreement on fundamentals and a belief on the part of each co-operating group in the sincerity of the other group. In tactics at least there is no agreement whatever between the Communist party and the C.C.F. . . . The overthrow of the C.C.F. rather than that of capitalism would seem to be the main object of the Communist party of Canada."

In the age of motivation research and image studies, the widespread confusion, even within its own ranks, about what the C.C.F. really stood for no doubt would have been solved quickly by men in flannel suits. As it was, the confusion lingered and spread.

In its first full-scale venture at the polls the C.C.F. won enough

seats in the British Columbia provincial election of 1933 to become
the official Opposition. In 1934 it was snowed under in Ontario but
got a quarter of the votes in Saskatchewan and became the Opposition there. In its first appearance on the federal ballot a year later,
the new party won only seven seats, most of which it held already
under different labels; five M.P.s of the United Farmers of Alberta
who had swung over to the C.C.F. were liquidated by that other
enigmatic but yeasty mission band, the Social Crediters.

Before the party's first national campaign was over, Woodsworth
found it necessary to remind even his sworn followers that the
manifesto meant exactly what it said. A C.C.F. paper in British
Columbia had chided him for embarrassing the west-coast membership with "an academic discussion" of discrimination against immigrants from the Orient. Woodsworth answered with a short, rueful
letter to the editor:

"Undoubtedly in British Columbia the application of our principles to the Orientals is rather inconvenient. So also in Quebec the
repeal of Section 98 of the Criminal Code, in rural Ontario the
setting up of a Labor Code, in Winnipeg the socialization of our
railways, in Alberta our attitude towards Social Credit. Does that
mean that in these places Opportunism shall be our guide? One
recalls the old rhyme:

> *A merciful providence*
> *Fashioned us holler*
> *So that we could*
> *Our principles swaller.*

Yours sincerely,
J. S. WOODSWORTH"

XXXIX

*The resurgence of the provinces—Social Credit
and William Aberhart—The astonishing
revolt of R. B. Bennett*

NOT even in 1917 had the country been in such political ferment
as in that seething year of 1935. At least half a dozen new acids,
unguents, soporifics, and abrasives were at work on the raw nerves
of the electorate. Between them the warring leaders of the Left,
Buck and Woodsworth, had already supplied enough new spice for
any normal campaign—the cloak-and-dagger disclosures of Sergeant
Leopold, the mysterious shots at Kingston, the riots at Regina, the
noisy debates over Section 98, the audacious challenge to capitalism
not merely by crackpots and foreigners but by respected college
professors, preachers, and sober grain growers.

There were other new elements of greater complexity. One of
them was a revolt against the growing weight of federalism.

By and large the provinces had been content from Confederation
until after the First World War to pattern their politics after the
politics of the Dominion. Thousands of people made it their habit
to vote one way federally and another way provincially, but in both
areas the two-party system was challenged only occasionally and
usually only briefly.

Between 1914 and 1918, when the most important functions of
government were concentrated in Ottawa, the provinces were little
more than satellites. This high degree of centralization had not been
intended by the Fathers of Confederation. It was not desired by the
populace at large, who agreed that in a country so various and
scattered the best government was the government nearest to home
—the provincial legislature and the city or town or rural council.
Centralization held no attractions even for those on whom it bestowed extra power. King and Bennett were both against it.

By the end of the twenties the provinces were well on the way to reclaiming their full rights under the British North America Act. Once more when an argument broke out in a barbershop or a tavern the subject was as likely to be those fellows at Queen's Park or those fellows at Regina as those fellows at Ottawa.

Then the Depression, with its endless bankruptcies in the provinces and municipalities, forced a return to centralization. But this time the provinces were uninhibited by the pressures of a war. They were free to express both their resentment at being dependent wards again and their anger at the behavior of their guardian.

New ideas, new parties, and new men exploded in all directions. In Quebec a tough young Tory lawyer named Maurice Duplessis began taking over from the discredited Liberal regime of Alexandre Taschereau. Before long he took over from the Tories too, established a principality called Union Nationale, and made himself its absolute ruler. In Ontario, Mitch Hepburn, a bouncy, wisecracking, hyperthyroid young onion farmer, burst like a comet into the office of premier, liked it, and began considering an advance on Ottawa and his fellow Liberal, Mackenzie King.

The most remarkable of the new stadholders was neither Duplessis nor Hepburn, but William Aberhart, of Alberta. For the first five sixths of his life Aberhart had two goals before him and was well content with them. He wanted to be a good schoolteacher and he was. He wanted to spread the word of God and, according to his lights, he did. He was well into his fifties before he gave any serious thought to politics. By then he was the much respected principal of one of Calgary's largest high schools and the much admired primate of a thriving organization called the Prophetic Bible Institute.

The Institute was his own creation, born of thirty years of preaching on a frontier that still thirsted for the fundamental gospel. Aberhart believed in the Old Testament to the letter and the comma, and more than a quarter of a million people sat beside their radios every Sunday evening to hear him say so; it was claimed that his local audience was slightly larger than that of Jack Benny, who came on right after him. Only a few of his listeners had seen him, but they all knew his likeness from the newspapers or from photographs sent out by the Bible Institute: a vast, globular, bald Buddha in coat and vest and rimless glasses.

The gospel made him famous and it made him sure and when

he saw the world crumbling in the hands of the cynics and the reprobates he set out as a matter of simple Christian duty to put it right. By chance, in 1932, he came across a book on Social Credit. He read further, established an acquaintance through correspondence with the Scottish founder, Major C. H. Douglas, and finally evolved an application for Alberta.

Though he buried his meanings in a jungle of words, Douglas was a monetary fundamentalist in the same degree that Aberhart was a religious fundamentalist. After due study, the Calgary prophet paraphrased him in words as easily understood as the story of Jonah and the Whale. The times were essentially times of plenty. The reason food, clothing, shelter, and jobs weren't getting to the people who needed them was solely that a sacred cow called money was getting in the way. Since straight barter was no longer practical, there had to be something like money. But did it have to be the same stacks of paper that the banks kept locked up in their vaults, the same reams of chits and checks and deposit slips that fluttered past the tellers while real wealth lay unused?

Aberhart's answer was no and his remedy was to set up a separate banking system for Alberta. The indispensable object was to get credit flowing again and keep it flowing. To this end he proposed to give every man, woman, and child twenty-five dollars' worth of provincial scrip a month.

The timing could not have been better. In the first flash of revelation Aberhart had no notion of seeking political office for himself. He hoped to usher in Social Credit by converting or coercing or somehow bypassing the existing governments.

R. B. Bennett had already made certain that, so far as the voters of Alberta were concerned, it didn't matter how Ottawa reacted; the Prime Minister's unflagging support of orthodox finance was the best argument possible for unorthodox finance.

As for opposition within the province itself, a solution as simple and tidy as a chapter from the Book of Proverbs had intervened already. John Brownlee, the respected premier of the province, had been successfully sued for sleeping with a youthful lady secretary. Brownlee's Minister of Public Works was in the process of divorcing his wife. Both men were forced to resign in 1934, about the time Aberhart felt he had the theories of Major Douglas distilled to a manageable quantity. And although a convention of their demoralized party, the United Farmers of Alberta, refused Aberhart's invitation to put Social Credit in their platform, the U.F.A. was in no condition to stand up to him in the presence of the electorate.

"Rats, sons of Satan, liars, fornicators!" Aberhart cried at them as he prepared to meet them head on in the coming provincial election. The U.F.A. sought to confound him by bringing Major Douglas over to Canada as an official government adviser, its obvious hope being to draw the founder of Social Credit and its Canadian disciple into a public quarrel. But Douglas, while he never fully endorsed Aberhart's interpretation of his theories, never fully repudiated them either. Aberhart thundered on against the money-changers in particular and the sinners in general.

His own name was not on any ballot on provincial election day, August 22, 1935. Officially he was not yet in politics, but the day brought him perhaps the most astounding triumph in all the history of politics in Canada. People were lining up to vote for his candidates an hour before the polls were open. For every three lackadaisical voters in 1930, there were now five eager ones and most of them voted Social Credit. Of a total of 63 ridings the new party carried 56. The outgoing Farmers' government, weighed down by bad times and its record on sex, suffered a total eclipse, ending up without a single seat. Aberhart allowed himself to be persuaded to enter the legislature through a by-election and took office as premier a month and a half before the coming Dominion election.

The modest surge of the C.C.F. and the Communists and the revolt of the provinces coincided with an upheaval more astounding than all the others put together. With his term of office nearing its close the rocklike pillar of the Right, Richard Bedford Bennett, suddenly stampeded to the Left.

There was almost no warning. Indeed, as 1934 turned into 1935 the Prime Minister seemed as certain as ever that his policy of the last four years was the only policy possible: protect the dollar, protect business, avoid new debt, see that no one actually starved, and tough it out from there.

It was on this precise issue, or so the public read it, that he had just had an acrimonious break with the Tory gadfly, Harry Stevens. Stevens' committee on prices and marketing, meeting in camera, had turned up so much hair-raising evidence of price fixing, sweatshops, and other forms of the squeeze that the chairman found it impossible to contain himself. Before the inquiry was over he disclosed some of the interim findings to a semi-private Conservative study group and later distributed them in a pamphlet. Bennett found himself besieged by wealthy businessmen who held, rightly enough, that their defense was being thrown out of court before it was even heard. The Prime Minister asked Stevens to retract some of the things he had said and correct some others. Stevens replied by resigning from Bennett's Cabinet and preparing to contest the election as leader of his own Reconstruction party.

It was against this immediate background that Bennett renounced everything he had championed for four bleak and bitter years and proclaimed himself a secret dreamer and do-gooder, a foe of the Interests and a friend to the common man.

The first intimation of the change occurred on a Saturday afternoon just before Christmas in 1934. Bennett's gifted brother-in-law and Minister to Washington, W. D. Herridge, was addressing the Canadian Club of Ottawa, and the more attentive of his hearers swore they heard him pronounce an almost unbelievable heresy. "The form of our economic society is unimportant," the Prime Minister's close friend, relative, confidant, and employee said, "so long as it responds to the one test of its effectiveness—the greatest good to the people as a whole. I would throw over our economic system in a flash if I thought there was a better one available."

A less sophisticated and knowledgeable audience might have concluded that Herridge was only disposing of a few harmless platitudes. But it soon became apparent there was far more to it than that; almost simultaneously Bennett himself, addressing another meeting in Montreal, began talking about the need for "a sane and regulated capitalistic system and a wise regulation of undesirable practices."

Here, in unmistakable and obviously considered terms, was a clear intimation that Bennett was preparing to strike his colors. Here was the freest of free-enterprisers talking like the most meddlesome of bureaucrats. Here was the stoutest of Tories speaking in the accents of a parlor pink.

Bennett barely gave his dumfounded constituents a chance to collect their thoughts before he launched a series of CBC radio broadcasts outlining a Canadian equivalent of Franklin Roosevelt's New Deal. If his speech in Montreal had left any shred of doubt about where he was heading, it was dispelled by the broadcasts. "I am for reform!" Bennett barked at the microphone at his swiftest, most decisive speaking gait. "And in my mind reform means government intervention. It means government control and regulation."

And again: "Canada on the dole is like a young and vigorous man in the poorhouse. The dole is condemnation, final and complete, of our economic system. If we cannot abolish the dole we should abolish the system." The veriest Red could scarcely have been more explicit: "The old order is gone. It will not return."

Spelling out his precise meaning in subsequent broadcasts, Bennett outlined a program of legislation calling for unemployment insurance, new laws on hours and wages, laws to control prices, marketing and mortgage foreclosures, and banking. Most of Bennett's customary supporters replied with a stunned silence or a cautious injunction to wait and see. Not so the Montreal *Gazette*, the unofficial voice of St. James Street and perhaps the most faithful of all the government's adherents. "Is Mr. Bennett endeavoring to humbug himself or the people of Canada?" the *Gazette* demanded hotly. His New Deal, it cried, did violence to every Conservative principle.

The reaction in other quarters reflected an air of real bewilderment. The Liberal Attorney General of Ontario sniffed Marxism. A prominent rabbi smelled Hitlerism. J. S. Woodsworth dismissed the whole matter as "a deathbed conversion," and another socialist solemnly invited Bennett to join the C.C.F. Numerous students of the Constitution pointed out, prophetically, that when and if Bennett sought to put his new legislation into the statute books, most of it would be declared *ultra vires* of the Dominion government anyway.

While Bennett, Aberhart, Woodsworth, Buck, Duplessis, Hepburn, and Stevens calculated their chances and arranged and rearranged their timetables, one man maintained an almost insulting calm. Mackenzie King was back in the catbird seat and left no doubt that he knew it.

His five years out of power had mellowed him. For the first time since the death of Laurier he was free to give his Borgia streak a long and complete rest. His cleverness, his adroitness at maneuver and debate, were temporarily superfluous. They could obtain him no office within the party or outside it. They could win no friends, unhorse no enemies, bury no scandals, carry no elections. His defeat in 1930 had been so resounding that only time could repair it, time and a train of events that, however regrettable they might be otherwise, were already on the way to ruining his chief opponent. King relaxed as he probably had not done since his earliest years at university.

He argued with Bennett interminably, of course, over the administration and dimensions of relief and over the tariff and finance, but there was far less rancor on either side than there might have been if Bennett's present majority had been less secure or its future disappearance less certain.

King devoted a portion of these five years to cultivating a part of his life that scarcely anyone knew of or understood until after he was dead. Behind his round, stodgy, ultra-orthodox façade there dwelt alone and secretly the spirit of a great adventurer.

For more than a decade, King was sure, he had been in contact with the world beyond the grave. He had talked with his mother, with his brother, and with Sir Wilfrid Laurier. In the years still ahead, with the help of a trusted little group of mediums in England and Scotland, he was to talk—he was equally satisfied—to the departed Franklin Delano Roosevelt and even to his beloved deceased dog Pat.

His years as leader of the Opposition left him time to pursue and reflect on these experiments, which his mediums all agreed gave him obvious contentment and peace of mind. They also agreed that he never asked the voices from the other world to advise him on public affairs or his part in them.

In the coming contest King needed no advice from any quarter, otherworldly or more local. Unless he made some blunder infinitely more egregious even than the Five-Cent Piece speech, there was no possibility that he would be defeated—or, to be more accurate, that Bennett would not be defeated.

Not since 1908, when Laurier was returned in spite of the scandals in his previous administration, had Canada actually voted *for* any Prime Minister. In 1911 the vote was against Sir Wilfrid, his navy bill, and his proposal to truck and trade with the Yankees; in 1917 against Quebec and its stand on conscription; in 1921 against everyone, but especially against Meighen and protection; in 1926 against Lord Byng and his handling of the constitutional issue and against Meighen's Chanak speech; in 1930 against the Depression. Now the issue was still the Depression and the people were still against it.

In the campaign King was satisfied to observe patronizingly that

Bennett's New Deal fell into three main divisions: the part that would be thrown out by the courts; the part that had been stolen from much earlier Liberal platforms; and the part—this applied to the proposed central but private bank—that was "Fascist."

Counting the hyphenated ones, a total of ten parties nominated a total of 894 candidates, by far the largest number in history. Of the 245 seats, the Liberals carried a stunning 171 while the Conservatives plummeted to 39. Harry Stevens, who had fondly dreamed of turning the country inside out by putting 174 of his brand-new Reconstructionists in the field, elected only one—himself. The C.C.F., considering its much greater seniority, did little better—7 elected in 118 tries. All 10 Communists were defeated. Among the rebellious new lairds of the provinces, Duplessis and Hepburn weren't quite ready to challenge Ottawa directly. Aberhart was, on the other hand, and his Social Crediters carried 15 of Alberta's 17 seats and picked up 2 more outside.

One of Bennett's many controversial actions while in office had been to re-establish the King's right to confer titles on his Canadian subjects whether the Canadian government recommended them or not. He himself shortly accepted the specially created Viscountcy of Mickleham, Calgary, and Hopewell and left Canada forever to live out his days in a South of England mansion beside his old friend Beaverbrook.

Canada saves and then helps destroy the League of Nations—Munich, Ethiopia, and the start of the Second World War

FROM 1919 and the heady months of Versailles through most of 1939 and the last weeks of peace, Canada suffered along with the rest of the world from an almost epidemic blight. It was, essentially, a blight of reason, a wish-turned-to-belief that fair words and small deeds could somehow wipe out war.

Germany and, following her example, Japan and Italy began turning away from the strange formula as soon as they could and getting ready for war. But elsewhere, even among the nations that remained in the League and paid it their annual tribute of rhetoric and resolutions, the same struggle that had paralyzed the will of the United States was being repeated on essentially the same terms. Within the nerve center of every sovereign state there dwelt side by side a Woodrow Wilson and a Henry Cabot Lodge: Wilson to make the noble promises, Lodge to make prudently sure they were not kept.

Canada's unsurpassed military effort between 1914 and 1918 had left the country rather in the position of a medium-sized boy who has set out to do the work of a man, has somehow done it, and then has discovered to his pride and consternation that he can't revert to being a boy again. The only possible course was to press on to still greater feats of manhood. Hence Borden's implacable insistence that Canada sign the peace treaty for herself and be represented separately at the League of Nations. Hence the steady affirmation by King and Bennett of full autonomy within the Empire until with only two or three minor *t*'s uncrossed it became binding and official in the Statute of Westminster.

Not everyone was agreed how this new and militantly—and at times obnoxiously—nationalistic Canada might best make itself heard and felt. Borden favored a common foreign policy for the Empire; King favored separate foreign policies and as few commitments as possible. Woodsworth supported old-fashioned Christian pacifism; Bourassa leaned on modern, fire-eating pacifism. Meighen at first stood for the ready-aye-readiness of Chanak and then for the no-war-without-a-plebiscite caution of the 1926 election. Bennett believed Canada could best extend its influence through aggressive trade policies.

But regardless of the differences in these prescriptions for peace, none of them—excepting only Meighen's passing urge to march against the Turks at Chanak—envisaged any real risk-taking or expense. Not that this was much cause for wonder, for Britain and France, the only strong guarantors of law and order after the U.S.A.'s return to isolation, were drifting in the same direction toward the ultimate catastrophe of Munich.

Even before the proud flourishing of pens was over at Geneva, Borden was trying to persuade the League to water down Article X of the Covenant, the provision that called for united action against an aggressor. In each of the first four Assemblies of the League, the effort was repeated, twice by Conservative governments and twice by Liberal governments. In 1923, King's delegation barely missed having the key article rewritten to say that (*a*) before the League called on any member for military support it would be bound to take into account "geographical situation and special conditions"; and (*b*) it was for each member to decide for itself whether it should answer an appeal to action or not.

As one of its earliest delegates to Geneva confessed later, Canada considered itself a producer rather than a consumer of security. Senator Raoul Dandurand, one of King's first emissaries to Geneva, put it even more bluntly: "We live in a fireproof house. . . ."

Canada had no special culpability in the League's sellout of Manchuria to Japan in 1932, but neither could it claim any special absence of guilt. While Bennett side-stepped a discussion at home on the ground that the matter was *sub judice*, his Geneva representative, C. H. Cahan, was questioning whether Japan's victim was strong enough for self-rule; that is, whether the Japanese weren't really doing the Manchurians a favor by conquering them. Moreover, Cahan added innocently, the delegate of Japan had himself assured the Assembly that his country had no designs on Manchuria. The marching battalions of the Rising Sun were marching only to protect their people's legitimate rights and interests. Young Pu-yi, the clearly visible puppet Emperor of Manchukuo, was no creature of Japan's. "It seems to me," Cahan said virtuously, "that this Assembly may not wholly disregard . . . the emphatic statements made by the delegate from Japan."

Ultimately Canada voted, along with the rest of the League, for a lukewarm rebuke to the Japanese, who thereupon politely walked out of the League and politely carried on with their invasion.

Europe was full of deeper pitfalls and complexities, particularly for a North American visitor still less than a generation old in the worldly business of world treaty making. Though this was no longer constitutionally necessary, Canada was still inclined to take its lead in foreign affairs from Britain. And Britain, along with France, had been lured back into the deadly form of Russian roulette called maintaining the balance of power.

The streets and prison yards of Germany were awash with blood. Madman or not, Adolf Hitler had won more than seventeen million votes in the Fatherland's last free election. In the dying flames of the Reichstag fire and the naked terror of the pogroms and the purges, the will and rights of the twenty million who had voted against him were simply melted down and reprocessed into the all-embracing will of the Nazi party and the state.

A promise made a dozen years before, even before the first words of *Mein Kampf* were put on paper, had come true: "We will incite the people, and not only incite, we will lash them to a frenzy. We will preach struggle, the inexorable struggle against this parliamentary brood, this whole system which will not cease before either Germany has been totally ruined or else one day a man with an iron skull appears. His boots may be dirty but he will have a clear conscience and a steel fist, he will put an end to the speeches of these matinee heroes and show the nation some action."

But Hitler, according to the zodiacal readings from Downing Street and the Quai d'Orsay, was not yet in the danger phase. The immediate problem was to come to an understanding with his senior, Benito Mussolini.

The two dictators were believed to be at loggerheads over the future of Austria. Britain and France wished to keep them there and calculated that, for the time being, the best method was to try to get along with Italy. Thus, in a special meeting, the three powers pledged themselves to oppose "any unilateral repudiation of treaties which may endanger the peace of Europe."

The two innocent words "of Europe" deceived no one. Mussolini was already making noisy plans to invade Ethiopia, solely because it happened to be the softest and most attractive article of imperial spoil within his reach. In return for his undertaking to help stop Hitler in Europe, Britain and France were content to place no immediate obstacle in his path to expansion in Africa.

When Mussolini marched in early October 1935, Canada was on the eve of an election. Its delegation to Geneva managed, however, to obtain Bennett's authority to join in condemning Italy as an aggressor.

The ensuing discussion of how to thwart Mussolini's adventure centered around economic sanctions. No one proposed or even hinted at anything so drastic as military sanctions, and the question of how far the League should go was still being debated when the Canadian delegation received the news that it was working for a new administration.

The permanent head of the delegation, Dr. Walter A. Riddell, asked the incoming King government for instructions, and in reply the Department of External Affairs cabled the summary of a statement the Prime Minister had just given to the press. Its substance was that Canada favored and would co-operate in economic sanctions but couldn't consider military sanctions without consulting Parliament.

Riddell took it that this was intended for his official guidance. He was already sitting on a League committee charged with recommending what goods should be barred to Italy and on what conditions. Though he had had considerable previous experience of the realities of international negotiation, he was learning new things every week. Aggression or no aggression, sanctions or no sanctions, the marble halls of the world government were still crowded with local patriots to whom all the lofty avowals of the Covenant were much less compelling that the three simple words Business as Usual.

Foreign Minister Pierre Laval was there in person from France, arguing against extending the embargo to iron, steel, coal, and oil. The convenient hairsplit was that League members did not control the world supply of these four products; to ban them would only give the United States, a non-member, a monopoly of the Italian market. The Canadian delegate reflected that France itself was a big seller of steel and iron to Italy; moreover, he was certain that Laval had been making secret telephone calls to *Il Duce* in Rome.

Almost everyone in this theoretically selfless concourse, it seemed, was playing some private angle. The Argentine delegate, recollecting that a million Italians lived in his country, asked the committee to remember the economic and social damage it might do to Latin America by opposing Mussolini too zealously. Norway, Poland, and Rumania demanded that they be allowed to send Italy any war goods already ordered. Spain argued that if other countries were allowed to sell Mussolini processed iron and steel she ought to be allowed to sell him iron ore. The United States, though not a League member, had sent observers and expressed sympathy with the aims of the embargo; nevertheless, Secretary of State Hull considered it necessary to issue a statement that "the people of the United States were entitled to know that considerably increasing amounts of oil, trucks, tractors, scrap iron, and scrap steel, which were essential war materials, were being exported for war purposes."

The most candid stand of all was that of the perennial neutral, Switzerland, which claimed a special exemption from any ban against shipments of war goods to Italy. To comply with the ban, the Swiss argued, would cost the country its best market and throw thousands out of work.

Amid these seamy proceedings, the Canadian delegate Riddell had to remind himself that his own country was not immune to temptation. Twenty-seven raw materials had been officially described by the League as essential for war purposes and more than half these were being mined from the Canadian Shield, some in vast quantities. One of them was copper.

On Saturday, November 2, as Riddell entered the Geneva committee room the delegate from Chile rushed over to him "much disturbed" and told him that copper was about to be proposed for addition to the embargo list. Riddell, still without detailed instructions and "not sure whether the new Canadian government would share the Chilean view on copper," was in a quandary. Finally, after hurried consultations with the Chileans, the Spanish, the Belgians, the French, and Anthony Eden on behalf of Britain, Riddell concluded he must act before the day was over or not at all; the debate was already near its conclusion.

Accordingly he drew up a resolution of his own. In it he added the four items he felt must be proscribed if sanctions were to work—petroleum, iron, steel, and coal. Copper was not mentioned. "If I left off copper," he explained a dozen years later in his book *Security by Conference*, "as the inclusion of copper at the time was not important, it might be more acceptable to my government as we were already as much affected as any other country by the key products proposal."

Before submitting his resolution Riddell cabled its substance to Ottawa and asked for approval. As the Geneva afternoon wore on and no reply came he felt free to obey his instinct. His motion was clearly in harmony with Mackenzie King's press statement in Canada. In any case, the powerful weapon now pointed at *Il Duce* had a safety catch; whatever recommendations the League of Nations committee made, they had to go back to the individual governments for final acceptance.

At first the safety catch seemed superfluous. Riddell's motion for oil sanctions went sailing through the Geneva committee unopposed and a world sickened by Mussolini's bombings of unprotected tribal villages suddenly took heart again. While others bargained and shilly-shallied in the presence of wholesale murder the courageous Canadians had shown the League the way to its salvation. Limited sanctions went into force in mid-November and neutral correspondents in Rome reported the pinch was felt so quickly and severely that Italy's total volume of trade was cut in half. Italian housewives were being urged to save waste paper and scrap metals and throw their wedding rings into a national pot of gold. When oil was added to the list of imports forbidden to Italy—as it now seemed certain to be—Mussolini's whole dark adventure in Ethiopia would be almost surely doomed.

The widespread admiration of what was now being described as "the Canadian resolution" did not, however, extend to Canada. King was on a holiday in Georgia, relaxing after the election, and he had left Ernest Lapointe, his indispensable Quebec lieutenant, in charge of the Department of External Affairs. Lapointe soon found himself under heavy pressure from two quarters, from the Italian consulate in Ottawa and from his own province.

The first time the Italian consul general called, Lapointe sent him packing with a polite assertion that Canada was only fulfilling its obligations to the League and the blunt suggestion that Italy might do well to do the same.

But the reaction of Quebec was more awkward to deal with, and Quebec offered the busy Italian propagandists a much more fertile field. Practically every French-language newspaper opposed action of any kind by Canada. What was the difference between Mussolini's foray into Africa and Britain's war of conquest against the Boers? Canada had joined in Anglo-Saxon hypocrisy then; must she repeat the error now? The Church took no official stand, but to most of its individual priests and bishops two facts stood out: Italy was Catholic, and Rome was Rome.

No one paid much attention when Canada's No. 1 Fascist, Adrien Arcand, led his little band of Silver Shirts through the streets of Montreal to deride the League and hail *Il Duce*, but it was a different matter when a pronouncement came from Camillien Houde himself. Houde, a sometime mayor of Montreal and leader of the provincial Conservative party, occupied a unique position among the urbanized habitants of Canada's largest city—part court jester, part paterfamilias, part beloved scalawag. When he spoke, French Canada often laughed but it always listened. This time he intended to be heard in dead earnest: "If war should come between Britain and Italy, French-Canadian sympathies will be with Italy."

Lapointe stood his ground until almost a month after the oil embargo had been endorsed by the League committee. Then he and his government made a dramatic and unexpected discovery. There had been a regrettable case of mistaken paternity. The so-called Canadian resolution at Geneva was in reality a sort of foundling whose sole discoverable ancestor was Dr. Walter A. Riddell. With his Prime Minister's full approval, Lapointe, the Acting Secretary of External Affairs, disavowed all responsibility for the motion to cut off Mussolini's oil, coal, steel, and iron. If some other country wished to make such a motion and if the rest of the League happened to be in favor, Canada would go along. But Canada had not taken the initiative and didn't intend to, and said so in a public statement: "The opinion which was expressed by the Canadian member of the Committee, and which had led to the reference to the proposal as a Canadian proposal, represented only his personal opinion and his view as a member of the Committee, and not the views of the Government of Canada."

Riddell, being a dutiful public servant, accepted the foundling as his own, as, indeed, in the narrowest sense it was. Another meeting of the sanctions committee had already been called for December 12 in the hope of moving the oil embargo through the next stage of the cumbersome League machinery. But now bereft of its sponsor—and an apologetic sponsor at that—it had little chance of finding another one.

Britain and France, which had felt compelled to vote for the embargo when it made its first troublesome and undesired appearance on the League's agenda, now considered themselves free to consummate the private deal with Mussolini which they had made possible in their "peace of Europe" declaration.

Three days before the next decisive League meeting Pierre Laval and Sir Samuel Hoare, his opposite number at the British Foreign Office, pronounced their Solomon's judgment: cut Ethiopia in two and let Ethiopia have one part and Italy the other.

The Emperor Haile Selassie rejected this solution. So did Mussolini, now completely secure in the knowledge that the League's brief show of serious opposition was at an end. He went on with his total conquest while the committee on sanctions proceeded to its predictable business of shoving the oil embargo into a pigeonhole.

By midsummer the capital, Addis Ababa, was in Italy's hands, the Emperor was in exile, and the League was back in session.

This time its purpose was not to get in Mussolini's way but to get out of it, finally and officially. Not only was there no further talk of the oil-and-steel embargo but the embargo on less important war materials was removed. By a genuine but happy coincidence Walter Riddell had a prior appointment in South America and it fell to a new delegate, Vincent Massey, to speak for Canada: "These sanctions having proved inadequate . . . continuance of the ineffective economic pressure would not secure the original objective and would be worse than useless."

The magic word in world diplomacy was now "reality." The companion word "appeasement" had not yet lost face. King referred to appeasement often, with approval, and practiced it with diligence and stubborn faith. When, undoubtedly under Communist direction, Canadian volunteers began enlisting with the Spanish Republicans in the war against Franco, the government invoked a sixty-year-old act forbidding foreign enlistments and sought to stop them. After attending the Coronation of George VI in 1937, the Prime Minister made a personal visit to Hitler and concluded wishfully—so confiding to Bruce Hutchison on his return—that the Führer was "a simple sort of peasant," not very intelligent and no serious danger to anyone.

When Chamberlain returned from Munich leaving the corpse of Czechoslovakia and the last remnant of collective security behind, King cabled him a message of thanks. "The heart of Canada is rejoicing tonight at the success which has crowned your unremitting efforts to peace. . . . Your achievements in the past month alone will ensure you an abiding and illustrious place among the great conciliators. . . . On the very brink of chaos . . . the voice of reason has found a way out of the conflict. . . . A turning point in the world's history will be reached if, as we hope, tonight's agreement means a halt to the mad race of arms and a new start in building the partnership of all peoples. May you have health and strength to carry your great work to its completion."

King was far from alone in his euphoria. In 1935 R. B. Bennett had handed over to him a defense budget of seventeen million dollars, or about one half of 1 per cent of the national income, and when the new administration sought a modest increase in these almost invisible military estimates, it ran into heavy going. J. S. Woodsworth moved that "in the event of war, Canada should remain strictly neutral regardless of who the belligerents may be." A group of Quebec Liberals abandoned their leader to support him. Their contention was that nothing had occurred to change things for the worse since the Italo-Ethiopian fiasco and Canada therefore was less justified than ever in increasing the defense budget. "Our boundaries are the same," Maxime Raymond asserted. "Our neighbors are the same and just as peaceful as they were. Our geographical position has not changed and we are still separated from Europe and Asia by oceans that mean an almost absolute security. We have no enemies that we know of. Moreover, the friction that existed by reason of the sanctions against Italy has disappeared since these sanctions have been removed."

Other voices, however, were raised in genuine alarm. While Mussolini was mopping up in Ethiopia and Hitler was marching into the demilitarized Rhineland, the Canadian government had before it a report from its Chief of Staff on the state of the military stockpile. Major General Andrew McNaughton summed it up in two terse sentences. "As regards reserves of equipment and ammunition, the matter is shortly disposed of. Except as regards rifles and rifle ammunition, partial stocks of which were inherited from the Great War—there are none." The detailed inventory he followed with disclosed that in all of Canada there was not a single modern antiaircraft gun of any sort, not a single operational military aircraft, not a single aerial bomb. There was enough field ammunition on hand for a total of ninety minutes' fire from the obsolescent guns inherited from the first war. The few coast-defense guns were not only obsolescent but so defective that "to keep some defence value in [them] . . . we have not dared for some years to indulge in any practice."

"About the only article of which stocks are held," McNaughton went on, making no attempt to conceal his disgust, "is harness. The composition of a modern land force will include very little horsed transport."

In 1937 Japan revived and stepped up its war against China. In 1938 Hitler grabbed Austria and the Sudetenland and then, with Munich behind him, took the rest of Czechoslovakia in 1939 and prepared to march on Poland and the old free port of Danzig. Mussolini, his bargain to break no treaties in Europe of no further use to him now that Ethiopia was safely digested, made a swift lunge into Albania.

By midsummer the statesmen and diplomats had begun to stir from their hopeful trance, but if hysteria was near it was not the hysteria of the warmonger but the hysteria of the peacemonger. In Europe they were a little quicker to face the bitter truth that what seemed to be happening actually was happening, but behind the great moat of the North Atlantic, under the friendly wing of the U.S.A., millions of Canadians were still practicing a kind of mass Couéism. Day by day in every way the world was getting better and better, and it *would* get better if enough people kept on saying so and believing it.

Seeking to harness these mighty forces of autosuggestion and help them to ignore the impending war right out of existence, the country's largest newspaper, the usually sensational Toronto *Daily Star*, embarked on one of the most remarkable performances in journalistic history. All through that final fateful August, right up to the twenty-ninth day, the paper's readers were invited to believe that the day's most important news was: MAN AND WIFE SLAIN, DAUGHTER WOUNDED; or GUNMEN ROB BANK, BEAT TRAIN TO ESCAPE; or BLAST BRIDGES, RUSH TANKS IN U.S. STRIKES; or 2 ROB BALA BANK, NAB ONE AT GUN-POINT. These were the actual front-page news banners the *Star* used on the first four publishing days of August 1939, and the top front-page feature stories were an unbroken run of:

"IDEAL WOMAN'S" IDEAL MAN
NOT "MAN-ABOUT-TOWN" TYPE

PRINCESSES PERSONALLY
BUY GIFTS FOR "MUMMY"

GOOD FAMILY LIFE GIVEN CREDIT
AS SISTERS WIN BEAUTY CONTESTS

BREATHE DEEP, GIRLS, AND HOLD IT
CORSETS ARE COMING BACK AGAIN

Parliament was not sitting, nor was a sitting planned until fall. Even as late as August 16, two weeks and two days before the shooting started, most Canadians had no idea where Danzig was and why Hitler and a man named Förster suddenly considered its immediate possession of such vast importance. In the *Star*'s judgment the things that mattered most that day to its vast audience were:

$11,004 NEEDED STILL BY FRESH AIR FUND

"CLARK GABLE SO SILLY"
TURKISH CO-EDS DECLARE

On the eighteenth Hitler briefly abandoned the Danzig front and the Polish Corridor and took final possession of his erstwhile "protectorate" of Slovakia.

FOIL GRIMSBY BANK HOLDUP, NAB SUSPECT

STOP TAKING QUINT PICTURES
FIRM SAYS CONTRACT BROKEN

On the twenty-second, after a pleasant weekend in most of the world, Berlin announced that Hitler and his greatest enemy, Joseph Stalin, were about to sign a ten-year non-aggression pact. Now, not two heavily armed dictators would be loose in Europe, but three.

SENATOR FRANK O'CONNOR DIES, LONG ILL

PRINCESS MARGARET ROSE, NINE
PINK BIRTHDAY PARTY ARRANGED

On the twenty-third Mackenzie King announced that Parliament would be summoned only "if efforts for peace were likely to fail." But in one of his most dazzling constitutional exercises he proclaimed a state of "apprehended war" and announced his intention of making use of the War Measures Act, a sweeping mandate for absolute rule of the Cabinet which no one had remembered to cancel after the 1914 war.

COBB SETS WORLD MARK, 368.85 M.P.H.

54 ENLARGED PHOTOGRAPHS WILL
AUGMENT MOVIE OF ROYAL TOUR

On the twenty-fourth Hitler's man in Danzig was head of the local government while the Wehrmacht wheeled new divisions to the Polish border.

TORONTO MAN NEW SALVATION ARMY HEAD

CELEBRATES 90TH BIRTHDAY
BY WINNING GAME OF BOWLS

On the twenty-sixth King cabled personal peace appeals to Hitler, Mussolini, and the President of Poland. He reminded the head of the trapped and doomed Polish state that "there is no international problem which cannot be settled by conference and negotiation," adding the helpful counsel that "force is not a substitute for reason" and appealing to him to use his "great power and authority . . . to prevent impending catastrophe."

WOUNDED FATHER AND SON ROUT THREE GUNMEN

STAR ROYAL PHOTOS
"BEAUTIFUL SOUVENIRS"
SAYS LORD MAUGHAM

After another weekend, the last peaceful August weekend until 1945, Germany imposed rationing.

BLAST WRECKS HOUSE, ALARMS NEIGHBORS

CROWDS LINE UP FOR HOURS
TO GAZE AT ROYAL PICTURES

On the first of September, Hitler introduced Poland and the world to Blitzkrieg. Two days later he was at war with France and Britain.

XLI

King meets two challenges—First from
Duplessis and Quebec, then from
Hepburn and Ontario

CANADA's entrance into the Second World War had none of the bustle and bravura of her entrance into the First. In 1914 the scene was one of bold and instant decisions made and carried out with a Plantagenet flourish. But 1939 brought no grave, determined Borden hastening from his summer retreat to take counsel with his ministers. It brought no fiery captain like Sam Hughes to declaim on the greensward of Parliament Hill. No Hughes thundering off to round up an immediate legion of thirty thousand, rush them through dusty encampments on the plains of Valcartier, stuff them pell-mell into the quickly assembled transports, and thrust them across three thousand miles of water to take their place, ill equipped, ill trained, but superbly present and willing, beside the mother country.

On September 1, the day Germany attacked Poland, Mackenzie King summoned Parliament for a special session to begin six days later. At the same time he issued a cautious statement that the government would seek authority to co-operate with the United Kingdom. To those who had paid attention to his earlier speeches on international affairs, his failure to mention a possible declaration of war was of no particular significance. He had been maintaining for years that when and if the country had to face such a decision again, it would be made by Parliament and only by Parliament.

For the time being the question was largely an academic one, for in spite of four more years of growing tension Canada's immediate military capacity had not changed much since General McNaughton pronounced it virtually non-existent.

A month before the official beginning of the war, the full-time army had just over 4000 officers and men. The Non-Permanent Active Militia, the theoretical reserve of "Sunday soldiers," numbered around 60,000. The total strength of the Royal Canadian Navy was barely 1800 and of the Royal Canadian Air Force less than 4500. The combined strength of the three services was just above 10,000, and most of these had never seen, much less been trained to use, the ships, planes, tanks, trucks, and guns with which they would soon be required to fight. Inventories taken either at the outbreak of war or just before showed that the Army possessed a total of 29 Bren guns, 23 antitank rifles, and 5 three-inch mortars. The Navy and the Air Force were armed on an equally pitiful scale.

A general mobilization order on September 1 brought a rush of recruits and another embarrassing discovery. Not only was there an insufficiency of equipment to train them on; there was an insufficiency of clothing, barracks, beds, blankets, almost everything. The colonel of one old and honored infantry battalion was reduced to accepting a kindly lady's offer to present his men with 130 pairs of boots. While the crises of procurement ebbed and flowed, defense headquarters was forced to slow down the rate of recruiting by closing most of its depots. Nevertheless, the Army alone had increased its active strength by 55,000 by the end of September and had turned enough would-be soldiers away to be certain that manpower was the least of its problems.

Parliament discussed the war for three days before voting formally to become a participant. It was less a debate than a series of careful expositions, for although J. S. Woodsworth and a handful of members from Quebec spoke in favor of neutrality, in the end only Woodsworth insisted on voting against the war and having his vote recorded.

The brief session marked the end of Woodsworth's career and a turning point in King's. After twenty years as the country's most persistent and effective champion of civil liberty and social reforms, the Chaplinesque little ex-clergyman and stevedore squared his thin shoulders, lifted his head, and went marching down his lonely road again. When he began his brink-of-war speech, the leader of the C.C.F. had six followers in the House of Commons. When he finished, he had none. Not a soul voted with him against the war, nor did he ask that any do so. He stated his position firmly and with a trace of sad apology: the last war had settled nothing, the next war would settle nothing. Others could confront him with all their realism and logic. They could call him a crank and a hopeless idealist, but they could not make him forget a scene he had witnessed a few days earlier near Blaine, Washington, at the Peace Arch between Canada and the United States. "The children gathered their pennies and planted a rose garden, and they held a fine ceremony in which they interchanged national flags and sang songs and that sort of thing: a beautiful incident."

And then Woodsworth said softly: "I take my place with the children."

Two days later, a new party leader, M. J. Coldwell, announced the C.C.F.'s official position: home defense and economic aid to Britain, but no military expeditions outside Canada. At his party's insistence Woodsworth remained its nominal head, but never again would he take an active part in forming its policies. He lost that right, he insisted without rancor, when he lost the party's confidence.

King, like his old friend and adversary, was getting on; his sixty-fifth birthday was two months away. But now, at last, he had come face to face with a situation that called not for the worst of his talents but for the best of them. He still had enough compromising and tough political infighting ahead of him to last most men a lifetime, but this time it had a better purpose than undoing another opponent, burying another trail of mismanagement or malfeasance, clinging to or scrambling back to office for four or five more years. From this point on, so far as the record has disclosed, King's trifling with principle was more for his country's benefit than for his party's or his own.

He launched Canada into the war in the wake of another compromise, as massive as it was unavoidable. He was ready to make his own kind of settlement with his own kind of belief. He had no more real faith than Woodsworth in war's ultimate power to achieve any useful end. While there was still a chance for peace it had been instinctive—and, in domestic political terms, safe—to back and fill and dissemble before the terrifying dangers of the League and anything that hinted at replacing words with action. But with peace already lost, the option was lost. Unlike Woodsworth, he could no longer meet an impossible problem with an impossible solution. Neither he nor his country could take a place among the children, and so they must take their place among the warring grownups.

The larger compromise was with Quebec and with conscription, and it, too, left no choice. King's long speech came to this essential matter only after hours of beating about the bush—as though the lifelong reflexes would not be easily or suddenly stilled—but when he came to it he did not try to build in loopholes or escape hatches. Weighing every word, King said slowly: "The present government believe that conscription of men for overseas service will not be a necessary or an effective step. No such measure will be introduced by the present administration."

Ernest Lapointe soon followed, hoping to finish laying the ghost of 1917. On the need for Canada to declare war he spoke with far greater force and conviction than King had done. Constitutionally and morally, it was impossible to remain neutral. As Minister of Justice, Lapointe cited a dozen hard, pragmatic reasons, based on law, trade, shipping, the existing diplomatic apparatus, and even the recent legislation to keep volunteers from going to Spain. As a Canadian, he had a dozen other reasons, the first of which rang forth all the more compellingly because the English in which he stated it was heavy with the accent of the lower St. Lawrence. "Our King, Mr. Speaker, is at war," he said, "and this Parliament is sitting to decide whether we shall make his cause our own."

As a French Canadian, Lapointe spoke with equal directness: "The whole province of Quebec—and I speak with all the responsibility and all the solemnity I can give to my words—will never accept compulsory service or conscription outside Canada. I will go farther than that: When I say the whole province of Quebec I mean that I personally agree with them. I am authorized by my colleagues in the Cabinet from the province of Quebec to say that we will never agree to conscription and will never be members or supporters of a government that will try to enforce it."

The debate continued through the last hours of a Saturday afternoon and the first hours of Saturday night, but Lapointe's decisive stand, backed by his personal stature in both Canadas, made all that followed superfluous. The proclamation was approved and dispatched by midnight. It reached Buckingham Palace in the early morning, and Canada was officially at war on Sunday, September 10.

There was barely time to rough out a loose and general plan of action before Lapointe's bridge between French and English Canada, which had looked so stout and dependable only a few days before, was threatened with total collapse.

After three years as premier of Quebec, Maurice Le Noblet Duplessis had laid the foundation of one of the most extraordinary and chilling public careers in Canadian history. Part demagogue, part tyrant, part old-fashioned political boss, he had administered a crushing defeat to the Liberal government of Alexandre Taschereau in 1936 and set out to make Canada's largest province a satellite of his Union Nationale machine. Like a Huey Long run riot behind the steamroller of a Tammany Hall, he combined prejudice with patronage to make himself, in time and until the end of his time on earth, almost invulnerable to the ordinary uncertainties of politics. But now, in the heat and excitement and confusion of September 1939, he made the mistake of believing that he was invulnerable already.

The belief was not without supporting evidence. Duplessis held 75 seats in the Quebec legislature to the Liberals' 15. It was true that, having put Taschereau to rout on the indictment of waste and graft, Duplessis had then doubled the province's debt inside three years. But some of the money could be honestly and innocently charged against the Depression and the rest could be charged —with great advantage to the party—to Union Nationale's willingness to reward its friends. "Help yourself," Duplessis was fond of counseling men who could be of use to him, "and heaven will help you. Or help yourself and the Union Nationale will help you. Which comes out the same in the end."

While the machine became its bedrock, his regime did not lack for other sources of strength. The break with the Conservatives meant fully as much to the Quebec-firsters as Borden's and King's well-publicized differences with England had meant to the Canada-firsters. Under the label of Union Nationale he made a far more convincing champion of provincial rights than he could ever have made as the sworn ally of any federal party. And provincial rights, provincial autonomy, and provincial isolation—with all of which Duplessis was fast making his name synonymous—had not been so close to his people's hearts in a generation.

Long before the war's approach became visible the Abbé Lionel Groulx, an immensely influential historian, author, teacher, and orator, had helped relight the ancient beacon of Laurentia. Duplessis did not wholly embrace the Abbé's vision of an independent French Catholic republic, but those who did easily recognized in him at least a fellow traveler.

And after the declaration of war, even with King's and Lapointe's guarantees against conscription still echoing on its own front pages, the French-language press remained suspicious and unenthusiastic toward the whole enterprise. In theory *La Presse* and *La Patrie* supported Ottawa, but neither foresaw or would condone any substantial sacrifice of men or money. *Le Devoir* took its stand approximately where it and its editor Henri Bourassa had stood a generation earlier; it was against any kind of participation. Even the Liberal voice of *Le Canada* cried that to send an expeditionary force abroad would "ruin our country."

L'Action Nationale, a monthly publication edited by Groulx and a dozen other well-known intellectuals, opposed compulsion in any form or any attempt to raise volunteers "by the Canadian government at Canadian expense for military operations outside Canada." Groulx and his colleagues were willing to tolerate an embargo on exports to Germany and they would permit individual Canadians to join the British Army. "Since Canada is divided on this question," they counseled, "let Canadian policy be to leave each individual free to act according to his own convictions."

L'Action Nationale found much to recommend in Charles Lindbergh's suggestion that if Canada refused to insulate herself from Europe, she might be forced to do so by the United States. Canada, Lindbergh had said, had no right to involve the Western Hemisphere in another European bloodbath "for the sole reason that it prefers the crown of England to American independence." The fading idol of the continent was talking the equivalent of a U.S. invasion across the famous undefended border; his nation, he insisted, "should not permit any American country to extend the use of its bases to foreign ships of war, or to fight abroad under our protection." Groulx and his fellow custodians of the Laurentian dream offered no objection.

It was small wonder that Maurice Duplessis saw this as the moment to make assurance doubly sure, to strike a stupendous blow at the forces of federalism and internationalism and to establish his own position as the true spokesman of his race. Two weeks after Canada became a belligerent he called a provincial election.

The issue was the war. The election would be "a battle for the survival of our popular liberties . . . a fight for the life and survival of French Canadians," a struggle for autonomy against the apostles of "participation, assimilation, and centralization."

National unity, even in the dubious and semi-fictional form into which Lapointe and King had managed to cast it, seemed in peril of an imminent and perhaps final breach. There were two courses open to Ottawa. The first, however dangerous and distasteful, offered some slight hedge against a total catastrophe: stay out of Duplessis's way. Concede that his corrupt and ruthless machine, plus his call to the ties of blood, had made him at least temporarily invincible. Since he was almost certain of victory, let the victory be diminished by being uncontested and hope somehow to muddle through until there was time to think.

The other course was to tackle Duplessis head on, under his own rules and in his own territory. The first course, the pretense of being too busy with more important events to join battle with the awful man from Quebec, was the one King himself found less dismaying.

But Lapointe and Charles Gavan (Chubby) Power, another Quebec cabinet minister of great influence, assured him he was wrong. They admitted the fearful risks of direct combat, but if Duplessis won his election either in open battle or by default, the war was over for Quebec. King took their advice and sent all four cabinet ministers from Quebec to the aid of the provincial party.

They all—P. J. A. Cardin and Raoul Dandurand as well as Lapointe and Power—deliberately and specifically staked their careers on the outcome. If Duplessis carried Quebec, then Quebec would have to find new men to speak for it in Ottawa. They all swore to resign from office before submitting to his "act of national sabotage," as Lapointe called it.

The argument proved more persuasive than any of them had hoped. For all its aversion to becoming involved again in what it saw as the private homicide of Europe, Quebec was still very much a part of Canada—in its own far from unnatural view the most steadfastly "Canadian" part of all. It, too, was willing to make concessions in order to protect what there was of national homogeneity. It, too, was profoundly shocked by the threat that the country might fly apart before it had ever given itself a fair chance to draw together. And if the choice had to be between the total isolation that Duplessis promised but could not guarantee and the limited isolation that Ernest Lapointe could both promise and guarantee, then it was Duplessis who, for the time being, had to go.

The Liberals, under the nominal leadership of a little-known man named Adélard Godbout, swept back to power with 69 seats of a total of 86.

But King's government, scrambling now to come to Britain's aid before it was too late, was not past its difficulties with the rebellious barons of the provinces.

William Aberhart and the Social Crediters of Alberta nagged about the way the war was being financed but did not question that it must be fought. When Aberhart called a provincial election for March 1940, the federal Liberals had no cause to intervene. Social Credit went back into office, even though court decisions had long since erased its famous twenty-five dollars a month along with most of its other fiscal schemes.

Mitch Hepburn, the rambunctious premier of Ontario, was far more troublesome. Hepburn had watched intently while Duplessis challenged Ottawa and failed. Far from being deterred in his own ambition to replace King as the strong man of the Liberals, the onion farmer from Elgin County became more impatient than ever. Moreover, since Hepburn desired a greater, not a lesser, concentration on the war, he could read it as an omen in his favor that Duplessis had been so roundly defeated.

While the protesting gears of mobilization and industry were still barely beginning to mesh, the head of the Ontario government was telling his legislature that in Canada's greatest emergency King had offered it only sloth and inefficiency in place of energy and leadership. And besides, he added, determined to squeeze the last inch of mileage from the issue of provincial rights, King had shown a "positive hatred" for Ontario.

On January 18, 1940, three months after the overthrow of Duplessis, Hepburn rose in Queen's Park and proposed a motion of regret "that the federal government at Ottawa has made so little effort to prosecute Canada's duty in the war in the vigorous manner the people of Canada desire to see." George Drew, leader of the Conservative opposition, hastened to second the motion, which carried by a vote of 44 to 10.

With the feud between the first- and second-ranking Liberals now fully in the open, the country had to wait another week for King's next move. Parliament had been summoned for January 25. King had seen to it that, contrary to custom, neither the leader of the Opposition nor the press gallery received advance copies of the Speech from the Throne. Consequently, his answer to Hepburn—and by inference to all other critics, including the block of Tories awaiting their chance to get at him from across the floor of the House of Commons—came as a complete surprise. He asked for the dissolution of Parliament—immediately. He asked for a new election—immediately. Since the legislature of the wealthiest and most populous province had seen fit to condemn his government, the people as a whole deserved an opportunity to throw him out of office or send him back for another term—immediately.

The shock was almost universal, for only the members of the Liberal Cabinet had been taken into their leader's confidence and then only at the last minute. When the full truth of what was happening dawned on them, even some of King's silent and ordinarily sheeplike army of backbenchers were seen to touch their brows in pain. Whatever else it meant, it meant precisely $3975 to each of them—the difference between their full-session indemnity and $25 for a one-day sitting. For Robert J. Manion, Bennett's successor as Opposition leader, the consequences were much more awkward. Manion had been looking forward to a full winter and spring of sittings in which to examine the government on its record, call for documents and departmental records, and at least coax a full statement from the Cabinet of what it had already done and what it proposed to do next. Amid the thickets of rule by order in council, Manion was lost and helpless, as many an abler man would have been. But now, King reminded him regretfully, not even the motion to dissolve was debatable.

In the ensuing election campaign the enfeebled and dispirited Tories could do no more than go on hacking at the underbrush of secret plans and absolute decrees, emitting an occasional cry of frustration or rage and seeking vainly for an issue. Failing to find one, Manion was thrown on his inventive powers. He renamed his Conservatives the National Government party and declared that anyone was eligible to stand for nomination whether he had been a member or supporter of the former party or not. This merely enraged the Tory faithful without attracting any new blood. Hepburn, the one potential new ally of any consequence, made it clear he preferred to carry on his own vendetta with King unencumbered by any side arrangements. When the smoke screen dissolved from the hustings, both he and Manion lay prostrate. King had 178 seats to Manion's 39, the largest margin since Confederation.

Manion himself was defeated and surrendered the leadership of his party to R. B. Hanson, who restored the Conservatives' original name. Hepburn, stunned and demoralized by his failure to prevent a King majority even in Ontario, resigned within two years as provincial premier. So complete was his fall that after three years of semi-hibernation he was unable to win a seat as a private member. "I'm going back to my farm to listen to the grass grow," the former wonder boy consoled himself. A total of four premiers, one Opposition leader, and one Governor General had now chosen to engage Mackenzie King in frontal combat, and they had all found themselves doing more or less the same.

XLII

The Canadian Army and its false starts—The Air Force and the Battle of Britain

CANADA made five major military contributions to the winning of the Second World War.

The Army, which reached a peak strength of five divisions and nearly half a million men, put assault and follow-up formations of various sizes into all the main campaigns of Western Europe. Its greatest victories, none won easily, were in Sicily, Italy, France, Belgium, Holland, and northwestern Germany. It suffered total defeats at Hong Kong and Dieppe, the first to no purpose, the second redeemed by the lessons in amphibious landings it provided for all the Allies. Its casualties numbered 81,000, including 23,000 dead.

The Navy played a part second only to that of the British Royal Navy in keeping the lifeline to Britain open during the dark and almost fatal years of the Battle of the Atlantic. It expanded its strength in officers and ratings almost fiftyfold to a hundred thousand and built, bought, and borrowed more than four hundred cruisers, destroyers, frigates, corvettes, mine sweepers, gunboats, torpedo boats, and landing craft to add to its prewar establishment of thirteen vessels, one of which was a sailing ship for training cadets. It convoyed twenty-five thousand merchant ships and nearly two hundred million tons of supplies either part of or all the way between North America and the United Kingdom. It sank twenty-seven U-boats and itself lost two dozen warships. More than four in every five of its two thousand casualties were fatal. There were not many second chances in the Battle of the Atlantic.

The Air Force put nearly a quarter of a million Canadians in uniform, steadily stepping up its striking power from a squadron of fighters during the Battle of Britain to forty-eight squadrons of fighters plus a complete bomber group. Of the 18,000 Air Force men listed as casualties, more than 17,000 lost their lives.

Canada brought into being, ran, and largely paid for a work of genius, cauldron of discord, and essential implement of victory called the British Commonwealth Air Training Plan. Designed to turn raw recruits from Great Britain and the dominions into qualified air crews, the Plan graduated more than 130,000 pilots, navigators, bombardiers, and air gunners, of whom 55 per cent served in the Royal Canadian Air Force. Canada and Britain quarreled almost constantly about the direction of the Air Training Plan and the destiny of its graduates, but in its results the Plan was a magnificent success.

From what amounted to a standing start, the country developed into a major supplier of munitions and war machinery of all kinds, not only for itself but for other nations of the Western Alliance. It accomplished this without financial help from outside, and while extending three and a half billion dollars in various kinds of aid to its allies.

The three armed services enlisted one and one third times as many men as in 1914–18 and lost only two thirds as many dead. In the old war the primary target had been the front-line soldier, imprisoned in his dugout or trench, pinpointed to the eighth reference point on a thousand artillery maps, under surveillance day and night by snipers and machine-gunners scarcely a hundred yards away, his only possible escape from death or injury through a chink in the law of averages.

In the new, portable war the destruction was much greater, but it was also less selective, and after two full years of it the total of killed and missing in the Army, the Navy, and the Air Force was just under a thousand, a fortieth of the ultimate sum. A part of the anomaly could be explained only by utter chance, a factor reflected in the early years by the bizarre adventures and escapes of the First Canadian Infantry Division.

The First Division sailed out of Halifax on December 10, 1939, expecting to be in the front line in Western Europe no later than the following spring. In fact, it did not engage the enemy until it landed at Pachino, Sicily, on June 10, 1943, exactly three years and six months after its departure from Nova Scotia.

But during its first year abroad, the division was committed willingly—and as the tedium of waiting mounted, eagerly—to four separate operations which in two cases possibly and in the other two probably would have ended in its suicide or decimation. And so variable were the currents of high command and so sudden the shifts of tide that it received three of its unwelcome reprieves only after it was about to embark, was already embarked, or had begun to disembark for its final destination. The fourth remission came when Hitler canceled his cross-Channel invasion of England in 1940 and with it the Canadian contingent's standing order to meet the first assault.

The division was proceeding with its training at Aldershot when the "phony war" ended in April 1940 with the German invasion of Norway. The British War Office, which itself had been on the verge of sending troops into Norway, now decided to seize the port of Narvik and the rail center of Trondheim. Two Canadian battalions, the Princess Patricia's and the Loyal Edmontons, were fitted out with winter gear, piped aboard their trains at Aldershot, drawn up before their waiting ships in Scotland—and then sent back to their base at Aldershot. In the end, unwilling to abandon the Norway operation entirely and unwilling to risk sufficient land and sea forces to give it a reasonable chance of success, the War Office dispatched an inadequate all-British expedition, which was soon withdrawn. The impatient British public was not mollified by the obvious fact that a potential disaster had been converted into nothing worse than a humiliating farce. Chamberlain was forced to resign as Prime Minister in favor of Winston Churchill.

As the perilous spring of 1940 brought the fall of Belgium and Holland, the miraculous escape of the British Expeditionary Force through Dunkirk, and the surrender of France, the Canadians became involved in two more plans far more deadly and quixotic than the fiasco in Norway.

With the shattered British Army falling back on its last beachhead in France, with its total destruction or capture apparently only days away, the War Office summoned the First Division's commander, Major General Andrew McNaughton, to a hasty conference in London. The British, already cut off from the main body of the French by the pursuing Germans, were desperately in need of protection for the road and railway on their exposed southwestern flank. McNaughton was asked to provide this with the help of a British brigade already at Calais and reinforcements from his own division.

The request was made early in the morning of May 23. By noon the First Canadian Brigade was ready to leave its bivouacs for Dover and by midnight McNaughton himself was across the Channel reconnoitering at Calais and Dunkirk.

He found the situation indescribably precarious and confused and, while the first wave of the Canadian Brigade awaited aboard ship, he hurried back to consult the War Office again. He told Sir Edmund Ironside, Chief of the Imperial Staff, that he didn't think the small Canadian reinforcement could materially improve the situation. "There seemed," according to the summary of his views in the Canadian Army official history, "little point in throwing the Canadians into the midst of a mass of dispirited soldiers and civilian refugees."

The operation was called off, but two days later it was on again, McNaughton having stipulated that arrangements must be made for the brigade's artillery to sail at the same time as the infantry. Then it was called off a second time after McNaughton told the British War Secretary, Anthony Eden, that his objection to the plan "was not based on any timidity but rather on a desire to get the best possible value for the effort made." McNaughton added that his brigade group "could go tonight complete with guns if the Prime Minister and War Cabinet decide that it should be sent." After this second cancellation Eden received an urgent appeal from Lord Gort, commander of the besieged and retreating force at Dunkirk, that at least one and if possible two Canadian brigades be sent to his aid at once. The plan had been before the British Cabinet once and now the military planners threw it back to their political superiors again. This time, Churchill, who had been in favor of sending the Canadians across the Channel all along, gave his reluctant consent to abandoning the project for good.

That it should have required a British Cabinet meeting to determine whether a Canadian brigade should go to the aid of the British Expeditionary Force in its darkest hour appears in retrospect as no more than a footnote to the larger tragedies and fantasies of 1940. Had McNaughton been a British officer and his division a British division, he would, of course, have had no choice but to accept his assignment unconditionally and carry it out at once. That he would have discussed it personally with the British

Prime Minister or the British War Secretary is almost inconceivable.

Yet all parties to the strange five-day-long hiatus had good legal and constitutional grounds to act exactly as they did. One of the many pieces of fine print which the post-1918 move toward autonomy had inserted in the contract between Britain and the dominions was an enactment headed "The Visiting Forces Acts, 1933." Under the Canadian interpretation of this agreement, Canadian troops were completely under the orders of superior British formations only when they were serving "in combination" outside Britain or had been specifically placed in their command within Britain. Otherwise—that is, when within the United Kingdom—they were officially designated as "serving together" with the British forces. And while the visiting forces remained in that state they were not under the control of the War Office or of any British commander. For their higher direction they were responsible to the government of Canada until the government delegated its authority elsewhere.

In April, McNaughton had committed part of the First Division to the abortive Norwegian sortie and placed it under British operational command without even notifying Ottawa. For this he had been firmly but politely ticked off by Colonel J. L. Ralston, his Defence Minister in Ottawa. His laborious and cautious approach to the operation at Dunkirk and the meticulous way in which the War Office abstained from giving him any outright "orders" were both a reflection of the political dynamite lurking in the Visiting Forces Act.

At the moment there was no time for brooding or reproaches.

While the first ships of the brave and motley rescue fleet were nosing into Dunkirk to save the First British Expeditionary Force from extinction, the irrepressible Churchill was already laying plans to send another expeditionary force to France at once. This time—even though the prospects of success or even survival had degenerated from the highly doubtful to the hopeless—there was no hesitation about the Canadian division's willingness to play a full part.

With 340,000 British and Allied soldiers streaming across the Channel, disorganized and unarmed, their transport smoking on the beaches of France, there were only two divisions in all of the United Kingdom fully ready and equipped to fight. One of them was the Canadian division, the other the Scottish Fifty-second.

Churchill proposed to send them both to France in the hope their appearance would stiffen the crumbling French armies and, more importantly, prevent the utter collapse of the French government and the morale of the civilian population.

It was a desperate undertaking, far more desperate than the abandoned sally into Dunkirk. It is doubtful that any Canadians except McNaughton and his brigadiers and the senior officers at Canadian Military Headquarters in Trafalgar Square fully realized they were embarking on a mission as valiant and as surely doomed as Balaclava. The two rescue divisions, supported by the remnants of two others trickling back from Dunkirk, were to deploy across a hundred and fifty miles of front at the neck of the Brittany peninsula. The object was to delay, somehow, the westward rush of four German armies long enough to permit the fleeing French to rally and form a redoubt and thus save the Allies at least a foothold in Continental Europe.

On June 2, Lieutenant General Sir Alan Brooke, just back from Dunkirk with the survivors of his Second British Corps, was called to the War Office, informed of the plan for a Second British Expeditionary Force, and appointed its commander.

Brooke later was to become Chief of the Imperial General Staff and carry for most of the war a burden of authority, responsibility, and trouble second only to Churchill's. But, he wrote after it was all over: "As I look back at the war this was certainly one of my blackest moments. I knew only too well the state of affairs that would prevail in France from now onwards. I had seen my hopes in the French Army gradually shattered throughout those long winter months; I had witnessed the realization of my worst fears concerning its fighting value and morale and now I had no false conceptions as to what its destiny must inevitably be. To be sent back into that cauldron with a new force to participate in the final stages of French disintegration was indeed a dank prospect."

Later in the day Anthony Eden sent for Brooke. "He was very charming and sympathetic and finished by asking me whether I was satisfied. . . . I think I astonished him by saying that I was far from satisfied. That the mission I was being sent on from a military point of view had no value and no possibility of accomplishing anything. . . . I continued by stating that possibly this move had some political value but I wanted him to be quite clear that the expedition I was starting on promised no chances of military success and every probability of disaster."

By the time McNaughton had digested Brooke's orders for the First Division, he too was without the slightest trace of illusion. He drafted an operations instruction which contained the laconic estimate: "A division may have to hold up to fifty miles of front." Then he had his staff bring the division's war diaries up to date and send them to London along with the bulk of the other divisional files. As Charles P. Stacey, the army historian, has noted: "The 1st Canadian Division was, in effect, making its last will and testament —as it had good reason to do."

On June 14 the main body of McNaughton's First Brigade under Brigadier Armand Smith began disembarking at Brest. Its transport, which had been shipped to France a day ahead, had been dispersed by the harassed port officers into a maze of roads already choked with civilians fleeing the other way. Smith got his three infantry battalions and his own headquarters aboard three trains and began moving them toward their allotted destination two hundred miles inland.

At approximately the same time, Brooke, the commander in chief of the British-Canadian expedition, was conferring with General Maxime Weygand, the seventy-three-year-old Supreme Commander of the Armies of France, under whose orders he had been placed. Brooke had spent the day before poking along three hundred miles of roads made almost impassable by refugees and abandoned cars and trucks and had concluded that the French could not hold out longer than a few more days.

The next day Brooke "went to see Weygand at 8.30 A.M. Found him looking very wizened and tired. . . . He said he would speak very frankly. That the French Army had ceased to be able to offer organized resistance and was disintegrating into disconnected groups. That Paris had been given up and that he had no reserves whatever left. He then stated that at the Inter-Allied Council it had been decided to hold a position covering Brittany in front of Rennes. That consequently I could concentrate the Canadian Division in the vicinity of that place."

The Canadian infantry force was now pushing eastward toward Rennes. Its artillery was already billeted in the final assembly area beyond the pivotal city.

In midmorning Brooke and Weygand drove to the headquarters

of General A. J. Georges, commander in chief of the French Armies of the Northeast. "He took me to a large wall-map with a line running across France, showing the latest fighting reports," Brooke recalled in the notes for his biography. "On this line was drawn in red chalk several sausage-shaped indentations. I asked what these represented and was informed by him that they were penetrations by German armed forces. . . . I asked him what reserves he had and, holding his hands up in a gesture of desperation, he replied: Absolutely none, not a man or gun left."

Brooke suggested they return to the question of how to defend that now very awkwardly thick neck of Brittany with a Canadian division not yet fully embarked from England, a British division, and the wreckage of two other partial survivors of Dunkirk. Weygand reaffirmed the original plan: the British-Canadian force was to hold a line stretching through Rennes from the western end of the English Channel to the northern fringe of the Bay of Biscay. "There were no existing defences on this line. No anti-tank ditch, no wire, practically no anti-tank guns to defend it with, and quite inadequate A.A. defences for the ports destined to act as bases."

Brooke placed a pair of pocket dividers on the map. The distance from coast to coast was 150 kilometers. "I drew Weygand's attention to this and he said that it could not be as much. I therefore measured the distance again under his eyes and said that to defend a front of 150 kilometers we should require at least fifteen divisions. . . . Weygand agreed that the plan was 'fantastic,' and Georges, I think, qualified it as 'romantic!' "

Weygand, nevertheless, insisted that the plan had to be carried out. But Brooke was now convinced the only course left was to take matters into his own hands. He sent a liaison officer flying back to London, returned hurriedly to his own headquarters to telephone the War Office, and finally late in the afternoon was given permission to start withdrawing.

The order to evacuate reached most formations of the Canadian brigade while they were aboard their trains going the other way. They still had seen no sign of the enemy, and when the 48th Highlanders, two hundred miles inside France in the forward train, received their instructions to retreat from a British transport officer, they mistook him for a fifth columnist. By the time the Englishman had established his *bona fides*, the French engineer had decided the whole enterprise had a fishy, dangerous smell and refused to turn his train around. He had to be persuaded to do so at gunpoint.

By various means the entire Canadian contingent got back to England with only two men lost, a dispatch rider who was killed in a crash and a straggler who was taken prisoner. The division's other two brigades were stopped as they were preparing to sail from England.

The companion Scottish division escaped through Cherbourg a bare three miles ahead of the German columns. Even after the withdrawal of the Canadians had been authorized, Churchill still stubbornly clung to the hope that the French would continue fighting so long as there was at least a token British force fighting beside them. When Brooke announced, over an uncertain telephone connection between Brittany and No. 10 Downing Street, that he proposed to pull the Fifty-second back to England, an acrimonious shouting match ensued. "He told me that was not what he wanted," Brooke recorded. "I had been sent to France to make the French feel that we were supporting them. I replied that it was impossible to make a corpse feel, and that the French Army was, to all intents and purposes, dead, and certainly incapable of registering what was done for it.

"Our talk lasted for close on half an hour and on many occasions his arguments were so formed as to give me the impression that he considered I was suffering from 'cold feet.' . . . This was so infuriating that I was repeatedly on the verge of losing my temper. Fortunately while I was talking to him I was looking through the window at Drew and Kennedy [two senior officers of the division whose fate was being discussed] sitting on a garden seat under a tree. Their presence there acted as a continual reminder of the human elements of the 52nd Division and of the unwarrantable decision to sacrifice them with no attainable object in view.

"At last, when I was in an exhausted condition, he said, 'All right, I agree with you.'"

Most of the Canadians arrived back at Aldershot quite unaware of the narrowness of their escape, complaining hotly about the indecisiveness and general lunacy of the higher brass. But the unbelievable summer of 1940 soon brought home the unbelievable truth: Britain might be and could be conquered by a hostile army for the first time since the day of William of Normandy, and if this were to be prevented, the job of preventing it might fall squarely on the Canadians, who were the closet approach to a mobile, armed, and fully manned ground division in all the British Isles.

The Royal Navy still stood guard over the Channel. The Royal Air Force, desperately outnumbered, was ready to defend the skies. But if the Germans broke through these outer palisades—as they almost certainly had the strength to do if they also had the will and ingenuity—then the fighting on the beaches and in the streets would have to be led by the First Division.

On June 25, a week after the last of his troops got back from France, McNaughton described the situation to a conference of his officers. The official summary read: "We are a mobile reserve with a 360-degree front, and may have to operate anywhere in Great Britain from the South Coast to Scotland or in Wales. The Canadian Force and two TK Bns of the 4 Corps with some Light Armed Units comprise the only mobile force immediately available in Great Britain. . . . It will be approximately ten days before the general situation regarding reserves improves. There are large numbers of troops in Great Britain but these are not yet organized in the re-constituted divisions. The degree of re-equipment is lamentably small."

Throughout that crucial July, August, and September—indeed for a full year after the fall of France—Canada was the largest and strongest nation on the Allied side next to Great Britain itself. And the First Division, ceaselessly maneuvering across the South of England to meet an army that never came, was Canada's largest and strongest military unit. The disasters on the Continent stepped up recruiting at home for the Second Division and led to the authorization of a Third, a Fourth, and, later on, a Fifth. None of these would be ready for action for many months to come.

But in this summer of 1940, the future was as meaningless as the past. The present engulfed and obliterated all else and the present was almost wholly in the hands of Adolf Hitler.

Hitler believed the thousand years he had promised the Fatherland had begun already. On the last day of Dunkirk, he began discussing plans for demobilization. Two weeks later, after the capitulation of France, his staff was organizing a victory parade in Paris and starting arrangements to send the Wehrmacht home.

Through most of July 1940 he clung to the hope that Britain would give up a palpably lost cause. He had no desire to possess

England physically and, indeed, wanted to maintain it as a buffer
state in a condition of nominal independence. Receiving one of
his generals on his mountaintop in Berchtesgaden, he confessed
himself "greatly puzzled by Britain's persisting unwillingness to
make peace." He was uneasily sure that Churchill recognized the
fragility of Germany's fake alliance with Russia and foresaw its
ultimate explosion. The disintegration of the British Empire "would
not be of any benefit to Germany," he said. "German blood would
be shed to accomplish something that would benefit only Japan,
the United States, and others."

Hitler never was able to make a consistent appraisal of the English. Nine days before he went to war he assured an assembly of
his commanders: "Our enemies are little worms; I saw them at
Munich." But now, with all of Western Europe in his grasp, with
Britain staggering from Dunkirk and only the dominions at its side,
his intuition told him the exact opposite. The final conquest, if
it had to come, would still be "hard and bloody."

He had the Luftwaffe drop peace leaflets on London. When the
incorrigible natives auctioned the leaflets off for the Red Cross he
knew they would not be beaten except by force. But he had lost
a whole month betting on the memories of Munich, and when he
called on his commanders to prepare for the capture of England,
he found them full of misgivings. For the assault wave and the
immediate follow-up, the Army told him it would have to land a
quarter of a million soldiers, nearly a thousand tanks, thirty-five
thousand trucks, cars, wagons, and tractors, and sixty thousand
horses. To get this great machine across the Channel, the German
Navy estimated it would need almost four thousand vessels.

On one thing Hitler's army and his navy could agree. Before any
invasion plan could succeed, the Royal Air Force must be defeated.
This did not seem at all impossible. In serviceable combat aircraft
the Luftwaffe outnumbered the R.A.F. almost three to one. Hermann Göring happily accepted an assignment to eliminate the
"English Air Force both as a fighting force and in its ground organization" and to "strangle England's supply lines by destroying her
ports and her shipping." Göring planned to begin the destruction
of the R.A.F. on August 10, which he designated as Eagle Day. The
corresponding code name for the invasion was "Sea Lion." The
secret signal the English had chosen to announce what might be
their nation's last battle was "Cromwell." Preposterous though it

seems in the efficient age of the atom, thousands of greengrocers, pubkeepers, and clerks really did make ready to defend their native soil with axes, pitchforks, fowling pieces, and family pikestaffs.

But "Cromwell" was not proclaimed until September 7, and then it was a false alarm. Göring's Eagle Day and the onslaughts that followed it failed—though only barely—to win command of the sky. Hitler never gave the order to put "Sea Lion" in motion. All his enterprises began cracking down in the Battle of Britain.

On the first day of the total air assault, postponed almost a week by weather, the R.A.F.'s Hurricanes and Spitfires shot down 76 of the invaders. On the last day they shot down 56. Counting the preliminaries of the battle in July and early August and the post-scripts in late September, the defenders destroyed 1400 German aircraft while losing half that number.

The victory was built of many things. The Hurricane was a tough and dependable aircraft. The Spitfire, equated to the time and place in which it served, was one of the most efficient military instruments ever built. The men who flew these planes, and, to an equal degree, the men who directed them from the ground, had brought their skills to a pitch neither required nor possible in the plodding Dorniers, Heinkels, and Junkers of the Luftwaffe. The new miracle of radar was at their command.

Göring spent his resources at a fixed 2 to 5 per cent a day trying to bring the British fighters to battle on his terms. He attacked their airfields and landing strips, their ports and harbors, and their fac-tories, and finally he threw everything he had left into a massive assault on London. By mid-September he had been turned back everywhere, and the inspired madmen of Fighter Command, not content with the wonder of their survival, were racing across the Channel to blow up the German invasion barges.

On September 17, the official diary of the German Naval Staff made this notation: "The enemy air force is by no means defeated; on the contrary it shows increasing activity. The weather situation as a whole does not permit us to expect a period of calm. The Führer has therefore decided to postpone Operation Sea Lion in-definitely."

The fledgling Royal Canadian Air Force, destined to a rate of growth and an importance no one then could have dreamed, re-ceived its baptism during the Battle of Britain. The first of its forty-eight fighter squadrons was in action through the last eight weeks of the main engagement and its aftermath, and was credited with thirty-one kills against the loss of sixteen Hurricanes.

The sparse, compact, sudden-death nature of this new kind of warfare was sometimes reflected in the combat reports of the pilots. Squadron Leader Ernest McNab, commanding officer of the Canadian Force, summed up one short mission fairly typically: "I was Caribou Leader leading 4 sections No. 1 Canadian Squadron, and leading squadron combined with 303. Ordered to intercept raid . . . sighted raiders 10 miles East at 18,000, turned and forced to make an astern attack. The bombers were in section three's stepped down. Attacked left hand JU. 88 in rear section. He broke away and dropped his bombs turning toward south coast and I followed in with section. Two parachutes came out but man in first fell away from his, the second was badly ripped. The aircraft continued to fly south, so I closed and gave 2-second burst, the aircraft dived straight down and burst into flames at Limpsfield. This is claimed for Blue section."

Another pilot of the Canadian squadron described a dogfight: "Took off with squadron but forced to return as wheels would not come up. Took second plane up in an effort to overtake squadron. Saw squadron above and about six miles away, at same time saw bandits to left (above) and ahead to the right. Started to climb and while climbing to right saw e/a below and ahead. Saw red, white and blue stripes on rudder but saw another Hurricane make an attack. Closed in behind e/a after Hurricane broke away. E/a was apparently not damaged by first attack, as I experienced extreme gunfire when I attacked. Attacked and held firing button for 275 rounds per gun. Pieces were flying off and one engine smoking as I broke and climbed to make second attack. E/a burst into flame and dove straight for the ground. Saw e/a crash 5 miles E. of Tunbridge Wells. No person jumped out of e/a. This enemy casualty is confirmed by F/L. Kent of 303 Sqn."

In the crowded skies of Surrey and Sussex the whole fate of man was at stake. Hitler chose to ignore his defeat and summoned Molotov, the Russian Foreign Minister, to discuss the division of the British Empire. In Berlin late on a November night, the Russian found himself going over the details with his opposite number, Ribbentrop. It was an unhappy meeting. Ribbentrop insisted that Germany had already won the war and, therefore, was entitled to say how the spoils should be distributed. "If England is in fact defeated and powerless," Molotov snapped back at him, "why have we been conducting this discussion in your air-raid shelter?"

The dictators, having banished ordinary trust from the conduct of human affairs, discovered that without trust they were lost. Hitler could have survived only by trusting Stalin. Mussolini could have survived only by trusting Hitler. Russia could have shared Western Europe only by trusting Germany. But the dictators were all absolutely and justifiably certain that they must either betray their allies or be betrayed themselves.

At the height of their love affair, Molotov could not refrain from warning Hitler that Russia intended to be "a partner and not a dummy." Hitler hinted darkly at the need to "prevent this war from becoming the father of a new war." They haggled over the last square inch of Bulgaria, Rumania, Turkey, and Finland. Hitler did his best to see that his two strongest friends, Russia and Japan, did not become friendly with each other, for he had already made his plans to demolish one of them and to use the other to help him do it. He was alternately bullying and coaxing Franco in Spain, trying to wheedle him into attacking Gibraltar and of half a mind to do it himself even if it meant bombing Madrid and Barcelona as well. He had given up on Mussolini, whose feeble attempt to seize Greece and the Balkans without Germany's permission had opened up a whole new war.

XLIII

The Royal Canadian Navy—The handy whaling
ship called the corvette—The Battle
of the Atlantic

THE problems of Britain and its allies were, though more pressing, a good deal simpler. Their worry was not how to partition the world, but how to stay alive in it. To England and the dominions the essential struggle was not diplomatic or political, not Hitler against Stalin, or not even Churchill against them both; it was the Spitfire against the Messerschmitt, the Cromwell against the Tiger, the 5.5-inch gun against the 88-millimeter, the destroyer against the U-boat.

In all these contests, the Commonwealth began at a disadvantage of either quantity or quality. Nowhere was the disparity so dangerous as in the war at sea.

Germany had almost won in 1917 by winning the Atlantic. Now, with the fight for the English Channel and the sky over Britain at least temporarily settled, the Atlantic became the main arena again. This was Britain's sole life stream, and if it were closed off even for a week or two the result would be fatal. Canada undertook the job of defending the life stream's source—the harbors and approaches of North America.

In the military sense the country had no seafaring tradition, no experience, equipment, or even pride. The mention of war at sea called up no memories more heroic than the parliamentary filibusters of thirty years before, the diatribes against a "tin-pot navy," the ill-famed sisters *Rainbow* and *Niobe*, the *I'm Alone* and other rum-runners of the twenties and early thirties. When Canada undertook the Battle of the Atlantic it had neither ships nor sailors. Moreover, it had no clear idea of the kind of ships and sailors it would need if it could get them.

This state of unpreparedness offered at least one compensation. Compelled to start from scratch, the Royal Canadian Navy was free to experiment. In the first emergency it had to use what was available, notably a share of the old destroyers Britain obtained from the United States in a trade for airfields and harbors. But in its long-range planning the Canadian Navy not only could but was forced to venture into the unknown.

Its basic task was to guard its own coastal waters and protect merchant shipping in the first thousand miles of the western Atlantic. With this in mind, the Navy risked everything on a ship that had just been built and had never been properly tried—the corvette.

The real father of the corvettes was necessity—the constant demand for vessels agile enough, numerous enough, and expendable enough to keep the U-boats down, or at least make them work and sometimes die for their massive kills against the sitting ducks of the British, Canadian, and neutral merchant marines.

Only through the great artery of the ocean could Britain receive its oil from South America and its food and arms from the United States and Canada. Only if this artery was kept open could the Middle East be saved and Russia remain a fighting force. Only with supplies from the Atlantic and the ability to win battles there could the coming invasions of North Africa, Sicily, Italy, and finally Normandy be committed and arranged. Ships were needed at once and in the water, not distantly and on the drawing boards. The corvettes became, in the phrase of a gambling man, "the only game in town."

The first of them were the work of a Tees-side shipbuilder named William Reed. Reed had been called upon to study submarines in the 1914 war, and as any reliable man from the Tees would have done, he came to the unruffled conclusion that there was nothing at all new or mysterious about them. They were really only a mechanized whale. On the surface they swam at high speed. They could dive quickly and deep, and once submerged, they maneuvered with great cleverness and a fine instinct for survival. The best way to kill a whale, Reed knew without wasting much time on theory, was from a whaling ship. He set out to create a fast, responsive little vessel that could hunt the U-boats as skillfully as the captains of Lunenburg and Nantucket had once hunted an older quarry.

The first corvettes were officially designated as "patrol vessels, whaler type," and Canada ultimately built and sailed more than a hundred of them. They were about the size of a good Manitoba barn, 190 feet long and 33 feet wide. They carried one small cannon, two machine guns, several tons of depth charges, and a crew of a hundred. They could do sixteen knots, the same as a surfaced submarine. They were easy to make, easy to handle, and most important of all, they were there.

It has often been said that Britain or Canada, or the two of them together, won the Battle of the Atlantic. It would be more accurate to say that they avoided losing it. The U-boats had the insuperable advantage of three million square miles of shipping lanes to hide beneath and an unending procession of targets plodding back and forth above. In the first year of the war, with the help of mines, planes, and surface raiders, they sank four million tons of Allied shipping, nearly a thousand ships in all, the equivalent in total size of fifty *Queen Elizabeths*. For every Allied merchantman built, three were being sunk. For every U-boat sunk, eight were being built. And appalling as was the damage they did in 1940, it kept growing in 1941, 1942, and 1943. In terms of losses and replacements, Germany was winning the Battle of the Atlantic hands down, and drawing further ahead every day and every hour.

It was into these disastrous seas that the Royal Canadian Navy launched its corvettes, its handful of destroyers, and its converted yachts and pleasure steamers, and began discovering new ways to use them. By the middle of 1942, Canada was doing 40 per cent of the escort work in the North Atlantic. By the end of the war, it was doing it all. And from the Atlantic war's turning point in mid-1943 the submarines were in retreat.

The reversal would not have been possible if Britain and the United States had not developed and largely provided a blanket of air support. Britain also supplied a mobile force of big ships and a series of new scientific wonders that kept the Allies abreast of, and for most of the time slightly ahead of, the enemy in the unending struggle of invention. The Canadian contribution on the high seas was, nevertheless, an impressive and essential one.

The convoy system worked in various ways. The "short-legged" corvettes—of which Britain as well as Canada had a number—could not go all the way across the ocean without refueling, and the destroyers could make the full voyage only by giving up their freedom to hunt and range. The pattern in the early years was that

Canada supplied protection for the western third of the ocean and Britain for the eastern third. For the middle third, where they had more room to deploy and the Germans less chance of intercepting, the cargo vessels were on their own. Tankers creeping north from the Caribbean along the United States seaboard had, at first, no escorts at all. Then the German admiralty moved twenty subs into the "U-boat paradise" between Trinidad and Newfoundland, and began torpedoing the coastal ships by the dozen, by the score, and finally by the hundred. Trying to hug the doubtful haven of the beaches from Key West up past Charleston, Cape Hatteras, Norfolk, and Boston, more than two hundred ships went down within easy sight of shore.

By late 1942 a system of north-south convoys chased most of the U-boats off the coastal run, but not before they had broken into the very heartland of Canada, the Gulf of St. Lawrence. A bare two hundred miles below Quebec, where Cartier, Kirke, and Wolfe had once dropped anchor, Lieutenant Commander Paul Hartwig and the U-517 set up a private shooting gallery. Between there and Newfoundland they sank more than thirty thousand tons in a single mission.

But the ultimate decision on the Atlantic was not reached near its shores. It came on the murderous gray prairie in between. The ocean, usually so friendly to and tolerant of men's enterprises, seemed itself to catch the merciless spirit of the war. It produced some of the worst weather in its history, and the ships had to go where the weather was worst. The convoy route was north, into savage gales and snow, up past Greenland and Iceland, through a world entombed in freezing cold and the dark side of the Midnight Sun. The winter storms lashed the convoys at fifty, sixty, sometimes a hundred miles an hour. Spray and sleet smothered their guns, their decks, and their superstructures in a foot or more of solid ice.

At least one ship thus weighed down simply rolled over and sank with all hands. Others buckled and broke apart. And whether the death of his ship was inflicted by the Germans or the sea itself, the individual sailor's chance of surviving it was never good. A man floating or swimming or clinging to a raft after a winter sinking in the North Atlantic had a life expectancy of five minutes. It seldom took longer for the subarctic wet and cold to paralyze and kill him. On the summer runs and in the coastal convoys from South America and, later, into the Mediterranean, a hazard just as deadly was oil—

oil burning on the surface or waterlogging clothes and lifebelts, until a sailor caught in it either suffocated above water or drowned below.

For Canadians the first war reached its depth of misery and entrapment in the trenches of Ypres and Passchendaele. In the second war the trenches were the cold, dark, rumbling bellies of the escort ships and the merchant vessels. The U-boats, at least at first, were a little better off. A submarine could do nine knots below the water and sixteen knots above. It had enough speed to keep up with a convoy by day, attack it by night, and still dive and run from the three-hundred-pound depth charges of the destroyers and corvettes.

Most of the submarines had two hulls, so that they might limp home on the inner one even though a depth bomb had wrecked or dented the outer one. They had no way of making a sure escape from asdic, the sound signal that bounced against them through the sea and told their enemies where they were. Nor when the planes of Coastal Command and the Fleet Air Arm joined the fight did they have a certain defense against radar and sudden attack from the sky. But a depth charge had to explode within twenty feet of a U-boat to break or cripple it. Many a submarine got away after being trapped and hunted for hours by the pings of enemy asdic and the crashing canisters of high explosive. Many a subchaser was fooled by the submarine commanders' trick, when caught and under fire, of emptying oil and waste through their torpedo tubes to create the illusion that they were destroyed already.

Long after the time of blackest crisis, long after Russia and the United States were in the struggle too, the fight in the Atlantic remained a matter of life and death for all the Allies. "The U-boat warfare," Churchill said as late as February 1943, "takes first place in our thoughts." In the previous June, General George Marshall had told the American naval commander, Ernest King, "The losses by submarines off our Atlantic seaboard and in the Caribbean now threaten our entire war effort. . . . I am fearful that another month or two of this will so cripple our means of transport that we will be unable to bring sufficient men and planes to bear against the enemy to exercise a determining influence on the war."

When the tide changed, it changed with almost unbelievable swiftness. More than half a million tons of Allied shipping were lost between Newfoundland and England in March 1943. But by April, long-ranging bombers and long-ranging cruisers, destroyers and frigates, and a new force of aircraft carriers had come to the aid of the battered escort ships and the cargo vessels in their custody. And the losses were cut in half. Although Hitler had given an absolute priority to submarines in the German economy, Grand Admiral Karl Doenitz was obliged to report to him that "the enemy by means of new location devices for the first time makes it impossible to carry on the fight." Hitler, nevertheless, would not break off the battle that had come so close to winning him all he sought for. He told Doenitz angrily: "There can be no talking of a letup in the U-boat campaign. The Atlantic is my first line of defense in the West and, even if I have to fight a defensive battle there, that is preferable to waiting to defend myself on the coast of Europe." But mere determination was of little avail. At the peak of the hunt, Germany had been able to count on destroying sixty thousand tons of Allied shipping for every lost U-boat. Now the return was down to four thousand tons. In March, Doenitz's Atlantic squadrons sank ninety merchantmen; in June, six.

The Royal Canadian Navy had other battles ahead or in the making in support of the great land campaign in Africa, Sicily, Italy, and Western Europe. But its greatest contribution to victory was made on the vital patrols out of Halifax and St. John's. Only when the summaries of supply were completed and the final analyses made of everything that went into the winning of the war as a whole could the Canadian Navy begin to know how well it had done.

XLIV

The R Men and the A Men—The start of another long dispute over conscription—The disaster of Hong Kong

WHILE the Navy was learning how to sail, the Air Force how to fly, and the Army how to stand and wait, the country behind them was still sorting out its motives and procedures.

No large nation ever came into so large a war with less obvious reason than Canada did when it entered the Second World War. It had no Pearl Harbor to force it in. Unlike France, it had no tanks and guns glowering from the Rhineland and the dragon's teeth of the Siegfried Line. Unlike Britain, it had no threat of being starved by sea, battered by air, and overrun by land. Unlike Russia, it had no vision of setting the whole world aflame and raking up the ashes. Unlike Germany, Japan, and Italy, it had no expectation of booty and more room. Unlike Australia and New Zealand, it was not marooned in the shadow of a hostile giant.

Of all the ultimate participants in the war, Canada had the least palpable and pressing stake of any. This—together with the memories of a not dissimilar situation in 1914 and the conscription troubles of 1917—was the background against which the country mobilized.

The early rush of volunteers was embarrassingly heavy and thousands of them had to be turned away. But when the first surge of excitement wore off, when the military establishment grew far beyond all prediction, and when civilian jobs grew more numerous and better paid, the task of keeping the forces up to strength became an immensely complicated one.

The government was committed to two propositions, each the exact opposite of the other:

1. Canada could not wait for the war to reach its shores, but must send men abroad to intercept it.

2. No man should be sent abroad unless he wanted to go.

King sought a remedy for this schizophrenia by proclaiming a National Resources Mobilization Act. The N.R.M.A. was modified several times, but its chief design was to conscript men of military age for training and home defense and then, if possible, to persuade them to volunteer for service overseas.

Often this process of converting the home-defense conscript into an overseas volunteer degenerated into sheer bullying. But it sustained the illusion of no-conscription-for-overseas, until just before the war's end.

In the fall of 1940 the government introduced compulsory training in the militia. Thirty thousand men a month were required to serve a month in military camps. They learned little more than how to march and peel potatoes in that short time and with the limited equipment available, and in early 1941 the compulsory training period was increased to four months. Then it was extended indefinitely. The men who were drafted were in the Army for the duration of the war, but only for home defense. They had the choice of staying in Canada or in outposts close to Canada, or of enlisting for service anywhere as members of the Canadian Active Service Force.

Thus the Canadian Army had two basic kinds of soldier. One was the R Man—the member of the Reserve—who had been conscripted for duty in Canada but had not seen fit to volunteer for service abroad. The other was the A Man—the member of the Active force—who had volunteered for service anywhere without being drafted or who, having been drafted for home defense only, decided to go all the way and make himself available for fighting wherever he might be sent.

Inevitably and quickly the existence of two such armies side by side led to frictions and differences of the ugliest kind. In their training camps it was the habit—and in many cases the deliberate policy—to mix the R Men and A Men in fairly close ratios and hope that by moral pressure and sometimes by actual physical violence the A Men would help persuade the R Men to "go active" too. Between the two groups there were small distinctions in such things as cap badges and service ribbons and quite often larger ones in their treatment by their officers and noncommissioned officers. Officially there was no discrimination against the R Men and none has ever been officially admitted, but as an Active Service volunteer—who at that time shared the general prejudice against the R Men—the present writer can testify from his own experience that there was. So can thousands of other ex-servicemen.

It was some time before anyone thought of a better epithet for the R Men than Mothers' Boys or Maple Leaf Wonders, the latter for their special insignia. Then some unknown master of invective gave them the name Zombies and the division between them and the rest of the armed services took on a bitterness that no one ever had intended.

It may conceivably be decided in time that the Zombies had as much right to be bitter as anyone else. Since they were called up by age groups, they were relatively young and many either had little idea what the war was about or had no urge to be destroyed in it. Some were idealistic young pacifists of the kind who had very recently been signing pledges and taking part in freshman or high school debates against the whole idea of war. Others were French Canadians whose whole instinct and training told them to avoid the far-off, perpetual bloodshed of Europe. Others were simply farm boys who wanted to stay on the farm, still others young men with girls they wanted to chase or marry.

Many of them were, of course, and not unnaturally, scared stiff of the whole idea of being shot at. Some—and perhaps more of them than has yet been realized—would have been willing to fight anywhere their country told them to if others like them had been told the same. As it was, thousands and tens of thousands of them rejected and continued to reject the mixed coaxing and coercion to which they were subjected by an army that was trying to conscript them without being allowed the machinery of conscription. Though in the end Canada raised and put in action a phenomenally large number of able and willing soldiers, some of the methods of raising them strongly resembled the fraternity rush and college haze, were quite unworthy of the solemn enterprise they supported, and not surprisingly led to immense trouble later on.

But in the first years of the war the problems of manpower in the Canadian land forces lay far ahead. With Russia neutral, Germany triumphant, France defeated, Britain on the defensive, and Mussolini floundering in the Balkans and North Africa, Europe had almost ceased to be a major battlefield.

On the ground the Canadians continued to grow in number and continued in their frustrating role of garrison troops. There were some Canadian engineers on duty at Gibraltar and another small force was sent to occupy Spitsbergen. A few Canadian officers were detached to acquire battle experience with the British in Africa, but with these exceptions the Army did literally no fighting until late in 1941. Then, ironically, the Army's first major engagement—the Navy and Air Force were, of course, already heavily engaged—was fought halfway around the world from its base in England.

The British suspicion that Japan would ultimately attack had begun to form almost a full year before the attack took place. When and if this happened, the crown colony of Hong Kong would obviously become a rich prize for the Japanese, and perhaps the most difficult of all places in the British Empire to defend. Sitting on and beside a tiny spur of China—part island and part peninsula—the colony had roughly the population and size of modern Toronto. It was not of vital importance in the military sense, but as Britain's best-known remaining foothold in the mid-upper Pacific, it was apparent that in any war involving Britain and Japan it would have tremendous psychological and commercial importance.

Winston Churchill nevertheless decided as early as January 1941 —eleven months before Pearl Harbor—that any serious attempt to reinforce the small Hong Kong garrison would be "all wrong." He wrote his Chief of Staff: "If Japan goes to war there is not the slightest chance of holding Hong Kong or relieving it. It is most unwise to increase the loss we shall suffer there. Instead of increasing the garrison it ought to be reduced to a symbolical scale. . . . I wish we had fewer troops there, but to move any more would be noticeable and dangerous."

The Chiefs of Staff were temporarily persuaded to Churchill's view and admitted that to send reinforcements to the colony in early 1941 would be to "throw good money after bad." But soon afterward they came to the view that even a token show of strength at Hong Kong might help to deter the Japs from going to war and accordingly, with Canada's full consent, two Canadian battalions were sent to the colony to reinforce the four British battalions already there.

No one, of course, was yet sure that they would have to fight, which furnishes whatever excuse there was for the fact that they were sent only partly trained and badly equipped. They arrived on the hills of Hong Kong Island and the Kowloon Peninsula with no transport at all. Their vehicles had been put on the wrong ships.

When the Japanese attacked, the two Canadian battalions—the Winnipeg Grenadiers and the Royal Rifles of Canada—were part of a total British fighting force of just over ten thousand. They fought well, but the far stronger invaders soon drove them out of their main line of defense, the picturesquely named Gin Drinkers Line, and the campaign was over in seventeen days. Ultimately, through battle casualties and mistreatment after capture, more than one in four of the total Canadian force of nearly two thousand lost his life.

Shortly after news of the disaster reached Canada, Lieutenant Colonel George Drew, leader of the Conservative party in Ontario, charged that the whole enterprise had been mismanaged and ill prepared. The government then began (but soon dropped) prosecution against Drew under the wartime regulations that forbade statements likely to prejudice recruiting. It also ordered an inquiry into the Hong Kong episode by Chief Justice Sir Lyman Duff of the Supreme Court. Duff found a number of things to criticize in the manner in which the expedition was equipped, but in authorizing the expedition, he decided, there had been "no dereliction of duty either on the part of the Government of Canada or its military advisers."

The Tory press joined Drew in crying "whitewash!" The one irrefutable fact seemed to be that, in asking Canada to send reinforcements to a position it had no real capacity or intention to defend, the British War Cabinet had fallen back into the practice that had brought on Borden's famous outburst of a quarter of a century before. Momentarily at least, Britain was again treating the government and military forces of Canada as "toy automata" to do as asked or bidden and be told as little as possible. For instance, the Canadian government was not told of Churchill's first realistic view of the impossibility of holding Hong Kong against a Japanese invasion, and as late as October 26, only six weeks before Pearl Harbor and eight days after the openly militaristic Tojo had become Premier of Japan, the British government was assuring Canada that war in the Far East was "unlikely at present."

The magnificent fiasco of Dieppe—Its costs and its returns

A MUCH more costly and a much more useful battle was fought by Canadian land forces eight months after Hong Kong, on August 19, 1942. This was the majestic fiasco of Dieppe, where a raid in force led by the Canadian Second Division ended in a bloody and almost total failure but provided many of the lessons which made the full-scale invasion of Normandy in 1944 a decisive and unexpectedly inexpensive success.

In a sense the military commanders of the West—and to an even greater degree the political commanders—were back where Haig, Foch, Lloyd George, and Clemenceau had been through most of the earlier war. Confronted with a stalemate, they were impelled toward the conclusion that a dubious battle was better than no battle at all.

Russia was now in the war, fighting for its life against the "ally" it had freed to overrun Poland in 1939 and France, Belgium, and Holland in 1940. Molotov, who had been so recently discussing the division of Europe with Hitler and Ribbentrop, was now in London and Washington demanding of Churchill and Roosevelt that they come to the Soviets' help—and of course their own—by launching an immediate second front in Western Europe.

Much as the Western Allies might have been tempted to let the Soviets pay the full price of their unholy bargain with Hitler, any such course appeared—at least then—to be out of the question. With a powerful Japan on the side of the Axis, the arguments for giving all possible relief and assistance to Russia were unanswerable. Although the United States was heavily engaged with Japan and was still in a relatively primitive stage of its military build-up, Roosevelt—against the advice of his chief military and diplomatic advisers

—gave Molotov what amounted to an undertaking that the second front would be opened in 1942. Churchill agreed to a tripartite communiqué that "full understanding" had been reached "with regard to the urgent tasks of creating a second front in Europe in 1942." But he added in an *aide-mémoire* to Molotov that no one could yet be sure whether the operation would prove feasible so soon and therefore that Britain could give no promise that it would actually be undertaken.

Nevertheless, the American military planners continued to press for an almost immediate assault on Western Europe. When Lord Louis Mountbatten visited Washington in June, Roosevelt suggested the possibility of at least a "sacrifice" landing before the year was over.

Churchill clung to his belief that the Western Allies should follow two main principles: "(*a*) No substantial landing in France unless we are going to stay; and (b) no substantial landing in France unless the Germans are demoralized by another failure against Russia. . . . We should recognize that, if Russia is in dire straits, it would not help her for us to come a hasty cropper on our own."

Canada was only on the extreme periphery of the argument, but Mackenzie King's instinctive position was similar to Churchill's. At a meeting of the Pacific War Council in Washington in April, Roosevelt spoke of the desired early invasion and added happily that the Canadian troops in England were "raring to go." So they were, but King wasn't. He feared the President was "crowding matters pretty strongly" and hastened to make it clear that Canada was not agreeing to "an immediate attack on Germany." Before such an attack took place, he emphasized, there "would have to be the strongest reasons" for believing it would be successful. If it failed "there would be no saving of Britain thereafter, with the consequences that would flow therefrom."

That was as strong an expression of Canada's views as anyone ever gave. The major Allies continued the debate among themselves and with growing heat. A closer look at the arithmetic involved revealed a shortage of landing craft so acute that a first-wave assault force of only five thousand men would have had to attack an Atlantic Wall behind which Hitler had twenty-five divisions. But the American commanders remained adamant. When the British planners remained equally so, the U. S. Secretary of War, Henry L. Stimson, joined his top subordinates, General Marshall and Admiral

King, in suggesting that the President lay down an ultimatum: either the British would agree to a Channel crossing in 1942 or the United States would withdraw its agreement that Germany must be defeated before Japan. Stimson's diary summarized his furious attitude: "As the British won't go through with what they agreed to, we will turn our back on them and take up the war with Japan." Roosevelt refused to accede to what Stimson later admitted was meant to be a "bluff."

When, at last, the decision against a 1942 invasion was taken on July 22, General Dwight Eisenhower, who was already in England to launch the preparations, thought it might well go down as "the blackest day in history." Later Eisenhower changed his mind and came around to the view that the decision to make substitute landings in North Africa had been a wise one.

But by now relations between the United States and Britain—at least at the senior military level—were almost as precarious as relations between Russia and Britain. The latter were to reach a climax three weeks later, when Churchill visited "this sullen, sinister Bolshevik state" to break the news in person to Stalin that there would be no second front in 1942. There followed their strange and now famous series of flowery toasts and angry quarrels, with Stalin railing: "When are you going to start fighting? Are you going to let us do all the work while you look on?" and Churchill pounding the table and roaring back in kind.

Knowing full well how Stalin would accept the news, Churchill had already given his consent to a number of small cross-Channel raids and to the much larger Canadian raid at Dieppe—which actually took place less than a week after his arrival in Moscow.

To say that Dieppe was a purely political battle would be a gross exaggeration, for it did have a serious military purpose and, in turn, a major military value. But its object was not purely military. Mountbatten, the Chief of Combined Operations and therefore the officer in supreme command of all the cross-Channel raids, admitted to some doubts about their usefulness, but he had been ordered to make them "as part of the general decision" come to by the War Cabinet and the Chiefs of Staff. "There are political reasons why I feel certain that they will not cancel them," he wrote one of his senior colleagues. The official biographer of Sir Alan Brooke, Chief of the Imperial General Staff, has written of Dieppe: "When, owing to unfavourable weather, it had to be postponed, the officer responsible for the military side, Lieutenant-General Montgomery, had recommended that it should be abandoned in view of the security risks in remounting it. But because of American and Russian feelings and the importance of obtaining data for later landings, the Prime Minister had favored proceeding with the landing."

Aside from mollifying the United States and Russia and spreading possible confusion among the Germans, the chief object of the Dieppe raid was to gain experience in an amphibious assault against a strongly held and fortified enemy coast. There were at least half a dozen questions about tactics and weapons which would have to be answered with at least partial accuracy if the second-front landings were to have a reasonable chance. Which the better gamble: to prepare the way or to dispense with the bombardment and try for surprise? Could a major, well-defended port be seized from the sea without so badly damaging it that it would be of no value in the critical first hours and days of the follow-up and the build-up? Could tanks be landed in the first wave and, if so, what chance had they of getting across the beaches and sea walls? What new engineering equipment and other weapons would be most useful? Was it best to work to split-second timing and an absolutely fixed plan, and if not, how much discretionary power should be left to the officers on the ground?

These problems and others almost as important had all been solved in theory and the solutions tested in unopposed exercises. But they had never been tried out in battle against the kind of defenses the Germans were known to have in Western Europe. Dieppe made sense only if it were considered as an exercise with live ammunition aimed to kill; considered thus, it made a good deal of sense, even after allowing for the haste imposed by political pressures.

All the senior officers and planners concerned were agreed on the necessity of the raid, or one similar to it, and—with the sole exception of Montgomery—all were optimistic about its prospects. Mountbatten said it would be "of great value as training." Canada's senior officer in Britain, General McNaughton, could have vetoed the participation of the Canadian Second Division, but after studying the outline plan he cabled Ottawa: "I am satisfied (*a*) objective is worthwhile (*b*) land forces detailed are sufficient (*c*) sea and air forces adequate (*d*) arrangements for co-operation satisfactory. I have therefore accepted this outline plan and authorized detail planning to proceed."

The Canadian corps commander, Lieutenant General H. D. G. Crerar, was assured by the divisional commander, Major General J. H. Roberts, that he and his brigadiers had "full confidence in their ability to carry out their tasks—given a break in luck." Crerar added on his own part: "I agree that the plan is sound, and most carefully worked out. I should have no hesitation in tackling it, if in Roberts' place."

As noted, Montgomery, who was at first in over-all command of the land forces, favored calling the operation off after weather forced a postponement. (As it happened, the security leak he feared did not occur.) Even his initial letter of approval was full of the hedges typical of the most careful and painstaking of all the Allied generals: "I am satisfied that the operation as planned is a possible one," he wrote, "and has good prospects of success, given: (*a*) Favourable weather. (*b*) Average luck. (*c*) That the Navy put us ashore roughly in the right places, and at the right times."

The total front to be attacked covered ten miles of cliff and beach and five major strong points, including Dieppe itself. The main assault force consisted of six infantry battalions of the Second Division and one regiment of the First Army Tank Brigade. The two flank operations were assigned to two British Commando units and a detachment of fifty men from the First U. S. Ranger Battalion. Of a total force of 6100, just under 5000 were Canadians. Air support, while heavy, was to be confined largely to fighters and reconnaissance planes and there was to be no preliminary bombardment of the town itself either by sea or air.

Allied intelligence on the German defenses, except in one or two minor details, was remarkably good. German intelligence on the Allied preparations was less efficient. As early as July the Germans had detected the first concentration of ships around the Isle of Wight; they were reasonably certain that some sort of cross-Channel attack was coming soon, but where and when they learned only when it began. After examining the German records, Charles P. Stacey, the Canadian Army's official historian, has concluded that "we can say with complete certainty that [the enemy] had no fore-knowledge whatever of the raid."

This is not to say that the enemy was unprepared. Hitler took the Roosevelt-Churchill-Molotov declaration in favor of a 1942 invasion to mean a little more than it said, and had been strengthening the Channel defenses and thickening up the reserves behind them throughout the spring and early summer. "A solid line with un-broken fire must be insisted on at all costs," he had decreed. "During the winter, with fanatical zeal, a fortress must be built which will hold in any circumstances." Between March and August, German ground strength in France, Belgium, and Holland increased by nine divisions, and in spite of the continued pressure on the Eastern Front, nearly half the Luftwaffe squadrons were either in the West or the Mediterranean.

Dieppe itself, besides the natural obstacle of high cliffs over-looking the beaches, was protected by a growing number of con-crete pillboxes and artillery positions and an unbroken line of barbed wire. There were nearly fifty field and coastal guns and howitzers, ranging in size from French 75s to German 150-millimeters, plus three antiaircraft batteries and a few antitank guns. Although the 302d Infantry Division, the area's first-line defender, had to stand sentry on a total frontage of fifty miles, there were ample reserves behind it.

Almost precisely an hour before the scheduled touch-down, the "break in luck" that Roberts, Crerar, Montgomery, and other officers concerned in the enterprise had considered so important began go-ing the other way. The time was 3:47 A.M. By now the assault troops had been transferred from their mother ships to small landing craft for the last ten-mile run to the beaches. There, in the darkness and to the surprise and consternation of both forces, twenty-three of the landing craft and their three armed escorts ran head on into a small German coastal convoy and its armed escorts. There followed a small naval engagement, short and indecisive in itself but still loud and confusing enough to alert the German shore batteries on the left and scatter the corresponding part of the landing fleet. The result was that fewer than a third of the British No. 3 Com-mando got ashore and most of them were pinned down and either killed, wounded, or forced to surrender by midmorning.

The other British Commando, No. 4, commanded by the dashing young Lord Lovat, met with a far different fate. Alone of the five landing groups, it achieved its full objectives and retired on schedule after capturing and destroying all the guns and killing most of the gunners of the German coastal battery on the extreme right. Lovat was able to report his mission accomplished as early as 8:50 A.M., when he sent the laconic and only slightly exaggerated wireless message to his friend Mountbatten: "Every one of gun crews finished with bayonet. OK by you?"

The disasters sustained by the seven Canadian units attacking on the three central sectors varied only in degree. Without exception the commanders of the landing craft carrying them in had difficulty meeting their exact time schedules and pin points of beach; many of the slow, sledlike, thin-skinned little vessels were blown up or badly damaged by the shore batteries before they reached land, and for the infantrymen and tank crews who got ashore—as the great majority unfortunately did—the attack became within minutes, or at most an hour or two, a hopeless defense. Nevertheless, each of the seven units made at least some slight penetration inland, and on the favored western sector, between Lovat's Commandos and the city itself, the South Saskatchewan Regiment and the Cameron Highlanders of Canada got between a mile and two miles inland before they were driven back with heavy losses.

Immediately to the east of the city, beneath the high sea wall and higher cliffs of the village of Puys, under close fire from mortars and a protected machine-gun position and cut off from retreat by the sea and from advance by barbed wire, the Royal Regiment of Canada suffered virtual extinction. Precisely one in every two of its 554 officers and men died either there on the beach or a little later of wounds or in prisoner-of-war camps. Of its total strength only 65 got back to England and of these only 22 were unwounded. Thus, during the three hours between the landing and the surrender of their last pitiful remnants under the littered and blood-strewn sea wall, the Royal's total percentage of casualties was over 96 per cent.

The attack in the middle, before the famous esplanade and casino at Dieppe itself, was made by two infantry battalions, the Essex Scottish and the Royal Hamilton Light Infantry, and one armored unit, the Calgary Tank Regiment. Two other units, the Fusiliers Mont-Royal and the Royal Marine "A" Commando, lay offshore in their landing craft as reinforcements.

Since this main part of the assault had been deliberately scheduled for half an hour later than the flank landings, surprise was neither hoped for nor intended there. Accordingly, as the landing craft drew to within a mile of shore four destroyers and five squadrons of Hurricanes laid down a barrage from their four-inch guns and smaller aerial cannon. This achieved its main purpose of forcing the enemy to keep his head down while the first waves scrambled to the beach. But unfortunately the three landing craft bringing in the first nine tanks missed their course slightly and touched down more than ten minutes late. By then the air and naval bombardment was over, the Germans had their heads up again, the whole beach was under heavy fire, and the infantry had already taken severe losses.

Altogether twenty-nine tanks left their landing craft. Two lurched down the ramps too soon and were "drowned" in deep water. Approximately half the rest bogged down in sand and shingle or were stopped by the sea wall. Those that struck for the wall's low-lying ends got over it to the esplanade only to find a row of concrete obstacles barring their way into the city proper. But although the armored regiment was virtually immobilized, it remained a valuable fighting unit. The thick hides of its Churchills were impervious, of course, to shrapnel and machine-gun fire and even to the light antitank guns commanding the beach, and the crews were able to remain in action, supporting the trapped Canadian infantry with machine-gun and light-cannon fire for more than seven hours and covering the re-embarkation of those who made it back to the water's edge. There some of the infantry and a few of the tank crews found a precarious haven in the battered but intrepid little landing flotillas that had braved the guns a second time to rescue whom they could as best they could.

Through faulty communications General Roberts sent in his reserves of infantry long after the main force had been beaten back and trapped in the ghastly shooting gallery between the edge of the sea and the promenade. They fared little better than the assault battalions.

Altogether 3367 of the 5000 Canadians who had embarked from England became casualties. About 900 were killed, 1946 were captured, more prisoners than the whole Canadian Army lost in almost a full year of action between D Day and V-E Day in Western Europe.

If these enormous POW figures suggest any lack of courage or efficiency the suggestion is quickly dispelled by the operations report of the formation that defended Dieppe. "The main attack," the 302d German Infantry Division recorded, "was launched by the Second Canadian Division with great energy. That the enemy gained no ground at all in Puys and could take only parts of the beach at Dieppe . . . and this only for a short time . . . was not the result of lack of courage but of the concentrated defensive fire of our division artillery and infantry heavy weapons. In Puys the efforts made by the enemy, in spite of heavy German machine-gun fire, to surmount the wire obstacles studded with booby traps on the first beach terrace are signs of a good offensive spirit. The large number of prisoners at Puys was the result of the hopelessness of the situation for the men who had landed, caught under German machine-gun, rifle, and mortar fire between the cliffs and the sea on a beach which offered no cover."

The German 81st Corps, reviewing the battle, concluded: "The Canadians on the whole fought badly and surrendered afterward in swarms." But this conclusion was rejected by the German Fifteenth Army, which warned: "The large number of English prisoners might leave the impression that the fighting value of the English and Canadian units employed should not be too highly estimated. This is not the case. The enemy, almost entirely Canadian soldiers, fought . . . so far as he was able to fight at all . . . well and bravely. The chief reasons for the large number of prisoners and casualties are probably:

"1. The lack of artillery support.

"2. The Englishman had underestimated the strength of the defenses and therefore at most of the landing places—especially at Puys and Dieppe—found himself in a hopeless position as soon as he came ashore.

"3. The effect of our own defensive weapons was superior to that of the weapons employed by the attacker.

"4. The craft provided for the re-embarkation were almost all hit and sank."

One English and two Canadian officers, all of whom miraculously survived to receive them in person, were awarded the Victoria Cross for their parts in Dieppe. The Englishman was an officer of Lord Lovat's Commandos, Captain P. A. Porteous, who, although twice badly wounded, raced through heavy machine-gun fire to lead the final assault on the German artillery positions on the right.

Another was the commanding officer of the South Saskatchewan Regiment, Lieutenant Colonel C. C. I. Merritt. When Merritt's forward troops were blocked by heavy enemy fire at a bridge in the village of Pourville, he walked calmly ahead past the dead and wounded waving his helmet like a flag and shouting back to the men behind, "Come on over—there's nothing to it!" Merritt got enough of his men across the bridge to lead them in several equally daring attacks on enemy positions on the hills beyond, and later he took personal charge of a small rear guard that fought slowly back to the beach, covering the evacuation. He was finally taken prisoner.

The third V.C. was Honorary Captain J. W. Foote, chaplain of the Royal Hamilton Light Infantry. Foote had little time or opportunity for conventional religious duties on the beach, but as an impromptu stretcher-bearer and first-aid man he performed prodigies. As the re-embarkation neared its end, he could have been one of the last men out of the beachhead, where there was now no more work for him to do. But he decided to stay behind and join the sad trek to the prisoner-of-war cages, where he knew he would be needed more.

As for the much discussed "lessons" of Dieppe, the politicians and generals made so much of them in the first aftermath of shock that many people felt they were simply trying to cover up a senseless blunder with a retroactive excuse. But although a single event or a single person is seldom solely or wholly responsible for a major advance in military science, the total evidence does indicate that Dieppe was not a total waste. Dieppe was a powerful contributor to the artificial harbors of D Day 1944; to the decision to give the assault troops overwhelming fire support from air and sea; to the formation of a special, permanent naval force highly trained in assault landings.

Just as importantly, Dieppe got Corporal Percy Hobart out of the Home Guard and back into the Regular Army, promoted him eleven grades to his old rank of major general, and brought him a knighthood.

Hobart was one of those brilliant mavericks whom their superiors find intolerable in times of peace and indispensable in times of war. During the halcyon, do-nothing years before and after Munich he had been one of Britain's senior tank officers. In its use and nature the tank had changed surprisingly little since 1917. Hobart was bursting with ideas on new equipment and new tactics, and he insisted on thrusting them at his more tranquil superiors at every opportunity, often with such impatience that he incurred their anger and resentment.

In 1938 the War Office sent him to virtual exile to Egypt, where he created the soon to be famous Seventh Armored Division but made so many more impossible demands on and complaints about the Establishment back home that he was virtually forced to retire in 1940.

Working on his own and other people's ideas, Hobart developed the miraculous swimming tank, the water-winged DD (DD stood for Duplex Drive, but to the troops who manned it or fought under its protection it had the affectionate name Donald Duck).

Hobart also developed the AVRE (Armored Vehicle Royal Engineers), a tank that could move right up to a pillbox and either lob a lethal charge of explosive at it or, if the concrete were especially thick, clamp the explosive right on the outer wall. He produced the Scorpion, or Flail, a wondrous device for beating a swift path through minefields. He produced the Crocodile, the fearful flame-throwing tank, as well as the bulldozer tank and two or three other varieties of tank for bridging shell craters and ditches under fire and helping other tanks to climb sea walls and ford canals. The Wasp was a small flame thrower.

And because all these weird machines worked, they spelled the final rout of the conventional military thinkers and led to the development and use of still other weird machines. The Alligator was an amphibious troop-carrying tank that proved to be one of the most potent of the Canadian Army's vehicles in the Battle of the Scheldt. The Buffalo was another land-and-water troop carrier. The Kangaroo, armored and land-borne, helped in the breakthrough at Falaise.

How many lives this Hobart-inspired or Hobart-encouraged menagerie saved before the war was over there is no way of guessing. But they were many more than the lives lost at Dieppe, and according to the impersonal cost accounting of war and in the jargon of the military-college blackboards, the final verdict may be that Dieppe was a tactical failure but a strategic success.

XLVI

Franklin D. Roosevelt and some important bargains
between Canada and the United States—Meighen
loses a by-election—The plebiscite

FOR all their much proclaimed understanding of the United States
there is one thing about the American people that few Canadian
people have been able to comprehend. How could so many of them
have hated Franklin Delano Roosevelt?

It is probably no exaggeration to say that at any time between
1932 and 1944, Roosevelt, had he been eligible, could have been
elected Prime Minister of Canada by a margin much more overwhelming than any of those by which he was elected President of the
United States. Canadians sensed only obliquely, if at all, the real
depths of alarm and disruption that Roosevelt was spreading among
his country's businessmen, isolationists, and conservatives. Not being
directly privy to the costs or risks of the New Deal, they recognized
only its rewards and returns. They saw it as a rallying point for
all humanity and heard its gospel as a mighty shout amid the sour
gloomy silences of Herbert Hoover, the uncertain waffling of Mackenzie King, and the ceaseless sermons of R. B. Bennett on the
sanctity of hard money and happy bondholders.

During the Depression years millions of Canadians had listened
as eagerly to Roosevelt's fireside chats as had his own countrymen.
And the Canadians had listened a good deal less critically. Neither
Bennett nor King had the magnetism to serve as a father figure in
an age during which the world cried for father figures (and got
as mixed a bag as Hitler, Mussolini, Baldwin, Chamberlain, and
Chiang Kai-shek). For Canada, Roosevelt was the natural and inevitable surrogate. After 1940 the larger part of the role was transferred to Winston Churchill, but even during the two years when
the Dominion was at war and the United States was not, many

Canadians had the paradoxical and illogical feeling that they were
fighting to make the world safe for F.D.R. and the id
seemed somehow able to sustain against every hazard and

Canada asked or took no direct financial aid from Roos——— or
his government during the war and, in the total cross index of borrowing, lending, giving, and receiving among the Allied powers,
ended up a benefactor nation second only to the United States. It
remains the simple fact, however, that the foreign and fiscal policies
of the United States gave almost indispensable support to Canada's
war effort. Canada's economic contribution to victory could not
possibly have been so great as it was without the co-operation of
the U.S.A.

A full year before the war began, in 1938, Roosevelt and King
publicly announced one point of agreement on foreign policy and
pledged that it would hold good however their countries' courses
might diverge in other matters. In a speech at Queen's University
following the opening of the Thousand Islands International Bridge,
the President proclaimed: "The Dominion of Canada is part of
the sisterhood of the British Empire. I give you assurance that the
people of the United States will not stand idly by if domination of
Canadian soil is threatened by any other empire." Two days later
King spelled out Canada's part of the bargain in another public
speech: "We, too, have our obligations as a good friendly neighbor,
and one of them is to see that, at our own instance, our country
is made as immune from attack or possible invasion as we can
reasonably be expected to make it, and that, should the occasion
ever arise, enemy forces should not be able to pursue their way,
either by land, sea, or air, to the United States, across Canadian
territory."

It was two years before these guarantees were repeated in doc-
umentary form. Then, on an August night in 1940, the President
and the Prime Minister met in Roosevelt's railway car in the border
town of Ogdensburg, New York, and signed a permanent agreement
on joint defense. The agreement concerned only the defense of
North America and did not officially affect America's neutrality in
the European war. But a parallel and simultaneous transaction—
in which King acted merely as the middleman between the United
States and Britain—took the United States a long step toward full
participation, just as lend-lease was to take it a longer one four
months afterward.

One of the many things the United States had but didn't need and Britain needed but didn't have was a pool of fifty serviceable but overage destroyers, quietly reposing in mothballs at their naval bases on the Atlantic seaboard. Roosevelt, fully certain of America's stake in a strong British Navy, was willing enough to give them up. But even though lend-lease still lay in the future, millions of his country-men felt he was already being too generous to Britain and playing too fast and loose with the U.S.A.'s standing as a non-belligerent. Besides, the Neutrality Act and the Constitution offered certain legal obstacles to handing over the destroyers as an outright gift.

To satisfy the requirements of public opinion and the law—and incidentally to improve his own country's defenses—Roosevelt pro-posed that Britain pay for the destroyers with military bases in Ber-muda, the West Indies, and Newfoundland. Churchill balked; the thought of surrendering a single inch of British territory to anyone for any reason was particularly distasteful in that year of perpetual crisis. But within two days of Ogdensburg, King, having been thoroughly briefed on Roosevelt's point of view, helped Churchill change his mind. The ensuing destroyers-for-bases trade was one of the straws that kept Britain and Canada afloat during the blackest period of the Battle of the Atlantic.

But it was in the economic field that Roosevelt and his adminis-tration did most to help Canada realize its potential during the twenty-seven months when one country was a neutral and the other a belligerent.

Industry in Britain and Canada ultimately performed prodigies in helping to win the war and made genuine sacrifices along with—in many cases—excellent profits. But in the final year of preparation and the first pre-Dunkirk months of the "phony war" the prevailing civilian motto on both sides of the ocean might have been a parody of the British shopkeeper's proud boast of 1914. This time it could have been: "Business as usual and let us get our full share of it."

Just before Germany marched on Poland the Canadian Manu-facturers' Association sent a deputation to the United Kingdom seeking contracts for military goods, and the government gave it quasi-official status by lending a group of advisers headed by Gen-eral McNaughton. Their reception was later described by the leader of the Senate and a member of the King Cabinet, Raoul Dandurand, in these blunt terms: "The industrialists of Great Britain were not disposed to allow plants to be set up in Canada that would be rivals to them in time of peace. . . . We were begging them for blueprints, for help to build war equipment that they wanted, but they were reluctant to send us the blueprints. They were living in a false paradise . . . there was no hurry to establish in Canada plants with which they would have to compete after the war was over."

King took a keen personal interest in the business politics attendant on the tooling up and early production for war. The cynical spirit of this whole part of the enterprise was reflected in his message to Chamberlain on the day Britain declared war. He made absolutely no promise of military help to Britain other than that it would be "considered." He was more specific when he referred to contracts. "We should also like," he cabled, "to have your government's present appreciation of the nature and extent of British and Allied requirements as regards supplies and particularly the relative urgency of the needs for various commodities which Canadian producers could furnish. As regards munitions, the dispatch of the British Mission now on its way and the consultations which have already taken place should make it possible to reach prompt conclusions on detailed arrangements. Presumably the negotiations which have been taking place in the United Kingdom for the purchase of war materials and foodstuffs will be completed and developed."

Chamberlain's response was politely aloof. Bent on protecting Britain's exchange position, he was determined to offset its heavy spending on Canadian food and raw materials by keeping every possible bit of war manufacture at home and selling every possible gun, shell, and tank abroad.

The fall of France and the Low Countries brought all this parrying to a sobering end. Suddenly, with the greater part of its land armament lost at Dunkirk, a terrifyingly outnumbered R.A.F. naked to the Luftwaffe, and its industry under attack or the constant threat of attack, Britain was in desperate need of imported munitions. Next to the United States, Canada was the most hopeful source of supply.

Within a few weeks blueprints, tool designs, and assignments of patent were pouring across the Atlantic in a bewildering torrent. They were accompanied by a small mountain of contracts, nearly all calling for the immediate production for which Canada had neither the necessary plant nor the necessary personnel.

Nevertheless, under the direction of the robust Minister of Munitions and Supply, C. D. Howe, existing factories retooled and new factories came into being at a sufficient rate to make Canada a major producer of war material long before the end of 1941. By then Howe was able to tell the House of Commons that Canada was making every one of the 2000-odd items of equipment needed for a modern army and making them fast enough to fit out a full infantry division every six weeks.

The cost of this industrial upheaval was a financial upheaval of alarming proportions. Buying component parts and tools in the United States to meet both her own requirements and some of Britain's, Canada incurred a deficit of almost half a billion dollars in her North American trade by the end of March 1941. Britain for a while was able to absorb her share, but shortly began running out of gold—a crisis recognized and partly solved by lend-lease.

Canada continued to pile up dollar deficits, both on her own account and Britain's. Had the process continued indefinitely the country's phenomenal growth as an arsenal would have had to slow down and level out at a ceiling set not by its capacity to produce but by its capacity to find U.S. currency.

It was this precarious and complex situation that Roosevelt and King met to discuss at Hyde Park, New York, on April 20, 1941. They solved it quickly, with the easy assurance and amiability of two dictators with a common goal and a long-established personal rapport. The formula was largely King's, but Roosevelt accepted it with enthusiasm. To alleviate the purely U. S.-Canadian part of the problem, each country would provide the other with the defense articles which it was best able to produce; Canada would still have a deficit but it might be cut by as much as a quarter of a billion dollars a year. And Britain would be allowed to pay in lend-lease dollars for the component parts Canada had to buy in the United States in order to fill British needs.

The Hyde Park Declaration accomplished in the economic sphere what the Ogdensburg Agreement accomplished in the military sphere. The two together freed Canada from any pressing anxiety about the defense of her own shores and from the danger of going bankrupt, not through any lack of resources but through the perils of orthodox bookkeeping. Thus, unshackled of two pressing worries with the help of the helpful F.D.R., the country went on learning new things about its own strength and using that strength on a scale that it would have been impossible to imagine in 1939.

Much of this, however, was invisible to the populace at large: where visible, it seemed commonplace and anticlimactic. After 1914–18 most Canadians were accustomed to thinking of war in terms of Wagnerian violence. They might rejoice now that there was no Ypres, Vimy, or Passchendaele to use as the measure of their national sacrifice and effort. At the same time that part of it which was on display in Canada moved drearily past a set of dreary mileposts—price controls, wage controls, national registration, high taxes, rationing, priorities, minor scarcities, sullen waitresses and haughty salesclerks demanding whether the customer knew there was a war on.

On the civilian front, 1942 did bring a brief flurry of political excitement. There had been no real political conflict in Canada since King's surprise election of 1940. All the important government actions were taken by order in council. All the important negotiations with other governments were conducted in secrecy or semi-secrecy. King, for once content to have strong men around him, had assembled an overwhelming array of talent in his Cabinet: Howe in Munitions, J. L. Ralston in Defense, Louis St. Laurent in Justice, James Ilsley in Finance, half a dozen other ministers adroit and experienced enough in debate to take on the combined forces of the battered and plaintive little Tory party almost single-handed. The Opposition was reduced to the role of a virtual by-stander in the nation's affairs, so much so that its parliamentary leaders, R. B. Hanson in the Commons and Arthur Meighen in the Senate, were trapped by ignorance of the Ogdensburg Agreement and its intent into denouncing it as anti-British.

Now that Bennett was retired in England, Meighen again was the party's uncontested head. Contemplating the dismal fact that Hanson had proved even more ineffectual than his predecessor, Manion, King's old university friend and parliamentary enemy decided to resume the Commons leadership himself. Accordingly, he resigned from the Senate and prepared to resume his seat as a member of the Commons.

First Meighen had to go through the formality of a by-election and he announced he would fight it on conscription. The Conservatives had, like the Liberals, taken their stand against the overseas draft in 1939 and 1940, but now Meighen and his party felt a new policy was needed and inevitable. Their platform called for a coalition government and "compulsory selective service over the whole field of war."

King's position was immensely complicated. He was opposed to conscription. In his Cabinet, the man most powerful next to him was a conscriptionist, Ralston. The third most powerful, after the death of Lapointe, was P. J. A. Cardin, an equally convinced anti-conscriptionist.

King was almost beside himself as he saw the tall, self-righteous figure of Meighen striding into his sea of woe and churning it up again. The threat that Meighen might soon be back on the other side of the Commons, parading his cleverness and scorn, filled him with dismay. "He will detract from the Government's record and myself in particular," King wrote uneasily in his diary.

"Every face will be directed against myself, to get me out of the leadership. . . . Meighen . . . will stop at nothing in seeking to bring conscription into force . . . with Quebec hating him, he will hate in return, be arrogant with Labour and will seek to stir up the farmers. . . . Life day by day will be made intolerable by his attacks, misrepresentations and the like."

The more he contemplated the return of Meighen, the more King acted as though he had seen a particularly horrible ghost. The whole prospect, he admitted, left him "sick at heart." Another bout with his old tormentor might wreck his health: "Mental fatigue and physical combined, but depression as well, and feeling of being left alone, old colleagues gone or going, no one to help, and alone . . . no one to talk with."

"I am getting past the time," King confessed again, "when I can fight in public with a man of Meighen's type who is sarcastic, vitriolic and the meanest type of politician. . . . To have as leaders of the Opposition . . . types of Conservatives I have had to contend with has been a real cross all the way. . . . No one will ever know how hard it has been to bear. That and the contemptuous attitude of the Tory Press, all of which I have borne pretty much in silence."

When Meighen's federal Tories made their alliance with Hepburn's Ontario Liberals, King considered the arrangement "truly vile and bad . . . as cruel as it can possibly be."

Toward political enemies who were not dangerous to him he was the soul of kindness: to such weak Tory leaders as R. B. Hanson, Gordon Graydon, and John Bracken he was always polite and deferential and he even gave a job to one of them, Robert Manion. But he was implacably hostile to the ones who showed real signs of strength. In one of his threnodies he noted: "I have had to endure a lot of very insulting and even vicious things at the hands of three men in particular: "Meighen, Bennett and Hepburn. The careers of all three have been ended by their own hatefulness."

King foresaw as early as 1943 the rise of another enemy worthy of his dislike. "The Tories seldom choose a decent man," he wrote. "They are likely to take Diefenbaker as being the most bitter . . ."

There were secret and open conscriptionists in King's own party, including Premier J. B. McNair, of New Brunswick, and, of course, Mitch Hepburn, of Ontario. The Manitoba legislature, theoretically Liberal, had unanimously voted for a resolution in support of the draft. A Committee for Total War, composed largely of well-heeled Torontonians, launched a strong propaganda campaign toward the same purpose.

After routing Duplessis at one extreme and Hepburn at the other in the early months of the war, King had expected that his middle position would not come under serious attack again. Now he perceived that although Quebec remained pacified, Ontario was stirring once more with the same pro-conscription feeling that had liquidated the Laurier Liberals in 1917. With the detested, persuasive Meighen fanning the flames there was no telling where it might lead before it was over.

King buckled on his pillow shield, his pneumatic armor, and his rubber sword and strode forth yet once more to confront Meighen and his hard but shiverable lance of steel. He had been meeting the challenges of that erect and antiseptic knight for more than two decades now and had learned how beautifully simple it was if you refused to meet them quite head on. Here was another problem that could not possibly be solved; therefore, the way to dispose of it was to smother it.

On January 22, 1942, eighteen days before Meighen was to fight his by-election in the Toronto constituency of York South, King announced what was perhaps the most ingenious of all his compromises. He would hold a national plebiscite in which the people of Canada would be asked to release the government from its repeated pledges that it would not invoke overseas conscription. But this did not mean conscription would automatically follow an affirmative vote. The proposed policy could be—and, somewhat later, was—summed up in seven words: "Not necessarily conscription but conscription if necessary."

The plebiscite was not taken until two and a half months after the York South by-election. But the mere announcement that it was to be held defeated Meighen's plan to fight for a Commons seat on a straight show of hands between pro- and anti-conscriptionists. King had fashioned a carryall large and elastic enough to hold almost any ballot; now only those who wanted conscription right away, whatever the military circumstances might be, were compelled to vote for Meighen.

And in this contest nobody was even given a chance to vote for the Prime Minister himself. The Liberals nominated no one, but put all their weight behind the candidate of the C.C.F., Joseph W. Noseworthy. There were two advantages to this course. First, the government couldn't lose a by-election in which it wasn't represented. Second, since his party's stand was the only completely unequivocal one, Meighen could be certain of some fairly fixed though unknown number of votes no matter who ran against him. Anything calculated to split the anti-Tory vote would help his chances.

The Liberal strategy worked flawlessly. Meighen lost York South to the C.C.F. candidate by more than four thousand votes.

"When I think," King reflected, "of Meighen trying to usurp his way into Parliament . . . and of his being now completely defeated and out of public life . . . and Hepburn out of the premiership in Ontario, Bennett safely out of the country altogether, and Manion anxious to help all he can, I have indeed reason to be thankful."

The subsequent plebiscite was more awkward. It was a foregone conclusion that Canada as a whole would release King from his promise of 1939 and 1940, but Canada as a whole had not wanted the promise in the first place. It had been exacted specifically by and made specifically to Quebec. It was King's earnest hope that Quebec would release him from it too, or at least give him enough votes to remove part of the sting of race and sectionalism from the country's thorniest issue.

When the ballots were counted on the night of April 27, eight of the nine provinces had voted with the government by an average of 4 to 1. But Quebec voted against, 72 per cent to 28. Allowing for English-speaking voters, this meant that French Canada was still almost solidly against a draft for overseas although the country was in favor of it, "if necessary," by almost 2 to 1.

Parliament was now asked to strike from the mobilization act of 1940 the clause prohibiting conscription for service abroad. This it did, but only after another long and painful debate in which forty-five Quebec Liberals voted against their party and P. J. A. Cardin resigned from the Cabinet.

Ernest Lapointe had died a few months earlier and thus Cardin had become the senior Quebec minister. With deep passion—though, as it proved, vainly—he had urged Quebec to vote affirmatively in the plebiscite: "I wish simply to say, without weakness and equally without shame, that it is better not to run the risk of isolating ourselves. We wish that confidence be shown to us; therefore we must show confidence to others. Let us speak not only of rights; let us also think sometimes of the obligations that guarantee them. . . . Be the first to reply 'yes' to the question of the plebiscite. It is in your interest to act thus, first as citizens and then as members of a minority which not only has need of the law and treaties to develop according to its ideals but must count on the good will of all and feel its soul surrounded by the respect and comforting friendship of the great majority of the people of the country."

Like King, Cardin had seen the plebiscite primarily as a means of stopping Meighen in his tracks and calming down the conscriptionists. Neither man really expected it to be followed—certainly not at once—by action. But no sooner had the votes been counted than half a dozen cabinet ministers, led by Ralston of Defence, insisted that if the draft was not to be proclaimed immediately the law forbidding it must at least be amended. King acquiesced rather than risk a major cabinet revolt. In the debate that ensued Cardin spared his former leader nothing, for he felt that he and the dead Lapointe had been betrayed into betraying their people. "We accepted 1939," he cried angrily. "We accepted 1940. We accepted the plebiscite . . . in order to preserve Canadian unity in Canada." King, he pointed out, still made no claim that conscription was necessary. "Then why in the name of God authorize it?"

Feelings began to approach the ugly peaks of 1917. Ironically the Catholic hierarchy, whom the Orangemen of Ontario persisted in holding responsible for all troubles in Quebec, took so moderate a position that thousands of their parishioners suspected them of trying to sell the habitant down the river to *les Anglais*. Even devoted churchgoers were known to have referred to Rodrigue Cardinal Villeneuve by his anglicized nicknames, "Newtown, O.H. M.S." and "Kid Villeneuve."

But aside from the flurries attendant on the plebiscite, party politics were virtually stagnant from early 1940 until well into 1943. Excepting only the Quebec dissidents, who remained obedient on all issues but conscription, the huge Liberal majority did as it was told. After his own last personal defeat, Meighen valiantly went searching for a new man to lead his party and settled on John Bracken. No one was quite certain of Bracken's politics, including himself. He had originally been a Progressive, but the coalition government he headed in Manitoba leaned heavily on Liberal support. When the Conservatives asked him to be their national leader, he naturally hesitated. But he was far from satisfied with the way King was running the war and accepted on the condition that his new party change its name to Progressive Conservative and make its tariff policies more acceptable to the West. The hope that so doubtful and reluctant a Tory could somehow bring the moribund Tories back to life was dead within a few months.

The C.C.F. and Social Credit parties had their heads buried in doctrinaire sand; every time conscription of manpower came up they insisted on arguing for conscription of wealth as well, thus turning an immediate and practical issue into a remote and academic one.

The Quebec nationalists were forming ranks around a new leader, Maxime Raymond, a new party, the Bloc Populaire Canadien, and the basic platform of Bourassa, which, King said in one of his rare flashes of wit, was "contained in a single word, *non*."

The busiest political figure outside the Cabinet was the little Communist, Tim Buck. Scuttling perpetually to keep up with the changes in the Moscow line, Buck was in and out of hiding, in and out of jail, in and out of the embrace of the conscriptionists, on and off and back on the ramparts of democracy.

Unfortunately for the Canadian comrades, communications with the Comintern were slow. When Hitler invaded Poland they had been stuffed to the ears by a decade of anti-Fascist instruction and the Russo-German non-aggression pact had gone right over Buck's head. On September 9, 1939, he wired Mackenzie King, in the name of his party, a pledge of "full support for the Polish people in their resistance to Nazi aggression." He urged Canada to press the war against Germany with all its strength.

Eight days later Russia struck at Poland from the east. Buck, having prudently gone underground, wrote and circulated a pamphlet headed: "The People Want Peace." It began: "The Mackenzie King Government and the bankers and the capitalists who were strangling national recovery in peace are now promoters of imperialist war." The party's clandestine propaganda apparatus rolled into high. Thousands of leaflets—all illegal under the Defence of Canada Regulations—were planted in war factories and military barracks. The slogans changed with the chronology and emphasis of Canada's war effort: "Not a man must leave Canada's shores to die in imperialist war!" Then: "No conscription!" And then: "Bring the Canadian boys back to Canada!"

One pamphlet read: "It is a lie that this war is a war against Fascism! It is a lie that the defeat of Germany by Britain and the Dominions will benefit the people. It is a cheap lie that we are fighting for 'Democracy.'" A special release on May Day 1940 urged a military revolt: "From the ranks of the armies the news arrives that the workers and peasants have not forgotten their class, that they know which way their guns have got to turn—against 'our own enemy,' against 'our own' capitalists and the state of oppression."

Buck was still in hiding when Germany attacked Russia. Now, overnight, the fire and eloquence of his rallying cry put more conventional patriots to shame: "Canada is in mortal danger. The future of our democracy and the safety of our homes and families depend on the outcome of the battles raging on the eastern front. At this critical hour the thoughts of all Canada are with our Soviet allies. To defend Canada and save world civilization, to keep faith with our heroic Soviet and British allies, to press for immediate invasion of the Continent—Join the Armed Forces!"

Buck issued a special encyclical on the eve of the plebiscite. "Unity for total war is the only pattern for victory," he wrote. "Defeat for Canada and her allies would mean fast invasion of our country by depraved hordes from Japan and Germany. Canada's war program must be accelerated. The way out of the conscription crisis lies in a great national movement uniting all classes to make democracy work for total war."

He stayed underground until September 25, 1942. Then, rightly sensing that a nation gone wild about Stalin would forgive his seditious words of 1939 and 1940, he gave himself up to the Mounted Police. After eleven days in the Don jail, he was released on a direct order from the Department of Justice. He spent the next two years—until the party line changed again—making speeches in behalf of national unity, total war, and Soviet-Canadian friendship. His utterances during this phase were filled with such capitalist aphorisms as: "Mackenzie King is right" and "Anthony Eden is so right." The figure Buck cut during his wartime adventures—for all the world like a man clambering in and out of windows in a French bedroom farce—was so preposterous that few Canadians have ever taken him or the Communist party of Canada as seriously as they may deserve.

XLVII

Goebbels views the R.C.A.F.—Some difficulties
over the Air Training Plan—The campaign
in Sicily

THE *damage is colossal and indeed ghastly. . . . Nobody can tell how Krupps is to go on. . . . It drives one mad to think that some Canadian boor, who probably can't even find Europe on the globe, flies here from a country glutted with natural resources which his people don't know how to exploit, to bombard a continent with a crowded population.* —Joseph Goebbels, *Diary*, February—March 1943.

If Goebbels knew how important a part Canada was playing in the war, he was better informed than most of the world, Canada included.

Censorship made it permissible for the press and radio to do little more than hint at the growth of the Royal Canadian Navy and its vast job in the Battle of the Atlantic. The Dominion's role in the air was even less well understood. Canadians were soon supplying the majority of the air crews from the Commonwealth Air Training Plan and the majority of that majority were being swallowed up more or less anonymously in the British R.A.F.

As the early complications of administration and combat control began to sort themselves out, it became possible to establish a separate Canadian bomber group and several separate fighter wings and to refer to them in the communiqués as R.C.A.F. units. A new Air Training Plan in June 1942 also placed the overseas commissioning of R.C.A.F. personnel in the hands of a special Canadian selection board and relieved the long-standing complaint that Canadian airmen were getting less than their rightful share of promotions. These and a number of other measures for "Canadianizing" the R.C.A.F. gradually won the Dominion's air and ground crews the recognition and sense of identity their superiors considered vital to their morale. Just as essentially—in the eyes of Mackenzie King, his Air Minister, Chubby Power, and most of the press—the world at large was reminded that if Canada was touchy and quick about asserting her place among the nations she was also paying the price for it.

King, as fierce a nationalist as his fierce little grandfather, found himself at hopeless odds with Britain on almost every detail of the Air Plan.

To get the scheme in motion the Chamberlain government had delegated its powers to two blimpish aristocrats, Lord Riverdale and Sir Gerald Campbell. They both made the mistake of trying to patronize King. King refused to be patronized but lacked the tough demeanor needed to convince Riverdale and Sir Gerald that he was not just another uncertain little man from the colonies.

They kept alternately pushing him and evading him. Riverdale made two—to King—outrageous suggestions: one that the Air Training Plan was a Canadian invention that Britain was willing to help out with; the other that the number of Canadian graduates designated as Canadians should be determined by the relative amounts of money spent by Britain and by Canada.

Finally King went into one of his controlled rages. Late on a cold December night in 1939, he telephoned Rideau Hall and asked to speak to the Governor General, Lord Tweedsmuir.

"I had quite a time getting anyone to answer the phone," King recorded. "Some boy went and searched for an A.D.C. and word came back that he was having difficulty finding an A.D.C. and that it was thought that the Governor was in bed. I said I wished to see the Governor whether he was in bed or not . . ."

When King arrived, according to his recollection, "the Governor was propped on his pillows, looking pretty frail." After a brief and not unfriendly talk they straightened out the first and worst of the differences between the two countries over the Air Plan.

But the Army was still the largest of the fighting forces. It was from the Army that the country instinctively expected most, even before McNaughton coined his famous description for it: "A dagger pointed at the heart of Berlin." After more than three years its combat record consisted of the hopeless little last stand at Hong Kong and the one-day massacre at Dieppe. A Canadian correspondent in London reported that some of the veteran members who had signed up in 1939 and 1940 expecting immediate action had begun to feel like "a sort of adjunct to the British Home Guard" while in the English countryside they were regarded as "the county constabulary."

Even the patient and unwarlike Mackenzie King was haunted by the thought of the effect on Canada's reputation and influence in the postwar world if its army should remain on garrison duty throughout the war. Although it was his hope—as it was, in a much greater degree, McNaughton's—that the Canadian ground forces might remain intact and ultimately serve as a unit under its own commanders, he did not insist on it.

As early as 1941, a few months before the overseas establishment reached its peak of five divisions, King declared in London that "so far as the disposition of the Canadian troops is concerned, Canada places no restriction whatsoever upon any decision that may be made, other than that the government itself shall have the opportunity of knowing what is contemplated and . . . of express-ing views." In October 1942, Ralston went in person to see Church-ill and assure him that there were no strings on the employment of the Canadian Army, either in whole or in part; that the gov-ernment of Canada wished it to be used where it would make the greatest contribution, and that the government was ready to con-sider any proposals. This was a few weeks before the Allied landings in French North Africa, but with the exception of a hand-ful of officers and men detached for special training, no Canadian ground troops took part.

Ralston began to wonder how much more idleness the Army could stand before its morale and efficiency began to suffer. King had some misgivings and was increasingly troubled by possible long-range consequences. At the start of 1943 one of his bright young men in External Affairs sent him a far from comforting reminder of Henri IV's famous letter to the great sixteenth-century captain Louis Balbis de Berton de Crillon: "Go hang yourself, brave Crillon, for we conquered at Arques and you were not there."

Two months later it was apparent that the full-scale cross-Channel attack for which the Canadian Army had been waiting and training would have to be postponed still another year, until 1944. King took matters into his own hands and cabled Churchill urging him to send at least some Canadian formations to North Africa before the campaign there was over. At the same time he had the Canadian

Chief of Staff in Ottawa wire McNaughton: "We should urge re-examination for one or perhaps two divisions going as early as possible to an active theatre."

McNaughton, of course, obeyed his instructions, but without enthusiasm. Reminded a few months earlier of Ralston's anxieties, he had assured Ottawa there was no reason to doubt that morale could be maintained even if the troops had to remain on guard duty for another year. Now he said, yielding to the dispassionate soldierly logic (or, as some called it, the stubborn ambition) that soon was to cost him his job: "I do not recommend that we should press for employment merely to satisfy a desire for activity or for representation in particular theaters however much I myself and all here may desire this from our own narrow point of view."

The army commander pointed out that the British Chiefs of Staff Committee was responsible for the strategic planning of the Commonwealth war effort and suggested that "proposals for use of Canadian forces should initiate with this committee." In short, Canada should not inhibit the planners by confronting them with awkward demands.

But whether he realized it or intended it, McNaughton had already confronted the Chiefs of Staff with his own awkward demands—or given them the impression he had. In a diary entry of February 10, 1943, Brooke, the C.I.G.S., noted a dinner conversation with Lieutenant General Crerar, the commander of McNaughton's First Corps. "A long harangue from him as to the necessity of getting some Canadians fighting soon for Imperial and political reasons. I fully see his point and his difficulties, but wish he could see mine in all their complexities." In a subsequent elaboration for his biography, Brooke explained that the difficulties to which he referred were "connected with the growing uneasiness amongst Canadians lest the war should finish without their having been engaged in any active operations." Crerar, he added, "was full of the fact that the present situation would strain Commonwealth relations and that something must be done at once. I had to remind him that the main factor that had up to date militated against their use in Africa was the stipulation made by the Canadian government that the Canadian army must not be split up and must only be used as a whole—a conception that McNaughton had always upheld with the greatest tenacity."

Obviously the liaison between the politicians and the generals left a good deal to be desired both in the Canadian and British services. Whatever the cause of misunderstanding about the conditions, if any, Canada attached to the use of its army, it was too late to send the Army or any part of it into action in Africa. Churchill so replied to King's cable but added: "I fully realize and appreciate the anxiety of your fine troops to take an active part in operations and you may be assured that I am keeping this very much in mind."

When, after a great deal of indecision, the Allies decided to follow up the conquest of North Africa with an attack on Sicily, Churchill kept his word. Brooke was instructed to fit the Canadians into the next operation. In a personal message to Eisenhower the C.I.G.S. said that on "both political and military grounds" it had been decided to withdraw two of the British formations already assigned to Sicily and replace them with the First Canadian Infantry Division and the First Canadian Army Tank Brigade.

Long before the end of the campaign in Africa, the Italian Army had demonstrated that it had no stomach for fighting abroad. Hitler suspected it would fight no better at home. Nor, so long as Mussolini remained their master and Italy remained in the shadow of Germany, was it safe to expect the civilian population to resist the invasion. Seven weeks before the attack on Sicily—when he believed the next blow would come in Sardinia or Greece but prudently canvassed the other possibilities too—the Führer conferred with several of his military leaders and political officers. Konstantin von Neurath, his former Foreign Minister, had just been to Sicily to talk to General Mario Roatta, military commander of the island. In Hitler's inner circle it was seldom considered wise to tell him unpleasant truths, but Neurath pulled no punches, as a transcript of their conversation later made apparent:

"*Neurath:* Among other things he [General Roatta] told me that he did not have too much confidence in the defense of Sicily. He claimed that he is too weak and that his troops are not properly equipped. Above all he has only one motorized division: the rest are immobile. Every day the English do their best to shoot up the locomotives of the Sicilian railroads, for they know very well that it is almost impossible to bring up material to replace or repair them, or not possible at all. The impression I gained on the crossing from San Giovanni to Messina was that almost all traffic on this short stretch is at a virtual standstill. Of the ferries there—I think there were six—only one remains. This one was being treated as a museum piece; it was said that it was being saved for better purposes.

"*Hitler:* What are the 'better purposes'?

"*Neurath:* Well, my Führer, sometimes the Italians explain, 'When this war is over'; others say, 'You never know what's going to happen next.'

"The German troops in Sicily have undoubtedly become rather unpopular. That can be explained very easily, because the Sicilians hold the view that we have brought the war to their country. First, we have eaten everything up that they had, and now we are going to cause the English to come themselves, although—and I must emphasize this—the Sicilian peasant really wouldn't mind that. He thinks that this will end his sufferings. The general opinion all over southern Italy is that the war will be over when the English come, and that the presence of the Germans just delays this.

"*Hitler:* What is the Italian government doing to counteract this attitude?

"*Neurath:* My Führer, as far as I know, the prefects and officials who are still around are not doing much about it. Whenever I directed their attention to it and complained that German soldiers were being cursed in the streets, I was told that they didn't know what to do about it, since this represented the popular view. They said, 'That's how the people feel; you have made yourselves unpopular; you have requisitioned things and eaten up all our chickens.' But I do think that the officials could make more of an effort, and make examples of the more flagrant cases.

"*Hitler:* They won't take action?

"*Neurath:* It is very difficult. They just won't take action."

The apathy of the Italian Sixth Army, the island's first line of defense, almost surpassed that of the weary half-starving peasants. One of its corps commanders, General Agostino Cinti, was repeatedly reduced to the verge of tears by the unquenchable incompetence of his coastal divisions. At least twice in the tense pre-invasion months he visited a section of the front near Syracuse expecting to see his troops busily training or improving the defense works; he found nothing but "soldiers idling and yawning in the sun, their mules torpid from lack of exercise and attention." Three or four weeks before the Allied landings the distraught corps commander sought to stir his men to a show of patriotic zeal by arranging to have them inspected by a prince of the royal blood. Although the royal car was equipped with two royal pennants in place of the customary one, many of the detachments the prince reviewed neglected to salute him and of those that did a number tried to present arms with heavy machine guns, an enterprise that made up in novelty what it lacked in neatness. The only outcome of the rededication visit was that several officers had to be court-martialed.

Far from apologizing for his unit's condition, the sixty-six-year-old commander of the 206th Coastal Division, General Achille d'Havet, added a special lament on his own behalf: "I have observed that units consider the bayonet as an object to be fixed on to the rifle only for presenting arms. If I summon a soldier, if I order a unit to move a few yards, the first thing anyone does is to unfix his bayonet as if it were not possible for a soldier to address an officer with the bayonet fixed, or for a unit to do a half-right turn or move five yards with the bayonet fixed. I cannot understand it. It would be perfectly easy to have a few hours' battle drill or even ordinary drill with fixed bayonets. Soldiers are not children two or three years old, who are afraid of cutting themselves if they carry a sharp instrument in their hands."

Thus the Canadian ground forces began their first continuous campaign against a comic-opera army and a tragically deprived and disillusioned citizenry. They made their landings in the early morning of July 10, 1943, on the extreme southeastern tip of Sicily, on the left flank of the British Eighth Army and to the right of the U. S. Seventh. The wind and surf were against them. There were awkward sandbars in front of the beaches, and although the ground overlooking them was not particularly well fortified, the Italians had enough pillboxes, machine-gun posts, barbed wire, and mines to have caused a great deal of difficulty if they had been in the mood. Fortunately they were not. Any vestigial interest they might have had in the war was soon erased by the heavy Allied bombardment from the air and the sea. The First Division took its main assault objective, the airfield at Pachino, without real opposition. With a single warning pistol shot a sergeant of the Royal Canadian Regiment captured an entire battery position and its three officers and thirty-five other ranks. As the willing prisoners streamed back toward the beaches the men plodding north through the semi-tropical sun and dust were already making half-sheepish jokes about waiting three and a half years to get into another phony war.

Their misgivings were unnecessary, for the real baptism of fire awaited them not far ahead. Alarmed by the Italian collapse in Africa and by his intelligence reports on the Italian indifference toward the defense of the homeland, Hitler had already made up his mind that the task of protecting the "soft underbelly" of Europe must fall to the Wehrmacht. Two months before the attack he offered Mussolini five fully equipped divisions.

But ever since his rash adventure in Greece, the Duce had chafed under the German dictator's patronizing offers of advice and help. Moreover, he was afraid of him; once he warned old Pietro Badoglio, his Chief of Staff, that if the Germans ever got a firm footing in Italy there'd be no getting rid of them. Happily for the Allied assault troops in Sicily, Mussolini replied to Hitler's latest offer with the lofty assurance that he didn't need five divisions but was willing to accept three. Two of these, the 15th Panzer Grenadiers and the Hermann Göring Panzer, were in Sicily on D Day.

With a dozen Allied divisions closing in and ten Italian divisions folding up, there was nothing the Germans could do but fight a delaying action. This they did with great skill and with the aid of some of the best natural defensive ground in Europe.

From the air or on a relief map, Sicily has the gingerbread-and-icing look of an illustration from *Grimm's Fairy Tales*. Above its stony river gorges, high hills and ridges rise as thick as pebbles in a bed of coarse gravel, every other one surmounted by a white or gray or saffron crown of stone-and-plaster buildings. Driven there by three thousand years of invasion from every corner of the compass, the little towns and villages sit on their fortress hilltops much as they did in the time of Hannibal and the Caesars. Beneath them a maze of donkey trails and usually a road or two of sorts list crazily down to the arid scraps of field and vineyard on the slopes and in the valleys.

Seen closer up, the hapless island loses its appearance of charming

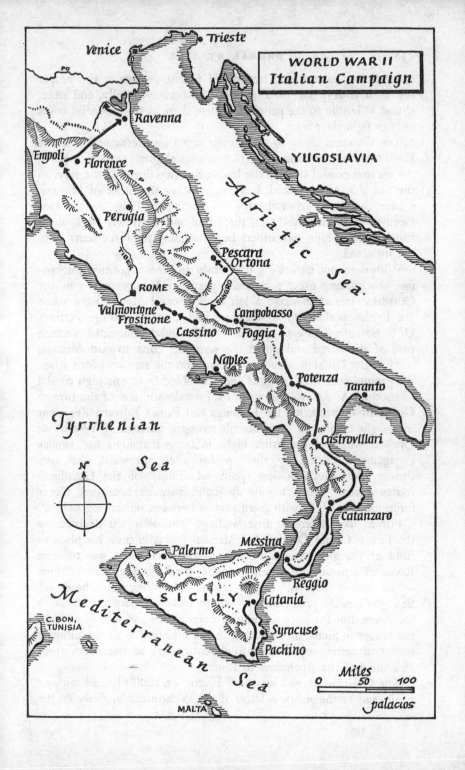

WORLD WAR II
Italian Campaign

Venice
Trieste
PO
Ravenna
Empoli
Florence
YUGOSLAVIA
Perugia
Adriatic Sea
Pescara
Ortona
ROME
Valmontone
Frosinone
Campobasso
Cassino
Foggia
Naples
Potenza
Taranto
Tyrrhenian
Sea
Castrovillari
Catanzaro
Palermo
Messina
Reggio
SICILY
Catania
Mediterranean
Syracuse
Pachino
C. BON,
TUNISIA
Sea
Miles
0   50   100
palacios
MALTA

eccentricity. Except in a handful of tourist retreats at the proper season, it is dry, hot, malarial, squalid, scrawny, smelly, and steep, almost as hostile to the people who live there as to those who come only to fight their wars.

The Germans chose to make their stand on the natural pivot of Etna, a massive volcanic peak that towers almost 11,000 feet above the narrow coastal strip of the Ionian Sea two thirds of the way up the east side of the island. Beyond Etna lay the Strait of Messina, a bare two miles from the toe of continental Italy. As the two German divisions already on the island moved slowly back along Etna's satellite hills, two others began sending reinforcements from the mainland.

With the front narrowing constantly and the opposition thickening, the fighting grew progressively stiffer. Montgomery sent the Canadians inland to make a left hook around Mount Etna while the British pushed up to the east and General George Patton's U. S. Seventh Army swept through the lightly defended western part of the island and down the northern coast toward Messina.

The First Division, aided by its tanks on the rare occasions when the ground permitted, slogged and scrambled from one high citadel to another. At Assoro, young Lord Tweedsmuir, son of the former Governor General, led the Hastings and Prince Edward Regiment in a night climb and dawn assault strongly mindful of Wolfe's at Quebec. Most of the other eight infantry battalions had similar engagements. Sizing up their performance afterward, the 15th Panzer Grenadier Division spoke admiringly of the Canadians' *Indianerkrieg:* "Very mobile at night, surprise break-ins, clever infiltrations at night with small groups between our strong points."

Fifteen days after the first landings, Mussolini was deposed by the Fascist Grand Council and Marshal Badoglio took his place as head of the government. Hitler's first wild impulse was to seize Rome with paratroops, arrest Badoglio, the King, the Crown Prince —"the whole bag of them"—restore Mussolini, and head off Badoglio's easily predictable efforts to make a separate peace with the Allies. But for once the Führer counted ten and instead ordered the troops in Sicily to withdraw to the mainland with the ultimate object of setting up a German defensive line in the north from Pisa through the Apennines to Rimini.

The Germans carried out their evacuation skillfully and without panic, and of the 70,000 soldiers of the Wehrmacht in Sicily on the day Hitler gave the order to start disengaging, some 60,000 made it to the mainland along with most of their weapons and transport.

Although Montgomery (who blamed muddled planning by his superiors) later said it was an "iniquity" that so many Germans had been allowed to get away, the thirty-eight days of the Sicilian campaign attained all the strategic goals the Allied had hoped for, and a little more. The Mediterranean was made much safer for Allied shipping; a firm base was established for further attacks in southern Europe; and Italy was virtually knocked out of the war. Excluding an estimated 137,000 Italian prisoners, the relative cost in casualties was about even. (The exact figures varied according to the source and method of reckoning; the ones Churchill finally accepted for all services on both sides were: Germans 37,000; Allies 31,158.) The official Canadian return was 562 killed, 1664 wounded, 84 taken prisoner.

XLVIII

The firing of McNaughton—Italy and the battle of Ortona

THE Sicilian campaign partly relieved the government's nightmare of maintaining a non-combatant army—however accidentally or unwillingly—throughout the most vital war in history.

But while the First Division and the attached Three Rivers Tank Regiment were still fighting their way up through Leonforte, Assoro, Agira, Adrano, and Regalbuto, the quiet and for the most part courtly battle between the politicians and the generals went into another phase.

As the one unreconstructed champion of a unified, self-contained Canadian Army, McNaughton had been forced more and more on the defensive. He had acquiesced in the dispatch of the Canadian contingent to Sicily only on the understanding that it would be returned to his command in England in time for the invasion in France a year later. Far from considering that it had disappeared permanently from his control, he had flown to Eisenhower's headquarters at Algiers four days before the landing and in mid-July asked Montgomery to arrange for him and a small party of his staff officers to visit the Sicily headquarters of the First Division.

Montgomery's reply could not have been more blunt. He not only refused to allow McNaughton into Sicily but let it be known that if the Canadian commander in chief tried to land there without permission he would have him arrested. Montgomery later explained his attitude in his postwar memoirs: "The 1st Canadian Division had not been in action before and officers and men were just beginning to find their feet. [Major General] Guy Simonds, the Divisional Commander, was young and inexperienced: it was the first time he had commanded a division in battle. I was determined that the Canadians must be left alone and I wasn't going to have Simonds bothered with visitors when he was heavily engaged with his division in all-out operations against first-rate German troops. However, to make sure, I went to see Simonds and asked him if he would like McNaughton to come to Sicily. His reply was immediate— 'For God's sake keep him away.' On that I sent a message to Malta asking that the visit be postponed."

After this humiliating rebuff, McNaughton returned to London and another unpleasant surprise. His government had decided that it wanted not only to leave the First Division and the Army Tank Brigade in the Mediterranean but to increase the Canadian strength there to a full corps. Early in August, Defense Minister Ralston and his Chief of Staff, Lieutenant General Kenneth Stuart, flew from Ottawa to communicate this wish direct to Churchill and the British Chiefs of Staff. When he broke the news to NcNaughton, Ralston explained that the Cabinet had four main reasons for adopting the course it had: "(a) giving a Canadian Corps HQ training, (b) battle experience for additional Canadian troops, (c) morale of Canadian Army in U.K., (d) morale of Canadian people."

McNaughton still held hopes that, even if a corps were constituted in Italy, it might be returned to the Canadian Army in time for the cross-Channel operation. But, he told Ralston, if the government had decided on or should decide on dispersion of the Army as a matter of policy then "it would be wise to put someone in control who believed in it."

McNaughton's threat of resignation was premature. Military logic was overwhelmingly on his side, even if political logic was not. Far from calling for more divisions in the Mediterranean, the grand strategy of the Allies called for fewer. Seven of the divisions already there were earmarked for return to Britain and the build-up for Normandy. Moreover, under an agreement made long ago, Burma and the Far East were to have a priority on shipping during the last half of 1943.

Although the Mediterranean was to remain an important theater with the coming assault on the Italian mainland, all but essential traffic there was to be avoided. Furthermore, another corps headquarters would add an administrative nuisance and cut down the ratio of combat troops to the total number of troops to be housed, fed, and supplied. In addition to this, the only way Canada could keep its two existing corps in balance would be to send one of its two armored divisions to Italy; Eisenhower and his ground commander, General Sir Harold Alexander, already had more armor than they could use.

All these objections were duly communicated to Mackenzie King and King knew there was considerable force behind them. He knew also that there had been considerable force behind the arguments against sending the First Division to Sicily, just as he knew that it, too, would still be idle if he had not answered the unanswerable generals with the stubborn obtuseness of a civilian. He was prepared to be obtuse again if that was the only way Canada could be protected from the ignominy that befell brave Crillon and be assured of a respectful hearing in the postwar world.

By the end of August, Churchill was in Canada for the Quebec Conference with Roosevelt. Before the conference opened officially, King asked the British Prime Minister to intervene with the military planners again. Churchill once more was sympathetic, although he doubted that anything could or should be done. However, he cabled a strong hint to the Deputy Prime Minister, Clement Attlee, and to the Chiefs of Staff: "At my meeting with Canadian War Committee to-day a strong desire was expressed that a second Canadian Division should be despatched to the Mediterranean area as soon as possible. . . . Pray let me know as soon as possible what can be done."

In mid-September, after his return to London and two weeks after the First Division had landed with the Allied assault troops on the Italian mainland, Churchill gave King what looked like his final reply: a regretful no. King was only moderately discouraged. He instructed Vincent Massey, the High Commissioner in London, to call on Downing Street and bring the matter up once more. Churchill (who according to Sir Alan Brooke often tried to bully his Chiefs of Staff into submission but never flatly overruled them on a major military question) obligingly agreed to "have another try."

This time it worked. On October 7 McNaughton heard the (to him) unwelcome news that his government's request had been granted. An extra British division would be brought back to Britain, thus making room in the Mediterranean for another Canadian division. The shipping difficulties could be eased by having the British division leave its tanks and other heavy equipment behind for the Canadians to take over. Transport and employment

could be found, if it was absolutely necessary, for a corps headquarters and supporting corps troops.

But Allied Force Headquarters and Fifteenth Army Group left
no doubt of their real feelings. Alexander, the ground commander
in the Mediterranean, cabled his superiors in London: "The proposed move of the Canadian Armoured Division has come as a
complete surprise to me. We already have as much armour in the
Mediterranean as we can usefully employ in Italy. I should have
preferred another Canadian Infantry Division. . . . I do not want
another Corps Headquarters at this stage. I shall be grateful if I
can be consulted in future before matters of such importance are
agreed upon. These decisions upset my order of battle, which in
turn affects my plans for battle."

Eisenhower, the supreme commander in the theater, signaled
the U.S and British Chiefs of Staff: "While the arrival of these
troops at this time is likely to cause us considerable embarrassment,
General Alexander advises me, and I agree, that, appreciating political considerations that may be involved, we accept the Canadian
Corps Headquarters, Armored Division and non-divisional troops.
In view of our total build-up we shall eventually be glad to have
this HQ. The aspect which causes me the most concern is the
pressure I anticipate will be put upon me to get these troops into
action at an early date."

It was hardly surprising that neither the Fifth Canadian Armored
Division nor Crerar's corps headquarters received a tumultuous
welcome in their new theater. Montgomery, who either hadn't
been given adequate directions by Alexander or chose to mis-
understand the directions he did receive, greeted Crerar in the
same cavalier manner in which he had received McNaughton a
few months earlier. The Eighth Army, he said, didn't want another corps; he suggested Crerar forget the whole thing and take
command of the First Division from Simonds, who was ill. (Crerar
replied politely that his instructions did not permit this.)

For several weeks a high proportion of the unwanted new boys
—who had come out thirsting for battle—were put to work on
glorified fatigue parties, running a transit camp for British combat
troops, filling in at other tasks on the line of communications, and
helping to look after civilian refugees. The old vehicles bequeathed to them by the departing British Seventh Armored Di-

vision were almost totally worn out and it was weeks before they had artillery of any kind.

By January 15, 1944, ten weeks after the Fifth Division had begun disembarking at Naples, Crerar felt justified in throwing a discreet quantity of weight around. He wrote Alexander: "I dislike intensely complicating in any way the difficult problem which already faces you . . . concerning the proper military employment of the several Dominion and Allied forces under your command, in which problem the 1 Canadian Corps is an important factor. This is a situation, however, unfortunately inherent in a heterogeneous, as opposed to a homogeneous, military command. On the other hand, my responsibility to my own government compels me to tell you that this combination of what appears to be a comparatively slow re-equipment and the recent large-scale employment of trained combatant Cdn. troops on L of C guard duties threatens to produce very undesirable reactions among the Canadian forces in this theatre and, indeed, among Canadians generally."

Events soon cleared up the delicate situation much more effectively than words ever could have done. More than a year's fighting still lay ahead of the Canadians in Italy, most of it hard enough to satisfy the most thoroughly brassed-off veteran of the long wait at Aldershot and on the downs of England. And by the time the war was over, the relations between the First Canadian Corps and its wicked stepfather of 1943 were so firmly rooted in mutual regard that Alexander's appointment as Governor General was one of the most popular ever made.

There was no happy ending for McNaughton. He and Ralston managed for a few weeks to sustain the fiction that the Cabinet had not really repudiated the Commander in Chief when it repudiated his advice. It is conceivable that if all the other circumstances had been favorable, the fiction might have survived and even have become a sort of fact when, in the last stages of the war, McNaughton's army was reunited in Western Europe. But if McNaughton's relations with his Canadian political superiors had become difficult, his relations with his British military superiors had become impossible. For four years he had been the man in the middle. Sometimes he believed himself required as a Canadian to pull his semi-ambassadorial rank on the British War Office and Chiefs of Staff. Sometimes, as in the Canadian expeditions to Italy, he felt compelled to side quite frankly with Whitehall against the East

Block in Ottawa. As the time drew nearer for the climactic battles in Western Europe one other consideration stood apart from past conflicts. McNaughton had never commanded a large formation in battle and was not acceptable to the British planners as the commander of an army in operations. Aside from everything else his health was failing; there was nothing organically wrong, but the doctors said he was in a state of fatigue and needed three months' rest.

When the War Office recommended his dismissal, King and Ralston complied with alacrity and relief. To the astonished country—which had been led by four years of propaganda to believe that McNaughton was an acknowledged military genius of whom even the Montgomerys and Alexanders stood in a certain awe—it was explained that the retiring Commander in Chief was in ill health. McNaughton returned to Canada to deny that he was anything of the kind, but he would say no more than that. The full reasons for his retirement remained a national mystery until the war was over.

The attack on the Italian mainland began in the early morning of September 3, 1943, four years to the day after Britain's declaration of war on Germany. At first the pattern of the landings was remarkably similar to that in Sicily. A massive bombardment of the enemy coast, this time heavily augmented by field guns firing across the narrow straits; a fast run in assault boats to virtually undefended beaches; not a German in sight; relieved Italian soldiers surrendering by the hundred as soon as it was safe to come up for air; anxiously smiling civilians emerging from their cellars to offer wine, ask for chocolate and cigarettes, and inquire about their inevitable cousins and uncles in Pittsburgh or Montreal.

Both the First Canadian Division and the First Canadian Army Tank Brigade were again assigned to the assault, along with the British Fifth Division. Their task was little more than a glorified feint; the main assault was planned for six days later in the Gulf of Salerno, just south of Naples and two thirds of the way up the west coast to Rome.

This was one of the enemy stratagems that Hitler's intuition diagnosed correctly. A week before the withdrawal from Sicily was completed, Field Marshal Albert Kesselring, German Commander in Chief South, began establishing a new Tenth Army with its headquarters less than fifty miles from Salerno. And the Führer himself issued the orders for the new army's commander on August 18: "(1) Sooner or later the capitulation of Italy before enemy pressure is to be expected. (2) In preparation for this, Tenth Army must keep the line of retreat open. (3) In the coastal area from Naples to Salerno, which at first is the most threatened, a strong group consisting of at least three mobile formations from the Tenth Army is to be assembled. All no longer mobile elements of the army are to be moved to this area. . . . In the case of an enemy landing the area Naples-Salerno must be held."

Ever since the fall of Mussolini the Allies had been negotiating a surrender with the new government of Italy. There were a dozen secret meetings and feelers put out on the neutral territories of Spain, Portugal, Tangier, and the Vatican. Italian emissaries flew under protection to Sicily and one of Eisenhower's generals slipped into Rome to see Badoglio in person. The outcome of these cloak-and-dagger excursions was an agreement that Badoglio and Eisenhower would announce Italy's surrender a few hours before the landing at Salerno. The new Italian Prime Minister tried to back out at the last minute, but Eisenhower made his announcement anyway. The harassed Badoglio followed suit in a radio broadcast an hour later and then fled with the King from German-occupied Rome to British-occupied Brindisi.

The hoped-for effect on the military situation did not materialize. The Germans had been pouring troops into Italy since early August and had eighteen divisions there by the time General Mark Clark's U. S.-British Fifth Army touched down at Salerno on September 9.

Badoglio had given a promise that, in return for unspecified concessions when it came time to write the peace treaties, his armies would help drive the Germans out of Italy. But in conformity with a prearranged plan Kesselring immediately sent one parachute and one panzer division into Rome; the five Italian divisions there meekly laid down their arms. Elsewhere the code signal *Achse*, "Axis," was the only order other German formations needed to begin disarming other Italian formations. There were few difficulties. The bewildered and demoralized legions of the broken Duce were by now willing to surrender to anybody.

On the morning after the capitulation Goebbels wrote in his diary: "The Führer, thank God, can rightly claim that he suffered

no disappointment. . . . Ever since Mussolini's exit we have anticipated and expected this development. We therefore won't have to
make essential changes in our measures." The next day he added
a less cheerful postscript: "The Duce will enter history as the last
Roman, but behind his massive figure a gypsy people has gone to
rot."

The Allies' Salerno assault went promisingly at first, but within
three days a series of heavy counterattacks threatened to push
Clark's four divisions back into the sea and give the Allies their
worst defeat in the West since Dunkirk.

Alexander appealed to Montgomery to step up his advance from
the south as quickly as possible with the object either of linking up
with the other bridgehead or drawing some of the besieging Germans down to meet him. What had begun for the Eighth Army as
a forced march in the wake of demolition parties now became an
urgent race, with two hundred miles of narrow roads still between
Montgomery's spearhead and Clark's beleaguered divisions on the
beaches.

This was not Montgomery's cup of tea at all. Despite the legend
that he was a commander of the go-for-broke, hell-for-leather
school, much of his genius depended on nothing more eccentric
than the proverbial capacity for taking pains. Before the campaign
now in progress he had repeatedly pressed on his superiors and
colleagues the need for more caution, better arrangements for
supply, a firmer long-range plan, more respect for the strength of
the Germans, less reliance on the beneficial effects of the Italian
surrender.

Two days after the Eighth Army landings in Calabria and four
days before the Fifth Army's touch-down at Salerno, Alexander
visited him at his headquarters in Reggio. As so many of the perpetually self-assured (and often maddeningly right) Montgomery's
diary entries did, the key extract for that day began with the three
words: "I told him."

"I told him," Montgomery recorded, "my opinion that when the
Germans found out what was going on they would stamp on the
Italians. The Italian Army morale was now very low; that Army
would not face up to the Germans. I said he should impress on all
senior commanders that we must make our plans so that it would
make no difference if the Italians failed us, as they most certainly
would. . . . The Germans were in great strength in Italy and we

were very weak. We must watch our step carefully and do nothing foolish. I begged him to be careful; not to open up too many fronts and dissipate our resources; and to be certain before we landed anywhere that we could build up good strength in that area. . . . If the landings at Salerno go against us we will be in for a hard and long fight. . . . Before we embark on major operations on the mainland of Europe we must have a master plan and know how we propose to develop those operations. I have not been told of any master plan and I must therefore assume there was none."

Now, equipped and supplied only for an initial thrust of sixty miles, Montgomery was asked to rush ahead three or four times that distance—and all because, in his estimation, nobody had listened to him. He considered it essential and no more than his duty to consolidate his "tail" before sending his advance columns into the blue. A day or two, and perhaps more, were lost and even then what Montgomery called the "administrative muddle" got progressively worse rather than better. His British Fifth Division, moving up the west coast, made contact with Clark's right flank on September 16, but the Salerno bridgehead had come through its last and most desperate crisis two days earlier.

Clark wrote the Eighth Army a letter of congratulation on the "skillful and expeditious manner" in which it had moved up to the north. But the whole enterprise continued to offend Montgomery's sense of order, and when he recollected it fifteen years later he made it clear that he had "never thought we had much real influence on the Salerno problem; I reckon General Clark had got it well in hand before we arrived."

For the Canadian division and tank brigade the first dash to the north had its frustrations too. It ended on September 20, with the capture of Potenza. After a long retreat up the central spine of the Apennines, strewing the high hairpin roads with wrecked bridges and buried *Tellerminen,* the Germans had reached the main lateral between Salerno on the west and the Gulf of Taranto on the east. Potenza, a town of 30,000, stood in its middle. To give it up would mean giving up any real hope in retaking Salerno. It would also increase the peril to Naples and to the immensely valuable Foggia airfields fifty miles to the northeast.

A flying column of infantry, tanks, and artillery hit Potenza from the south about the time Lieutenant General Richard Heidrich's First German Parachute Division began reinforcing it from the west. But the small detachment Heidrich could spare from Salerno merely postponed the fall of the town by a few hours. By the beginning of autumn the Fifth and Eighth armies were firmly joined. In seventeen days the Allies had taken over a third of Italy. As the crow flies, the Canadians' progress measured about two hundred miles. As the mountain roads wandered, it was more than four hundred and fifty.

Though the tide was slowly turning against him, Adolf Hitler remained the most powerful man in the world. While Churchill, Roosevelt, Stalin, and their military staffs were compelled to treat every major decision as an occasion for debate, the Führer still consulted only whom he chose and argued when he chose. In one of his terse decrees on the day before Naples fell, he settled the kind of winter it would be for the twenty-odd German divisions and the dozen-odd Allied divisions now regrouping on the Italian peninsula. "I order as follows for further warfare: . . . a delaying action only as far as the line Gaeta-Ortona. This line will be held."

The Allies considered refusing the gambit and either launching their next large attack across the Adriatic into the Balkans or sitting still in their fall positions in Italy. The ultimate decision was to drive on for Rome.

For two more months the Fifth and Eighth armies nudged ahead as much according to Hitler's plan as their own. In a sweep much like the rush from Reggio to Potenza the First Division seized the mountaintop road centers of Campobasso and Vinchiaturo. Another month of hide-and-seek against the German sappers and their covering fire parties put the Allies on the Sangro River, almost halfway between the Strait of Messina and the Alps. For the first three months of this hit-and-run combat the total Canadian casualties were about 1200, of which 300 were fatal. In five months in Sicily and Italy the Dominion's ground forces had lost only a few more officers and men than in the single morning at Dieppe.

But now, along with the whole advance wave of the Allies, they had arrived at the threshold of Hitler's winter line. From this point on—right up to the time of the First Canadian Corps's departure for France fifteen months later—they were to be in almost constant contact with an enemy determined and able to fight for every foot of ground.

The Gaeta-Ortona lateral was ideally suited for defense. From the mile-high backbone of the Apennines, two river gorges fell to the coasts, the Sangro to the Adriatic Sea on the east, the Garigliano to the Tyrrhenian on the west. This was the narrowest and, excluding the Alps, almost the highest part of the country.

The roads were bad, even for the mountain roads of southern Italy, and the rivers, dry or almost dry in summer, were coming into flood. On and behind the eastern part of this natural barrier Kesselring built his Bernhard Line of wire, concrete, log breastworks, rock caves, dugouts, and gun emplacements. In a relatively small area his engineers laid 75,000 mines and blew up 7 miles of bridges and 400 miles of railway track. The Sangro was not the strongest part of the Bernhard Line, which was anchored on the mouth of the Moro, ten miles further north. The task of forcing the first firm crossing into the country between fell to the British Seventy-eighth Division. Early in December the Canadian First Division passed through the Seventy-eighth and made its way to the steep ridge overlooking the Moro and the seaport town of Ortona. This set the stage for one of the most savage and punishing battles of the whole war.

It lasted a month and went through three stages—the seizure of the Moro, then a difficult little gully in front of the town, and finally Ortona itself. The fighting it produced was an agonizing throwback to 1917—to the mud and rain and icy waters of Flanders, the blasted slopes of the Somme, the bloody little advances and bloody little withdrawals and counterattacks, ditch by ditch, house by house, yard by yard.

To the traditional tortures and hazards of close infantry fighting in the winter, there were a few additions and refinements: flame throwers, more efficient tanks and anti-tank guns, more cunning and deadlier booby traps and mines, better methods and instruments of demolition for the defending engineers. To get down streets hopelessly clogged with rubble and thick with machine guns, mortars, and concealed tanks and close-support artillery, the attacking battalions used the technique of mouseholing. Almost every one of the stone houses and tenements beside the impassable roadways held enemy infantry or gunners. The only way to get at them was to blow an opening through the wall from the dwelling next door with a small explosive charge called the Beehive, or with the infantryman's portable anti-tank gun, the PIAT, and then pour through with grenades and submachine guns. Mouseholing parties sometimes fought their way down whole blocks—often at the level of the third or fourth story—without ever seeing open air.

There were classic deeds of valor on both sides. In a week's fighting in the town itself the Edmonton and Seaforth infantry battalions and their support groups won a total of five Distinguished Service Orders, three Military Crosses, and seven Military Medals. On the way through the gully in front of the town a captain of the Royal 22d Regiment, Paul Triquet, led a company already torn to shreds into a ring of tanks, machine guns, snipers, and self-propelled artillery. His assessment of the situation was concise and simple: "There are enemy in front of us, behind us, and on our flanks. There is only one safe place—that is on the objective." Triquet got there with two sergeants, fifteen riflemen, and four tanks of the Ontario squadron that had started out with him. When the counterattacks came in, he and his theoretically doomed little party met them with the cry of Verdun: "*Ils ne passeront pas!*" Triquet won the first Canadian V.C. in Italy.

As the battle raged with undiminished fury through the last week of 1943, the two battalions in Ortona insisted on remembering Christmas Day. Both ate their Christmas dinners in relays in whatever shelter they could find, a company at a time, and then crept back into the blackened broken streets to resume the war. The Seaforths were particularly fortunate to find a reasonably suitable hall in the church of Santa Maria di Constantinopoli; there, with their officers serving, as officers always serve the men at Christmas, they ate from white tablecloths. There was no turkey, but the ration parties had arrived with roast pork, apple sauce, four kinds of vegetables, plum pudding, mince pie, candies, nuts and fruit, and a bottle of beer per man, and the church organ played Christmas carols.

Three days later the Germans, who had fought with as much reckless heroism as their attackers, made a night withdrawal, and the attack with which the Canadians began the morning of December 28 found nothing in its way. The enemy has simply been bled and worn to the verge of collapse, as, to an only slightly lesser degree, had the Canadians. With winter closing in, the only real question since mid-December had been who would break the battle off. "It is clear we do not want to defend Ortona decisively," Kesselring had complained to his Tenth Army commander, "but the English have made it as important as Rome. . . . It costs so much blood that it cannot be justified. . . . You can do nothing when things develop in this manner; it is only too bad that the world press makes so much of it."

The Allied high command saved its doubts until later. Montgomery's Chief of Staff, Major General Sir Francis de Guingand, wrote of Ortona after the war: "The fighting during this period had been fairly costly, and one rather wondered what we achieved. Enemy formations were certainly pulled over from opposite 5 U. S. Army, and heavy casualties had been inflicted on the Germans. With snow in the mountains and mud everywhere else, we began to think about Passchendaele. Had we gone on too long? Were the troops being driven too hard? I feel very definitely that a mistake was made in pressing the Sangro offensive as far as it was. When once the weather had broken it was extremely unlikely that we could have advanced across the mountains, even if we had reached the Pescara-Rome road. Perhaps we were still not prepared to give the weather best, resenting her behaviour after the dryness of the desert. Who should have stopped the operations—the Army or Army Group? The Army Group, I suppose, for its job was to assess whether our contribution was worth while within the bigger picture."

In the closing stages of this "minor Stalingrad" (as the Associated Press called it) the fighting strength of Heidrich's First Paratroop Division was down to one company to the battalion, and Kesselring, lacking replacements at the divisional, corps, or army level, had been driven to the extremity of throwing in his Army Group reserve. Major General Chris Vokes, who had succeeded Simonds as commander of the Canadian First Division, reported at the end of the month that the rifle companies of every one of his nine infantry battalions had suffered 50 per cent casualties. Counting cases of sickness (which included battle exhaustion, formerly called shell shock), the Canadians had lost just over 4000 men since descending into the valley of the Moro. Reinforcements fell far below requirements, and of the reinforcements that did arrive almost none had previous battle experience and some, at least, had not even completed their training. Not far behind them in time, though several thousand miles away, there lurked a political crisis far greater than the military crisis they had been sent to meet.

Vokes did not think his division could go beyond Ortona without a period of rest for its veterans and training for its newcomers. The other Eighth Army divisions to the Canadians' left—the British Fifth, the Eighth Indian, and the New Zealanders—had not suffered so severely, but their prospects of continuing anything resembling a serious offensive were no better. For the next three months the campaign on the Adriatic consisted largely of probes and feints.

The static winter did at least enable the depleted battalions to build up their strength again and the pending shifts in the high command to be completed without dislocation. Eisenhower and Montgomery went back to England to make ready for the invasion of Normandy. And finally, on February 1, 1944, Crerar's much wrangled-over First Canadian Corps came into the line with the First Infantry Division on the coast and the Fifth Armored in the mountains further inland. Before spring Crerar went back to England to take command of the still existing though divided First Canadian Army. He was succeeded as corps commander by Lieutenant General E. L. M. Burns.

On the other, more promising, sides of the central mountains the offensive continued and grew in ambition and intensity. With "Overlord," the long-delayed attack through France, now definitely scheduled for the spring, it became doubly important to keep as many German divisions as possible pinned down in the Mediterranean. The capture of Rome would be an immense blow to the morale of the enemy and might finally convince Stalin that his allies were not deliberately dragging their feet. Moveover, although there was no practical road to Rome from the Adriatic, there was one on the western coast. It led up the broad valley of the Liri River past the mountain town of Cassino and the Benedictine monastery near by.

Clark was ordered to attack in mid-January. He had two almost simultaneous objectives: one the Liri and the other the seaside town of Anzio, sixty miles ahead of him and only forty miles short of Rome.

At first everything went exactly right. The Fifth Army launched its massive offensive toward Cassino. Kesselring rushed his armor and infantry down to meet it. Two Allied divisions, going north by sea while the Germans were going south by land, landed at Anzio almost unopposed. For a few hours Rome was at their mercy.

But the Allied corps commander paused to consolidate. Whether it was a sound and proper decision his military and political superiors have not agreed to this day. In any case, Kesselring had a few hours to think and begin regrouping his Tenth and Fourteenth armies.

Within a week the Anzio beachhead had been completely sealed off. To the south the first of the many assaults toward Cassino was beaten back with heavy losses. As it became more and more apparent that Anzio could neither be abandoned nor exploited, Churchill pronounced a sour and highly confidential summary: "We hoped to land a wildcat that would tear out the bowels of the *Boche*. Instead we have stranded a vast whale with its tail flopping about in the water!"

Now, where they had intended to be moving on at least one front, the Allies were stalled on three. At the end of February, Alexander and General "Jumbo" Wilson, Eisenhower's successor as theater commander, decided to try breaking the deadlock by massing their strength in the Cassino-Liri sector. Leaving only enough troops to hold the dormant Adriatic front, the Eighth Army moved across to join the Fifth.

Kesselring had four lines in front of Rome. His Fourteenth Army was jammed against the Anzio beachhead, obeying Hitler's personal injunction to "fight with inspired hatred against an enemy who is carrying on a pitiless war against the German people." Below Anzio there were three other defense systems. The Gustav Line rested on Cassino and the Garigliano River. Ten miles behind was the Hitler Line, not so well favored by geography, but bristling with wire, steel, tunnels, concrete, guns, tanks, and mines. And behind that, and just in front of Rome, was the last ditch, called the Caesar Line; it was fated to be overrun before it was finished.

In the spring offensive, the main task of the Canadian Corps was to take the Hitler Line. Cassino had been bypassed and enveloped by the middle of May. Everyone had had a crack at the mighty redoubt hinged on the Benedictine monastery—Frenchmen, Englishmen, Indians, Canadians, New Zealanders, Moroccans, Poles. Now they had opened Highway 6 to Rome and the Canadians were assigned to make the follow-up. On May 24, after a costly battle of infantry and tanks, they broke through. Traffic complications and decisions at a higher level denied them the satisfaction of moving beyond the Hitler Line to the Caesar Line and entering the city itself. But in the fighting still ahead the First Canadian Corps continued to add to its battle honors until its dispatch to France in 1945.

XLIX

The question of a unified Empire again—The disastrous speech of Lord Halifax

AS military history repeated itself at Ortona, on the Hitler Line, on the Gothic Line, and in the muddy valley of the Po, political history was being repeated elsewhere. The conscription issue was approaching its boiling point of 1917. And the question of the bravely battered Empire and where it was going to go stood forth again in all its old complexity.

In perhaps the most eloquent and generous speech he ever made, King in 1941 had addressed a notable assemblage at the Mansion House in London. There, in the darkest hour of all, he had pledged for Canada: "We will be with you to the end."

There was not time then to analyze rhetoric, but as the pivotal year of 1943 turned into the victory year of 1944, Britain and the dominions began searching for their future. As it had been in the time of Laurier, Borden, and a younger Mackenzie King, the point under examination was whether the ties between Britain and the dominions should be firmer or looser or remain as they were.

Jan Christiaan Smuts, still as highly respected in the councils of the Empire as when he and Borden had sat in the Imperial War Cabinet, put forward a twofold plan. Under it Britain would seek closer associations with smaller European democracies and the administration and tutelage of the colonies would be transferred, wherever geography recommended it, to the self-governing dominions.

Smuts foresaw and thought he knew how to avert the coming upheaval in Africa. He also foresaw that the world was shaking down into two kinds of nation—the Colossi and the rest. Germany, France, and Italy were finished as great powers. So, probably, was

Japan, and China had not yet arrived. The two assured Colossi of the postwar years were Russia and the United States. Great Britain and the Commonwealth might make a third, but only if they closed ranks.

John Curtin, the Prime Minister of Australia, wanted to go further. He advocated a permanent Empire Council with a full-time secretariat and a concerted foreign policy.

Late in January, Lord Halifax was given the difficult task of trying out these lines of thought on Canada. A former Foreign Secretary and now ambassador to Washington, he was, excepting only Churchill, the most imposing civilian in the Commonwealth. He had an almost equally imposing audience, the traditionally Imperialist and Tory Board of Trade of Toronto.

His speech was a brilliant disaster, a political Balaclava. Where Smuts had used the word "Colossi," Halifax spoke of Titans. He saw three of them emerging, Russia, the U.S.A., and China. Britain could be the fourth, but only if she had in peace "the same strength that has sustained her in the war."

"Not Great Britain only, but the British Commonwealth and Empire must be the fourth power in that group upon which, under Providence, the peace of the world will henceforth depend." Halifax went on to draw the blueprint for reconstituting the Empire as one of the Titans. "It is plainly a loss if, with our essential unity of ideal, the responsibility of action which represents that unity is not visibly shared by all. It is an immeasurable gain if on vital issues we can achieve a common foreign policy expressed not by a single voice but by the unison of many. So, too, in the field of defense, while there must be individual responsibility, there must also be a unity of policy."

This was the proposition that Laurier, Borden, and King had had to ponder a dozen times before. Their findings had all been difficult and contentious, but they had always been the same. In nearly all their mutual enterprises Canada and Britain saw almost exactly eye to eye, but that did not mean they always would. Anything like a common parliament, a common council, or a common policy would mean the loss for the dominions of their status as sovereign nations and a reversion to the standing of minorities committed to courses of which they might or might not approve.

This had been the country's feeling throughout the twentieth century. Now the feeling was reinforced by the high hopes everyone held for the new United Nations Organization. The UN ideal was a total rejection of Colossi and Titans. Canada had no desire to help build a Titan or even to become herself a fraction of a Titan.

King put his own and his party's position to the House of Commons. He deplored any policy based on "inevitable rivalry between the great powers."

"Could Canada," King asked, "situated as she is geographically between the United States and the Soviet Union, and at the same time a member of the British Commonwealth, for one moment give support to such an idea? What would seem to be suggested is that the prime Canadian commitment should be to pursue in all matters of external relations . . . a common policy to be framed and executed by all the governments of the Commonwealth. . . . Apart from all questions as to how that common policy is to be reached or enforced, such a conception runs counter to the establishment of effective world security and therefore is opposed to the true interests of the Commonwealth itself. . . . Collaboration inside the British Commonwealth has, and continues to have, a special degree of intimacy. When, however, it comes to dealing with the great issues which determine peace or war, prosperity or depression, it must not in aim or method be exclusive. . . . Our commitments on these great issues must be part of a general scheme, whether they are on a world basis or regional."

For once—perhaps, indeed, for the first time in the country's short but argumentative history in foreign affairs—there was no real dissent. The Tories, still partly under the spell of Arthur Meighen and his Imperial cry of "Ready, aye, ready!" did not at first announce any position. Finally their new leader, John Bracken, condemned the "balance of power doctrine," endorsed the Empire as an instrument of the "first possible consultation and collaboration," and rejected the notion of "any permanent agency which would centralize the influence or increase the rigidity of the Commonwealth structure." In brief he stood approximately where King stood.

The Social Credit party considered Lord Halifax's proposals "good" but observed skeptically that he hadn't said how they could be put into effect. Through its new parliamentary leader, M. J. Coldwell, the C.C.F. proclaimed total opposition. "Empire isolationism and power politics!" Coldwell objected. "Canada should

. . . support . . . a policy which, based on . . . the Atlantic Charter, will win the co-operation not only of the members of the Commonwealth but equally of all other small and great peace-loving nations. The international order . . . must not be based on power groups . . . but on full participation by all states."

The Halifax speech might well have been the epitaph of the British Empire. It forced the Empire into unready, hasty choices. Canada and the other dominions had lived in felicity with England long after they had won their independence. It was essentially a common-law arrangement, a shrine to pure, unregulated love. Now Britain wanted it put in writing, wanted it stamped and official. Required to say yes or no, Canada—and soon the other dominions and colonies—said no.

L

The assault into Normandy—The advance to the Scheldt

ON June 5 and the early morning of June 6, 1944, four United
States divisions, three British divisions, and one Canadian division
crossed the English Channel into the fortress of Europe.

This, at last, was the second front. Here at last was the rendez-
vous with Utah, Omaha, Gold, Sword, and June, with Nan Green,
Mike Red, and Oboe Amber, the land of the Normandy beaches.

The first airborne troops landed at fifteen minutes after midnight. The five divisions coming by sea waded into their beaches
just after dawn. The Canadian Third Division had average luck,
no better than average, no worse. It had to fight hard to get ashore
at the little resort towns of Bernières-sur-Mer, Courseulles-sur-
Mer, St.-Aubin-sur-Mer, and Graye-sur-Mer. By D-plus-1 its Seventh Brigade had crossed ten miles of wheat and poppies to the old
highway of William the Conqueror, the road from Caen to Bayeux.
It was the first of all the Allied formations to reach the objective
set forth for it in the original plan.

But there were no easy successes anywhere—except for a while
at Utah—and there were some cruel failures. The assault all along
the coast had been preceded by huge air and naval bombardments.
These momentarily stunned the enemy but they did not defeat him.
Throughout the Normandy campaign and the eleven months
ahead in Belgium, Holland, and Germany, the belief was abroad
that the use of heavy bombers in close support of infantry had
relieved the foot soldier of his old perils and discomforts. This
was largely a myth. It happened repeatedly that four or five hundred Lancasters of British Bomber Command or Flying Fortresses
of the U. S. Strategic Air Force prepared a ground attack by

dropping several thousand tons of bombs only to have the battle below them settled by a few tiny bullets from Schmeissers, Stens, Lee-Enfields, and Lugers.

The communiqués created the impression that it was an antiseptic, automated, cleanly "modern" kind of war, but it was nothing of the kind. It was a mean and intimate war. No better glimpse of it has been given than the official report of what happened to one of the American assault battalions at Omaha Beach.

The weather on D Day was bad, almost bad enough to call the attack off if there had been time. In the churning choppy seas at Omaha one battalion tried to land twenty-nine tanks. All but two either "sank like stones" or were blown up by mines or shells from the heights above.

The 1st Infantry Battalion of the U. S. 116th Regiment landed on its own. Hardly any of the supporting bombs and shells came within half a mile of the enemy.

Smoke and dust obscured the beaches, and the gunners and bombardiers fired short rather than risk hitting their own men. The American infantry went ashore waist-deep, shoulder-deep, neck-deep, in water boiling with shrapnel and the killing spat of rifles and machine guns.

And then, as the 1st Battalion's history has put it: "All boats came under criss-cross machine-gun fire. As the first men jumped they crumpled and flopped into the water. Then order was lost. It seemed to the men that the only way to get ashore was to dive head first in and swim clear of the fire that was striking the boats. But, as they hit the water, their heavy equipment dragged them down and soon they were struggling to keep afloat. Some were hit in the water and wounded. Some drowned then and there. . . . But some moved safely through the bullet fire to the sand, finding they could not hold there, went back into the water and used it as cover, only their heads sticking out. Those who survived kept moving forward with the tide, sheltering at times behind under-water obstacles and in this way they finally made their landings. Within ten minutes of the ramp being lowered, A Company had become inert, leaderless and almost incapable of action. Every officer and sergeant had been either killed or wounded. It had become a struggle for survival and rescue. The men in the water pushed wounded men ashore ahead of them, and those who had reached the sands crawled back into the water pulling others to land to save them from drowning, in many cases only to see the rescued men wounded again or to be hit themselves. Within 20 minutes of striking the beach A Company had ceased to be an assault company and had become a forlorn little rescue party bent upon survival and the saving of lives."

To the east of Omaha the British and Canadians met their crises a day or two later. Montgomery had been much more adventurous than the American commander, Omar Bradley, in the use of the new Flails, AVREs, Crocodiles, and Donald Ducks, and most of the British and Canadians were from three to nine miles inland when the counterattacks began. On this sector the Germans were led by the 21st Panzer and 12th S.S. divisions, the latter the famed and fanatical Hitler Youth. The Germans could not roll the front back but they stopped its advance and for more than a month the thrust for Caen was stalled.

By the middle of June there were half a million men in the bridgehead. The Americans made gains to the west, toward the Cherbourg peninsula, but a second spell of bad weather slowed down the supply of ammunition and the chance of a quick, decisive breakthrough anywhere was gone. Indeed, if Hitler had not held his reserves back in the fear of new Allied landings in the Pas de Calais, the whole "Overlord" operation might have ended in disaster.

As it was, the Allied exploitation was laborious and painful. It was also contentious, made all the more so because it was commanded by that most contentious of all military leaders, Bernard Law Montgomery.

Under Eisenhower—whom he obviously considered a thoroughly decent but not particularly competent Boy Scout—Montgomery was in charge of the land battle. On his left, facing Caen, was Miles Dempsey's Second British Army; on the right, Bradley's U. S. First Army, soon to be joined by George Patton's U. S. Third.

Montgomery's first hope—though not a fully confident one— was to get to Caen on D Day and then go as far beyond as further developments would permit. His long-range plan, whether he took Caen or not, was to draw the German armor to the British and Canadian front and allow the Americans to wheel around it from the west.

Whether this was the best plan or not, it had been approved by Montgomery's superiors, including Eisenhower, and it worked. In

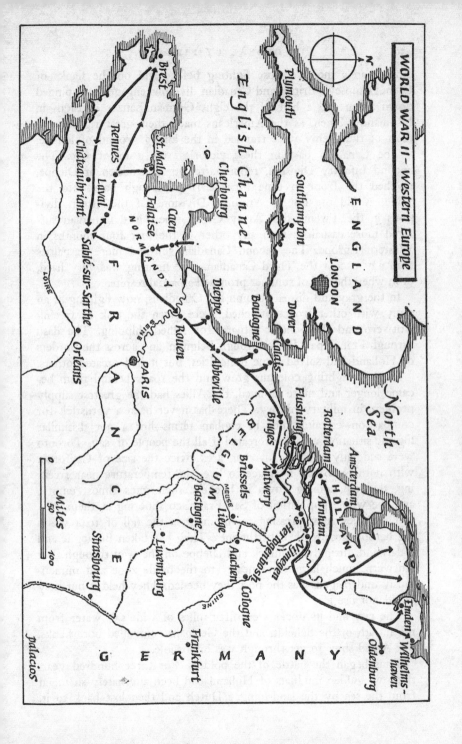

WORLD WAR II – Western Europe

English Channel

North Sea

ENGLAND

Plymouth
Southampton
Dover
LONDON

Brest
St.Malo
Cherbourg
Caen
Falaise
NORMANDY
Dieppe
Rouen
Abbeville
Boulogne
Calais
Flushing
Bruges
Rennes
Laval
Châteaubriant
Sablé-sur-Sarthe
Orléans
LOIRE
SEINE
PARIS
FRANCE
BELGIUM
Brussels
Liège
Bastogne
MEUSE
Luxemburg
Aachen
Cologne
RHINE
Frankfurt
Strasbourg
GERMANY
's Hertogenbosch
Nijmegen
Arnhem
Antwerp
Rotterdam
Amsterdam
HOLLAND
Emden
Wilhelms-haven
Oldenburg

Miles
0
50
100

N

palacios

more than a month's close fighting before and on the flanks of Caen, Dempsey's British and Canadian divisions engaged and pinned down seven and a half of the eight German panzer divisions in Normandy. Then, as the Americans made their great right hook, most of the enemy were trapped in the killing ground of Falaise.

The Canadian part in these victories was a major one. The Second Infantry Division, rebuilt after its destruction at Dieppe, reached the front in time for the rush through Falaise to the Seine, as did the Fourth Armored Division. Of the fifteen divisions in the Twenty-first Army Group, the Third Canadian suffered more casualties than any other in the first four months in Western Europe. The Second Canadian suffered more casualties than any except the Third Canadian. The fighting was very hard, even when the end of summer promised a partial respite.

In the gray and dismal autumn the Canadians, now fighting as an army with other troops attached, were given the task of freeing Antwerp and the Scheldt estuary for Allied shipping. The dash through France past Paris, through Belgium, and across the borders of Holland had solved some difficulties, but it had created others.

As their fighting columns grew and the roads behind them became longer and more jammed, the Allies had the greatest supply problem in military history. There has never been a yardstick for comparison—certainly not in civilian terms—but a not dissimilar logistic situation would be created if all the people of, say, Toronto were suddenly scattered over an area twice the size of California with nothing to eat, no place to live, the temperature near freezing, the rain coming down in buckets, their guns almost empty, and the whole population of San Francisco shooting at them.

The Allies' most pressing requirement in the fall of 1944 was a big harbor close to their battle lines. They had taken Boulogne and Calais and, fittingly, Dunkirk and Dieppe on the way through. But Antwerp, much larger and nearer to the battle zone and miraculously undamaged, was the port they needed. They held it but they could not use it.

The city and its docks were fifty miles of wide salt water from the mouth of the Scheldt, and the Germans controlled both banks. For Allied ships to get through was impossible.

Thus began the battle of the polders. For three hundred years the low, sodden mudflats of Holland had been alternately snatched from the sea by the land-hungry Dutch and then lost back to it.

Now at the island fortress of Walcheren and elsewhere on the frowning shores, both the Allies and the Germans were blowing up dikes to let the sea in again. The polders were of no use as land or water; they were good only for fighting over, for the gun positions that had survived the flooding.

Montgomery's operational order to the First Canadian and Second British armies said bluntly: "We must accept heavy casualties to get quick success."

LI

The reinforcement problem—McNaughton
re-enters and Ralston departs

THE Canadians did take heavy casualties in Holland, and these, together with the still formidable losses in Italy, gave them an almost impossible task of reinforcement.

In this fifth year of war the armies of both sides found it hard to keep up to strength. One problem they all shared was a hazard not yet defined but later made famous as Parkinson's Law. The old-fashioned citizens' army—and by 1944 they were all citizens' armies—had been founded on the principle that anybody handy and able grabbed a musket and started shooting at the nearest stranger.

But with the exception of the desperate and driven Russians, this spartan rule did not apply to the armies of the early 1940s. All of them were clogged to the verge of smothering by their administrative overhead. They had NAAFIs (for tea, sausage rolls, and Woodbine cigarettes), ENSAs (for elderly dancing girls and music-hall comics), and PXs (for Lucky Strikes and Lifebuoy soap), and in addition to these amenities all the Allied formations had almost incredible numbers of headquarters and line-of-communications troops.

The question of the "teeth to tail" ratio in the various armies is never likely to be settled beyond dispute, but one of the best-informed insights has come down from the late Lieutenant Colonel Nicholas Ignatieff. A Russian by birth and a Canadian by adoption, Ignatieff dealt closely with his former compatriots as a British intelligence and liaison officer.

"I attended a meeting," he wrote after the war, "at which a group of British and Soviet tank experts were discussing the Red

Army's medium tank, the T34. The British experts conceded the Russian tank had a fine engine, good armament and was hard to hit. But they pointed out that it had a very unwieldy clutch. The Russians agreed: 'But this is a simple clutch to make and we needed a lot of them in a hurry.' The British said the hatch on the Russian tank was extremely heavy and cumbersome and provided the only means of escape if the tank was hit. The Russian reply was: 'If the tank gets hit what good is the crew anyway?' Finally the British said: 'Your tank had cramped quarters. Where does the crew store its blankets and rations?' The Russians replied: 'They don't need blankets and the food is back in the kitchen.' "

Ignatieff's main conclusion—supported by many other sources —was that "it takes seven non-combatants to keep one man fighting in the British Army, whereas in the Red Army the ratio is no more than 2 to 1."

The present writer has two vignettes of personal experience which bear on the topic. In 1942 a formation of Zombies came to the west coast of Vancouver Island to replace an active service unit about to go overseas. Autumn rains—said to be the heaviest in the British dominions—were driving down in brutal gusts. There was nothing in sight—or in prospect—but mud, water, drowned and porous tents, and jerry-built Bofors-gun positions designed to repel the sensibly absent Japanese. As I turned over my part of this drenched and forgotten wilderness to a gun crew of the Zombies, I asked if there was anything more I could tell them about the local conditions of warfare and subsistence. "Yes, Sarge," said the most wet and dispirited man I have ever seen in war or peace. "Where do they sell cupcakes?"

Three years later an almost identically water-shrunk young Russian came over the last rise of ground before the east bank of the Elbe River near Torgau, Germany. He was wearing a filthy bandage on his head and he was riding on the back of an ox, which was pulling a small ammunition truck, which had run out of gas. He maintained, with the sense of romance common to all soldiers of experience, that he had been riding the ox and pulling the truck all the way from Stalingrad, and that if he hadn't been, the Allies might still be in fairly serious trouble. I asked him what he intended to do with the ox now that the war was nearly over. "Eat it," he said, and there can't be the slightest doubt that he did.

This contrast between the non-fighting Canadian Zombie who

expected someone to deliver him coke machines in the wilderness and the front-line Russian who was supplying both his own transport and his own food could have been repeated, with only a few of the details changed, in any comparison between any of the democratic armies and any of the totalitarian armies. But no nation—not even the notoriously self-indulgent and opulent U.S.A.—needed so many men to keep one man in action at or near the front as did Canada.

For good reasons or bad, for reasons of nationalism, honest pride, and politics, Canada had clung to the goal of a self-contained, self-controlled, self-administered army of its own. The army was relatively small, but it still required the appurtenances and paraphernalia of a large one. There was a big National Defence Headquarters at Ottawa, a big Canadian Military Headquarters in London, a big Canadian Army Headquarters in Surrey and later on the Continent, and there were two substantial corps headquarters in Italy and Western Europe. Maintaining so big an office and supply organization for the five excellent fighting divisions was made more troublesome by the absence of conscription.

One of the officers who had to concern himself with these matters and maintain a strong fighting unit in the face of them was Lieutenant General E. L. M. Burns, commander of the First Canadian Corps in Italy. In his postwar book *Manpower in the Canadian Army*, Burns made some sardonic but well-documented observations:

"Two curious units listed among those authorized by Ottawa were the 1st and 2nd Canadian Tobacco Depots—13 officers and 262 men. They were to handle the traffic of cigarettes sent to the troops by relatives and friends in Canada."

Burns also noted with little enthusiasm the number of men in "auxiliary units, bands and shows." "Attempts," he observed, "to preserve the soldier from the deleterious effects of his traditional recreations of wine and women by providing alternative 'wholesome' entertainment can cost a great deal without achieving their object."

Burns claimed he encountered only one officer who, of his own accord, concluded that he had too many men on his establishment for the job to be done, and reduced their numbers. This little-known hero was Brigadier E. A. McCusker, Burns's senior medical officer.

Parkinson's Law, heavy fighting in northwestern Europe and Italy, and the government's continued refusal to send the Zombies overseas aggravated the Canadian Army's shortage of men every day. Any figures that can be used in this context run the danger of being oversimple. But there are some criteria for objective comparison. One is the number of military personnel needed to man, supply, and keep a division in action. This figure is called the "divisional slice," and it has special significance because the division is the largest ground unit with a fixed size.

The divisional slice in the Canadian Army was 93,150, in the British Army 84,300, and in the American Army 71,100. The Canadian division was a large one (18,000 compared with 14,000 for the American division in infantry and 15,000 compared with 10,000 in armor), but however such figures are interpreted it becomes apparent that all the Western Allied armies were preposterously inefficient.

The reinforcement crisis in the Canadian Army was entirely a crisis of infantry. Each division had nine battalions. Each battalion had four rifle companies of just over a hundred men. In a division the number of men who could see the whites of the enemy's eyes and engage him with rifles, grenades, submachine guns, or bayonets was around 4000. These 4000 were by no means the only true combat troops within a divisional slice of more than 90,000, but it was among them that three quarters of the casualties were incurred. An artilleryman or a truck driver of the Army Service Corps or a repairman of the Ordnance Corps could not be turned, overnight, into a qualified foot soldier. And so it came about that an army with nearly half a million men in all its services and branches could be threatened with disruption because of a shortage and continued rate of loss in one relatively small department. As other armies were doing in the face of their continuing and not wholly foreseen infantry casualties, the Canadians were remustering thousands of men, retraining others, breaking up some formations and assigning their personnel as replacements to others.

These measures were not enough. The government remained in the curious position of having repeatedly promised Quebec never to introduce conscription, then persuading the other eight provinces to "release" it from its promises to Quebec, and now, while knowing the Army was in trouble over manpower, pretending it was not.

The man who bore the hopeless burden of squaring this equation was Layton Ralston, the Minister of Defence. Ralston made a personal trip to the two fronts in late 1944 and there heard from the field commanders what the headquarters staffs had been trying to conceal or minimize. The troubles of reinforcement, Ralston learned, were far more serious than mere figures going across office desks. They involved the effectiveness and morale of the Army and, in his belief, the honor of the men responsible for it.

Now he came back home on a gray October day, bearing gray and fateful news. He rushed to see King and told the Prime Minister there was only one remedy for the conditions he had found. Conscription. Conscription at once, with no further hedging or reservations. There followed thirteen days of argument, much of it in secret meetings of the Cabinet, much of it in private debate between the black hats (as the generals sometimes described the politicians) and the red tabs (as the politicians described the generals).

To the country's shame its great dilemma soon boiled down to a question not of military arithmetic but of political arithmetic.

The military arithmetic was devastatingly simple. As early as August, in the aftermath of the battles of the beachhead, Caen and Falaise, Canadian Military Headquarters had reported to Ottawa that the twenty-one Canadian battalions in northwestern Europe were below establishment by an average of 150 men. Five battalions were short between 200 and 330 (on the natural assumption that nearly all these casualties were in the rifle companies, this meant that their average fighting strength had been reduced to something between 25 per cent and 60 per cent).

The brief late-summer lull made it possible to plug most of the holes (though the reinforcements were not always properly trained), but the vicious fighting on the Scheldt left matters worse than ever. Ralston's summation of the military arithmetic—which endorsed the demands of the General Staff—was that 15,000 trained infantry reinforcements must proceed overseas at once if the Army was to recover from the wounds of summer and autumn and be ready for the winter battles ahead. And the only place to find them was in the ranks of the Zombies.

The political arithmetic was at the root of all King's calculations. He had not the slightest intention of sending a single Zombie overseas, no matter what his Defence Minister and his generals said. And so the questions on which the pending decisions hinged had very little to do with the bitter questions on the Scheldt. Suppose Ralston resigned; how many members of the Cabinet would resign with him? Suppose conscription were forced to the floor of the House; how many Liberals would cross over to join the Opposition? Suppose there were enough to force a general election; how many seats would the government lose, how many gain, how many hold?

Day after day King fought a delaying action in the non-stop cabinet meetings—coaxing, cajoling, calling for new plans, new figures from the generals, new explanations for the mess he insisted was of their making, not his; sometimes threatening darkly that if these hints of resignation did not cease he himself would resign and leave his colleagues and the country to their own devices.

It was a skillful exercise in stalling and if it accomplished nothing more it created a certain indecision among the four or five other ministers who at first had been wholly on Ralston's side. But it was still apparent that, although Ralston might be induced to compromise and even try one more crash drive for volunteers from among the trained Zombies, he had no more intention of surrendering on the main issue than had King himself.

Ralston, then, must go. Once that matter was settled in King's mind, the only thing to be decided was the manner of his going, and that called for careful arranging.

His departure must be on King's terms, not Ralston's. The initiative must be with the government, not with the departing minister. The unavoidable and awkward element of martyrdom must be kept to a minimum. There must be no suggestion that Ralston was anything less than an honorable man leaving on a point of principle; still, it would ease the government's difficulties if his exit could be accompanied by just the barest suspicion that he was also a stubborn man being booted out for clinging to wrong and harmful policies. Finally—and most important of all—a strong successor must be ready to replace him at once, someone whose prestige was at least as high as Ralston's.

Such a man existed and such a man, King discovered discreetly, was available. He was the very man King and Ralston had so recently and willingly fired, partly on the advice of the British War Office and partly because of his reluctance to divide the khaki empire that now lay at the root of all the trouble.

Andrew McNaughton was back in Ottawa, retired with the rank of general. Three massive considerations recommended his as Ralston's successor. He was a declared foe of conscription. His public reputation was immense; if anything, it had been enhanced by the cloudy reasons offered to the public for his retirement. And it was a known fact that the Tories were trying to persuade him to become their national leader in place of the ineffectual John Bracken; if he accepted he would be King's first dangerous political enemy since R. B. Bennett.

On the thirteenth day of the mounting crisis in the Cabinet, King telephoned McNaughton and asked him to call that evening at his residence in Laurier House. It took only the single meeting for them to come to a full understanding. McNaughton promptly assured his host that he could get all the reinforcements needed without invoking conscription. King as promptly offered his guest the Ministry of National Defence, and it was accepted.

When the Cabinet met again the next afternoon, the afternoon of November 1, 1944, Ralston had not the slightest inkling of what was in store. Indeed, for almost an hour he held forth on the possibility—of which he was skeptical but was willing to explore—of solving the crisis by a last-minute appeal to the Zombies.

Then, during a pause in the round-table discussion, King fired him.

Nominally he merely accepted the resignation Ralston had placed in his hands two years before the turmoil of the plebiscite. But in fact it was a discharge, as flat and peremptory as the discharge of a lackey. In the next breath King announced to a stunned Cabinet that General McNaughton would succeed the late minister and maintain the Canadian Army in the field without departing from the voluntary system.

Ralston rose, shook hands around the table—with King as with the others—and walked out the door. If the thought of inviting others to follow him crossed his mind, he did not show it, and no one did follow. King had won his point and his government still stood firm. For the time being the political mathematics of conscription had fallen into place as neatly as the balls of a well-managed abacus.

LII

Conscription again—The Zombies go to war—
The end of the battle in Europe

BY patience and prestidigitation, King had now solved an insoluble problem seven different times: at the parliamentary session of 1939; in the Quebec provincial election that followed; in a snap general election of 1940; in the plebiscite of 1942; in the by-election rout of Arthur Meighen; in the changes in the mobilization act—and now against the threat of insurrection in his own Cabinet.

But to his dismay and disbelief the problem still was there. The Army still needed qualified infantry reinforcements, and McNaughton, it became apparent almost at once, could not get them.

The former army commander had completely misjudged the power of his own name, and he had completely misjudged the temper of the Zombies. In his first week in office he made two public addresses, both in effect recruiting speeches. In each case he was booed by the pro-conscriptionists. In neither case was there any ensuing increase in the enlistments for overseas. McNaughton admitted that in the past the home-defense troops had been "pressed rather than led"—a veiled acknowledgment of the clumsy psychological warfare and occasional outright strong-arming the reserve army had been enduring for more than four years.

Of the 70,000 Zombies then included in the land forces' total strength of almost 450,000, a third were from Quebec and most of this third bore the epithet not with shame but with defiance and a certain pride. Even the outright slackers, from Quebec and elsewhere, had had time to build up a wall of scar tissue and an impregnable rationale: *If they want me, let them conscript me—and all others like me. . . . If they haven't got guts enough to send for*

*me, why should I have guts enough to go? . . . I'll give my life for
my country but not for the politicians.*

The Zombies' resentment and cynicism were directed largely
against the two very men who now sought to convert them with a
few fatherly words. McNaughton's first two appeals for volunteers
were followed by a third in which King spoke over a national
radio network. It failed just as dismally. In the week before the
Prime Minister and the new Defence Minister launched their personal recruiting drive, the average number of reserve soldiers
switching to active service was twenty-four a day. During the week
of their three major speeches it was twenty-four and five sevenths
a day.

King returned doggedly to his political arithmetic as he prepared
to meet Parliament on November 22. It looked much worse now.
Ralston's departure had not seemed a fatal hazard so long as the
tall and reassuring figure of McNaughton stood athwart the crisis,
promising to make it disappear. But with McNaughton's prospects
of success fading by the day, the beads on the abacus began rearranging themselves into highly ominous patterns.

As King read them, he could, in a pinch, command some sort
of majority if it came to a vote of confidence on the floor of the
House of Commons. But in the Cabinet there were now at least
six members certain to follow Ralston to the back benches unless
McNaughton found the 15,000 needed soldiers at once or the government enforced the draft.

The pressure mounted from without as well as from within. War
correspondents covering the Canadian Army overseas were permitted by censorship to give only the vaguest hints of the reinforcement situation at the front, but a number of soldiers inva-
lided back home or returning on leave were able to put it more
clearly and critically. Demands for action dinned in on King from
the press—and not only from the Tory press.

At the height of his agonized attempts to keep the Cabinet in
line—and only two days before the sittings of Parliament began—
one of the Army's most respected and senior commanders threw
in an added harassment. Major General George Pearkes had won
a Victoria Cross in the First World War and now, as commander
of the Sixth Canadian Division, a home-defense unit, he had been
handed the thankless task of badgering several thousand Zombies
into enlisting for service in Europe.

Pearkes called a press conference in the hope of enlightening an unsympathetic public on his problems and those of the troops under his command. The general line of testimony was that even the Zombies wanted conscription, provided it were applied across the board and without discrimination.

King took Pearkes's action as a disturbing invasion of politics by the military. But something far more disturbing was to come.

On the morning of the parliamentary session, McNaughton, the new Minister of Defence, met the Army Council, consisting of most of the senior staff officers at National Defence Headquarters. He was informed that volunteers were coming forward a little better, but not in large enough numbers to make any substantial difference. The reinforcement position was largely as before and the only way the army staff could see to correct it was to draft the home-defense reserves. Moreover, if the government did not see fit to accept this advice, the Army Council—or at any rate most of its members—would feel obliged to resign.

McNaughton was shaken by the ultimatum. King, whom he informed of it at once, was shattered—or professed to be. Was this the beginning of some Central American-style *Putsch?* Was a military junta trying to dictate to the government, perhaps even take it over? King alone, of course, was the judge of his own deepest thoughts; some people who were close to the events doubt that his alarm was nearly so grave as he pretended. Their contention was that he now recognized the failure of his no-conscription dream but reckoned, accurately, that the best way to sell the necessary amendments to the Cabinet, Parliament, the country, and particularly French Canada, was to plead that he had no choice.

That, at any rate, was what he did plead, and plead successfully. He still refused to accept total conscription, but he did consent to the immediate drafting of the 16,000 home-defense soldiers who were qualified to take their place in battle as infantrymen.

He brought the decision to the Cabinet on November 22 and to Parliament on November 23. He mentioned his anxious speculation about a "revolt" in the Army's Ottawa staff neither to the Cabinet nor to Parliament.

According to his own thus far uncorroborated account (which he later gave to Bruce Hutchison and a few Liberal intimates), the only man in whom he confided his fears at the time was Louis St. Laurent. With the death of Lapointe and the defection of Cardin,

St. Laurent had become the "second Prime Minister," the strong, respected French Canadian whom King regarded as indispensable to any Cabinet that hoped to keep the nation in a state of even approximate unity.

It was essential to win St. Laurent over to his new policy. Apprised of the red-tabbed, brass-hatted skeleton King was concealing in the closet, St. Laurent agreed that there was, indeed, no choice. He fell in behind conscription as reluctantly as King.

The partial-conscription enactment, which King immediately introduced as an order in council, satisfied no one. As the House of Commons stormed into the inevitable motions of no confidence, St. Laurent could only soften the opposition of the Quebec members. He could not overcome it.

The content and, occasionally, the decibel count of the two-week debate recalled the forensics of 1910–11 and 1917, over the Navy and an earlier conscription bill. King's position was not a comfortable one, but it was not an unfamiliar one; on the equator between two volcanic poles.

In tabling the new order in council he reminded the House blandly that it was in "entire accord" with the government's previous policy. When an unfriendly M.P. asked whether the order in council would have been necessary if the government had listened to Ralston to begin with, he replied magnificently: "There are some things which can be done or which may be necessary at one time which cannot be done or which may become unnecessary at another, and if the government had attempted to do a month or two ago what at that time did not appear necessary or what has been done today, I venture to say that its action would have frustrated the ability of the Defence Department to give to the men fighting on the other side the reinforcements needed at the time they may be needed."

In seeking to drown the Ralston episode in this soothing bubble bath, King was being unnecessarily cautious. Ralston had no intention of going over to the Tory enemy and taking the risk of unseating the government. When he said so, clearly and finally, there was little left for the House to do but finish the oratory and get on with the war. A Quebec anti-conscriptionist motion was defeated 168 to 43. A Conservative full-conscription motion was defeated 170 to 44. The main motion approving the dispatch of the 16,000 draftees was passed 143 to 70.

If they had accomplished nothing else, the four years of inde-cision, maneuver, and harangue had taken at least a little of the bitterness out of conscription. Through a sort of intellectual and emotional attrition, both sides had been worn down to the verge of reasonableness.

In 1942 King had whispered darkly to a Liberal caucus that if the draft were brought in then "we would have to enlarge our jails and use our tanks and rifles against our own people." Now the civil strife that he and the other anti-conscriptionists had so long and successfully used as their strongest argument simply failed to materialize. The bloody race war that so many proponents of the voluntary system had feared—or pretended to fear—produced far less real violence than the Winnipeg strike or the Regina riots.

The new generation of Quebec nationalists, the leaders of the Bloc Populaire, cried predictably for "independence" and against the ancient ogres of Ontario Toryism, Ontario Orangeism, St. James Street, Fascism, big business, and cliques of colonels. Union Jacks were burned at Rimouski and Chicoutimi and two thousand aroused French Canadians marched through Montreal, breaking the windows of the National Selective Service office and several banks. More windows were broken in Quebec City at the offices of the local English-language newspaper and the home of Louis St. Laurent.

But the physical outbreaks were brief and perfunctory. Even *Le Devoir*, which, as in Bourassa's great days, remained the most intransigent of the nationalist newspapers, scolded that "burning and tearing down flags gets us nowhere, is of no use, and can do much harm to the cause it claims to serve," and contemptuously dismissed the window breakers, not as aroused patriots, but as silly youngsters out for a lark.

L'Action Catholique came perhaps as close as any paper to ex-pressing the province's general mood: "We prefer this verdict to an overthrow of the government for three reasons: we like a govern-ment that is conscriptionist 'in spite of itself' better than a con-scriptionist government angry because compulsion has not been used sooner; we like a government which has reluctantly sacrificed Quebec better than a government which might have sought to sacrifice us still more, if not to be revenged upon us for our anti-conscriptionist stand; we like a government which has approved the recall of French-Canadian recruits to Quebec better than a government which might have canceled this recall and ordered a repressive discipline very dangerous for peace in military camps and elsewhere."

Fittingly enough, the ex-Zombies, having been so long the accepted symbol of a national schizophrenia, proceeded to the war in a highly disordered and inconsistent state. Some of them simply sighed with relief and went on doing what their country ordered them to do, as before. But of the first 10,000 warned for sailings in early January, 7800 either went absent without leave or deserted. A few drifted back in time to catch up with their units, but more than half were still missing when their ships sailed. A later summary, coaxed from the government with obvious reluctance, showed that of the first 14,500 men struck off for overseas duty, more than 4000 were still unaccounted for at the beginning of April 1945. Of these, 2400 were from Quebec and 1000 more from the prairies, where there had been considerable anti-draft feeling from the start.

Eventually almost 13,000 of the reserve soldiers went overseas and 9500 got as far as the Continent. But the war was already breaking up fast, and fewer than 2500 actually got beyond the transit camps and reinforcement depots into the front line. Their total battle casualties were 313, of whom 69 were killed. Allowing for the fact that none of them, by definition, had had previous experience in battle, it was generally concluded that they fought as well as anyone else.

Their reception at the front was almost wholly impersonal. As a contemporary account described their appearance to the frontline battalions: "The men who had been there before watched the new reinforcements come and go, and often wondered which of them were Zombies and which were not. They never really found out. For the reinforcements who came in February and afterwards were much the same as the reinforcements who had come in June. They wore the same uniforms, the same insignia and the same expressions. In battle, or in moving about their lines between salvos from the enemy guns and mortars, they often did things wrong, but when they did it was more likely to be the result of greenness than of cowardice. Often, for the first few days, they were braver than it was sensible to be. Sometimes there was no time to size them up at all before they were gone. Sometimes the men they fought beside would not even learn their names before they were dead. The sergeant would be taking a roll call after an attack and he would say: 'Jones!' There would be no answer and the sergeant would say: 'Jones!' again. Then he would say, with something like exasperation in his voice: 'Does anybody know what happened to Jones?' Somebody else, perhaps warming himself over a stove home-made of old ammunition boxes, would say: 'Was that the short guy with the sandy hair?' The sergeant would say: 'Yes, I think that was Jones. It was either Jones or Smith. Come to think of it, it couldn't have been Smith because Smith went to company headquarters.' The other man would say: 'Jones got it over by that first little house. The one where the machine gun was, I seen him. He got it in the guts.' The sergeant would make an entry on a paper and call the next name. Perhaps the man who had identified the blurred memory that went with the other name would whisper to the soldier warming his hands nearby: 'That Jones was all right. He shoulda kept his head down but he was all right.' And this would be the full recorded impact of Jones on the ken of those who saw him die. In his battalion only the padre and the adjutant would know whether Jones was married or single, what town in Canada he called home, and whether or not he paid formal homage to a God, and they would learn these things only from another piece of paper. Among the men he fought beside there would be none to bear witness whether he sang baritone or tenor, whether the worn snapshots he carried in his pocket were of his wife or of his girl, whether his preference in the way of breakfast was for bacon and eggs or for real pork sausages well grilled, whether he liked his music hot or sweet, or whether he deemed it more desirable, at the end of his service in the army, to work for wages or to try setting up a business for himself. Least of all would it be known whether the stranger Jones was a volunteer or an unwilling conscript."

The strange, costly, and vital battle of the Scheldt ended some two weeks before the reinforcement debate in Ottawa. Any thin hope that it might be followed by the final collapse of Germany was ended by Hitler's wild gamble to break out of the Ardennes in his massive December counterattack.

By January the Ardennes offensive had been contained and forced back and the Canadians were deployed for their last great attack, the clearing of the Allied left flank southwest of the Rhine. All through the early winter they sat in the soggy evergreen forests between the Maas and the Waal, looking toward the flooded flats of the Rhine itself and the drowned weirs and thick, bristling forests between.

The preparations went on until the second week of February. The ammunition dumps piled up; the Engineers hewed corduroy roads and railway spurs through the forests and threw long sagging pontoon bridges across the swollen rivers.

At the height of the attack Crerar had nine British divisions under command of his First Canadian Army, and a total fighting strength of nearly 400,000 men, the largest battle force ever led by a Canadian. Behind the first outposts, the enemy had two other main positions: the legendary Siegfried Line running through the evergreen anchor of the Reichswald and then a strong support line based on the Hochwald and covering the Rhine itself. "Probably no assault in this war has been conducted under more appalling conditions of terrain," Eisenhower said in congratulating Crerar afterward. By the time Crerar's army made its junction with the U. S. Ninth, 90,000 Germans had been killed, wounded, or captured.

Under British command, the Second Canadian Corps went on to help in the difficult crossing of the lower Rhine. The First Corps, after its long campaign in Italy, arrived on the Western Front just in time to take part in the final cleanup on the North German Plain and in western Holland and accept the surrender of General Johannes Blaskowitz's German armies in the Netherlands. Although some 80,000 Canadians answered a call for volunteers for the Pacific, it was in the lobby of a small hotel near the Zuider Zee at 8 A.M. on May 5, 1945, that Canada's military participation in the Second World War really came to an end.

LIII

The departure of the Aging Turks—Ontario
gets a new school reader

THROUGH the habit of a century, Canada emerged from the Second World War lamenting its modesty, decrying its inferiority complex, and asking itself quite audibly why it was so timid about raising its voice.

But the half-true stereotypes of a half generation before were no more than the roughest, most approximate sort of fit for the Canada of 1945.

Canada had learned to recognize the sound of its own footsteps. If, in this first year of what passed for a new peace, they seemed to be taking many directions, they still had a firmer ring than ever before. In another decade they might lose some of their sharpness amid the muffling sounds of Hollywood, NBC-TV, and a new rush of U.S.A. investment money. At times they would disappear entirely amid the thunder of the cold war and the overwhelming pronouncements of Washington. But in this confident year of 1945, no country in the world was more confident than Canada, or had better cause to be.

The first war had established Canada as a tough little military nation, precocious and resourceful. In spite of the red herring of conscription the second war confirmed this part of the country's place in the world. And economically and industrially it had grown beyond imagining.

Thanks to efficient price and wage controls, heavy taxation, and war-bond drives, the treasury had spent more than eighteen billion dollars on the war—an average of six thousand dollars for every family of four—and emerged at least theoretically solvent. It had paid its own way (or assumed its own debts) and in addition had spent two and a half billion dollars on Mutual Aid to its allies, plus another billion as an outright gift to Britain. In dollars the second war cost Canada nine times as much as the first war. (The price in lives, as noted earlier, was about three fourths as great.) The cost of living had risen only by a fifth; the standard of living awaited only the release of consumer goods to rise much higher.

The fleeting signs of political conformity began to disappear long before V-J Day. In 1944 an engaging little Baptist minister named Tommy Douglas led the C.C.F. into office in Saskatchewan, thereby creating the first and, to date, only socialist government in the history of Canada. Another Baptist minister, Ernest Manning, had succeeded William Aberhart as leader of the ultra-capitalist, ultra-conservative, though still nominally Social Credit administration in Alberta.

The voters of Quebec made it abundantly clear that their wartime separation from Maurice Duplessis and the isolationist Union Nationale had been only a separation of convenience. Duplessis squeaked back into power just before the final explosion over conscription and was to remain there for fifteen grandiloquent years. In Ontario the last vestiges of Mitch Hepburn's Liberal machine fell apart and an even longer Conservative reign began.

None of these portents of unrest was lost on King, who called another federal election at the earliest possible moment after the victory in Europe. With the help of a number of welfare measures borrowed from the C.C.F., he led the Liberals back into power with a reduced but still comfortable majority.

There remained a historic act of irony to place the final climax on those climactic years. While the leonine Winston Churchill was defiantly proclaiming his refusal to "preside over the liquidation of the British Empire," the deceptively meek Mackenzie King was doing that very thing.

A few weeks before the D-Day invasion the Commonwealth Prime Ministers met again in London. From the first post-Borden years to the wreckage of Lord Halifax's trial balloon, King (with the country quite demonstrably behind him) had almost continuously rebuffed attempts of various kinds to set up some kind of common policy for the Commonwealth and Empire, with or without a permanent secretariat, a permanent Imperial Cabinet, an annual conference of the Prime Ministers, or something of the sort. But Churchill still clung to the dream—even more strongly than ever now that it was apparent the United Kingdom alone could not hope to take a place of parity with the United States and the Soviet Union in settling the peace and the affairs of the postwar world. King rejected it as stubbornly as ever, even while proclaiming his sincere and unbounded admiration of the Empire and his faith in its future as a fraternity of free and friendly but not necessarily unanimous or invariably united communities.

During the meetings of 1944 King was invited to address the two English houses of Parliament. As the two Prime Ministers entered the Robing Chamber, Churchill said he hoped his friend would say "something of the Empire." The ultra-cautious King pointedly refrained from doing so, and as the conference limped to its end he blocked every attempt to reach any sort of common decision or to provide for common decisions in the future. The strongest statement of Commonwealth unity to which he would agree was that its strength lay "not in any formal bond but in the hidden spring from which human action flows." For better or for worse Canada was committing itself voluntarily to the United Nations and involuntarily to the United States.

During this London trip King had a fleeting last encounter with his old enemy Bennett. "I said to him," he noted later, " 'Well, Bennett, how are you?' and put out my hand to shake hands with him. He shook hands and said: 'Very well, how are you?' or some such expression. But that was all. Not the slightest look of even normal recognition. His face struck me as that of a man who must be suffering a great deal in his own mind. Had a sort of cut-to-pieces appearance, much as I have seen him look when he has been very much overwrought in Parliament. He looks considerably older."

All the Aging Turks who had made this tumultuous age their own were considerably older now—older or departed to rewards that, however mixed they might have been, could not possibly have lacked in zest and relish. King—as unshakably sure of meeting them all again as he was sure of meeting his beloved mother and his tempestuous little grandfather—went to join Laurier, Borden, Sam Hughes, Woodsworth, Aberhart, Lapointe, and other old friends and foes on the night of July 22, 1950.

Meighen outstayed him by a full decade. The unquenchable old Roman, Henri Bourassa, remained for one last angry joust with the bishops of his mother church; when he received the last rites it was from one of the two sons he had given her.

Each member of this lively, storm-tossed company had left far more than his mortal clay in the deep, fermenting soil of Canada. In the thirty-five crowded years between the launching of the "tin-pot navy" and the day of victory in Europe they and their countrymen had learned much of the price and the risks of nationhood. Together they had also learned more of its responsibilities and rewards than any generation of Canadians since the time of Jacques Cartier.

The Ontario Fourth Reader of 1910 had long since disappeared. Another volume on the way to the printer's still ended with Kipling and *Recessional*. But there was no more *Breathless Hush in the Close Tonight*, no more *Private of the Buffs*, no *Balaclava*, no *Drake's Drum*, no *Rule, Britannia*, no *Home Thoughts From Abroad*, no *Elizabethan Seaman*, no "*England, My England*," no hymn of Empire, no Wordsworth, no Keats, no Southey, no Browning. There were, perhaps to no one's disadvantage, "The Celebrated Jumping Frog of Calaveras Country," Thomas Alva Edison's recollections of the making of the incandescent lamp, and Samuel F. B. Morse's recollections of the first successful telegraph, plus a generous selection of Walt Whitman, O. Henry, Henry Wadsworth Longfellow, Washington Irving, James Whitcomb Riley, James Russell Lowell, and William Cullen Bryant, and an unsigned newspaper article about a baseball game between Cleveland and the Detroit Tigers.

Note on Sources

There are obstacles to any review of Canadian history in this century. Many of the sources of information can be seen only by official or semi-official biographers.

The papers and diaries of Mackenzie King have been left to a board of executors, which in turn has been supported by a foundation. Their compilers have been inhibited by King's order to burn a substantial part of them. Whether history properly belongs to trustees, foundations, heirs, and approved images and idols is open to question. But for the time being an indispensable part of Canadian history is being treated as private property and the residue is destined to be destroyed.

The papers of R. B. Bennett—next to King the most important Canadian political figure of the early twentieth century—are in the hands of his old friend Lord Beaverbrook. They can be seen only by persons who will undertake to adapt or describe them in a manner satisfactory to Beaverbrook.

The papers of Sir Sam Hughes were destroyed long ago by a government agency whose excuse was that it needed more filing space. The letters of Hughes and other documents pertaining to him that are quoted here have, in the main, been discovered in the available papers of Laurier, Borden, Minto, and Foster.

The diaries of Sir Robert Laird Borden are in the hands of his nephew, who has published only those parts that support the picture of a man who was infallible and unfailing.

These are only a very few of the many examples of the Canadian people's determination to prettify, sissify, censor, and regulate their history. There are, fortunately, many reliable historical sources even within these limits, and the writer has consulted many of them.

Those that are too large to be classified by date include:

The official debates of the Canadian House of Commons, better known as *Hansard*.

The Canadian Annual Review of Public Affairs, founded and edited in its best years by Castell Hopkins.

Reports of various Royal Commissions and parliamentary committees.

Newspapers, chiefly the Toronto *Globe,* the Montreal *Gazette,* and the Ottawa *Citizen.*

Periodicals, chiefly *Maclean's,* the *Canadian Magazine,* and the *Canadian Historical Review.*

Other works that have provided or verified material in the present volume include these:

Allen, Frederick Lewis, ONLY YESTERDAY (New York, 1931).

——, SINCE YESTERDAY (New York, 1940).

Archer, John H., HISTORIC SASKATOON (Saskatoon, 1948).

Armstrong, E. H., THE CRISIS OF QUEBEC, 1914–18 (New York, 1937).

Barck, O. T., Jr., and N. M. Blake, SINCE 1900—A HISTORY OF THE UNITED STATES IN OUR TIMES (New York, 1947).

Bean, C. E. W., AUSTRALIAN OFFICIAL HISTORY OF THE WAR OF 1914–18 (Sydney, 1935).

Beard, Charles A., and Mary Beard, THE RISE OF AMERICAN CIVILIZATION, 4 vols. (New York, 1927–42).

Beattie, Kim, DILEAS (Toronto, 1957).

——, 48th HIGHLANDERS OF CANADA, 1891–1928 (Toronto, 1932).

Beaverbrook, Lord, CANADA IN FLANDERS, 2 vols. (London, 1917).

——, MEN AND POWER (London, 1956).

Blake, Robert (ed.), THE PRIVATE PAPERS OF DOUGLAS HAIG, 1914–18 (London, 1953).

Borden, Robert L., CANADA IN THE COMMONWEALTH (Oxford, 1929).

——, MEMOIRS, 2 vols. (Toronto, 1938).

Bradley, Omar N., A SOLDIER'S STORY (New York, 1951).

Brady, Alexander, DEMOCRACY IN THE DOMINIONS (Toronto, 1957).

Brebner, J. B., CANADA, A MODERN HISTORY (Ann Arbor, 1960).

——, NORTH ATLANTIC TRIANGLE (Toronto, 1945).

Bridle, Augustus, SONS OF CANADA (Toronto, 1917).

Bruchési, Jean, A HISTORY OF CANADA (Toronto, 1950).

Bryant, Sir Arthur, THE TURN OF THE TIDE (London, 1957).

——, TRIUMPH IN THE WEST (London, 1959).

Buck, Tim, THIRTY YEARS (Toronto, 1952).

Burns, E. L. M., MANPOWER IN THE CANADIAN ARMY (Toronto, 1956).

Butcher, H. C., MY THREE YEARS WITH EISENHOWER (New York, 1946).

Campbell, Marjorie Wilkins, THE SASKATCHEWAN (New York, 1950).

CANADA IN THE GREAT WORLD WAR, Various authors, 6 vols. (Toronto, 1921).

Churchill, Winston, THE SECOND WORLD WAR, 6 vols. (London, 1948–53).

Ciano, Count G., CIANO'S DIARY (London, 1946).

Creighton, D. G., DOMINION OF THE NORTH (2d ed.; Toronto, 1957).

——, JOHN A. MACDONALD, 2 vols. (Toronto, 1952–55).

Currie, J. A., THE RED WATCH (Toronto, 1916).

Dafoe, J. W., CLIFFORD SIFTON IN RELATION TO HIS TIMES (Toronto, 1931).

——, LAURIER: A STUDY IN CANADIAN POLITICS (Toronto, 1922).

Dawson, R. MacGregor, CANADA IN WORLD AFFAIRS—TWO YEARS OF WAR, 1939–41 (Toronto, 1943).

——, CONSTITUTIONAL ISSUES IN CANADA, 1900–1931 (Oxford, 1933).

——, THE DEVELOPMENT OF DOMINION STATUS, 1900–1936 (Toronto, 1937).

——, WILLIAM LYON MACKENZIE KING, A POLITICAL BIOGRAPHY, 1874–1923 (Toronto, 1958).

De Guingand, Sir Francis, OPERATION VICTORY (London, 1947).

Eisenhower, Dwight D., CRUSADE IN EUROPE (New York, 1948).

Ferguson, G. V., JOHN W. DAFOE (Toronto, 1948).

Foch, Marshal, MEMOIRS, 2 vols. (Paris, 1931).

Foster, George E., MEMOIRS, ed. by W. S. Wallace (Toronto, 1933).

Fuller, J. F. C., THE SECOND WORLD WAR (London, 1948).

Glazebrook, G. P. de T., A HISTORY OF CANADIAN EXTERNAL RELATIONS (Toronto, 1950).

——, A HISTORY OF TRANSPORTATION IN CANADA (Toronto, 1938).

——, CANADA AT THE PARIS PEACE CONFERENCE (Toronto, 1942).

Goebbels, Joseph, DIARIES (New York, 1948).

Grant, Douglas, THE FUEL OF THE FIRE (London, 1950).

Griffin, Fred, VARIETY SHOW (Toronto, 1936).

Hardy, H. R., MACKENZIE KING OF CANADA (Toronto, 1949).

Haydon, Andrew, MACKENZIE KING AND THE LIBERAL PARTY (Toronto, 1930).

Heiden, Konrad, DER FUEHRER (London, 1944).

Hodder-Williams, Ralph, PRINCESS PATRICIA'S CANADIAN LIGHT INFANTRY, 2 vols. (Toronto, 1921).

Hughes, E. C., FRENCH CANADA IN TRANSITION (Toronto, 1943).

Hull, Cordell, MEMOIRS, 2 vols. (London, 1947).

Hutchison, Bruce, THE FRASER (Toronto, 1950).

——, THE INCREDIBLE CANADIAN (Toronto, 1952).

——, THE STRUGGLE FOR THE BORDER (Toronto, 1955).

——, THE UNKNOWN COUNTRY (Toronto, 1943).

Ingersoll, Ralph, TOP SECRET (New York, 1946).

Irving, John A., THE SOCIAL CREDIT MOVEMENT IN ALBERTA (Toronto, 1959).

Keenleyside, H. L., and G. S. Brown, CANADA AND THE UNITED STATES (New York, 1952).

King, William Lyon Mackenzie, INDUSTRY AND HUMANITY (Toronto, 1918).

Lingard, C. C., and R. G. Trotter, CANADA IN WORLD AFFAIRS, SEPTEMBER, 1941, TO MAY, 1944 (Toronto, 1950).

Laporte, Pierre, THE TRUE FACE OF DUPLESSIS (Montreal, 1960).

Leacock, Stephen, CANADA, THE FOUNDATIONS OF ITS FUTURE (Montreal, 1941).

——, MY DISCOVERY OF ENGLAND (London, 1922).

Le Bourdais, D. M., CANADA'S CENTURY (Toronto, 1951).

Lemonnier, Leon, HISTOIRE DU CANADA FRANÇAISE (Montreal, 1949).

Liddell Hart, B. H., THE OTHER SIDE OF THE HILL (London, 1948).

Lloyd George, David, WAR MEMOIRS, 6 vols. (London, 1933–36).

Lord, Walter, DAY OF INFAMY (New York, 1957).

Lower, A. R. M., CANADA, NATION AND NEIGHBOR (Toronto, 1952).

——, CANADIANS IN THE MAKING (Toronto, 1958).

——, COLONY TO NATION (2d ed.; Toronto, 1957).

Lucas, C. (ed.), THE EMPIRE AT WAR, section on Canada by F. H. Underhill, Vol. II (London, 1921).

Ludendorff, Erich, LUDENDORFF'S OWN STORY (New York, 1919).

Lysenko, Vera, MEN IN SHEEPSKIN COATS (Toronto, 1939).

McArthur, Peter, SIR WILFRID LAURIER (Toronto, 1919).

MacDonald, Thoreau, THE GROUP OF SEVEN (Toronto, 1944).

McHenry, D. E., THE THIRD FORCE IN CANADA (Toronto, 1950).

McInnis, Edgar, CANADA, A POLITICAL AND SOCIAL HISTORY (Toronto, 1939).

MacInnis, Grace, J. S. WOODSWORTH, A MAN TO REMEMBER (Toronto, 1953).

MacLean, Andrew D., R. B. BENNETT (Toronto, 1934).

McNaught, Kenneth, A PROPHET IN POLITICS (Toronto, 1959).

Malone, Richard S., MISSING FROM THE RECORD (Toronto, 1946).

Masters, D. C., THE WINNIPEG GENERAL STRIKE (Toronto, 1950).

Meighen, Arthur, UNREVISED AND UNREPENTED (Toronto, 1949).

Mongomery, Viscount, MEMOIRS (London, 1958).

Morton, A. S., HISTORY OF PRAIRIE SETTLEMENT (Toronto, 1938).

Morton, W. L., THE PROGRESSIVE PARTY IN CANADA (Toronto, 1950).

Munro, Ross, GAUNTLET TO OVERLORD (Toronto, 1945).

Nevins, Allan, STUDY IN POWER: JOHN D. ROCKEFELLER, INDUSTRIALIST AND PHILANTHROPIST, 2 vols. (New York, 1953).

Nicholson, G. W. L., THE CANADIANS IN ITALY, 1943–45 (Ottawa, 1956).

Pacey, Desmond, CREATIVE WRITING IN CANADA (Toronto, 1952).

Pickersgill, J. W., THE MACKENZIE KING RECORD (Toronto, 1960).

Pugsley, W. H., SAINTS, DEVILS AND ORDINARY SEAMEN (Toronto, 1945).

Raddall, T. H., HALIFAX, WARDEN OF THE NORTH (Toronto, 1948).

Riddell, W. A., WORLD SECURITY BY CONFERENCE (Toronto, 1947).

Roberts, C. D., CANADA IN FLANDERS, Vol. III (London, 1918).

Robertson, Sir William, SOLDIERS AND STATESMEN, 1914–18 (London, 1926).

Rolph, W. K., HENRY WISE WOOD OF ALBERTA (Toronto, 1950).

Ross, Malcolm (ed.), OUR SENSE OF IDENTITY (Toronto, 1954).

THE R.C.A.F. OVERSEAS, 3 vols. (Toronto, 1944–49).

Rumilly, Robert, HENRI BOURASSA (Montreal, 1953).

Sandwell, B. K., THE CANADIAN PEOPLES (London, 1941).

Schlesinger, Arthur M., Jr., THE CRISIS OF THE OLD ORDER (Boston, 1957).

Schull, Joseph, THE FAR DISTANT SHIPS (Ottawa, 1950).

Scott, F. R., CANADA TODAY (London, 1939).

Shapiro, Lionel, THEY LEFT THE BACK DOOR OPEN (Toronto, 1944).

Shirer, William L., BERLIN DIARY (New York, 1941).

——, THE RISE AND FALL OF THE THIRD REICH (New York, 1960).

Shulman, Milton, DEFEAT IN THE WEST (London, 1947).

Simonds, Peter, MAPLE LEAF UP, MAPLE LEAF DOWN (Toronto, 1947).

Skelton, O. D., THE LIFE AND LETTERS OF SIR WILFRID LAURIER, 2 vols. (Toronto, 1921).

——, THE RAILWAY BUILDERS (Toronto, 1916).

Soward, F. H., CANADA IN WORLD AFFAIRS; FROM NORMANDY TO PARIS, 1944–46 (Toronto, 1950).

——, CANADA IN WORLD AFFAIRS; THE PRE-WAR YEARS (Toronto, 1941).

Speidel, Hans, WE DEFENDED NORMANDY (London, 1951).

Stacey, C. P., THE CANADIAN ARMY, 1939–1945 (Ottawa, 1948).

——, SIX YEARS OF WAR (Ottawa, 1955).

——, THE VICTORY CAMPAIGN (Ottawa, 1960).

Stanley, G. F., CANADA'S SOLDIERS, 1906–1954 (Toronto, 1954).

Steele, H. E., THE CANADIANS IN FRANCE, 1915–18 (Toronto, 1920).

Thompson, R. W., DIEPPE AT DAWN (London, 1956).

THE TIMES HISTORY OF THE WAR IN SOUTH AFRICA, Vols. III and IV (London, 1900–1909).

Tucker, G. N., THE NAVAL SERVICE OF CANADA, 2 vols. (Ottawa, 1952).

Wade, Mason, THE FRENCH CANADIANS (Toronto, 1955).

Willison, J. S., REMINISCENCES, POLITICAL AND PERSONAL (Toronto, 1919).

——, SIR WILFRID LAURIER AND THE LIBERAL PARTY, 2 vols. (Toronto, 1926).

Wilmot, Chester, THE STRUGGLE FOR EUROPE (London, 1952).

Winter, C. F., LIEUTENANT-GENERAL SIR SAM HUGHES (Toronto, 1931).

Wolff, Leon, IN FLANDERS FIELDS (New York, 1958).

Woodsworth, J. S., ON THE WATERFRONT (Ottawa, 1918).

Wright, J. F., SLAVA BOHU (New York, 1940).

Wrong, G. M., THE UNITED STATES AND CANADA (New York, 1921).

Young, Desmond, ROMMEL (London, 1950).

Index